African Literacies and
Western Oralities?

American Society of Missiology
Monograph Series

Chair of Series Editorial Committee, James R. Krabill

The ASM Monograph Series provides a forum for publishing quality dissertations and studies in the field of missiology. Collaborating with Pickwick Publications—a division of Wipf and Stock Publishers of Eugene, Oregon—the American Society of Missiology selects high quality dissertations and other monographic studies that offer research materials in mission studies for scholars, mission and church leaders, and the academic community at large. The ASM seeks scholarly work for publication in the series that throws light on issues confronting Christian world mission in its cultural, social, historical, biblical, and theological dimensions.

Missiology is an academic field that brings together scholars whose professional training ranges from doctoral-level preparation in areas such as Scripture, history and sociology of religions, anthropology, theology, international relations, interreligious interchange, mission history, inculturation, and church law. The American Society of Missiology, which sponsors this series, is an ecumenical body drawing members from Independent and Ecumenical Protestant, Catholic, Orthodox, and other traditions. Members of the ASM are united by their commitment to reflect on and do scholarly work relating to both mission history and the present-day mission of the church. The ASM Monograph Series aims to publish works of exceptional merit on specialized topics, with particular attention given to work by younger scholars, the dissemination and publication of which is difficult under the economic pressures of standard publishing models.

Persons seeking information about the ASM or the guidelines for having their dissertations considered for publication in the ASM Monograph Series should consult the Society's website—www.asmweb.org.

Members of the ASM Monograph Committee who approved this book are:

Paul V. Kollman, Associate Professor of Theology and Executive Director Center for Social Concerns (CSC), University of Notre Dame

Alison Fitchett-Climenhaga, Research Fellow, Institute for Religion and Critical Inquiry, Australian Catholic University

Recently Published in the ASM Monograph Series

Samuel Lee, *Faith in the Marketplace: Measuring the Impact of Church Based Entrepreneurial Approaches to Holistic Mission*

Leanne M. Dzubinski, *Playing by the Rules: How Women Lead in Evangelical Mission Organizations*

"Has Western Christianity been too book-centered for African tastes? There is plenty of evidence to support this oft-repeated contention, but Coppedge's fascinating analysis of the reception of the Orality Movement in a Ugandan church turns on its head any simple juxtaposition between Western literacy and African orality."

—**Brian Stanley**, Professor of World Christianity, University of Edinburgh

"William Coppedge provides a major clarion call to reconsider the whole relationship of materiality in the contexts of orality. Coppedge challenges many widely held assumptions about the relationship between material-based and orality-based churches and, in the process, shows the interconnectedness of these two worlds in remarkable and insightful ways. While his focus is on Africa Gospel Church of Uganda, this research should be read widely by all those interested in the vibrancy of the gospel in oral contexts."

—**Timothy C. Tennent**, President and Professor of World Christianity, Asbury Theological Seminary

"Coppedge's research of the interplay of orality, ritual, and material components in discipleship is of utmost significance. Though some might presuppose that Christians in the Global South predominantly prefer orality and storytelling, Coppedge's study demonstrates an interesting cultural association between literary education and economic empowerment. Simply put, we must not underestimate the holistic benefits for those individuals and communities who can access the written word for themselves. I highly recommend this insightful work."

—**E. D. Burns**, director, MA in Global Leadership program, Western Seminary

"The modern-day Orality Movement (OM), claims Coppedge, inadvertently transfers Western proclivities. He then masterfully peels back layers of the onion that sometimes bring tears to the Majority World, in this case, Ugandans. While seeking a script/print world identity that adds social and material value to their lives, they find themselves under the tutelage of regressive oral champions. *African Literacies and Western Oralities?* offers constructive criticism to the renascent OM in this well-researched read. Timely."

—**Tom Steffen**, coauthor of *The Return of Oral Hermeneutic*

"In this book, William Asbury Coppedge has made significant contribution to the study of missions in the twenty-first century. He provides very clear analysis of the tension between Protestant evangelical commitment to the literary text and the personal and oral embodiment of the message of the gospel in the communication process. . . . As an insider, he has capably demonstrated in this research how Orality Movement's approach has worked well through storytelling and narratives in improving Bible literacy and discipleship for members of the Africa Gospel Church in Uganda. I highly recommend this work for readership by seminarians, missions theorists and practitioners, church and mission leaders, Bible scholars, and those interested in studies in global Christianity."

—**Robert K. Lang'at**, Bishop, Africa Gospel Church, Kenya

African Literacies and Western Oralities?

Communication Complexities, the Orality Movement, and the Materialities of Christianity in Uganda

WILLIAM A. COPPEDGE

American Society of Missiology Scholarly Monograph Series 54

☙PICKWICK *Publications* • Eugene, Oregon

AFRICAN LITERACIES AND WESTERN ORALITIES?
Communication Complexities, the Orality Movement, and the Materialities of Christianity in Uganda

American Society of Missiology Scholarly Monograph Series 54

Copyright © 2021 William A. Coppedge. All rights reserved. Except for brief quotations in critical publications or reviews, no part of this book may be reproduced in any manner without prior written permission from the publisher. Write: Permissions, Wipf and Stock Publishers, 199 W. 8th Ave., Suite 3, Eugene, OR 97401.

Pickwick Publications
An Imprint of Wipf and Stock Publishers
199 W. 8th Ave., Suite 3
Eugene, OR 97401

www.wipfandstock.com

PAPERBACK ISBN: 978-1-7252-9037-2
HARDCOVER ISBN: 978-1-7252-9038-9
EBOOK ISBN: 978-1-7252-9039-6

Cataloguing-in-Publication data:

Names: Coppedge, William A., author.

Title: African literacies and western oralities? : communication complexities, the orality movement, and the materialities of Christianity in Uganda / by William A. Coppedge.

Description: Eugene, OR: Pickwick Publications, 2021 | American Society of Missiology Scholarly Monograph Series 54 | Includes bibliographical references and index.

Identifiers: ISBN 978-1-7252-9037-2 (paperback) | ISBN 978-1-7252-9038-9 (hardcover) | ISBN 978-1-7252-9039-6 (ebook)

Subjects: LCSH: Christianity—Uganda. | Orality.

Classification: BR1443.U33 C67 2021 (print) | BR1443.U33 (ebook)

09/29/21

To:
Joanna Marie Coppedge
My Wife and Best Friend

Contents

List of Figures | viii
Acknowledgments | ix
Abbreviations | xii

1. Introduction: Communication and Material Complexities in Ugandan Christianity | 1
2. Protestantism's Enduring Communication Complexities: The Tension between Protestants' Commitment to the Biblical Text and the Pervasiveness of Illiteracy | 38
3. "Washing in the Word": Situating the Orality Movement in Protestant History | 66
4. Africa Gospel Church: Antecedents, History, and People | 115
5. Communication Complexities in the Africa Gospel Church | 167
6. Analysis: Material Complexities in AGC's Reception of Orality | 218
7. Conclusion: The Material Implications of Orality | 254

Appendix A: Oral Sources | 267
Bibliography | 271
Index | 287

List of Figures

Figure 1: The seven disciplines of orality | 72

Figure 2: Locations of Africa Gospel Church congregations in Uganda | 142

Figure 3: Organizational structure of Africa Gospel Church | 145

Figure 4: Stephen Steward Mukisa's pastoral training binder | 159

Figure 5: A printed page from Mukisa's former pastoral training lessons | 160

Figure 6: An older man and woman with their Bibles | 169

Figure 7: A Swahili Bible wrapped in newsprint | 171

Figure 8: Bulyango Africa Gospel Church | 176

Figure 9: Kenneth Hopson and Leonard in *The Print Shop* | 190

Figure 10: Four different styles of digital audio players (DAPs) | 200

Acknowledgments

THERE IS A BIBLE story told about a group of ten men who were healed of leprosy. Surprisingly, out of the ten, only one man ever expressed his gratitude. While I may not be able to remember all who have made this book possible, I do want to make a different choice than those other nine.

This book originated as a doctoral thesis at the University of Edinburgh and I am very grateful to Prof. Brian Stanley for his supervision throughout the process. He has been patient and gracious, providing a wealth of resources and knowledge along the journey. Likewise, I want to express sincere gratitude to Prof. Jolyon Mitchell and Dr. Naomi Haynes for their advice, counsel, and kind words of encouragement. I wish all three of them all the best in their endeavors, both academic and otherwise.

I want to express my heartfelt thanks to the men and women of Africa Gospel Church Uganda. So many of them opened their homes, churches, and stories to me. I sincerely appreciate their generosity, hospitality, and fervor. I want to express a particular word of thanks to Bishop Joseph Ogweyo and his wife Evelyn, James and Caroline Ouma, David and Judith Dhikusooka, Martin and Rose Owor, Steward and Miria Mukisa, Kennedy and Lillian Kirui, Benson Omri, Joshua Kinaalwa, Winnie Mugisha, and the former bishop Kefa Masiga. Other friends helped out along the way, and I am grateful for their time and expertise, particularly Father Tonino Pasolini, Imam Otafiire, Fred Okello, and Rhys Hall.

I am deeply indebted to my colleagues at World Gospel Mission. They were all very gracious in sharing their hearts and experiences with me. I want to say a particular thank-you to Jonathan Mayo, Jeff and Christine Stanfield, John and Beth Muehleisen, Larry and Joy McPherson, Nathan Metz, and Kenneth Hopson. Our family is also grateful to Josh and

Kelly Hallahan for allowing us to live in their house while conducting fieldwork. Hubert Harriman, Tim Rickel, and Dan Schaffer are also a part of World Gospel Mission and were instrumental in encouraging us in our educational endeavors.

I also want to express my appreciation to many within ION for their generosity, patience, and willingness to answer many questions amidst many other responsibilities. I am deeply grateful to Samuel Chiang, Grant Lovejoy, Linda Bemis, Chuck Madinger, Jay Moon, Ellen Marmon, Andrea Menkin, Bryan Thompson, Jerry Wiles, Melissa Dueck, Djibo Apollos, Abiel Herrera, Charlie Fletcher, Calvin Chong, Jason Boetcher, David Swarr, Tom Steffen, J. O. Terry, and Stan Wafler. The passion of these men and women is contagious and I am thankful for their friendships.

There are innumerous other champions who cheered and carried our family through the PhD process; their e-mail responses and messages were a source of great strength and encouragement while living abroad. I particularly want to express a deep gratitude to Pat and Ed Daigle and their caring about our home. Likewise, Laurence and Jessica Coppedge were tremendous allies, making so much possible. We are forever grateful to them.

Some of our closest champions were friends we made in Scotland. We are so grateful for Pastor Andrew Rollinson and all the dear friends from St. Andrews Baptist Church who loved our family. They showed us genuine kindness. I also want to thank our Thursday night small group for their love and encouragement. I am so grateful for Michael and Francina, Tamara and Ethan, David and April, Greydon and Erin, Max and Jessica, Eric and Bethany, Brett and Amber and all of the extended little people. They were tremendous friends, both to me but also my wife and children. Along with them, I am grateful to be not only cousins but also friends with Denny and Lauren Kinlaw, who loved all of us so graciously.

My extended family also played an incredible role in seeing this project to its completion. Blake and Nancy Neff were particularly gracious. I thank them for loving us. For Dan and Katy Beth, Cricket and Matt, and Susannah and Josh (and all their extended people), I am so appreciative of their love and prayers for us. More than once they were wonderful soundboards for various thoughts and ideas. I want to offer a particular thank-you to Cricket for her reading various chapter drafts along the way.

My father and mother, Al and Beth Coppedge, have been fixed reference points for me throughout this research endeavor. They have cheered, wept, prayed, laughed, called, encouraged, visited, and prayed some more. I am so grateful for their investment in my life, this process, and our family.

In April 2017, while our family was in Uganda for my research, my grandfather, Dr. Dennis F. Kinlaw, passed away. Second only to my wife, did Papa believe in me. He, perhaps more than all of us, will be celebrating this book's publication.

Teammates make all the difference. I am so grateful for my team, namely our children, Elsie Jayne, Lucy, Sophia, Chloe, and Blake, for all that they endured for daddy to finish his "paper." Their cheers, notes, hugs, and prayers have been more helpful than they will ever realize. I love them with all my heart.

Lastly, I want to express my appreciation to the Father for my wife, Joanna. Apart from Jesus himself, she is my greatest gift and this endeavor would never have been possible without her sacrifice.

William A. Coppedge
Entebbe, Uganda

Abbreviations

AGC	Africa Gospel Church Uganda
CBS	Chronological Bible Storying
CBT	Chronological Bible Teaching
CHE	Community Health Empowerment
CMS	Church Mission[ary] Society
CRU	Campus Crusade for Christ
FGW	Farming God's Way
GS	God's Story
IMB	International Mission Board of the Southern Baptist Convention
ION	International Orality Network
LCWE	Lausanne Committee for World Evangelization
NTM	New Tribes Mission (*Ethno360*)
OM	Orality Movement
SIU	Scriptures In Use
STS	Simply the Story
TWR	Transworld Radio
WBT	Wycliffe Bible Translators
WGM	World Gospel Mission
YWAM	Youth With A Mission

1

Introduction

Communication and Material Complexities in Ugandan Christianity

INTRODUCTION

THIS BOOK INVESTIGATES THE complexities of communication within a contemporary local reception of Christianity. Many, perhaps most, adherents to Christianity have historically recognized the medium of the written Bible as being the authoritative word of God, while varying in the theological meaning they have attached to such recognition. With ever-changing media developments and technology updates, the question emerges of how adherents of Christianity today reconcile the relationship between the spoken, the printed, and the digitalized word of God, particularly when different modes of communication have certain cultural associations with either traditional or modern ways of communicating. This is compounded when one recognizes the ways in which each mode's material form (or apparent lack thereof) contributes to these cultural sensibilities. In essence, in what way does the interplay between these various modes of communication and different cultural perceptions of modernity and materiality affect Christian engagement with the Bible? In light of these communication complexities, this project investigates how Africa Gospel Church, a mission-founded Ugandan denomination with some reservations about the traditional associations of orality, has been encouraged by their founding mission to appropriate particular oral communication methodologies into their literate-oriented pastoral training program. These communication methodologies derive from and are championed by the Orality Movement, an international evangelical mission network with strong Western affiliations. Therefore, the question that this book sets out to answer is: "In what ways have members and leaders within Africa Gospel Church Uganda responded to the appropriation of the oral communication principles of this Orality Movement, and what wider conclusions might be drawn from the interchange between this church and movement about the complexities and materialities of communication for the reception and development of Christianity within other Majority World contexts?"

The research that informed this book argues that material culture, far from being secondary in Ugandan Christian communication, plays a more influential role than perhaps has been previously recognized. On the one hand, this book investigates how oral communication privileges *material embodiment* in a special way, namely in the material body of the communicator. On the other hand, oral communication offers no *material artifact* such as is present in a literate-based event or even a digital one. This carries significant implications for proponents of the Orality Movement. While they have intuited the way bodies foster more affective (and often, effective) communication, at times, there seems to be an underestimation of how material artifacts convey meaning in powerful ways in certain contexts. Orality's lack of a material artifact means that some within Africa Gospel Church interpret it as failing to achieve certain educational, economic, and social values that are upheld by members of the communities in which Africa Gospel Church is seeking to communicate. Such failings have been interpreted as limiting the spiritual impact that these church members are trying to have in their communities. Furthermore, as becomes evident, the lack of a material artifact in oral methods of communication complicates issues for members of the Orality Movement, particularly in regards to questions of authority, interpretation, and conceptualizing personhood.

In the introduction of their book *Mediating Religion*, Mitchell and Marriage describe how "conversation lies at the heart of our human existence, at the heart of our cultural understanding and at the heart of our religious experience." They continue, quoting Gadamer, "A conversation is the process of two people understanding each other"; however, they note that "real understanding of the other does not come easily in conversations." Mitchell and Marriage express their interest in conversations that are happening on the borderline of "what I understand and what I don't, with people who are different from myself."[1] Such an introduction brings to the forefront several key motifs that help introduce this book. In many ways, it is an investigation into a conversation that is happening between

---

1. Mitchell and Marriage, *Mediating Religion*, 1–2.

a national Ugandan denomination and a global, albeit, heavily Western-influenced network of evangelical mission organizations. As Mitchell and Marriage have mentioned, understanding in conversations cannot be taken for granted; furthermore, such communication events are often, if not always, attempting to bridge borders. The heart of this project is indeed an attempt to understand better how (mis)communication between a local church and an international network has transpired. Certainly, there are numerous borders complicating the communication process, including geography, culture, and language, in addition to ethnic, economic, and educational differences represented within the network and the church. Such differences result in the various players, whether within the movement or the church, having to navigate different roles and expectations. In certain ways, many of these characters are cultural brokers, mediators trying to navigate various pressures (such as donor or missionary expectations) even as they seek to establish, at times, similar but also different versions of what might be called a *flourishing life*. While this theme is elaborated on in chapter 6, such understandings of the flourishing life, or what one interviewee labeled as the *achieved life*, differ. Some missionaries seem to interpret a flourishing life (or compartmentalized it) as achieving spiritual milestones, while church members' interpretations seem to bear a more holistic outlook, that is spiritual, but also material, social, and even political in character. That miscommunication should transpire between these parties, where unbalanced power relations, financial tensions, cultural differences, and spiritual expectations are all woven together, is not surprising and offers fertile ground for scholarly inquiry.

Before progressing, it is necessary to provide an initial taxonomy of the different understandings of orality within this book.[2] In a broad sense, orality can be any communication that relies on the spoken word. In this sense, an oral message can be organized according to any stylistic form (whether narrative, proposition, lyric, proverb, etc.) as long as the delivery of the message is via the spoken word. This generic understanding of orality, or what I am labeling as **orality$_1$**, is most often juxtaposed with literacy or what is typically interpreted in such contexts as communication that relies on the written or printed word. However, the orality that receives center stage within this study is more precisely defined. I have chosen to label orality as understood within the Orality Movement as **orality$_2$**, denoting an ideological conception of communication that relies on the spoken word (in a similar way to **orality$_1$**), but which in addition tends to be closely

---

2. It should be noted that this taxonomy of orality reflects my own understanding and is not emic to the Orality Movement.

4   African Literacies and Western Oralities?

associated (if not, at times, exclusively associated) with the message's content being organized in a narrative or story form. Furthermore, within this framework, the term *orality* is stretched to incorporate not only non-textual reliant communication such as verbal speech between interlocutors but also other communication acts such drama, dance, and singing that do not necessarily incorporate printed texts. Where such events happen without relying on the printed page, within this **orality**$_2$ ideological framework, they would be considered oral. Granted, on such occasions, differentiating between this ideological **orality**$_2$ and any non-textual reliant artistic expression becomes difficult. Nevertheless, it needs to be recognized that this particular ideological understanding of oral communication is what members of the Orality Movement have in mind when they talk about orality. This book investigates how Africa Gospel Church members react and respond to their encounters with **orality**$_2$ and for this reason, when the term "orality" appears throughout this work, it should typically be understood as **orality**$_2$ unless otherwise indicated. It should be readily acknowledged that there is overlap between the two categories; however, this classification provides some initial definitions to keep in mind.

With that taxonomy in place, this investigation into the church's encounters with the Orality Movement's particular orality promises to fulfill several interrelated objectives. First, this thesis explores the tension (for many) throughout Protestant history between a commitment to the printed Bible as being the authorized word of God and a pragmatic desire to overcome any communication barrier, including illiteracy, so that people could understand and respond to the Christian message. Second, this project provides an overview of the antecedents, history, people, and ideas of the Orality Movement (OM). This research is particularly important within the wider field of scholarship on world Christianity, for while several doctoral theses of a missiological kind have appeared from North American evangelical institutions (see examples cited shortly), this project offers an initial contribution to rectifying the complete dearth of scholarship on the movement itself within major research universities.

Third, this work explores the significant relationship between early Ugandan Christianity and literacy, probing into how the relationship between Christian faith, education, and social standing has a long, complicated history in Uganda. With the historic precedent established, this study accomplishes a fourth objective by investigating the complex reception of the OM's practices (and principles) within Africa Gospel Church Uganda (AGC). Analysis draws on the responses of church stakeholders (e.g., leaders, trainers, lay congregants) to the appropriation of particular oral methodologies into AGC's pastoral training program. Fifth, this research evaluates whether the claims, ethos, and enthusiasm of the OM correspond with the expectations and experiences of the AGC community. This evaluation necessitates investigating how, for those within the AGC community, communication is embedded in a broader social imaginary than that conceptualized by some members of the OM. This social imaginary (or imaginaries) includes a high evaluation of material culture, resulting in, among other things, certain educational and economic expectations. Furthermore, church members face pressure to obtain particular social standings within their communities that often are evidenced by material artifacts. This is related to the fact that many Ugandan Christians appear to understand "modern" modes of communication, including print and electronic media with their material or artifactual nature, as carrying a particular value for shaping one's identity. In contrast, orality, with its apparent lack of any material artifact, often carries negative associations with "traditional" or "premodern" communication. Some within the OM seem unaware of such complicating factors or have minimized their significance, yet such factors are impinging on local Ugandan Christians' perceptions of **orality$_2$**. Sixth, this research, in exploring the broader social imaginaries in which Ugandan communication transpires, offers an academic analysis of prosperity gospel theology—by considering "the theology of the belly." Exploration into this on-the-ground phenomenon offers a granular account of a theology of prosperity practiced in a particular Ugandan socioecclesial context, and its linkage with materiality and communication. Finally, this investigation explores the broader implications of this research and offers possible appropriate recommendations for the role of oral communication in modern communication practice among similar Christian groups within Majority World contexts.

KEY ORGANIZATIONS

While a more complete understanding of each of the key entities (or organizational groups) with which this story is concerned appears in subsequent chapters, it is important to provide at this point an introduction to the main characters. The organization that established Africa Gospel Church in Uganda is World Gospel Mission (WGM), an evangelical mission agency that is based in Marion, Indiana (USA). The mission was started in 1910 and, by 2017, the organization had about 230 missionaries serving in approximately twenty-four locations on five continents with an estimated annual revenue of twenty-three million dollars.[3] This inter-denominational organization

---

3. See the World Gospel Mission annual report from 2017 for a further breakdown on the mission's finances.

self-identifies with a Wesleyan (Arminian) theological position, and has historically maintained a strong emphasis on personal holiness (as is elaborated at length in chapter 4). In an attempt to encourage faithfulness to this theological tradition, the mission has traditionally expected its missionaries to have at least a Bible college education, although increasingly, WGM missionaries have exceeded this by achieving graduate and even terminal degrees in a variety of fields, including missiology and theology as well as agriculture, development, education and medicine.

Regarding the makeup of the WGM's missionary workforce, the 2018 gender ratio was 41.3 percent male and 58.7 percent female.[4] The average age is approximately forty-eight years old with over 90 percent of the missionaries being white Americans. The remaining percentage includes African Americans and representation from Honduras, Ukraine, Hungary, Eritrea, Bolivia, and Japan, Cambodia, and Peru. Regarding their socioeconomic standing within a United States context, the missionaries would probably be described as lower middle (if assessment included the benefits they receive such as a housing allowance, etc.) but below middle class if assessed only on their salary.[5] The faith-based nature of the mission means that the missionaries themselves, rather than the organization, are responsible for raising the necessary resources (both in financial and prayer commitments) before going to their designated ministry locations. Missionaries are expected to raise their necessary support either from churches or individual "champions" (donors). While each missionary's (or family's) financial budget maintains some common variables such as salary, insurance, and administrative tariffs, the actual budgets vary, depending on size of the family and differing expenses related to different ministry locations.

This project is immediately concerned with WGM's work in Uganda, which began in 1992. By early 2019, there were approximately fifteen WGM missionary units (five single women and ten families) living in Kampala, based primarily in the Kansanga, Muyenga, and Kiwafu neighborhoods. While approximately a third of the missionaries worked at Heritage International School, which is located in the Kiwafu neighborhood, the remaining numbers served in a variety of ministries, including caring for refugees, widows, and orphans, teaching at a local Christian university, and working alongside Africa Gospel Church.[6]

4. Kevin Zirkle, email, January 31, 2019.

5. I am indebted to Kevin Zirkle, assistant vice president of the international ministries of WGM, for this information. The socioeconomic assessment of the missionaries is based on Zirkle's evaluation, although his assessment concurs with my own observations and experiences. Zirkle, January 31, 2019.

6. Several of the WGM missionaries worked with ministries that care for refugees

Africa Gospel Church (AGC) was planted in 1992 by WGM missionaries and, as of 2019, had approximately 185 congregations with another 30–35 preaching points.[7] The church officially received its registration from the Ugandan government in 2011 and now operates as a separate entity from WGM, although the two continue to be in partnership (as discussed shortly). While the denomination has only about 3650 official members on record, it is estimated that approximately another 8760 people regularly worship in its congregations.[8] Figure 3 in chapter 4 shows that the denomination has typically been concentrated in the more central and eastern regions of the country, with perhaps its strongest representation being in the Kayunga/Kamuli, Amudat, and Masese/Buvuma Island areas, while its weakest being in and around Soroti, Nebbi, and Namayingo.[9] Rough estimates for the population demographics within the denomination are as follows: 15 percent adult males, 20 percent adult females, 25 percent youth, and 40 percent children. The vast majority of those who attend AGC would come from the lower level of Uganda's socioeconomic structure being non-professional casual laborers or small-scale farmers. Estimates put the number of working professionals involved in the church at no more than 10 percent of the church population.[10]

As already mentioned, AGC and WGM have a close partnership, exhibited in several ways. The denomination has struggled to raise its annual budget from its local churches and so for the last several years, the mission has provided a grant to the church to help with their financial needs.[11] In 2018, monies given specifically to AGC included $14,325 for pastoral training, $3,060 for constructing a new training center, $57 for the development of other church buildings and properties, $5,800 for church administration

---

or widows and orphans, yet those are not associated with AGC.

7. James Ouma, personal interview, March 31, 2017. David Dhikusooka and Jonathan Mayo, email, January 31, 2019.

8. I am grateful for Revs. David Dhikusooka and Jonathan Mayo for their working on the church's demographic and sociological information, both here and below. Dhikusooka and Mayo, January 31, 2019.

9. Dhikusooka and Mayo, January 31, 2019. Bishop Joseph Ogweyo, WhatsApp, February 4, 2019.

10. Dhikusooka and Mayo, January 31, 2019.

11. The following information represents an approximation of the numbers provided by David Dhikusooka, the church's general secretary, and WGM missionaries, Jonathan Mayo and John Muehleisen. Although they did not match up exactly, the figures were roughly the same and I credited the discrepancy to the difference in currencies since the church figures were in Ugandan shillings and the mission report was in US dollars. David Dhikusooka, WhatsApp, February 4, 2019. Jonathan Mayo and John Muelheisen, email, February 8, 2019.

support, $1,503 for camp meetings and other conferences, $3,900 in leadership scholarships for church leaders to pursue further education, and $7,000 in emergency and famine relief, amounting to a total of $35,645. Furthermore, WGM has been heavily involved in a relief and development project that has included partnering with AGC and Kikongo Primary School on Buvuma Island in Lake Victoria. In 2018, this ministry's budget was approximately $27,800 for scholarships for orphans and $7,140 for building development. In 2018, WGM also spent an additional $15,800 on their development program called Community Health Empowerment (CHE), which operates in partnership with AGC (and is discussed in due course). These numbers (totaling approximately $86,385) indicate that the mission is heavily invested economically in the area, although, significantly, the mission does not pay the salaries of AGC pastors or the CHE staff. Such realities are discussed in more detail in chapter 6 with particular reference to the economic differential between the missionaries and the church personnel. For now, it should be noted that while orality was originally conceptualized by the WGM missionaries as a spiritual resource tool, it was incorporated into a denominational context that involved substantial economic factors such as the mission's annual grant, which naturally brings with it its own political and material dynamics. The fact that WGM's faith-based missionaries are, likewise, having to rely on others' support for their livelihood indicates that both the missionaries and church personnel are operating within particular socioeconomic constraints, though these differ in nature and scale.

Although it is related to the finances, one other major way that the church and the mission partner is in the area of training. The history of AGC's pastoral training is provided in chapter 4, but it is necessary to highlight at this point that the church has often relied on missionaries to help organize, fund, and facilitate both pastoral training and other development types of training, such as Community Health Empowerment (CHE) and Farming God's Way (FGW). It should be acknowledged that the denomination has their own pastoral training coordinator and, in 2018, the pastoral training was conducted by Ugandan trainers (rather than missionaries). Even so, the church continues to utilize various WGM missionaries to help write curricula, plan training courses for leaders and trainers, and think strategically about future opportunities for both pastoral and development training. It is through this training partnership that WGM missionaries introduced AGC to the third major character in this book, namely, the OM.

The third major entity in this project is the Orality Movement. In the early 1980s, there was a group of dissatisfied evangelical, American missionaries, working in the Philippines and greater South Asia, who were looking for more effective ways to communicate the Bible. In frustration and reaction to the reception of their print-based, systematically organized presentations of the Christian message among particular groups, these missionaries began experimenting with oral performance. Developments occurred and chronological Bible storytelling began to grow as a viable communication tool. In 2004, a group of key organizational leaders, made up of primarily of American evangelical mission agency representatives, wrote a seminal paper called *Making Disciples of Oral Learners* at a Lausanne Movement consultation in Thailand; this officially birthed the International Orality Network (ION). While initially focused exclusively on oral Bible storytelling, ION's vision has grown, namely to *make disciples* of *all* oral communicators through a wide spectrum of oral and also digital means.[12] At an institutional level, the network intentionally maintains its network status, rather than becoming an incorporated legal entity. Consequently, there are minimal internal financial structures, but rather the network depends on partner organizations to volunteer their personnel, energies, and financial resources for everything from administrative responsibilities and costs to hosting consultations around the world related to the use of orality in mission communication.[13]

Regarding the reception of this championing of oral communication in mission endeavors, ION's leadership claims that the movement now includes over two thousand different entities from around the world, involved in some way with their oral-related initiatives.[14] Those entities include individual churches, denominations (e.g., Africa Gospel Church Uganda), denominational mission agencies (e.g., the Southern Baptist International Mission Board[15]), Bible translation agencies (e.g., SIL, Wycliffe, The Seed Company[16]), and other mission organizations (e.g., New Tribes Mission, Cru, TWR, Youth With A Mission). While representatives within ION originate from several of the mainline denominations, such as Anglicans, Lutherans, and Methodists, it is worth noting that such mainline denominations have not officially endorsed the movement and involvement is at a personal and not denominational level. As an indication of the geographical breadth of the movement, it should be noted that in the period from 1994 to 1997, oral-related mission activities were already being discussed in over forty different

---

12. David Swarr, interview via Skype, August 18, 2016.

13. Samuel Chiang, WhatsApp message, January 25, 2019.

14. Samuel Chiang, personal interview, August 1, 2016; Swarr, August 18, 2016.

15. The International Mission Board of the Southern Baptist Convention is often called IMB.

16. These agencies have a unique relationship and interrelated histories. While closely associated, they currently are separate entities. SIL was formerly Summer Institute of Linguistics.

countries.[17] Likewise, in my personal interviews of people within the OM, representation came from North America, South America, Europe, Asia, Africa, and Australia. Several areas of the world already have adopted their own regional orality networks, including North America, Latin America, East Africa, West Africa, and Southeast Asia. Several others are in formation, including South Asia and South Pacific.[18] Significantly, this global presence seems to be entirely evangelical Protestant in orientation.

The movement's emphasis on discipleship is important to highlight because the members understand the process broadly, incorporating both evangelism and instruction of Christian believers to maturity. They are committed to seeing this discipleship process worked out among their three specific and, at times, overlapping audiences: the least-reached people groups, that is, those with no Christian outreach among them; Bible-less people groups, being those with no access to the Bible at all; and all oral-reliant communicators, including those who cannot read (often called primary oral communicators by those within ION) but also those who may possess the skills and yet still prefer not to read (referred to by those within the movement as secondary oral communicators). Such a broad understanding of their target audience means that according to ION members, approximately 80 percent of the global population should be understood as preferring to communicate via oral means. Such claims imply that the growth of the worldwide Christian church in the twenty-first century depends on the distinctive communication strategies of the OM.

A final comment is necessary regarding the lack of specific demographics and sociological data on the movement's members. Although a broad survey of the movement was not possible, the movement's leadership is actively trying to diversify its membership, which has hitherto been predominantly white, American, and middle-class, with its leadership being almost exclusively male. David Swarr, the former executive director of ION,[19] discussed how incorporating women into the leadership has proved problematic as until recently, much of the leadership was coopted (or seconded) from other American evangelical mission organizations' personnel, which has typically been male-dominant.[20] While female involvement at ION's leadership level has been almost exclusively limited to one person—Linda Bemis, the senior associate for prayer—numerous women have been or are currently

---

17. See Terry, *Chronological Bible Story Newsletter*, 1.1–4.4.

18. https://orality.net/networks/regions.

19. Swarr resigned as the executive director in March 2020 and Charles Madinger was appointed as the interim executive director.

20. Swarr, August 18, 2016.

incorporating oral methodologies in their mission endeavors, several of whom carry leadership roles within their organization. Several examples of women who have had leadership roles include Dorothy Miller (deceased 2017), who founded the organization *God's Story* and developed their oral Bible storytelling methodology called *Simply The Story*. Miller was followed at *God's Story* by Andrea Menkins, who is now its current executive director.[21] Carla Bowman (along with her husband, Jim) founded *Scriptures In Use* in 1986, an organization with a vision to "make disciples of oral learners" and she has written *Building Bridges to Oral Cultures*.[22] A final example is Tricia Stringer, who is a Scripture resource strategist with IMB. Swarr commented that he is actively attempting to incorporate more women and persons from the Majority World as reflected in recent addition of an International Council into the ION administrative structure.[23]

THE SCOPE OF THE RESEARCH PROJECT

Broadly, this project examines one case study in which a Ugandan denomination has had to decide how far it wishes to appropriate a particular form of oral communication as opposed to literate-based methods for the purposes of the dissemination and teaching of Christianity. There is a long history of interest in the way that Christianity and its sacred written text, the Bible, have influenced individuals and communities. Recently, with the majority of self-described Christians living outside of the traditionally defined boundaries of northern and Western Christendom,[24] scholarship has turned attention to the role of the printed biblical text in contexts that maintain strong oral traditions.[25]

Africa is one of those regions that often provokes association with oral culture.[26] Historically, what might be termed oral praxis has played a dominant role in many African societies, yet scholarship has strongly challenged the former binary stereotype that strictly associated African

---

21. http://www.gods-story.org.

22. Bowman, *Building Bridges*. See also http://www.scripturesinuse.org/pages/about-us/. Regarding the quote, this is the organization's motto. See the homepage at https://www.scripturesinuse.org.

23. Swarr, August 18, 2016.

24. Jenkins, *Next Christendom*.

25. By strong oral traditions, I am speaking generally of societal contexts wherein the spoken word maintains a high degree of authority. For examples of biblical engagement with such cultures, see Arrington, "Hymns of the Everlasting Hills"; Handman, *Critical Christianity*.

26. Barber quotes Zumthor, describing Africa as the "continent of the voice." Barber, *Anthropology of Texts*, 30.

communication with orality and Western communication with literacy.[27] While the introduction of literacy to many African communities has strong historical ties to Western colonial and missionary endeavors, several recent African anthropological studies of a spectrum of African Christian communities have explored how African communicators have appropriated, adapted, and exploited print-based communication methodologies for a variety of spiritual, social, and political purposes.[28]

This project challenges the other half of that false stereotype that associates Western communication with literacy. Since the early 1980s, there has been a movement within a number of evangelical Protestant mission organizations and churches, many with direct or indirect American affiliations, to propagate orality; however, it is a particularly defined orality (or what I am calling **orality$_2$**). One of the distinct features of Protestantism has been its emphasis on the preached sermon, yet this self-identified OM is not merely calling for more oral proclamation. They believe that oral proclamation (or delivery) is only half of the equation, with the other equally important half being an orally constructed message, which, they argue, is typically narrative in style. Within their understanding, orality is defined to incorporate both a mode of communication (via the voice) but also a particular way of organizing information. They argue that too often Protestants' oral forms (e.g., sermons) are mere oral drapery over highly literate-styled, propositional messages. Thus, for members of the OM, a truly "oral" communication event has to be oral in both form (medium) and style (content).

The theoretical structures of such an understanding of orality invite further questioning and analysis.[29] Nevertheless, for now, what is important is that for these oral enthusiasts, today's global audience needs another reformation, only it needs to be an oral one. They are advocating against the alleged privileging of abstract, propositional, and monological forms of communicating the gospel and instead are championing an oral-friendly, narrative-centered, dialogically structured, full sensory approach to gospel communication. Whether this phenomenon is in reaction to particular styles of American evangelical Protestantism that tend to (over)emphasize certain conceptual or doctrinal Christian frameworks, or whether this group's concern does indeed have transcultural implications, this network of people is challenging the existing authority they believe has been wrongly

---

27. A good introduction to a variety of scholars dealing with these issues is in Barber, *African Hidden Histories*.

28. Barber, *Anthropology of Texts*; Cabrita, *Text and Authority*.

29. Vries, "Views of Orality," 141–55.

attached to the printed word and propositionally organized communication in Protestant mission and church-related endeavors.

Questions regarding the nature of communication practice, the biblical text, and divine authority have significant historical precedents. Not insignificantly, low literacy levels have been the norm throughout much of the history of Christianity, beginning with its first-century adherents.[30] Furthermore, some estimates project that only 5 percent of German speakers could read in Martin Luther's day.[31] Nevertheless, Luther leveraged the relatively new printing press and vernacular languages as communication strategies that enabled a shift in the locus of authority from the Catholic religious elite to the general populace.

Indeed, the question of authority was a central matter of dispute during the time of the Reformation. The Catholic Church maintained that its so-called unwritten traditions originated in the oral sayings and proclamations of Jesus and the apostles.[32] While understood to have been originally oral, such teachings had been preserved in writing by the faithful so as to share with future generations. One of the questions at the heart of the Reformation was whether the written tradition (i.e., the Bible) and what can be called the unwritten tradition (i.e., these once oral but since written apostolic teachings upheld by the Catholic Church) were of equal divine authority regarding the question of salvation. The Council of Trent (1545–63) reaffirmed that, along with the Scriptures, these "unwritten" traditions and customs of the Catholic Church were indeed necessary for salvation.

The Protestant Reformers denounced this unwritten tradition, proclaiming that the written tradition, the Scriptures alone, offered all that was necessary for salvation. This exclusive understanding of the relationship between divine authority and the written biblical text, an association that tends to remain in many Protestant branches today, stimulated an increasing desire among many early Reformers for believers to be able to read the Bible for themselves. Not surprisingly, without the guidance of the sacred tradition of the Catholic Church, right interpretation of the written text quickly became an immediate concern for the early Protestants and their spiritual descendants. This concern, in turn, fostered a high-value association between literate-based communication, Protestant education, and Protestant spiritual formation. Concern for investigations into original biblical languages, commitments to Bible translations into vernacular languages, personal devotional reading, printed hymnals, textual décor in

---

30. Harrison, *Art of Listening*, 3.
31. Edwards, *Printing, Propaganda, and Martin Luther*, 37–38.
32. Burghardt, "Catholic Concept of Tradition," 47–48; Evans, "Authority," 387–417.

homes, and biblical commentaries that provided Protestant-approved interpretations reiterate the Protestant tendency to affiliate divine authority with the written biblical text.[33]

Certainly, both Catholics and Protestants have historically utilized written and unwritten (i.e., printed and oral) communication strategies. Nevertheless, while possibly overstating the strong correlation between Protestantism and literacy, there is some legitimacy behind the following assertion: "Luther made necessary what Gutenberg had made possible."[34] No clearer historical example of this privileging of the written word can be seen than in early Protestant mission endeavors in Uganda, where, in the evangelical Anglican mission, the Church Missionary Society (CMS), being able to read, was "literarily the road to salvation."[35] Oral methodologies, that is, those reliant on the spoken word, have undoubtedly played a role in the history of Protestant spiritual formation, theological education, and mission praxis, yet this strong historical and theological association between divine authority and the written (and printed) biblical text makes the OM stand out as a phenomenon worthy of investigation.

This work evaluates the impact of the OM, with its enthusiastic commitment to oral communication methodologies, on the pastoral training program of Africa Gospel Church Uganda (AGC). Such research fulfills the multifaceted purpose of assessing the complex communication and material environment in which local receptions of Christianity are taking place, constructively analyzing the OM as a contemporary phenomenon in evangelical Protestant mission praxis while also paying due attention to intriguing historical precedents, and considering the wider implications for Christian communication strategies amidst similar Majority World contexts. Whether the appropriation of "orality principles" by AGC is simply about efficacious religious communication practice or represents a subtle form of imposition of Western (American?) missiological ideas, this project promises to make a unique contribution to contemporary religious studies and communication and media scholarship. Furthermore, as this research contributes to the interface incorporating oral, literate, and digital complexities, particularly in regards to biblical engagement and modern cultural expectations, it promises to be a stimulating dialogue partner for scholars interested in the study of the local receptions of Christianity. With the recent interest among Africanist anthropologists regarding texts,

---

33. Evans, "Authority"; Gordon, "Bible in Reformed Thought," 462–88; Walsham, "Holy Families," 122–60.

34. Furet and Ozouf, *Reading and Writing*, 58–59.

35. Manarin, "And the Word Became Kigambo," 269.

both oral and literate, this study desires to contribute a unique Ugandan case study to the conversation for purposes of fostering comparative study. Finally, this investigation affords greater clarity for understanding the interrelationships between differing modes of religious communication and materiality within a contemporary African context.

LITERATURE REVIEW

Regarding a review of the literature of relevant disciplines, the history of orality studies as a discipline finds its roots in classical studies, particularly the analysis of the oral dynamics in Homeric epics. Scholars such as Milman Parry, Albert Lord, and Eric Havelock have all been influential in drawing attention to oral communication, the formulaic nature of oral performance, and, among other things, orality's historical relationship with and transition to literacy. These scholars consequently influenced others, such as Marshall McLuhan[36] and Walter Ong. More than the others, Ong has played a formative role in the development of the theoretical understandings of both primary and secondary orality for many within the OM and thus receives extended treatment later in this work.

While oral tradition has historically played a significant role in biblical studies, recent scholarship has highlighted the significance of orality for the composition, performance, and reception of the biblical text.[37] Expressing frustration with scholarship's seeming inability to think outside of its textual bias, scholars such as Kebler, Dewey, Dunn, Rhoads, and Botha have sought to rediscover and reassert the value, role, and authority of the spoken word in ancient contexts. Consequently, such inquiries have turned to issues of interpretation and how sensitivity to such dynamics as oral performance influenced the way texts were originally interpreted and how they should be understood today.[38]

Significantly, this resurgence of interest in ancient orality and its implications have not been unanimous as voices such as New Testament scholar Larry Hurtado have expressed strong concerns.[39] For Hurtado, the

---

36. McLuhan, *Gutenberg Galaxy*. While McLuhan wrote extensively, his phrase "Gutenberg Galaxy" has become a part of the Orality Movement's verbal discourse. See Madinger, "Literate's Guide to the Oral Galaxy," 13–40.

37. For an excellent overview of the influence of Parry, Lord, and Ong on New Testament scholarship as well as an introduction to the major players who have given attention to orality and biblical studies, see Iverson, "Orality and the Gospels," 71–106.

38. Kelber, *Oral and the Written Gospel*; Dewey, "Oral Methods," 32–44; Dewey, "Gospel of Mark," 145–63; Dunn, *Jesus Remembered*; Rhoads, "Biblical Performative Criticism," 157–98; Botha, *Orality and Literacy in Early Christianity*.

39. Hurtado, "Oral Fixation and New Testament Studies," 321–40.

recent interest in oral performance appears to rely on romantic notions of orality and oversimplified understandings of the actual role of texts in the Roman era. While Hurtado acknowledges the prevalence of the spoken word during this timeframe, he cautions against an emphasis on orality that relegates the importance of texts. Hurtado's criticism has not gone unheeded and scholars such as Kelly Iverson, speaking from within the performance criticism community, have, likewise, countered Hurtado's challenge.[40] While reconciling such disputes falls beyond the scope of this study, it is worth highlighting that orality has been a topic of renewed interest and debate within biblical studies.

In regard to relevant anthropological studies, in the last decade or so, scholars such as Robbins, Haynes, Cannell, and Bialecki have sought to establish an anthropology of Christianity.[41] Out of this scholarship, a number of substantial Africa-based social anthropological studies, including Engelke, Kirsch, and Hawkins, have considered the dynamic relationship between spoken and written texts within Christian communities, particularly the construction, adaptation, and influence of texts in both colonial and postcolonial societies.[42] These studies have all contributed to investigating issues of identity, authority, bureaucracy, personhood, and the construction of meaning that emerges out of the confluence of oral and literate modes of communication.

Along these lines, in recent years, there has also been a renewed scholarly interest in the role of materiality within various Christian contexts. Scholars such as McDannell, Keane, and Meyer have sought to foreground the centrality of both material objects and embodiment in conversations regarding the central role that the bodily senses play in meaning-making practices.[43] Such explorations have led to fresh considerations of how the senses can mediate religious experience. This emphasis on embodiment and materiality informs much of the analysis undertaken in chapter 6.

Ironically, the OM has recognized the value of utilizing print to substantiate its oral claims. Numerous articles have appeared across a spectrum of

---

40. Iverson, "Oral Fixation or Oral Corrective?" 183–200.

41. Robbins, "Continuity Thinking," 5–38; Bialecki et al. "Anthropology of Christianity," 1139–58; Cannell, "Anthropology of Christianity," 2–50.

42. Engelke, *Problem of Presence*; Kirsch, *Spirits and Letters*; Hawkins, *Writing and Colonialism*.

43. For a helpful overview of some of these developments, see Morgan, "Religion and Media," 347–56; see also McDannell, *Material Christianity*; Keane, "Materialism, Missionaries, and Modern Subjects," 137–70; Keane, "On the Materiality of Religion," 230–31; Houtman and Meyer, *Things*.

evangelical missiology journals[44] as well as several popular-level books.[45] Desiring to influence literate-oriented educators, ION has hosted several consultations related to theological education and orality, the compiled papers from which have produced several books.[46] Within the last decade, a number of doctoral theses have also been written related to orality and mission, awarded primarily by American evangelical Protestant seminaries.[47] Finally in 2012, ION launched the *Orality Journal*, a semi-annual, online publication that seeks to promote dialogue around orality.[48]

Before progressing, two points of interest are worth further consideration, namely a British thesis and Walter Ong. As previously mentioned, I found no substantial work within the British academy specifically related to OM. I did find a semi-recent thesis (2002) related to the ownership of knowledge in theological education within Uganda by a former Baptist missionary, Brent Slater.[49] This thesis explicitly draws attention to the seeming contradiction between oral environments and literary education and pedagogical practices. Naturally, Slater's work and this current project have some parallels, but while sharing similar emphases, they go in different directions. Slater's concern was how theological educators can intentionally draw on indigenous, oral dynamics to ensure that adult learners are not just passive recipients in the educational process but active, critical owners (and creators) of knowledge. He constructed a theoretical framework by drawing on discourse and critical literacy theory, interrogating data drawn from studying three different formal theological institutions (Catholic, Anglican, and Baptist) within Uganda.

I found Slater's work to be insightful and of tremendous practical value for the broader church community within Uganda. However, while Slater shows awareness of such phenomena as oral Bible storytelling, his work was prior to the forming of ION in 2004. Furthermore, while both theses share a theological education motif, this current project explores how such education is embedded in particular socioeconomic expectations that cannot be ignored. In addition, it encompasses a wider scoop, focusing

---

44. Vries, "Views of Orality and Translation"; Prior, "Orality," 143–47; Seng, "Symposium."

45. Box, *Don't Throw the Book at Them*; Koehler, *Telling God's Stories with Power*; Willis and Snowden, *Truth That Sticks*.

46. See Samuel E. Chiang and Grant Lovejoy's *Beyond Literate Series*.

47. Jagerson, "Transformation through Narrative"; McIntyre, "Using Ceremonies to Disciple Oral Learners"; Yoakum, "Spoken Word"; Hartnell, "Oral Contextualization"; Thigpen, "Connected Learning"; Lee, "Bible Storytelling."

48. https://orality.net/library/journals/.

49. Slater, "Ownership of Knowledge."

on engagement with the Bible among a whole denomination and not exclusively among the trained leadership. Not incidentally, Slater's research took place within a formal education environment; his concern was institutionalized adult learning. On the contrary, this current project offers a comparative assessment of differing modes of communication from within an informal, non-institutionalized context. Therefore, while acknowledging similar interests and even contexts, both projects have clearly different scopes, audiences, and methodologies.

The second issue warranting extended consideration is the pivotal influence of Walter J. Ong in the development of orality studies as well as the OM itself. In 1982, Ong (1912–2003), an American Jesuit priest and cultural theorist, published *Orality and Literacy: The Technologizing of the Word*.[50] Southern Baptist missionary Jim Slack[51] introduced Ong's seminal book into the OM's consciousness as Ong's description of oral communication provided categories for what the movement's early pioneers had already discovered through oral storytelling. The reliance of many within ION on Ong's psychodynamics of orality expresses itself clearly in the influential ION text *Making Disciples of Oral Learners*.[52] The book refers to Ong as the father of the modern orality movement,[53] and the short annotation of *Orality and Literacy* in the bibliography is worth quoting in full.

> This is a technical treatise covering the modern discovery of primary oral cultures, some psychodynamics of orality, and oral memory, the story line, and characterization. It is more suitable for those interested in a deeper study of orality and its role in communication. This is the basic scholarly work in the field to date. No other work has superseded it. Ong takes account of all the major scholarly investigations through 1980.[54]

The reader should note the reference to the "psychodynamics of orality," and with acclamations such as, "this is the basic scholarly work . . . to date," and

---

50. My personal copy lists over thirty different reprints since it was originally published, testifying to the demand of Ong's most popular work. Ong, *Orality and Literacy*.

51. J. O. Terry and Grant Lovejoy suggested that Slack discovered Ong while reading for his doctorate of ministry degree from Southwestern Baptist Theological Seminary. After much searching, I was finally able to secure a copy of Slack's thesis through the help of the Southern Baptist Convention archivists in Richmond, VA. It is apparent that Ong was a major source for Slack's thinking with references to Ong starting to appear by p. 3. Slack, "Development of Chronological Bible Storytelling."

52. Lovejoy, *Making Disciples of Oral Learners*, 34.

53. Steffen also makes this claim, identifying Ong, Lord, Albert and Havelock as part of the Secular Story Movement. Steffen, *Worldview-Based Storying*, "Introduction."

54. Lovejoy, *Making Disciples of Oral Learners*, 54.

"no other work has superseded it," one can sense the level of high regard that those within the OM at the time maintained for Ong. *Making Disciples of Oral Learners* originated as a Lausanne[55] Occasional Paper and, thus, can be understood to represent (at the time) a general consensus within the broader evangelical mission community.

From his earliest research, beginning with his MA thesis on the poetry of Gerald Manley Hopkins and through his doctoral research on pedagogy, Ong exhibited a developing interest in oral/aural communication. Like many scholars, Ong's thinking evolved, particularly in regards to orality. His doctoral work on Ramism[56] led to a desire to understand how different information handling processes work, whether oral/aurally based or writing/printing based. He observed that different media influence the ways information is handled; consequently, how people and cultures communicate "and store knowledge changes how people (and cultures) think. Each culture develops a kind of bias for a particular type of knowledge."[57] In Ong's thinking, two significant historical examples were Hebraic thought, which he associated with aural–cognitive mind-set, and Greek thinking, which he argued tended to operate on a visual–cognitive register. In grappling with the implications of how different media influenced such cognitive processes, Ong developed an evolutionary understanding of how peoples' (and cultures') relationship with the word moves through successive stages of human expression, from the primary oral word, to written and printed word, to electronic word.[58]

Ong's evolutionary model has proved to be problematic, for, as members of the OM assert, certain peoples are skipping from primary orality to electronic means, or what Ong later labeled as secondary orality.[59] Secondary orality is communication that has been influenced by writing and the printed word but relies on electronic media. This concept is discussed at length in chapter 3, but for now, it only needs to be recognized that Ong's secondary (or digitalized) orality informs much of what the OM understands in its own conceptualization of "orality." Such an understanding is a good example of how the movement has, on the one hand, tried to move beyond some of Ong's thinking as sharp demarcations between

---

55. For a brief historical introduction to the Lausanne Movement, see Stanley, *Global Diffusion of Evangelicalism*, 151–80.

56. Ong, *Ramus, Method, and the Decay of Dialogue*.

57. Soukup, "Walter Ong and the State of Theology," 825; Ong, *Presence of the Word*, 3–6.

58. See chapter 1: "Transformations of the Word," and chapter 3: "Media Transformation." Ong, *Presence of the Word*, 17–49, 82–91.

59. Ong, *Orality and Literacy*, 3, 134.

evolutions or stages have proved elusive, while, on the other hand, members have drawn on other aspects of Ong's thought, such as his general categories and terminology.

To return to Ong's own development, *Orality and Literacy* represent a summation of Ong's multifaceted thinking on these transformations of the word within different contexts as he explores "the differences in 'mentality' between oral and writing cultures."[60] His exploration of the historical discovery (or scholarly rediscovery) of orality, his outlining of the psychodynamics (characteristics) that mark primary oral communication, and his discussion of how writing restructures human consciousness offered readers broad categories for understanding how different media afford different paradigmatic ways of thinking. It should be reiterated that Ong was not necessarily calling for a return to some romantic notion of a pre-script era but was highlighting a fundamental shift in sensory emphasis made possible (he argued) through the written and printed word, from the oral/aural to that of sight. "Writing has reconstituted the original oral, spoken word in visual space. Print embedded the word in space more definitively."[61] Such developments affect sensory hierarchies whereas, in eras past, the spoken word possessed an effervescent quality, print objectified words. With the moveable type printing press, words were literally assembled together from typeset letters, producing a typographic control that conveyed "tidiness and inevitability."[62] Over time, people came to trust their eyes more than their ears. Far from being incidental, Ong was convinced this sensory shift from *hearing* to *seeing* words as fixed "things" had far-reaching implications for understanding numerous issues, including space, certainty, and meaning,[63] as well as for a whole stream of other disciplines, including literary studies, social sciences, biblical studies, and philosophy.[64]

In the final paragraphs of the book, Ong explicitly states what would naturally seem to attract members of ION with their evangelical appreciation for both Jesus and the Bible:

> For in Christian teaching the Second Person of the One Godhead . . . is known not only as the Son but also as the Word of God. In this teaching, God the Father utters or speaks His Word, his Son. He does not inscribe him. . . . Yet Christian teaching also presents at its core the written word of God, the

60. Ong, *Orality and Literacy*, 3.
61. Ong, *Orality and Literacy*, 120.
62. Ong, *Orality and Literacy*, 115–20, 121.
63. Ong, *Orality and Literacy*, 121–35.
64. Ong, *Orality and Literacy*, 154–70.

Bible, which, back of its human authors, has God as author as no other writing does. In what way are the two senses of God's "word" related to one another and to human beings in history? The question is more focused today than ever before.[65]

While no evidence has emerged that Ong was ever aware of the OM, one might suggest that its members see their endeavors as a partial attempt to address Ong's final question regarding the relationship between the word of God as the person of Jesus and the written Bible. This issue is addressed in chapter 3's discussion of the OM's ideological understanding of the Bible. For now, it suffices to note that Ong's scholarly tone and Christian values provided a "legitimate" academic and theoretical platform to undergird a paradigm shift that was already in motion. As Lovejoy has described, Ong offered generalizations for those within the OM to get their literate minds around the preferences of many of their oral audiences.[66]

Not incidentally, Ong's oral–literate hypothesis has provoked vigorous critical conversation,[67] both directly and indirectly.[68] In 1984, Brian V. Street wrote *Literacy in Theory and Practice*,[69] and while his main dialogue opponent was Jack Goody and not Ong, Goody's autonomous view of literacy (Street's designation) was rejected. Goody, a Cambridge social anthropologist, greatly influenced Ong.[70] Street criticized Goody and, thus, indirectly Ong for essentially universalizing characteristics of literacy that, Street argued, failed to appreciate social context. In essence, differing ideas within a particular culture will influence the development and impact of literacy. Literacy is not value neutral and neither are its impacts autonomous of contextual ideologies.[71] Furthermore, the Africanist Ruth Finnegan has strongly cautioned against the dangers of technological determinism—an unintended implication for theorists such as Ong, Goody,

---

65. Ong, *Orality and Literacy*, 175–76.

66. Lovejoy, *Making Disciples of Oral Learners*.

67. While Ong uses phrases "oral-literacy shift," "oral-literacy studies," and "oral-literacy polarities," Farrell refers to Ong's "oral-literacy hypothesis." See Ong, *Orality and Literacy*, 153–54; Farrell, "Early Christian Creeds," 132–49.

68. Soukup, "Orality and Literacy," 3–33.

69. Street, *Literacy in Theory and Practice*.

70. Ong makes references to two of Goody's texts in *Orality and Literacy*. See Goody, *Domestication of the Savage Mind*; Goody and Watt, "Consequences of Literacy," 27–68.

71. Street describes what he calls the autonomous approach to literacy, which relies on strong generalizations or universals (Goody, Ong, etc.). Street argues instead for an ideological approach, which allows for local contributing factors. See chapters 1, 2 and 4 respectively. Street, *Literacy in Theory and Practice*.

and McLuhan.[72] Furthermore, "the technological model" (her phrase) tends towards reiterating the unhelpful concept of the great divide between those having literacy and those who do not, a divide that Finnegan acknowledges has influenced much of Western thought but that does not necessarily rely on empirical evidence. Thus, she, like Street, suggests that communication is not just about technology but requires sensitivity to factors within sociocultural contexts.[73]

As already indicated, the OM has not been completely naïve in ignoring criticism of Ong and the tendency of his appreciators to form clearly demarcated lines between oral and literate cultures. Lovejoy reported that at an ION meeting in 2006, special guest Lourens de Vries[74] criticized Ong for his overgeneralizations and warned the group to be careful of overreliance on his ideologies. While Vries's critique necessitates further elaboration (see chapter 3), subsequently other voices have begun to emerge from members of the movement, voicing the need for a more robust understanding of orality that acknowledges a greater appreciation of contextual factors in regards to the oral–literate interface.[75]

One of the questions that emerged in the research, which appears not to have been previously discussed, was whether Ong's Catholic sacramental thinking may have possessed a certain appeal to the evangelicals constituting the OM. In other words, did merely scholarship attract these Protestant missionaries, or was there something in the way Ong theologically conceptualized communication that these Protestants intuited was missing from their own paradigms (and practices)? In an article on Ong's religious foundations,[76] Paul Soukup outlines how Ong was influenced by H. Richard Niebuhr's model of "Christ above culture," and "the Catholic imagination."[77] While a full exploration of either or both issues is well beyond the scope of this work, Soukup sketches how, in Niebuhr's schema, Catholics understood Christ as being above culture but also as acting in and

---

72. Finnegan, "Communication and Technology," 113–16.

73. Finnegan, "Communication and Technology," 115–16.

74. Vries is professor of Bible translation and general linguistics at Vrije Universiteit Amsterdam. While I was not able to obtain a copy of the 2006 paper, one can discern Vries's primary concerns and explicit critiques in Vries, "Views of Orality and Translation."

75. For a very in-depth explanation and comparison of Ong and Street, see Yoakum, "Spoken Word," 48–76; likewise, Jagerson voices strong concern that Ong's ideas eliminate the importance of meaning, which has dramatic consequences. See Jagerson, "Transformation through Narrative," 54–56.

76. Soukup, "Contexts of Faith," 175–88.

77. Soukup, "Contexts of Faith," 181; Greeley, *Catholic Imagination*.

through culture. Consequently, Soukup suggests that for Ong, all creation follows a pathway of hominization that finds its realization in the Person of Christ, the God–man.[78] Furthermore, Soukup discusses how the Catholic imagination is one that allows for a sacramental orientation that seeks to cultivate awareness to the presence of God and signs that might point to the divine presence. This Catholic imagination emphasizes community and mediation, wherein persons, signs, and presences are interconnected in a "world of communication."[79] While there is danger in overgeneralizing what might be more accurately labeled as Catholic imaginations and understandings of culture, if nothing else, Soukup's thoughts highlight the fact that Ong possessed a different theological paradigm from that used by the Protestant members of the OM.

I propose that this different theological paradigm, one that tends to operate more on a sacramental register, has proven attractive to various members of the OM. Put in a different way, even if one rejects Ong's orality–literacy theory as tending towards unhelpful (if not untrue) binary opposites, one wonders if Ong's sacramental perspective, wherein persons live in interconnected worlds of communication, has struck a resounding cord among these Protestant members of the OM. Certainly, both Catholics and Protestants have historically utilized multipronged communication strategies, which have included, among other things, written and unwritten (printed and oral) elements. Yet an argument has been made that Catholicism, with its wider acknowledgement of the non-written or oral tradition already mentioned, has allowed for a more oral and, consequently, multimodal communication event in emphasizing the drama of its mass.[80] The sight of visual images, the smell of incense, and the carefully rehearsed liturgical choreography of the priestly celebration of the mass, including the tastes of the Eucharistic elements, all afford greater opportunities for congregants to engage in a multisensory and thus more holistic religious experience.

While this hypothesis has been unacknowledged by those within the OM, there has been an emphasis on orality and the arts. Curiously, the recent articles within the *Orality Journal*[81] depict worship experiences that bear remarkable commonalities with the Catholic mass. Thus, the *Journal* articles

---

78. Soukup, "Contexts of Faith," 181.
79. Soukup, "Contexts of Faith," 180–81.
80. Duffy, *Stripping of the Altars*.
81. Chiang and Coppedge, "Arts & Orality Part 1"; Chiang and Coppedge, "Arts & Orality Part 2."

described the movement of dance,[82] the smell of incense,[83] a sensitivity to space,[84] and the adaption of local festivals and rituals,[85] echoing not a stereotypical Protestant text-based (or propositional-oriented) communication event but a Catholic sacramental, communal communication experience. While refusing to concede on their evangelical privileging of the authority of the Bible, could it be that these OM Protestants are seeking an implicitly Catholic sacramentality not necessarily afforded by a worship experience structured around assent to rational propositions? In some ways, such inquiries are outside the direct scope of this study. Nevertheless, such tentative probings, while not definitively answered here, are a helpful way to prime the pump, not only in acknowledging the debt the OM owes to Ong, but also in helping to set the stage regarding the multifaceted complexity of communication dynamics under consideration.

METHODOLOGY

This project utilized an interdisciplinary approach that blended historical, ethnographic, and qualitative methods with a comparative analysis. This was accomplished by first, investigating the historical relationship between Protestantism, print, and learning by dialoguing with multiple relevant disciplines, including historical studies of Protestantism, print culture, and preaching. Second, in attempting to gain a true portrayal of the ideological values of the OM, as described by members of the movement themselves, I employed a modified grounded theory process,[86] seeking to distill the movement's core ideologies from the raw data of twenty interviews with members of the OM.[87] The interviewees included both male and female voices, representing active orality champions in as diverse locations as the

---

82. For examples of combining music, dance, drama and visual art in Tibetan and Indonesian contexts, see Chiang and Coppedge, "Arts & Orality Part 1," 43–46, 47–50.

83. Chiang and Coppedge, "Arts & Orality Part 1," 31–42.

84. Chiang and Coppedge, "Arts & Orality Part 1." For discussion regarding the role of Christian-themed mural art in public space, see pp. 55–58. For discussion of dance and music in public space, see pp. 63–66.

85. Chiang and Coppedge, "Arts & Orality Part 1." For two brief comparative case studies from Kenya and India, see pp. 51–54.

86. Glaser and Strauss, *Discovery of Grounded Theory*; Glaser, *Doing Grounded Theory*.

87. All interviewees, for the Orality Movement, WGM, and AGC, signed a written consent form prior to being interviewed. While the form did ask if the individual wanted to remain anonymous, no one requested it. In fact, particularly among the church personnel, people expressed an eagerness to be identified with their comments.

Introduction   25

United States, Venezuela, Niger, and Vietnam.[88] In addition, senior leaders from within the OM were interviewed, including two former executive directors of ION. Interviews were conducted either in-person or by means of Skype (or FaceTime).[89] Notes from the interviews were typed up and then coded line-by-line while memoing was employed simultaneously. This approach resulted in initial categories, which led to subsequent recoding and memoing and slowly, key ideas emerged. This material was supplemented with resources already published on the OM's history and thought and follow-up communication with differing interviewees.

Third, historical research was used to explore the longstanding relationship between Christianity and literacy in Uganda. For compiling the history of AGC, which remains largely undocumented, I drew on personal interviews and documentary analysis. The interviews drew on personnel both from within World Gospel Mission (the agency that founded AGC) and members of AGC for constructing a brief history of the denomination. Documentary analysis was used in consideration of relevant mission documents and church papers.

Fourth, data regarding the impact of the OM on AGC was accumulated through field research conducted in Uganda from March to May 2017 and again in December 2017. I was based in Kampala near to the church office but also traveled to various locations throughout the country, visiting AGC churches and their communities in the northern region (Nebbi), the western region (Kafu, Bulyango, Kahara), and the eastern region (Masese, Bugiri, Buwagi). Due to the extensive and integral nature of this field research process for the entire thesis, further description is appropriate. Several issues that deserve comment are the basis of data sampling, my reflexivity as the researcher, and the limitations of my data collection.

Sampling

A theoretical or purposive sampling approach was employed with both World Gospel Mission (WGM) missionaries and AGC personnel.[90] This

---

88. The gender ratio of interviewees was 80 percent male and 20 percent female.

89. In August 2016, the Lausanne Movement hosted the *Young Leaders Gathering* in Jakarta, Indonesia (August 3–10), which I attended. One of the workshops was focused on orality and I was able to facilitate a number of interviews with participants from around the world who are utilizing orality in mission endeavors. I attended the International Orality Network regional conference in Houston (September 12–14, 2016). This, likewise, provided an ideal occasion to interview a variety of active members in the movement.

90. Bernard, *Research Methods in Anthropology*, 145; Barbour, *Introducing Qualitative Research*, 52.

purposive sampling meant that I did not engage random Ugandans about AGC's communication praxis. Instead, while I was not able to connect with every AGC church member, I did intentionally seek opportunities to engage and observe as many AGC church leaders, local church congregations, and local church members as possible. This approach included intentionally connecting with WGM missionaries who are (or have been) involved with the church, whether through face-to-face interviews in Uganda, Skype conversations, e-mail correspondence or messaging via Whatsapp.[91] I organized many of these engagements, such as personal interviews or Sunday morning site visits, but others happened through serendipity, such as spontaneous lunches with church personnel. Overall, I sought every opportunity to spend time with church leaders or members, whether traveling, eating, worshiping, attending Bible study, or being involved in casual conversation. These activities resulted in a sampling that included the expected church visits, personal interviews, both unstructured and semi-structured, focus group conversations, and attendance at a weekly Bible study. It also included some unexpected opportunities, such as listening with a church member to Joel Osteen preach on the radio, traveling with an area overseer on a four-day training visit, navigating Kampala's taxi park with the denomination's pastoral training coordinator, and traveling from Jinga to Kampala with the senior missionary and church trainer for the *Farming God's Way* training program.[92]

Two other aspects of the sampling need highlighting, namely differences between rural and urban communities[93] and the inclusion of AGC women's voices. Due to the tendency of communication practices to vary between rural and urban environments, a mixture of perspectives was intentionally sought through visits and conversations with numerous rural church communities and pastors (Nebbi, Kafu, Kahara, Bulyango, and Bugiri), several semi-urban church communities and pastors (Masese and Bukasa), and finally several urban churches, namely Kisugu and United Faith Chapel (UFC).[94] This varied exposure to differing communities provided a rich repertoire of perspectives from across the rural–urban spectrum.

---

91. Hennink et al. calls this purposive recruitment, as in it deliberately recruits "information-rich" people. Hennink et al., *Qualitative Research Methods*, 84–85. Not all WGM missionaries work alongside AGC as several work exclusively with an international school in Kampala. Therefore, I did not bother to interview them.

92. John Muehleisen (WGM) and Simon Taliire (AGC) are the two senior trainers for the Christian agricultural development approach called *Farming God's Way* (FGW).

93. See the map of AGC locations throughout Uganda on page 142.

94. While UFC is technically inter-denominational because it is a university student-initiated congregation, it essentially functions as an AGC church with significant

I was conscious that my male gender might limit engaging women perspectives. Furthermore, many of the AGC pastors are male, including the church's entire executive committee. Nevertheless, I did intentionally seek to include female perspectives in the sampling by interviewing several female church members and women leaders, as well as spending travel time with Rev. Miria Mukisa.[95] Rev. Maria[96] is the only ordained woman in AGC and serves as the area overseer for "Kampala and beyond." She graciously welcomed me on a four-day safari with her and her husband to visit three different churches near Masindi.[97] That occasion and other conversations allowed for women such as Miria to provide valuable insight into AGC's communication context. Therefore, while the presented data cannot account for all AGC churches, it does provide a good range of perspectives from the participating parties.

Reflexivity and Data Collection Limitations

This study acknowledges that it draws on both the advantages and disadvantages of an "insider" and "participant" perspective. From 2007 to 2013, my wife and I lived in northern Uganda, serving with WGM. We were initially involved in establishing an AGC pastoral training center in the Nebbi district, and then in 2009, we were heavily involved in facilitating the AGC oral pilot training program. These activities led to our working alongside the AGC Training Committee to incorporate oral methodologies, primarily Bible storytelling, throughout the other training centers. Before leaving in 2013, we assisted with the launch of an integrated curriculum that sought to leverage oral- and literate-based practices for training AGC pastoral leadership. Therefore, there is an acknowledged "practical" sense to this project as it grapples with questions that were generated, not in the classroom, but out of the frictions of everyday communication complications within a particular Ugandan Christian context.

My proximity with those involved in the primary research resulted in a unique blend of limitations and opportunities. Being heavily involved

---

financial and personnel involvement by WGM.

95. Maria Mukisa and Steward Mukisa, personal interview, April 22, 2017.

96. AGC differentiates between the titles of "reverend" and "pastor," the former being ordained by the denomination while the latter has not. Maria Mukisa is unique in AGC in that while both she and her husband, Steward, serve as AGC pastors, she is ordained as reverend while her husband is not yet. To avoid the cumbersomeness of differentiating between "Rev. Mukisa" and "Pastor Mukisa," I have opted to refer to these important interlocutors by their first names.

97. Mira Mukisa and Steward Mukisa, personal communication, while traveling together on overseer visit, April 27, 2017.

in AGC's encounter with orality predisposed me to certain sympathies as well as criticisms. Having lived extensively in East Africa, I am also aware of some cultural tendencies wherein certain people try and provide what they believe is "the right answer" for the "visitor." Furthermore, there was a risk that neither missionaries nor church members would speak openly about matters of communication or even, more specifically, about the pastoral training because of their existing close associations with me. Although I acknowledge my own identity as a Christian, a missionary, a sponsor (at times) of various church activities and personnel, and even former trainer within the church,[98] I sought to establish that my return was in a new role, that of researcher.

Herein, I found the consent form to be an asset. Every time, with both missionaries and church personnel, the pulling out and explaining of the consent form brought a shift in the relational dynamics. Sometimes this change was as slight as the person shifting in his or her chair or, more often, people's voices becoming slightly more formal in response to the initial questions. While personally, these changes felt awkward for me, it was a professional gift because it clearly communicated that the "familiar missionary friend" was now operating from a new role as "researcher." Therefore, I acknowledge that my history of personal relationships with various other missionaries, church leaders, training facilitators, and pastors has had the potential to limit my objectivity. Nevertheless, conscious of these dangers, I have actively sought to avoid preconceived notions or presumptuous conclusions.

The "insider" limitation is also a unique opportunity. As an active participant in AGC's encounter with orality, I was aware of assumptions and tendencies both within the missionary community and the church context that need critical reflection. Furthermore, since the AGC community values relationships, the fact that I have traveled extensively, enjoyed meals together, and held discussions over many cups of tea with these various church affiliates suggests a relational depth to this research that would not be possible to an outsider. This strong relational network involves a personal trust that has allowed me to access data regarding the impact of orality at all levels of the church. Thus, there was indeed a degree of formality in conversations, with the consent form and my pulling out my recorder, notebook, and pen and yet, overall, I would count my relational history with many of the church and mission personnel as an advantage to this investigation.

---

98. On the legitimacy of acknowledging one's position as a Christian in doing ethnography, see Bielo, *Words upon the Word*, 32; Howell, "Repugnant Cultural Other," 371–91.

While acknowledging there is no precise way to measure how far my previous history did or did not impact dialogue partners, I was quite shocked by the emotion that emerged in conversation with members of both the church and mission. It was not reticence that I encountered in personal interviews or conversations but often a torrent of opinions that revealed concerns, grievances, and questions. Any apprehension that parties would not feel comfortable offering criticism, either of each other or those responsible for communication and pastoral training, was quickly removed as both missionaries and church personnel shared quite freely and even critically (albeit for the most part respectfully). Open critique was offered by both missionaries and church members of the orality programs, which many of them still associated with me, because of my previous role as a trainer. Often such critique included an inquiring look as if to make sure I really wanted their honest opinion (to which I would nod yes), before the individual shared plainly how he or she saw the issues at stake.

In his anthropological study of evangelical Bible study in the United States, James Bielo describes the question of whether his presence in a Bible study altered the conversation. In his case, he suggests that overall he did not believe his attending the study changed the discussion dynamics considerably.[99] That issue was likewise a concern for me. There were times when I was conscious that my presence might alter the dynamics of a situation, such as being called upon to answer a question while attending a Bible study.[100] On such occasions, I risked an honest but also as abbreviated answer as possible.[101]

When, on occasion, an episode or incident from my prior experience in Uganda was discussed, I consciously tried to discern where matters stood for the church "at this point," rather then merely reflecting back on my earlier experience. Having said that, there was one other area where my previous history played an important role, namely regarding questioning. Due to my experience with the pastoral training program, I was able to adapt my interview questions as appropriate. While this adaptation meant not everyone was asked the exact same questions, I believe a more nuanced rapport transpired between the interviewees and myself. One example is Pastor Benson Omri from Nebbi who had previously been heavily involved in the orality training, including AGC's original oral pilot program. He is currently pursuing a degree in theology, so I spent substantial

---

99. See Bielo treatment on being reflexive in chapter 2, "Doing Bible Study Ethnography," Bielo, *Words upon the Word*, 21–45.

100. Kisugu AGC Bible Study (4th), participatory observation, May 18, 2017.

101. For a discussion on risking dishonesty, see Bielo's justification in his *Words upon the Word*, 37.

time asking him to compare his experiences, having now participated in both an informal, oral training model and a formal, highly print-reliant training model.[102] Such questions would have been irrelevant for other pastors who have not had the occasion to pursue further studies. However, they did allow for a unique comparison by a senior pastor whose communication reflections were directly relevant. Thus, while acknowledging such reflexive concerns, the overall sense I perceived was that people were open, frank, and even, at times, surprisingly grateful for the chance to talk about issues that concerned them.

Two other comments are necessary regarding the limitations of my data collection. First it is necessary to acknowledge that when I was interviewing members of the OM, by and large, they provided me with a favorable account of their experiences with orality. This is particularly evident in chapter 3 and I have allowed this attitude to stand in order to offer a opportunity for members of the movement to express their own self-understanding. Nevertheless, the church's ensuing assessment, discussed in chapters 5 and 6, reveals that its personnel do not necessarily align themselves with the same positive tone that reverberates throughout much of the OM members' rhetoric. The critical space created by this differential in evaluations of orality is integral to this book's argument.

Second, if I had known my conclusions or my final reflections from the beginning of the study, I would have crafted my data collection differently. While I set out to explore the oral-literacy tensions (and those are reflected in my research evidence presented in chapters 5 and 6), what I did not expect was how important embodiment and material culture would be in my final analysis. Members of the church expressed appreciation for orality, yet they also expressed critiques. However, these concerns seemed to be based less on the actual oral communication event and more on other factors impinging on the communication context and their perception of these social and economic forces. In trying to interpret this "yes, we like orality" but "no, we don't" dynamic, I found myself needing additional conceptual tools to understand not only what the church members were saying but what the evidence meant. Surprisingly, for me, the theoretical apparatuses that helped me interpret the mixed reaction of church members were material and embodiment discourse. While I ended up leaning heavily on these disciplines, I did not necessarily start out that way. Thus, there is an element of development to this investigation as I seek to provide reflection on how to understand the mixed research evidence. In hindsight, had I known that the thesis's main

---

102. Benson Omri, interview (1st), March 19, 2017; Omri, Benson, interview (2nd), May 12, 2017.

intellectual dialogue partners would be materiality and embodiment studies, I would have crafted my data collection differently from the beginning. While granting that caveat, I submit that the theoretical reflections throughout shed valuable light on how to understand what the evidence does suggest concerning the ways in which the Africa Gospel Church has interpreted the OM's particular strand of orality.

Research Methods

A three-pronged, mixed-method approach was adopted for gathering relevant information: participant observation, personal interviews, and focus group discussions. Russell Bernard, in his epic work on research methods, describes participant observation as "stalking culture in the wild."[103] Such a description was the motivation behind wanting to spend time in Uganda for fieldwork in order to experience how AGC communicates in today's world. Practically, whenever I went out, I carried a local exercise book in which to record observations and, on occasion, took pictures with my iPhone.

Bernard describes the difference between "observing participants" and "participating observers," with the former being insiders who pay attention to what is happening around them and the latter being those, having entered from outside, who participate and take notes.[104] Due to my previous history with the church and the concern that too much participation might evoke former roles or expectations, I sought to remain a participating observer as much as possible. While not hiding, I did try to minimize drawing attention to myself.

The second research method used was focus group discussions. Monique Hennink describes a focus group discussion as simply "a *focus* on specific issues, with a predetermined *group* of people, participating in an interactive *discussion*."[105] Over the course of the fieldwork, I was able to facilitate nine of these interactive focus group discussions.[106] The primary purpose of these focus groups was to try to hear from the church members

---

103. Bernard, *Research Methods in Anthropology*, 258.
104. Bernard, *Research Methods in Anthropology*, 260.
105. Hennink, *Understanding Focus Group Discussions*, 1; for another helpful overview of the Focus Group process, including some of the challenges, see Makosky Daley et al., "Using Focus Groups," 697–706.
106. Focus Group: Nebbi AGC, March 19, 2017; Focus Group: AGC Church Leaders, April 5, 2017; Focus Group: Kamuli Area Pastors, April 7, 2017; Focus Group: Masese AGC, April 23, 2017; Focus Group: Kafu AGC, April 27, 2017; Focus Group: Bulyango AGC, April 28, 2017; Focus Group: Kahara AGC, April 29, 2017; Focus Group: KIU Students, May 5, 2017; Focus Group: Bugiri AGC, May 14, 2017.

themselves and not just the church leadership.[107] While there was one explicit incident where the congregation seemed to parrot what the pastor said, the nature of most of the questions was related to observations or personal preferences and thus, people seemed to answer quite freely and did not seem to mind responding differently from the pastor.

The two main areas of discussion within the focus groups were regarding how Ugandans, and more specifically AGC members, communicate their Christian faith and how they interact with the Bible. The questions were primarily open-ended and semi-structured as I sought to balance guiding the conversation towards the main particular topics but also allowing for the group's own interest to shape the discussion. This approach was conditionally successful as these discussions provided a wealth of data from the grassroots level. People talked freely about issues such as why the Bible was important to them, how they studied the Bible, what they found difficult in Bible study, and whether they preferred topical or story-based sermons and why. Each group maintained a mixture of male and female voices, although recording the exact size of the groups remained elusive as, often times, people would come and join the group (or even step out) in mid-discussion.

The discussion was usually a blend of English, Swahili, or the local vernacular, whether Luganda, Lusoga, or Alur. The wide range of languages is indicative of the wide variety of ethnicities represented within AGC Uganda. The multiethnic nature of AGC Uganda was intentionally cultivated by the WGM missionaries to counter the pattern they had witnessed while working in Kenya where the AGC Kenya denomination, while in theory supposed to be a national denomination, was, in reality, predominately made up of the Kipsigis people.[108] One of the consequences in AGC Uganda today of the missionaries intentionally cultivating a multiethnic denomination is that there is no one language that everyone speaks.[109] Thus, in the case of vernacular, I was dependent on interpreters, whether the pastor or another church member, but enough of the participants in each group spoke the

---

107. Two of the groups were exclusively pastors and I was grateful for the opportunity to hear from such a concentration of leadership voices. Focus Group: AGC leaders, April 5, 2017; Focus Group: Kamuli, April 7, 2017.

108. Jeff Stanfield and Christine Stanfield, personal interview, May 9, 2017. It should be noted that today, due to intentional missionary efforts by the AGC Kenya leadership—particularly among the Pokot and Maasai peoples, the denomination boasts a much broader ethnic representation.

109. While it would be natural to assume that different ethnic groups interpret oral genres such as storytelling differently, such ethnic-based differences did not appear in any vivid way throughout the discussion with church members.

vernacular and English that I did not worry that what was being interpreted was in any way being intentionally distorted or "bent."

The challenge presented by the focus groups was twofold: numbers and follow-up. Due to the distance between the churches, both from each other and from Kampala (where I was based), for both scheduling and funding purposes, it proved necessary often to combine a Sunday morning visit to a church with a focus group meeting. The advantage was that I was able to engage with a large group of local church members. However, the groups ranged from approximately eight to fifteen adults. This number is slightly larger than the ideal focus group size of six to eight.[110] Despite the size of the groups, often every person answered almost every single question. The disadvantage meant that time did not allow me to ask as many questions.

Furthermore, due to the excessive geographical distance, follow-up became impractical.[111] While individual follow-up was possible with various pastors (many who traveled to Kampala on a semi-regular basis, whether for work or attending to business in the church office), I was not able to schedule any follow-up focus group discussions. In the end, different groups discussed related but not always identical topics. The result was that although the groups provided ample data for me, because of these differences, straightforward comparison between groups proved challenging. Overall, I appreciated the interactions afforded by the groups (although at times wishing for more) because they did provide a sense of how local church members view communication practices in the church. The members' perspectives, at times, were in tension with what the pastor or church leaders alleged, and such contradictions proved illuminating, as discussed in chapter 5.

The third research method employed was personal interviews.[112] Interviewees were selected partially on their role or responsibility within the church, but their accessibility was a factor as well. Furthermore, I sought representation from both leaders and church members as well as female and male voices. The interview format was semi-structured with what Rubin and Rubin refer to as a topical approach.[113] I would begin with some background inquiries (if unknown) but would then shift to asking open-ended questions regarding areas of particular interest, including denominational history, personal history with AGC, communication practices of Ugandans and specifically AGC, personal experience (or exposure)

110. Robson, *Real World Research*, 295.
111. Robson, *Real World Research*, 294.
112. See Bernard, *Research Methods in Anthropology*, chapter 8, "Interviewing I: Unstructured and Semi-structured," 156–86; see also Hennink et al., *Qualitative Research Methods*, chapter 6, "In-depth Interviews," 108–32.
113. Rubin and Rubin, *Qualitative Interviewing*, 6.

with AGC's pastoral training program, and perspectives on oral Bible storytelling and the pastoral training program (if relevant). The table below presents the number of interviews conducted with persons belonging to the church, the mission, and other voices.[114]

Church and Mission Interviews

Personnel	Number of Persons Interviewed	Repeat Interviews	Total Number of Interviews	Gender
Africa Gospel Church	11	5 second interviews 1 third interview	17	7 men 4 women
World Gospel Mission	9	3 second interviews 1 third interview	13	6 men 3 women
Other	4 (2 Ugandans, 2 missionaries)	0	4	4 men
Total	24	8 second interviews, 2 third interviews	34	17 men 7 women

While the rationale behind interviewing the church and mission personnel is self-explanatory, I also interviewed four other interviewees who were neither AGC nor WGM personnel. These interlocutors afforded additional perspectives that I found helpful in trying to process and understand the research data. For example, Fred Okello, a faithful member of Arua Baptist Church, is a fierce champion of oral Bible storytelling because he suffers severe visual impairment. A printed Bible is inaccessible to Okello; thus, he relies either on others to read to him from the Bible or he uses a digital audio player, which can play an audio recording of the Bible. Another voice was Tonino Pasolini, an Italian Catholic priest who has worked in Uganda since 1966. He was tasked with establishing a Catholic radio station for West

---

114. It should be noted this table does not include interviews with the members of the OM.

Nile in 2000, *Radio Pacis*, and thus, offered not only a Catholic theological perspective but also a wealth of experience for communicating the Christian faith in Uganda. The third "other voice" was Rhys Hall, an Australian missionary who has worked in and on behalf of the Episcopal Church of South Sudan for over twenty-five years. His career has included running a publishing company producing resources related to spiritual and education matters for use in South Sudan as well as training primary education teachers in South Sudan in the use of oral storytelling and digital media devices. The fourth "other voice" was Imam Otafiire, a chef in Kampala who has actively sought to incorporate Bible storytelling into his urban-setting church.[115] Several of his concerns mirrored those raised by AGC church members; thus, including Otafiire's voice was a helpful "outside" perspective.

Thus, overall, I was able to conduct thirty-four interviews. These included talking with the AGC's bishop,[116] the assistant bishop, the general secretary, and training coordinator, as well as other pastors and lay members. The WGM interviews included the founding WGM Uganda missionaries, the field director responsible for launching the pastoral training program, the current field director, and other missionaries who have been involved in various capacities, including operating WGM's print shop and coordinating the mission and church's joint venture in what is called *Transformational Ministries*. These outreaches are intentionally aimed at addressing physical as well as spiritual needs and include programs such as *Community Health Empowerment* (CHE), the denomination's women's training (called *Cycle of Life*), children's CHE, and *Farming God's Way*. Therefore, this broad spectrum of voices from both the mission and the church provided me with a well-balanced and in-depth perspective on the role of communication in issues such as biblical engagement, theological education, and church–mission relations.

Notes from interviews, focus group discussions, and personal observations were analyzed through a process of identifying key words, repeated phrases, interesting mini-case studies, other repetitions, and outlying comments or examples. These pieces of information were then coded, sorted, and scrutinized as patterns developed that begged additional questions which helped clarify emerging themes that then needed to be cross-checked and confirmed as accurately portraying the data. From this collection and analysis process, two meta-themes emerged that received additional analysis, namely, specific communication practices

---

115. Otafiire attends Healing Broken Hearts Church in Muyenga, Kampala.

116. Kefa Masiga's term as bishop has since expired (December 2017) and Joseph Ogweyo is the current AGC bishop.

and the responses to such communication practices. Thus, while this approach was not exhaustive of the AGC denomination, it did allow for both personal and communal responses, providing a healthy sampling from a particular local Ugandan denomination.

OUTLINE OF BOOK

Chapter 2 delineates the historical context out of which the OM has emerged. This historical setting is particularly important for delving into the communication dynamics and the interplay between Protestants' established affinity for the printed word even alongside their ubiquitous employment of oral and material methodologies. Chapter 3 introduces the OM, tracing its antecedents, history, demographics, and core ideologies, all in an attempt to discern whether its members are articulating a revolutionary track in Protestant discourse or merely offering an "oral" echo of traditional Protestant practice. Chapter 4 shifts the scene from the international movement with its strong Western affiliations to a local, Ugandan denomination. The relationship between literacy and early Christianity within what has become Uganda and how it has shaped modern sensibilities is considered before Africa Gospel Church Uganda is introduced in detail. Among other things, this introduction includes charting the church's historical relationship with WGM, the denomination's current demographics, its holiness theological orientation, and an overview of its unique pastoral training scheme.

Chapters 5 and 6 offer the heart of the research, specifically exploring how the denomination, its pastors, and members have responded to the implementation of oral Bible storytelling into the church's pastoral training program. This assessment includes a rigorous comparison of the affordances and hindrances of orality as understood by the OM, as well as textuality and digitality. As already mentioned, a surprise that emerged from the research was the difference between the respective valuations that the church and the mission placed on the role of materiality in communication. Thus, analysis incorporates insights drawn from religious materiality studies to understand how the church has appreciated and appropriated, yet also critiqued, orality, specifically in relation to different types of materiality. The final chapter probes into how the church's interpretation of orality and its unique relationship with these different types of materiality, whether embodied or artifactual, carries significant implications for issues of identity and personhood within the church's social imaginary. Such considerations relate practically to AGC's context but also maintain an eye for application in similar contexts in the Majority World (and beyond).

This investigation, therefore, explores the complex nature of communicating religious faith amidst international and local pressures. What emerged from the research was that while oral communication affords numerous communication advantages, its Western promoters have not always appreciated the complex way that communication modes, whether oral, print, or digital reliant, are embedded in historical and socioeconomic as well as materialistic imaginaries. Without an appreciation of this complex embedding, a limited understanding of communication has resulted that essentially divorces communication practice from the societal forces in which it is seeking to operate. Such a paradigm has resulted in missed opportunities to recognize how different modes of communication in contexts such as in Uganda afford different ways of shaping or forming personal identity. The connection between communication, materiality, and identity is no more evident than with regard to how different modes are associated with or fail to convey a "modern" sensibility. Simply put, orality is perceived as not achieving such modern realizations. Thus, while the AGC members did appreciate numerous aspects of orality, members of the OM are going to have to continue the hard work of re-conceptualizing, promoting, and adapting their understanding of orality if they desire such Majority World Christian communities to validate orality as a mode that can carry them into the future.

2

Protestantism's Enduring Communication Complexities

The Tension between Protestants' Commitment to the Biblical Text and the Pervasiveness of Illiteracy

INTRODUCTION

THIS CHAPTER CONSIDERS HOW Protestants have historically navigated the ambiguous tension between their commitment to the printed biblical text and people's lack of literacy skills. Such an exploration provides the necessary foundation upon which the ensuing introduction and analysis of the OM in chapter 3 can be established, affording consideration of the ways in which the movement both echoes and deviates from historical Protestant communication patterns.

The complex issue of literacy and church leaders' concern for local congregants to access textual messages is as old as the early church.[1] By the time of Luther's Reformation, worship within the Roman Catholic Church had developed into a multisensory communication experience that afforded, at least in theory, worshipers without proficiency in literacy skills the opportunity to experience worship and communion with God on a variety of nontextual registers.[2] When Luther and the other early Reformers replaced magisterial authority with their doctrine of *sola Scriptura*, the Scriptures were infused with an authoritative status for all matters pertaining to doctrine and piety. Rather than recognizing the "unwritten" tradition of the Catholic

---

1. See Colossians 4:16.
2. For a Catholic perspective, see Duffy, *Stripping of the Altars*.

Church in addition to the Scriptures, the biblical text alone was understood as mediating divine revelation. Thus, the association between divine authority and the textual medium became embodied in the printed Protestant Bible. The early Reformers were conscious that the majority of Europe could not read, a sociological characteristic evident throughout much of the history of Christianity (and discussed later in this chapter). Thus, these leaders and their subsequent descendants have had to navigate this tension between their typically authoritative understanding of the biblical text and people's lack of ability and, at times, lack of preference to read the text.

There is a complexity or, more frankly, a messiness to Protestants' relationship with text that this project seeks openly to acknowledge. Protestantism has been known as a religion of the word, and it has often been associated with the printed Bible. Nonetheless, this emphasis on the word has resulted in Protestants having a reputation for emphasizing the preached word; thus, their faith became one with strong oral associations. This investigation's interest in communication complexities foregrounds this tension in dramatic relief, considering how members of the OM are rediscovering and popularizing oral approaches and alternatives to the printed medium, specifically the printed biblical text, in their twenty-first-century mission strategies. While on the one hand, such oral enthusiasm seems natural for those of Protestant lineage, on the other hand, there have been questions and even resistance, particularly by those within American evangelicalism for whom the supreme authority of the Bible is indissolubly linked to the textual and, consequently, the printed medium.

The objective of this chapter is to prepare the ground for chapter 3 by considering the complex historical precedent within Protestantism for upholding a commitment to or affinity for the printed medium, even as many Protestants have utilized oral and other nontextual media for engaging people with the Christian message of salvation. To excavate this apparent tension or complexity within Protestantism, the first section of the chapter begins with a discussion regarding Protestants' relationship to the textual medium, exploring the theological importance of the biblical text for the Reformers, their utilization of the printing press, and their concern regarding hermeneutics, specifically for ensuring that the common worshiper would rightly interpret the biblical text. With that in mind, the second section of the chapter probes how Protestants have historically used various nontextual media, including preaching, singing, visual art, and mass media, to overcome literate barriers. However, rather than being an easy distinction between textual and nontextual media, the issue is further complicated by the exposed reality that these supposed nontextual media maintain varying degrees of reliance on textuality. Therefore, the chapter concludes with several relevant observations that help to identify key questions regarding these complexities that this book seeks to explore.

Before progressing, it is necessary to acknowledge an ambiguity that runs through this book. Oral communication within much of the Protestant history has been associated with evangelistic efforts to communicate the gospel, as this chapter highlights. As chapter 3 reveals, such an evangelistic understanding is how proponents of the OM initially became interested in orality; they saw it as an effective counter-strategy to overly print-reliant methods in mission endeavors. In time, these oral champions also began to advocate for incorporating orality into theological education to prepare missionaries and pastors for oral-preferenced audiences. As the story progresses, the reader will notice a development from consideration of orality as an evangelistic means to a focus on orality within the domain of theological education. It is specifically the socioeconomic concerns of orality within the theological education program that garner such a reaction from the AGC church members. Thus, from the outset, I acknowledge this shift and, as appropriate, along the way will identify the ways in which orality is being primarily understood, whether evangelistically or educationally. Having said that, this distinction should not be interpreted as replacing our earlier discussed taxonomy regarding **orality$_1$** and **orality$_2$**. **Orality$_1$** describes a generic understanding of any spoken communication and this chapter focuses on how Protestants have historically utilized oral means (within an **orality$_1$** framework) to communicate. The primary purpose for such oral approaches has been for evangelistic persuasion. The OM, with its own developed **orality$_2$** ideological paradigm, likewise started out using oral approaches for evangelistic purposes, but has also actively sought to incorporate them into its theological education endeavors.

PROTESTANTISM AND PRINTED TEXT COMMUNICATION

In order to recognize Protestants' apparently complicated relationship with both text and nontextual strategies and to appreciate fully the OM and its communication endeavors, this story begins not at the end of the twentieth century but towards the beginning of the sixteenth century. This section of the chapter picks up that story, exploring three key facets of early Protestants' relationship with text and, even more specifically, with the printed medium. This exploration is necessary for establishing the historical context out of which the OM eventually emerges.

The Importance of the Biblical Text for Early Protestantism

The Protestant Reformation established the Bible as the final arbiter in all matters related to Christian doctrine and piety in what has often been referred to as *sola Scriptura*. This teaching essentially cut across the grain of the Roman Catholic Church's self-authorized religious power. While Martin Luther promoted the Bible as authoritative, what split Western Christendom was his de-authorization of the "unwritten" traditional interpretations of the Bible and subsequent teachings based on those interpretations as maintained by the Catholic Church.[3] The doctrine of *sola Scriptura* maintains that "whatever the Catholic Church had instituted, taught, and practiced through the centuries could only be upheld if a particular institution or mode of worship was authorized in the Bible."[4] Thus, while the medieval Catholic Church had revered the Holy Scriptures, with the coming of the Reformation, the Bible was sanctioned as authoritative in a new way.

For Luther, the Bible was the *written* word of God, containing the *spoken* word of God, that is, the apostolic gospel proclamation of which the central theme was salvation for sinners through faith in the *personal* word of God, Jesus Christ alone. David Lotz notes that Luther's "entire approach to scripture is consistently Christological and soteriological." Lotz continues, "Luther submitted himself totally to the authority of Holy Scripture because in and through that biblical Word the God and Father of Jesus Christ had encountered him in judgment and mercy, disclosing himself in Christ as friend of sinners."[5] Through the biblical text, Luther encountered Jesus Christ; thus, while Luther lamented that ideally the gospel should not be written but, instead, orally proclaimed as exemplified by Christ and the apostles, he recognized that the written biblical text made it possible for future generations to know Christ as revealed in the gospel and for those generations to maintain and proclaim the gospel faithfully in the future.[6]

In addition to his adhering to the word of God as the final authority for understanding the gospel of Jesus Christ, Luther also maintained belief in the *priesthood of all believers*, effectively democratizing clerical authority that had been tightly maintained by the Catholic hierarchy. This belief had tremendous implications, no more clearly demonstrated than in the

---

3. Lotz, "Sola Scriptura," 267. It needs to be acknowledged again that these originally "unwritten" oral traditions were eventually written down by the church for preservation purposes.

4. Puff, "Word," 392.

5. Lotz, "Sola Scriptura," 269.

6. Lotz, "Sola Scriptura," especially 264–65; for a more recent discussion, see also Cox, "Martin Luther on the Living Word"; Kreitzer, "Lutheran Sermon," 42.

common person's relation to the Bible. Clergy no longer had control over the reading of the Bible, and, consequently, Bible reading became an occasion experienced by various groups, families, and even the individual.[7] Thus, while risking oversimplification, it is worth reiterating that the textual nature of the Holy Scriptures received fresh attention and appreciation with the emergence of the Protestant Reformation. Practically, such lay engagement with the biblical text was, at least in theory, made possible for the common masses by Protestantism's aggressive and strategic utilization of the printing press.

The Importance of the Printed Text for Early Protestantism

The biblical text led to Luther's theological discovery of justification by faith alone and Luther wanted that discovery to be available to others. The printing press afforded common folk the opportunity to encounter that same biblical text and have similar salvation experiences. It needs to be readily acknowledged, as Ulinka Rublack has discussed, that the printing press presented its own problems, as most of the common worshipers in sixteenth-century Europe were illiterate.[8] In spite of this concern regarding the wide extent of illiteracy, the association between the biblical message and the printed (as opposed to the scribal or manuscript) text became inseparable. The two informed and fed each other as people began to clamor not only for printed biblical texts themselves but also, among other things, for helps in interpreting those biblical texts as discussed briefly in this introduction.

Peter Horsfield, in his work on Christianity and media, elaborates on two factors that played a key role in Luther's phenomenal success, namely his strategic employment of the various Wittenberg print shops and, closely associated with that, his writing in the vernacular language. This communication strategy confounded the Catholic hierarchies who shored up their institutionalized authority by maintaining that religious communication had to be in Latin, further expecting such communication to be typically kept within the sphere of the church. By contrast, Luther's utilization of local printers shifted the site of dialogue (or conflict) from the church to the market and from the elitist Latin to the local vernacular. As Horsfield notes, in Luther, the printers recognized a tremendous opportunity to take advantage of the vernacular market.[9] Luther, likewise, recognized in the printing press a grace from God to disseminate the biblical text and other Protestant writings to the masses.

7. Horsfield, *From Jesus to the Internet*, 199.
8. Rublack, *Reformation Europe*, 66–68.
9. Horsfield, *From Jesus to the Internet*, 192, 194.

Thus, whereas the doctrine of *sola Scriptura* had centralized the biblical text in Protestant thought, the printing press centralized the biblical text in society, making printed biblical texts and other printed materials available for the common person. The premier example of such printed, biblical texts was Luther's own German translation of the New Testament, which appeared in 1522, and his translation of the entire Bible that appeared in 1534, both of which emphatically reiterated his belief that it was the right of all Christians to read and interpret the Bible.[10] Furthermore, Luther strategically perfected the small pamphlet, using a quarto format, which enabled his writings (and that of others) to move more quickly through the printers. Such a length afforded a quicker and easier read, ideal for situations and audiences that demanded oral exchange.[11]

Therefore, while Luther did not invent the printing press nor even initiate its use for doctrinal and polemical purposes, the sheer volume of his over three million publications and reprints alone played a central part in both salvaging and ensuring the success of the still relatively new print medium.[12] With the emphasis on the Bible and with the prolific use of the printing press, Protestantism came to develop a deep association among biblical authority, religious practice, and the printed medium.

The Challenge of Reading and Interpreting the Printed, Biblical Text for Early Protestantism

The gift of the printed, biblical text presented two practical challenges for the early Protestant audiences, concerns that have endured throughout Protestant history. The first has already been mentioned, namely the need of literacy skills to access the biblical text. The second is the need for interpretation skills to understand the Bible properly. Alister McGrath acknowledges both of these concerns: "Aware of the difficulties that many experienced in reading and making sense of the Bible, Protestant theologians and pedagogues produced a rich range of material that aimed to make an engagement with the Bible as simple and productive as possible."[13] The printing press itself allowed for the ready production of a variety of helps, albeit textual in nature, namely Bible translations, biblical commentaries, lectionaries, and works of biblical theology such as Calvin's *Institutes of Christian Religion*.

---

10. McGrath, *Christianity's Dangerous Idea*, 53.
11. Horsfield, *From Jesus to the Internet*, 193.
12. Pettegree, *Brand Luther*.
13. McGrath, *Christianity's Dangerous Idea*, 202.

Significantly, in light of this project's overarching interest in exploring communication complexities, Luther and other reformed leaders took oral-preferred communicators seriously by using textual media in nontextual ways to ensure all of society had the opportunity to engage the biblical text. For example, as mentioned previously, Luther was aware of the concern for oral-preferred communicators from the beginning, adopting printed text sizes (the quarto format) that afforded easy vocal reading and listening. Further discussion on these methods is elaborated in section two, but for now, the complex matter of interpreting the printed, biblical word deserves attention.

Lotz, in his discussion on Luther and biblical authority, makes the following observation: "In Luther's eyes, then, the exigent issue of biblical authority was not simply a matter of appealing to Scripture as a formal norm (since every orthodox teacher conceded its formal authority). It involved, rather, the *right understanding* of Scripture, the proper comprehension of its true content, in the light of which Luther judged traditional church teaching and found it sorely wanting. For Luther, in short, the question of biblical authority was above all a question of biblical interpretation and orientation, rather than of biblical citation."[14] Lotz's quotation helpfully ties together the discussion on *sola Scriptura* and the significance of interpretation for Luther.

Luther's critique of the doctrine of indulgences, among other things, was based, at least in part, on his personal interpretation of the biblical text rather than the magisterium's interpretation. Herein lies the root of the Reformation, for in challenging the medieval abuses and encrustations that had accumulated over the biblical text and its interpretations, Luther was postulating that every individual has a right to interpret the Holy Scriptures as he or she sees fit. McGrath has aptly labeled this thought as "Christianity's dangerous idea": "In its formative phase, Protestantism was characterized by a belief—a radical, liberating, yet *dangerous* belief—that scripture is clear enough for ordinary Christians to understand and apply without the need for classical education, philosophical or theological expertise, clerical guidance, or ecclesiastical tradition, in the confident expectation that difficult passages will be illuminated by clearer ones."[15] Several comments are relevant for considering how this potentially "dangerous" understanding of Scripture had immediate implications for the early Reformers, implications that continue to maintain reverberations for issues concerning the OM.

---

14. Lotz, "Sola Scriptura," 267. Original emphasis.
15. McGrath, *Christianity's Dangerous Idea*, 208. Original emphasis.

Protestantism's Enduring Communication Complexities   45

The first matter of concern regarding this dangerous idea of personal interpretation is which Bible to interpret. While the canon of Scripture had been traditionally understood as closed since the patristic era, questions began to emerge regarding numerous books in the Old Testament. These books, which became known as the Apocrypha, while appearing in the Greek and Latin versions, were not found in the Hebrew Bible. Thus, while the Catholics decided at the Council of Trent in 1546 that the Old Testament included the Apocrypha, the Protestants ruled that such books bore no direct influence on matters of doctrine.[16] Thus, in one fell swoop, Protestantism reconfigured the very composition of the biblical text.

Those within the OM are not explicitly calling into question the boundaries of the canon of Scripture as the early Reformers did; nevertheless, when people have learned of my doctoral subject, I have been asked on numerous occasions about the OM's commitment to Scripture. The concern has run along the lines of whether members of the OM are truncating the biblical canon by essentially reducing it to easily reproducible narratives. Members of the OM whom I interviewed confessed to having experienced similar accusations.[17] Part of the justification behind such accusations is the phenomenon called the *Oral Bible*. The early pioneers in the OM originally developed the phrase *Oral Bible* to describe the cache of biblical knowledge that was being accumulated by people through learning oral biblical stories. Over time, an *Oral Bible* became associated with a set of typically sixty to seventy stories, adapted from the Bible, translated into an indigenous language, and recorded for use among a particular community.[18] In recent years, the phrase has been used less frequently due to concerns generated by those outside the movement that proponents of orality were soft on their evangelical commitments to the inspiration of the entirety of Scripture.[19] What is relevant is that, on the one hand, the early Protestant Reformers were trying to define the universally, applicable deposit of divine revelation for all people at all times. In this sense, the OM wholeheartedly affirms the Protestant canon. On the other hand, members of the OM are bumping into questions of how to contextualize the communication of the canonical Scriptures in particular situations. While they are asking contextual questions, their probing has raised canonical questions among the movement's detractors. This delicate balance of exploring

---

16. McGrath, *Christianity's Dangerous Idea*, 206–7.

17. Linda Bemis, personal interview, July 26, 2016; Grant Lovejoy, email (1st), January 26, 2018.

18. Leatherwood, "Case and Call for Oral Bibles," 37–39.

19. Grant Lovejoy, email (4th), April 23, 2018.

contextual questions while remaining within canonical perimeters is an ongoing theme that reemerges throughout this study.

The second issue of concern regarding the dangerous idea of personal interpretation returns to the question of who decides what is or is not a "proper" interpretation of Scripture. The root of the problem is that without a pope or church council, there is no fixed voice authorized to determine what is orthodox interpretation and what is heresy. Thus, McGrath discusses numerous emerging Protestant authoritative voices, namely city councils, denominational councils and synods, and popular theologians and preachers. Naturally, these different Protestant authorities handle the relationship between biblical interpretation and church tradition differently. While arguing that any traditional church practice or doctrine must be subservient to Scripture, some leaders, such as Luther and Calvin, saw a vital place for appreciating voices and teachings from within church history. Others among the Anabaptist tradition sought to maintain only what was explicitly mentioned within the biblical text. In the end, McGrath concludes that there really is no unified Protestant hermeneutic.[20]

This lingering question of authorized interpretation has direct relevance for further exploration in chapters 3 and 4 in relation to the OM's employment of oral Bible study. Numerous methodologies for biblical oral exegesis are being developed and tested, yet one of the contentious issues that emerged from the research, and was regularly voiced by the missionaries interviewed, was a concern that the church members should remain orthodox in their understanding, even as they are empowered with the exegetical tools to determine their own interpretations of the biblical text. Thus, the dual objectives of promoting personal engagement with the Bible on the one hand and the concern for maintaining personal biblical interpretation on the other provokes a tension that is as old as the early days of the Reformation and continues to manifest itself in communication endeavors among Protestant descendants five hundred years later.

The third issue regarding this dangerous idea of personal interpretation relates to the nature of the "helps" provided to ensure proper exegesis. The printing press enabled the Protestant leaders to produce a variety of exegetical tools to help guide new Protestants in their fledgling understandings of Bible. Horsfield notes that these were often included in the biblical texts themselves as exemplified in Luther's German Bible and William Tyndale's English translation. Rather significantly, Horsfield highlights that for 401 pages of scriptural text, Luther provides the equivalent

---

20. McGrath, *Christianity's Dangerous Idea*, 199–241.

of 298 pages of gloss, illustration, and interpretation.[21] One cannot help but sense the anxiety in the great Reformer that the lay reader not miss the "plain reading" of the text.

Another example, that of Calvin's *Institutes of Christian Religion*, epitomizes the emerging textual tendency within early Protestantism to employ the printed word readily to instruct Christians, both young and old, in their biblical knowledge and understanding. The *Institutes* began as a book with only six chapters, published in 1536, only to swell to eighty chapters covering four books by 1559. Calvin developed one hundred aphorisms to help summarize his substantial theological but also literary work.[22] The necessary observation regarding both Luther's interpretative aids within the biblical text and Calvin's systematic theological instruction external to the Bible is simply to note the prominent textual nature of such interpretative helps. They were printed texts, accessible to those who could read or for those who could find someone to read such helps to them.

Such examples reinforce the emerging associations that can be observed between Protestant faith and practice and the printed word. As has been introduced and as is elaborated at length later in this chapter, both oral and material communications were present from the dawn of the Protestant Reformation. This project is not arguing otherwise. What this first section has sought to accomplish is to highlight that, while oral methods were also employed, the authorizing of the Bible, the printing press, and the textual nature of many interpretative aids helped to infused the printed word with a weighty importance within Protestantism from its beginnings. While writing and text carried significance for the medieval Catholic scholastics, Protestantism shifted the printed biblical text not only into the center of religious attention but also into the hands and lives of laypeople. The challenges of reading and interpretation were offset by attempts to include oral methodologies; however, such oral-friendly methods did not prevent a prolific outpouring of printed texts related to the Bible, Christian piety, and other topics from establishing a print legacy within Protestantism. Thus, it is imperative to understand this strong association between print and Protestantism, particularly in relation to the Bible, its authority, and its interpretation, if one is to understand properly the various dynamics and even questions that have transpired around the OM's promotion of oral methodologies in their twenty-first-century

---

21. Horsfield, *From Jesus to the Internet*, 199.

22. Horsfield, *From Jesus to the Internet*, 196; Rublack notes that Calvin's *Institutes* expanded from a pocket-size edition to a tome of approximately half a million words. Rublack, *Reformation Europe*, 132.

mission endeavors. Attention now turns to how Protestants have tried to compensate for their affection for the printed word.

PROTESTANTISM AND ORAL (AND MATERIAL) COMMUNICATION

This chapter's interest in how Protestants have negotiated their multiple and, at times, complex commitments to the authority of the Scriptures, the printed word, and the renewed impulse to reach the masses necessitates considering what I call *Protestant orality*. *Protestant orality* is simply a shorthand way to describe the historic oral processes and practices that Protestants have employed in attempts to overcome people's inability to read and understand the printed, biblical text. This phenomenon orbits around two central elements, the first being the typical Protestant desire for *biblical engagement*, which can be understood broadly as the process of accessing, interpreting, and applying (or obeying) biblical truth to one's life and/or community's circumstances. The second feature of *Protestant orality* is that in spite of its "oral" description, it assumes an inherent textuality. In other words, even Protestants' attempts at non-print-reliant communication strategies continue to exhibit a printed medium influence. This is important for placing *Protestant orality* into our already introduced orality taxonomy. In many ways, *Protestant orality* is a qualified **orality**$_1$. On the one hand, it needs to be clear that it is not the particular **orality**$_2$ as interpreted by the OM. On the other hand, while *Protestant orality* carries a generic sense of any communication that relies on the spoken word and thus corresponds with **orality**$_1$, it is a qualified **orality**$_1$ because as will become evident, *Protestant orality* assumes a prior textuality.

While the first portion of the chapter established Protestants' affinity for print, this second section explores *Protestant orality*, considering several ways in which Protestants have attempted to overcome literacy barriers by orally communicating their gospel message. These attempts have only been partially successful as will become evident. Such historical exploration also throws into relief the materiality of the seemingly immaterial spoken (or sung) word, a topic that has direct relevance for the communication complexities discussed in chapters 5 and 6.

One way to approach *Protestant orality* is by considering communication as persuasion. In his work, *The Reformation and the Culture of Persuasion* Andrew Pettegree investigates why people chose the Reformation.[23] How did the Reformers convince people of the day to abandon the security and familiarity of their Catholic religion for the still developing

---

23. Pettegree, *Reformation and the Culture of Persuasion*.

Protestant faith? In essence, he wants to understand how the Reformers persuaded people to take the Protestant risk.[24] He acknowledges the traditional association between Protestants and print; however, he suggests that Reformers were seeking to engage not only "the individual Christian" but also "the wider collective religious consciousness." To do this, Pettegree argues that the printed text had to be situated into a much "broader range of modes of persuasion that used every medium of discourse and communication familiar to pre-industrial society."[25] These modes of persuasion included, among other things, preaching, drama, music, and visual images. Thus, Pettegree's discussion of different modes of persuasion offers a starting point, and the following mini-studies highlight several of the different non-print methods that have been employed for Protestant persuasive purposes since Martin Luther.

Before commencing, Protestant communication, in general, and *Protestant orality*, in particular, exhibit a complexity that resists simplified categorization between print and non-print (i.e., oral) categories. In spite of Pettegree's justified curiosity to explore other media, I believe that they all have been influenced in some degree by print. Therefore, *Protestant orality*, in spite of its oral delivery nature, retains (or continues to reaffirm) the deep affinity among Protestantism, print, and religious practice.

Communicating the Word through Preaching

In his chapter on preaching, Pettegree writes, "There is little doubt that from the first days of the Reformation preaching played a formative role in shaping the new movement; and it would continue to play a vital part in shaping the new Protestant congregations in the generations ahead. The sermon provided the ideal vehicle to express the bibliocentric core of Protestantism: in its turn it swiftly became the core of all Protestant worship."[26] Pettegree continues, "Most of all, sermons adopted a method and pattern entirely appropriate for *illiterate and semi-literate populations*: the purposeful use of lists, paired contrasts, repetition, summary and reiteration. It was the bedrock around which the churches harnessed other communication media."[27] There is no doubt that the proclaimed word has been of bedrock importance within Protestantism over the last five hundred years.

While up until this point, the discussion has focused primarily on the early Protestant Reformers, Harry Stout, in his biography of George

24. Pettegree, *Reformation and the Culture of Persuasion*, 1–3.
25. Pettegree, *Reformation and the Culture of Persuasion*, 8.
26. Pettegree, *Reformation and the Culture of Persuasion*, 38.
27. Pettegree, *Reformation and the Culture of Persuasion*, 38. Emphasis added.

Whitefield, compares the similar commitment to the rigors for spiritual piety in Whitefield with Martin Luther's spiritual journeys.[28] Therefore, it is apropos to broaden the lens for consideration of Protestant history and consider Whitefield as a prime example of the power of Protestant preaching.

The influence of George Whitefield (1714–70) and his power as an orator in the eighteenth century was on par with celebrity status. Whitefield, an Oxford-trained Anglican clergyman, began his preaching career in London and from the earliest days was recognized as possessing a unique ability to communicate. Stout attributes the secret of Whitefield's success to his early love for and involvement in theater. While later in life he renounced the theater, Stout maintains that Whitefield's experiences as a young actor marked him for life, transforming sermon treatises into pulpit performances.[29] Historian Mark Noll records one witness recounting how Whitefield "seemed to kneel at the throne of Jehovah and to beseech in agony for his fellow-beings."[30] Such description alludes to one of Whitefield's trademarks: the embodied nature of his preaching where "the words were the scaffolding over which the body climbed, stomped, cavorted, and kneeled, all in an attempt . . . to startle and completely overtake his listeners."[31] For Whitefield, what mattered was not that his audience knew about the "New Birth" but that they *experienced* it for themselves.[32] While Stout is quick to note that Whitefield aggressively promoted his self-image and popularity through the printed press,[33] Whitefield's preaching provides a model of how the persuasive powers of the Protestant sermon can bring together the spoken and dramatized word of God.

Within recent times, the precedent and pattern of persuasive Protestant preachers such as Whitefield was further amplified in the towering legacy of Billy Graham (1918–2018). It is hard to overstate the role that Graham played in popularizing evangelicalism, not only in the United States but also throughout the world.[34] Upon his death, a *Wall Street Journal* newspaper article noted that Graham preached a "simple, optimistic message of redemption" to approximately two hundred million people throughout the course of his life.[35] Furthermore, Graham and his team aggressively experimented

---

28. Stout, *Divine Dramatist*, 14, 26.
29. Stout, *Divine Dramatist*, xix–xx, 1–15.
30. Noll, *Rise of Evangelicalism*, 98.
31. Stout, *Divine Dramatist*, 39–43.
32. Stout, *Divine Dramatist*, 38–39.
33. Stout, *Divine Dramatist*, 44–48.
34. Stanley, *Global Diffusion of Evangelicalism*, 32–34.
35. Lovett, "Will There Ever Be Another?"

with emerging mass media possibilities, including radio, television, and satellite broadcasting. While the issue of mass media is discussed later in the chapter, what is relevant for now is that Graham personified the Protestant evangelical preacher, orally proclaiming, "The Bible says," in an impassioned plea for people to make a personal decision for Christ Jesus. Thus, for both Whitefield and Graham, the orally proclaimed sermon afforded the opportunity for people to experience the word of God and make a choice based on their hearing and understanding.

In his study of preaching, Arnold Hunt identifies the heart of Protestant preaching theory with Romans 10:14–17, the apostle Paul's strong rhetorical question regarding who can believe if they have not heard, for "faith cometh by hearing, and hearing by the word of God."[36] Thus, far from being a minor appendage to historical Protestant communication endeavors, preaching such as that of Whitefield and Graham has been understood as essential for people making decisions of faith. Furthermore, the oral repetition of sermons has been considered, at times, a means not just of proclaiming the faith but also of rooting people in a greater knowledge and understanding of that faith, as exemplified by the English conventicles in the seventeenth century. These private meetings were sites of Christian education, wherein believers memorized the main heads (or points) from recently preached sermons, and so were "edified one by another."[37] Such incidents reiterate that not only has the orally proclaimed sermon been used for evangelistic purposes as a pillar in Protestant communication strategies, but it has also, at times, been utilized for discipleship and educational purposes as well.

Significantly, having established the high priority and power of Protestant proclamation, not all Protestant sermons have matched Whitefield or Graham's quality, for not all sermons are proclaimed with equal power. A sermon's makeup includes its *method* of delivery as well as the *style* of the language used to convey the message. Pettegree hinted at style in the previously referenced quotation wherein the Reformers adopted different rhetorical patterns or devices within their sermons that were appropriate for illiterate and semi-illiterate populations (e.g., paired contrasts, repetition). The style of the content was arranged with illiterates (or oral-preferred) communicators in mind. Such intentionality raises several interesting points, the first being that Protestant preaching has often presumed that the preacher will work from a printed copy of the biblical text.[38] Second, if a sermon is written

---

36. Hunt, *Art of Hearing*, 22.
37. Collinson, "English Conventicle," 241, 243.
38. Similarly, in spite of their using oral memorization, Collinson indicates that

and not just preached, it contains literary stylistic features as well as an inescapable oral component in its delivery. In his research on Victorian preaching, Robert Ellison notes that by the Victorian era, sermons were no longer understood primarily as orations but as written pieces; "consequently, they were to follow the rules of all other writing."[39] Furthermore, Ellison suggests that, rather than doing away with oral practices, there was a conflating of oral and literary elements in such a way that Ellison argues Victorian preaching is a good example of *oral literature.*

This tension between the oral and literary nature of a sermon is worth highlighting as evidence of the residual textual tension within *Protestant orality* but also because the sermon has been a source of confusion for people trying to understand the OM. Is not the Protestant legacy one of the proclaimed sermon? The OM is trying to promote orality in what way, if not through methods such as the sermon? Grant Lovejoy, the current director for oral strategies for the International Mission Board of the Southern Baptist Convention (IMB), is a former homiletics professor at Southwestern Baptist Theological Seminary. In trying to clarify what the OM distinguishes as truly oral, he, like Ellison, emphasizes the difference between the communication delivery method and language style. A PhD dissertation can be read aloud and, thus, in an etymological sense, can be an oral event; however, "the vocabulary, syntax, sentence length and complexity, section and paragraph arrangements, degree of conceptualization, etc., used in the dissertation are much more characteristic of print than of ordinary spoken language. Most PhD dissertations do not sound like someone speaking; in that sense, they are not characteristically oral in style." Lovejoy, speaking as a member of the OM's advisory board, explains that, "for clarity and improved effectiveness in missions strategy, we frequently go further to insist that *by 'oral' we mean both produced by the mouth and stylistically characteristic of speech composed as speech.*"[40] Having established this distinction, Lovejoy acknowledges that the sermon remains problematic.

A sermon can be oral in delivery but with a heavy literary style, or it can be literarily composed but with oral stylistic features in mind.[41] He adds that conversation within the movement has debated whether such oral

---

the conventicle leaders worked from their own written sermon notes. The point in highlighting this is only to recognize the textual-reliance present even in a communication event that appears to value oral rhetorical practices. Collinson, "English Conventicle," 244.

39. Ellison, *Victorian Pulpit*, 31–32.

40. Grant Lovejoy, email (2nd), January 30, 2018. Emphasis added.

41. Hunt affirms the difficulty of considering preaching as a merely oral event, disassociated from both written and printed texts. See Hunt, *Art of Hearing*, 56–59.

or literary styles are always discernible even for playwrights, novelists, and scriptwriters, for both radio and television broadcasts utilize a literary mode but are attempting to create a stylistic dialogue that sounds like "natural speech."[42] In this regard, a sermon may not necessarily be "oral enough" if it fails to convey the naturalness of speech that Lovejoy notes.

Furthermore, an additional facet to this complexity relates to the fact that such oral proclamations often assume a textual life of their own. The famous London Baptist pastor, Charles Haddon Spurgeon (1834–92) used only a few roughly sketched notes for his Sunday morning preaching. The sermon itself was transcribed while Spurgeon preached, and then, his first act on a Monday morning was to edit the transcribed sermon for publication by Thursday. Consequently, these oral-to-textual publications became widely influential on both sides of the Atlantic.[43] Thus, while at first blush, sermons appear to be the epitome of orality, such dynamics indicate they represent a problematic genre, often including various and, at times, explicit literary influences. Likewise, they have historically been dependent on textuality for their ongoing survival.

The complexity of this tension between oral and literary dynamics lies at the heart of *Protestant orality*. At this point, it is important to affirm that the OM is trying to reconcile an understanding of orality that is oral both in delivery *and* style with a continuing evangelical belief in the authority of the scriptural text. This reconciliation is not always easy to maintain as further exploration reveals, but the sermon is one of the primary, if not the primary, ways that Protestants have historically sought to persuade people towards Christian faith as well as to promote their maturing within it.

Communicating the Word through Song

Communicating the Word through song has also been a persuasive Protestant communication strategy since the days of Martin Luther. Granted, it needs to be understood that singing was indeed part of preindustrial society, but at the time of the Protestant Reformation, "congregational singing played no necessary part in the regular Mass."[44] Luther himself saw the power and goodness of music as witnessed in his reformed liturgy, wherein he included numerous occasions for congregational singing. Pettegree quotes the Reformer: "The gift of language combined with the gift of song was only given to man . . . that he should praise God with both word and music, namely by proclaiming [the Word of God] through music and by

---

42. Lovejoy, January 30, 2018.
43. Ellison, *Victorian Pulpit*, 59.
44. Pettegree, *Reformation and the Culture of Persuasion*, 40–42.

providing sweet melodies with words."[45] This association between singing and the word of God was exemplified in the Swiss Reformation, primarily through John Calvin's appreciation of metrical psalms.

While Luther was open to refurbishing secular songs and melodies for enabling people to remember the tunes and to understand the gospel truth, Calvin resisted the employment of profane music, even for sacred purposes. He, likewise, saw music as playing an important part in "his conception of reformed liturgical practice," but he essentially desired only songs based on the words of Scripture, specifically new metrical translations for each psalm.[46] These new metrical psalms became immensely popular and assumed an almost canonical status alongside Scripture, becoming a "staple of French Calvinist culture."[47]

For certain contemporary sensibilities, singing unaccompanied metrical psalms may conjure up negative connotations of sobriety or sterility. John Witvliet's account of the use of the psalter within Geneva's Reformed worship counters such misconceptions. Witvliet describes one visitor who recounted the affective impact of the singing, which caused the visitor to break down weeping, not from sadness but from the joy of hearing the singing. As the visitor said, "No one could believe the joy which one experiences when one is singing the praises and wonders of the Lord in the mother tongue as one sings them here."[48] Such a testimony from Calvin's Geneva hints towards a reoccurring theme in Protestantism's relationship with music, namely singing has often afforded occasions for spiritual experiences that are affective (note the reference to joy) as well as embodied (note the physical acts of singing and weeping). Rublack affirms the affective and, at times, almost mystical characteristic of singing when she describes how singing for Calvin in Geneva was a means for "the pious to attain a special connection with the divine and almost taste their heavenly state as elect."[49] This affective, yet embodied association (note also Rublack's reference to taste) with singing is worth highlighting at this juncture as a way of introducing a recurring theme that emerges in this book, for issues of materiality and embodiment become important points of dialogue in subsequent chapters.

This embodied musical participation in congregational worship was not limited to the continent, for the metrical psalms also became a powerful force for the laity in reformed Scotland. Jane Dawson notes that in Scotland the

---

45. Pettegree, *Reformation and the Culture of Persuasion*, 44.
46. Pettegree, *Reformation and the Culture of Persuasion*, 55–56.
47. Pettegree, *Reformation and the Culture of Persuasion*, 58.
48. Witvliet, "Spirituality of the Psalter," 276.
49. Rublack, *Reformation Europe*, 233.

psalter became the most memorized book of the Bible, used in a variety of ways, from militarized contexts to those of prayer. Relevantly, she explicitly links the use of singing the psalms to the issue of oral culture: "The psalms and religious singing were an essential method of disseminating the new Protestant culture, because they cut across the literacy divide."[50] Dawson's discussion of Scotland illustrates how the metrical psalmody carried significant influence over Reformed Europe; however this would not always be so.

Over time, this strong adherence to metrical psalms began to show strain in certain contexts as Protestantism's affinity for personal piety encouraged those with musical gifts to consider other possibilities for singing the faith. While space limits a full exploration of Protestantism's historic developments from strict psalmody to the more experiential hymnody, a few observations are worthwhile to understand Protestantism's use of song better but also some of the complexities in attempts to communicate biblical truth. J. R. Watson's study of the English hymn serves as a natural guide, highlighting numerous key figures, including George Wither, Isaac Watts, and Charles Wesley.[51]

George Wither (1588–1667) was an Anglican song writer of Puritan leanings who sought to utilize the principles employed in the creation of the metrical psalms for other portions of Scripture, beginning with those that lend themselves to being originally lyrical, such as the songs of Moses, Deborah, and Hannah. Watson notes the tension under which Wither wrote: "Because of the particular reverence attached to the sacred text of the Bible, Wither had to follow it closely, even to the extent of using the same figures of speech."[52] Ultimately, Watson notes that in spite of Wither's concern to adhere to the biblical text, Wither was, in fact, not merely translating the biblical text into a lyrical text but was actually creating a new text. Wither was conscious of the dangers such steps might elicit from "some atheists and sensual men," and employed warnings and offered interpretations so as to hinder anyone from impious use of his songs.[53] While Wither himself was not as influential as George Herbert, Watts, or others, Watson's discussion of Wither illustrates the pressures and, at times, constraints of Protestant theological and ecclesial expectations regarding adhering to the biblical message, even as Protestants tried to translate the biblical text from the printed to the sung medium, from a literary biblical text to a lyrical biblical song. The challenge of translating the biblical text,

50. Dawson, *Scotland Re-formed 1488–1587*, 226–27.
51. Watson, *English Hymn*, 57–69.
52. Watson, *English Hymn*, 58–59.
53. Watson, *English Hymn*, 59–60.

not only from one language to another but from one medium to another, is an underlying theme of this book and is elaborated in the following section and appears again in chapter 3. For now, Wither provides an example of the ongoing tension regarding the attempt to define what is and what is not an acceptable or "authorized" translation or representation of the biblical text and its interpretation, highlighting a concern that the OM in later generations would, likewise, experience.[54]

If Wither (and others such as Herbert) were precursors to a fully accepted hymnody, Watts was the turning point. Watts possessed a masterful understanding of the metrical psalm tradition yet was not satisfied that existing metrical translations captured either all possible emotions or all pertinent Christian doctrines. Daringly, and yet not altogether surprisingly in light of Protestant historical precedent, Watts believed David's psalter needed to be recast "as if the psalmist were writing in the Christian era." Watts called this development "'an evangelic turn to the Hebrew sense,' and 'to accommodate the book of Psalms to Christian worship.'"[55] Watson notes that for Watts, this worship so often centers on the crucifixion and resurrection of Jesus Christ, brought together with wonder and energetic life. The premier example being "When I Survey," which, Watson suggests, affords an almost mystical experience.[56]

Similar mystical or affective experiences were encountered in the hymnody of Charles and John Wesley. Isaac Watts, while drawing on the past, provided a clear break with the strict adherence to metrical psalms and, thus, forged a new hymnodist tradition. Charles Wesley, and to some degree, his brother John, gave this emerging hymnody forward momentum by adding a spontaneity and freedom.[57] J. Ernest Rattenbury discusses how influential the Bible was for Charles Wesley,[58] yet, in writing his hymns, Wesley also drew on a rich repertoire of other sacred and secular sources. Thus, his work brings together biblical text, doctrine, and experience into well-crafted, worshipful art.[59] Mark Noll records the recognition that several American Congregationalists granted to the Methodists, saying of the Methodist hymns that they "strike at once at the heart, and the moment we hear their animated thrilling choruses, we are electrified."[60]

---

54. Grant Lovejoy, email (3rd), February 27, 2018.
55. Watson, *English Hymn*, 137, 153.
56. Watson, *English Hymn*, 170.
57. Watson, *English Hymn*, 231; see also Rattenbury, *Evangelical Doctrines*.
58. Rattenbury, *Evangelical Doctrines*, 231–32.
59. Watson, *English Hymn*, 233–51, 255–60.
60. Noll, "Defining Role of Hymns," 5.

Protestantism's Enduring Communication Complexities 57

Significantly, echoing Pettegree's discussion of persuasion, Watson notes that through Wesley's potent use of rhetoric, his hymnody "seems purposive, articulate, expressing what it wants to say in a form which allows it to *persuade* as fully as possible."[61]

This reminder of the evangelical nature of hymns, that they were sung words, intended to persuade and even electrify the heart, is fitting in light of the fact that in the second half of the eighteenth century, "the movement of hymnody, through the Wesleys and through others, was away from the general towards the individual and the particular situation, away from reason towards an authenticating personal experience."[62] Thus, once again, singing afforded affective, spiritual experiences. This association was no more clearly manifested than in the high value that American evangelical Christianity placed on hymns.

In his study of American hymnody, Stephen Marini notes, "It is no exaggeration to claim that for evangelicals only the Bible itself surpassed the hymnal as a definer of religious beliefs."[63] Noll, drawing on Marini's research, comments that there is virtually no record of an evangelical event that did not include the singing of hymns.[64] Likewise, in Candy Gunther Brown's discussion of printing and reading in nineteenth-century America, she observes that singing became a means for evangelicals to "solidify their membership in a pilgrim community traveling from this world toward the holiness of heaven."[65] For Brown, these evangelicals were seeking to navigate the, at times, tenuous position of remaining pure (holy) even while promoting the presence of the word of God in the world. Singing was an important component of their strategy. Hymns were seen as inextricably linked to both the word of God as the second person of the trinity and the word of God as the Bible, affording occasions for personal (and subjective) spiritual experience and maturity that, could be, even more influential than a tract or a tome of theology. Furthermore, a high value was placed on the memorization of hymns, which afforded oral recall and, thus, was helpful when printed texts were less suited or not practical.

The association between singing and memory is significant and relevant because it reinforces the value of hymns as oral methodologies. Furthermore, these themes of pilgrimage, holiness, and spiritual experience, all seen in conjunction with manifesting the word of God both in the

61. Watson, *English Hymn*, 255–56. Emphasis added.
62. Watson, *English Hymn*, 267.
63. Marini, "Hymnody and History," 137.
64. Noll, *Rise of Evangelicalism*, 260.
65. Brown, *Word in the World*, 190–91.

person of Jesus Christ and in the Bible, reinforce this affective theme associated with singing as witnessed by Witvliet, Rublack, Watson, and Noll. Whether through joyful weeping, feeling electrified, or seeking personal holiness, singing had (and still has) a way of mediating spiritual and even mystical experiences for evangelical Protestant believers. Contemporary evangelical mission endeavors, specifically among associates of the OM, continue to be animated by a belief in the experiential power of making and sharing worshipful music.[66]

Hence, the sung word has been a meaningful and powerful oral ancillary to Protestant faith, particularly as a vehicle for expressing the emotive, or affective, nature of one's faith. In spite of its apparent oral nature, singing in the Protestant tradition has typically been deeply embedded in a community of believers devoted to biblical and inspirational texts. This commitment is manifested in the ubiquitous presence of the biblical text in Protestant music and in the reality that songs, like sermons, can and have exhibited strong literary style influences. The most explicit textual feature to this supposedly non-print-reliant medium is the printed hymnal, a staple in most Protestant contexts since the days of Luther, although increasingly being supplanted by digital media. In this regard, Protestant songs have often followed a rough literary-to-oral trajectory, being written down before being printing and published. Curiously, the more a hymnal is read, the more the songs are remembered and, consequently, the printed text becomes less necessary. The result is that while initially print-reliant, songs and hymns often become increasingly more oral. In chapter 4, discussion includes an East African experience where an English hymn from the Keswick hymnal developed an oral existence on its own throughout Uganda (and beyond), becoming the distinctive anthem of the East African Revival movement. For now, it is only necessary to reiterate that singing, like preaching, is a complex facet of *Protestant orality* that includes appreciation and appropriation of oral methodologies yet never seems to sever the tether to the printed medium.

Communicating the Word through Image

In summarizing preaching, music, and drama, Pettegree writes,

> All helped ensure that the challenge of the new evangelical movement would touch all members of society, both those who had access to the new Protestant teachings *through reading—the literate*—and those who had not. That there should be no gulf in

66. Anonymous, "Participatory Approach to Song-Crafting," 43–48.

> understanding between these two groups was of course a huge concern to contemporary churchmen, aware as they were of *the bookish and cerebral tendency* of the theological debate inspired by Luther, and the difficulties of teaching even the barest essentials of the new Christian principles to the population at large: a concern to which the great outpouring of pedagogic literature inspired by the Reformation bears eloquent testimony.[67]

Pettegree is acknowledging the tendency within even the earliest Protestant communication to bend itself towards literate modes of discourse. As already mentioned, such "bookish and cerebral tendency" did not escape the Reformers' attention, and they sought ways to close the gulf of understanding between those who had access to Protestant teaching through literate means and those who did not. This bookish tendency did not originate with the Reformers, as New Testament scholar Larry Hurtado notes. In his recent study *Destroyer of the Gods*, Hurtado entitles one of his chapters "A 'Bookish' Religion," in which he discusses the complex relationship between orality and textuality in the early church.[68] Identifying this pattern is pertinent in light of the OM's claims that twenty-first-century Protestant mission endeavors are essentially too bookish and cerebral.[69]

Pettegree's quotation comes at the opening of his chapter on Protestantism and visual imagery in which he assumes a rather negative view of how effective visual imagery was in persuading the masses to convert to Protestantism. Protestantism has had a tenuous relationship with visual imagery since its emergence in the early sixteenth century. Theologically, the tension stems from an apparent ambiguity within the Bible itself in regards to images, forbidding them on the one hand ("You shall not make for yourself a graven image") yet, on the other, depicting Jesus Christ as the brightness of God's glory and the express *image* of his person.[70] Consequently, Christian history has included a continuum of beliefs regarding the role of imagery, from complete aversion to images being intentionally incorporated into worship experiences. Traditionally, Protestants have been thought to land closer to the "averse" end of that spectrum as Pettegree's caution regarding the extent of the persuasiveness of imagery in the early Reformation days and beyond illustrates. Having said that, some scholars have challenged that interpretation. Bridget Heal argues that the caricature of Protestantism being only about the word is incomplete, arguing that visuality played a more

---

67. Pettegree, *Reformation and the Culture of Persuasion*, 102. Emphasis added.
68. Hurtado, *Destroyer of the Gods*, specifically pp. 105–42.
69. This is developed below and reiterated in chapter 3.
70. Exodus 20:4; Hebrews 1:3.

significant role in sixteenth- and seventeenth-century Lutheran practice than has been previously appreciated.[71]

One English example of a successful attempt to overcome the Protestant tensions found at the nexus of textuality, orality, and imagery is "The Wordless Book." This small "book" relied not on text but color to communicate, having its origins in Bishop Gervase Babington's (1550–1610) morning and evening meditations. Babington's use of this unique form of media seems to have been the inspiration for Charles Spurgeon who, in January 1866, preached a sermon entitled, "The Wordless Book."[72] His text was Psalm 51:7,[73] and in his sermon, Spurgeon discussed a book that had no words but was simply three pages, each a different color: black, red, and white. Spurgeon explained that reflection on the black page reminded one of one's sinfulness, the red page, the "precious blood of Christ," and the white page, God's perfect righteousness available to whoever believes in Christ's atoning work. Shortly thereafter, Spurgeon shared his wordless book with Dwight L. Moody (1837–99), the American soul-winning enthusiast who is credited with adding a fourth page, gold, to represent the glory of heaven.[74] Thus, "The Wordless Book" was a book but did not require alphabetic literacy; instead, it communicated the gospel message through color imagery. As Dominic Janes writes in his investigation of "The Wordless Book," "It is through the complimentary reading of colors as symbolic that the viewer becomes transformed through faith in the power of Jesus Christ."[75] Janes suggests an historical precedent among Protestants for the use of color-symbolism "as a way of assuaging their thirst for the visual whilst avoiding the dangers of idolatry."[76] Such comments reflect the typical Protestant tension with imagery, a tension that Spurgeon was attempting to navigate in offering an aniconic tool that avoided the pitfalls of both the sensational and, at times, considered inappropriate printed Protestant tracts of the day and the "Catholic visual culture."[77]

Over time, "The Wordless Book" became increasingly popular, not only domestically in Britain in schools and among sailors but also by missionaries with accounts of it being used in various countries, including

---

71. Heal, "Catholic Eye and the Protestant Ear," 321–55; Heal, *Magnificent Faith*.
72. Janes, "Wordless Book," 33.
73. "Wash me and I will be whiter than snow."
74. Janes, "Wordless Book," 28; Spurgeon, "Wordless Book," vol. 57.
75. Janes, "Wordless Book," 31.
76. Janes, "Wordless Book," 33.
77. Janes, "Wordless Book," 32, 37.

Japan, China, and Nigeria.[78] Such a tool was easy for those with limited (or no) English literacy skills or for missionaries with limited local language abilities. Practically, it was cheap to produce, easy to carry, and could be expanded or adapted in the form of banners or fabric versions.[79] In spite of "The Wordless Book's" apparent usefulness in a variety of contexts, at least one scholar has observed that the book necessitates a certain amount of "proper interpretation" by an authorized interpreter.[80] Thus, once again, the issue of interpretation emerges, for while the removal of physical text was intended to remove literate barriers, the absence of text creates ample space for questions of meaning to proliferate.

Such brief observations suggest that "The Wordless Book" is a prime historical illustration of *Protestant orality* that attempts to negotiate the tensions found at the confluence of text, speech, and image. In John Butcher Wheeler's explication of "The Wordless Book," published in 1882, he includes the story of "a deaf, illiterate woman" who explains the meaning of the pages of "The Wordless Book" to a new clergyman. While chapter 5 touches on the ways orality affords advantages for the marginalized, such as this woman, what is important to highlight at this point is Wheeler's comment following the story that the "inability to read will not shut anyone out of Heaven if his sins do not."[81] In some way, this is the daunting theme that runs throughout this chapter. As discussed in the first section of the chapter, Protestants are committed to the biblical text, and in spite of their reverence for the proclaimed word, they continue to have an affinity for the printed medium. Consequently, in spite of Wheeler's claim that the inability to read will not keep anyone out of the kingdom of heaven, this chapter's discussion has questioned whether non-printed media, such as the orally proclaimed sermon or the visual imagery of "The Wordless Book," in fact, succeeds in overcoming literacy barriers. If these media do indeed struggle to overcome literacy barriers, then the implication could be quite dramatic—that literacy and texts are necessary, or essential, in the spiritual and physical life of a Christian. At the heart of such inquiries is whether the biblical message and the printed medium can be prised apart or perhaps more accurately, to what degree can they separated and spiritual change or maturity still be experienced. These are fundamental concerns that echo throughout this project, but at the present, it suffices to observe that the visual imagery

78. Peel, *Religious Encounter*, 168–69.

79. Janes, "Wordless Book," 39. For discussion regarding *Wordless Book* and China's ancient color cosmology as compared with Western interpreted color interpretation, see Austin, *China's Millions*, 4–10, 167–68.

80. Kent, "Books and Bodices," 71–74.

81. Janes, "Wordless Book," 42.

of "The Wordless Book" is understandable only by reference to the Bible. Even without any printed words, "The Wordless Book" is informed by a printed text. Thus, "The Wordless Book" exemplifies yet another mode of persuasion, that of imagery, albeit qualified, that Protestants have employed in seeking to overcome barriers in the promoting and cultivating of their message of faith.

Communicating the Word through Mass Media

One final form of non-print media that deserves attention is American Protestant evangelicals' use of electronic mass media, beginning in the early part of the twentieth century.[82] In his survey of evangelical engagement with both radio and television broadcasting, Dennis N. Voskuil writes, "The story of religious broadcasting in America is largely a tale of how evangelicals eventually came to dominate the airwaves."[83] They have actively pursued funding for prime time slots and won over respected audiences.[84] Through such proactive communication strategies, leveraging both the oral (or aural) and visual (or imagery) senses,[85] evangelicals have mediated their gospel message to American culture. Graham and his team exemplified this evangelical media fervor. There were times when Graham's team would purchase prime-time viewing for Graham's preaching on all three of the major stations, essentially monopolizing the airwaves for the gospel.[86] This is a good illustration of how multiple communication dynamics come together, namely the printed, biblical text, preaching, and electronic mass media. Furthermore, if one thinks of how Graham's team incorporated singing into the evangelistic services, then another component is added. Here is where the fierce pragmatism of American evangelicals shines brightly, for they have sought to communicate their Protestant faith through as many modes and media as possible in the hopes of reaching the widest audience.

Not insignificantly, Voskuil and Richard Ostling have questioned whether evangelicals, at times, have been too utilitarian, "caught in the spell of American evangelical optimism" and seemingly unaware of how the medium has a tendency to influence the message.[87] This concern regarding how

---

82. Ostling, "Evangelical Publishing and Broadcasting," 46–55; for a more contemporary introduction, see Schultze and Woods, *Understanding Evangelical Media*.

83. Voskuil, "Power of the Air," 69–70.

84. Voskuil, "Power of the Air," 79–92.

85. For an analysis of Pat Robertson's "The 700 Club" and its affective (and numerically extensive) power, see Lesage, "Christian Media," 21–49.

86. Lovett, "Will There Ever Be Another?"

87. Voskuil, "Power of the Air," 90–92; Ostling, "Evangelical Publishing and

Protestantism's Enduring Communication Complexities 63

the medium shapes the evangelical message could easily be extended in further discussion regarding evangelicals and digital media. Such consideration deserves further reflection, which follows in chapters 3 and 5.

The second section of this chapter has demonstrated that from the sixteenth century onwards Protestant Christians have pragmatically sought to employ a variety of non-print media for their persuasive purposes. Whether these persuasive attempts have been through sermons, songs, images, or, in modern times, some combination of these broadcasted electronically, Protestants have employed a variety of non-print media in attempts to overcome literacy barriers and communicate their "good news" as effectively as possible. While readily acknowledging the prevalence of these oral methods, this second section has raised the question whether these methods ever actually escaped the influence of the printed medium.

CONCLUSION: REFLECTIONS ON HISTORICAL PROTESTANT COMMUNICATION COMPLEXITIES

In her study of evangelical reading and printing in nineteenth-century-America, Brown uses the phrase "Evangelical textual community" to describe how a textual canon, consisting of biblical and approved non-biblical texts, shaped the assumptions, practices, and, ultimately, identities of conservative communities of Christians. While it would be dangerous to read Brown's conclusions anachronistically over Protestant tradition at large, her concept of an evangelical textual community is valuable as it highlights this chapter's discussion of Protestants' affinity for printed texts. Such is this print-reliant pervasiveness that even attempts at non-printed (oral) media have belied a textual influence. The phrase suggested to capture this qualified or "textual" orality is simply *Protestant orality*, the implementation of oral communications for purposes of overcoming literacy but with acknowledged textual influences. This textual influence finds its locus first in the printed, biblical text and then, second, around other approved, non-biblical texts. Together, these evangelical textual canons have shaped Protestant communities' theological (or denominational) identities.

Several examples of how printed texts have interfaced with the oral methods have already been discussed, including sermon publications and hymnals. These printed artifacts have become respected and influential commodities for evangelical publishers and denominational leaders alike.[88] Such examples find their inspiration from Protestants' premier text, the printed Bible, which has informed and shaped the words, imagery, and theology

---

Broadcasting," 55.
88. Brown, *Word in the World*, 190–212, 213–42.

behind Protestant sermons and songs down through the centuries. This phenomenon illustrates a print-centered intermodality inherent in *Protestant orality*, wherein even methods intended to be oral cannot seem to escape the gravitational pull of the printed medium. This chapter has helped establish that this tether to the printed medium is an underlying result of the theological position that Protestants have traditionally upheld, namely that the Bible, manifested most often since the days of Luther as a printed text, is the final authority in matters of piety and doctrine. One of the implications of such an observation is that while no one may be explicitly denied entering the kingdom of heaven due to the inability to read, there seems to be a consensus that quickly learning to read would be strongly recommended.

The second main observation is that, in spite of the prevalence of printed, textual influence, the oral methodologies, such as sermons and songs, tend to create (or afford) affective experiences. This affectivity is not always available in the same way through the printed medium because oral approaches have a heightened ability to engage people's hearts and imaginations due to their tendency to engage multiple senses simultaneously. Protestants from Luther onward have recognized this and sought to leverage oral methods for affective impact. This affective power has tended to operate more on an embodied or physical register whereby, for example, people are reduced to tears (as in the example from Geneva previously cited). Likewise, as Mark Noll acknowledges, hymn singing "was the most *physical activity* that all evangelicals shared, just as it was the single experience that bound them most closely to each other."[89]

With regard to preaching, a sermon may, at times, appear to be more of a literate-reliant event than an oral one, particularly if a monotone voice is used to read demurely from a dense manuscript. In such events, albeit oral, the role of the body is rather constrained, and the fixation of attention is on the text. On the other hand, the best of Protestant preachers, such as Whitefield and Graham, have been dynamic communicators who have incorporated their entire bodies into their exhortations. While further discussion of the role of the body in communication appears at length in chapter 6, what is being suggested here is that part of what made Whitefield and Graham and others like them so persuasive was precisely because they imbued their oral messages with passion, movement, and energy by using their bodies, whether clapping their hands, raising their voice, walking the stage, or pointing their fingers. Such embodied drama lent itself to affective experiences that have impacted listeners. Although not denying that printed texts can generate emotional experiences, the printed medium does not necessarily lend itself to multisensory engagement in quite the same way if a text serves as proxy for one party's embodied presence. Thus, while this chapter has only

---

89. Noll, *Rise of Evangelicalism*, 260. Emphasis added.

briefly introduced these issues of affectivity (and embodiment) in relation to oral communication (e.g., singing), this initial discussion foreshadows the elaborated attention that affectivity and embodiment receive in chapter 5's consideration of AGC's assessment of orality. For now, it is only necessary to recognize that amidst Protestants' privileging of print, they have historically recognized an affective power in oral communication.

The third observation does not need much elaboration here but deserves recognizing, namely, that there is an inherent tension between texts and their interpretation. This tension begins with the nature of the text itself. The early Protestants' dangerous idea was that every Christian had a right to access the biblical text with the consequent implication that authoritative interpretation rested with the individual. Not incidentally, the Reformers ended up not just granting new authority to the biblical text, but they ended up redefining the very form of what the biblical text included, demoting the Apocrypha from holy writ. While the Reformers' concerns were canonical, and the members of the OM's concerns have been contextual, the oral approach by members of the movement has raised questions by critics regarding whether the OM is in danger of jeopardizing the canon of Scripture with their oral storytelling and other methods.

While members of the OM are not trying to challenge the canonical status of any portion of the entire Scriptures, their desire for a contextualized oral approach leads straight into questions regarding biblical interpretation. Who is authorized to pronounce the validity of an interpretation? Does that happen by a denominational body, a church congregation, the local pastor, or merely the individual believer? As already hinted and as discussed further in chapters 3 and 5, concern for different opinions regarding interpretation between missionaries and national church leaders can be an area fraught with anxiety. Furthermore, in light of the explored precedent for Protestant biblical interpretation to be strongly wedded to printed explanation and instruction, the matter of interpretation is further complicated by the OM's attempts at "oral hermeneutics," exemplified in numerous oral Bible storytelling methods promoted by various members of the network. If engagement with the Bible is loosened from its printed moorings—both the biblical text itself and the companion texts offering interpretative guidance—who defines the perimeters and practices for conducting "orthodox" oral exegesis? Such a complex question emerges out of the confluence of Protestants' elevation of the printed text and their desire to create opportunities for people to engage and interpret the Bible for themselves. They, likewise, serve as background music for this story, emerging in the next chapter in full relief.

3

"Washing in the Word"

Situating the Orality Movement in Protestant History

INTRODUCTION

WHEREAS CHAPTER 2 EXPLORED the historic complexity found in the tension between the active use of oral methodologies and an inherent, printed textual orientation within historic Protestant communication, this chapter stands on the shoulders of that investigation by narrowing the focus to a particular phenomenon within Protestant missions, namely, the Orality Movement. While discussion of the OM has already begun in earnest, the objective of this chapter is twofold. It aims to provide an in-depth introduction to the OM, as well as to consider the ways in which the movement is both a similar and distinct phenomenon within historical, evangelical, Protestant communication endeavors. In other words, is the OM merely a contemporary expression of *Protestant orality*, the traditional use by Protestants of oral strategies though still bearing textual influences (as discussed at length in the previous chapter) or are they actually doing something new and unique in Protestant history? A quick conclusion might lead one to assume these strategies are merely an echo of historic Protestant oral approaches, yet such an assessment fails to appreciate the OM's emphasis on using oral methods not only for evangelism but also for discipling and theological education. While there have been occasions, such as the English conventicles discussed in the previous chapter, where individuals or groups have utilized oral methods for educational purposes, traditionally, Protestant oral strategies have been understood as appropriate, more or less, for evangelistic purposes. The general tenor has been that subsequent education and Christian maturity often depends on the rapid adoption of literary tools, such as in the case of Uganda as described in chapter 4. The OM's desire to train oral disciple-makers pushes against such stereotypes, probing the limits of how effective oral instruction can be in forming not only Christian disciples but also church leadership. Such inquiry exposes the complexity of these issues but runs the risk of jumping to analysis before a proper introduction.

For all practical purposes, the OM is synonymous with the International Orality Network (ION). Although ION has some characteristics of an institutionalized organization, it does not have a 501c3 non-profit registration in the United States, but rather, it is a self-described network of other evangelical institutions, such as mission organizations and churches, as well as individuals. Together, those within the network desire "to influence the body of Christ to make disciples of oral learners"[1] by using oral, audio (i.e., electronically recorded), and audiovisual means. They see themselves as standing within the historical church's trajectory (or pattern) of using various media, whether oral, manuscript, print, or non-print digital means. Nevertheless, just as the printing press sparked a "Scripture literacy revolution," they likewise see themselves as participating in something unique, albeit, this time, in a scriptural oral–digital revolution.[2]

The chapter is divided into three sections with the first providing an opening snapshot of the movement as well as giving attention to its antecedents and historical development. The second portion considers its demographics and core ideologies. In light of such explorations, the concluding section of the chapter suggests that instead of either sounding a contemporary echo or announcing a revolution, these activists are aiming to facilitate an *oral renaissance*. This chapter focuses on how members of the OM understand themselves. Chapters 5 and 6 provide the necessary critical distance from these accounts by investigating how local recipients of the movement's activities are responding to orality and reflect critically on the differences between the perspectives of the movement and those of its audiences.

THE ORALITY MOVEMENT: AN EVANGELICAL PHENOMENON

Members of the OM see themselves as situated well within the historic Protestant tradition and even more specifically, as within the broad evangelical tradition, affirming, among other conservative tenets, the importance

---

1. https://orality.net/about/.
2. "Audio Scripture Engagement Declaration."

of faith for salvation and the Bible as the inspired word of God.[3] It is the evangelical appreciation for the connection between these two tenets that motivates much of the activities of members of the OM: the word of God is the primary means for understanding and experiencing a relationship based on faith with God through Jesus Christ. While they do believe that the sixty-six books of the Protestant Bible are the supremely authoritative word of God, they are concerned that the majority of the world does not, cannot, or will not read a printed biblical text.[4] Proponents of the OM bemoan that twenty-first-century gospel communications and discipleship methods tend, according to them, to rely on or assume the printed medium. Furthermore, even where reading abilities exist, proponents argue that information or the gospel message tends *not* to be presented in holistic, narratival, or embodied ways but in fragmented, piecemeal ways that tend to focus on the propositional parts. These oral enthusiasts believe that the high literary standards assumed by Western educational institutions are producing missionaries, evangelists, and preachers who process information in highly literary, systematic ways.[5] As one pioneer of the movement argued, Western culture has tended to denarrativize knowledge since the Enlightenment, "replacing narrative with philosophy, events with ideas, and characters with concepts."[6] The result, according to many within ION, is a tendency to over-rationalize the Christian faith, distilling the metanarrative of the Bible to sequential, abstract propositions. The concern, expressed by those within the movement, is that effective communication and spiritual transformation is less likely among people in contexts not familiar with processing information in this more Western, sequential, abstract way. An example comes from missionary-turned-professor and OM pioneer, Tom Steffen, who testifies to his disappointment after trying to communicate from a systematic theology approach while working among a group in the Philippines: "However, to my great surprise, Ifugao narrative logic did not perceive this approach to evangelism as free flowing or intuitively sequential. In fact, they found it extremely boring, difficult to follow, and hard to communicate to others. So much for starting a church-planting movement."[7] Steffen contrasts his sequential and systematic logic with the narrative logic of the Ifugao. What seemed free flowing to him was not as easily accessible to others. While

---

3. Lovejoy noted that ION ascribes to the National Association of Evangelicals' statement of faith. Lovejoy, February 27, 2018.

4. Lovejoy, *Making Disciples of Oral Learners*, 6.

5. Willis, *Following Jesus*, disc 1, track 3.

6. Steffen, "Clothesline Theology for the World," 254.

7. Steffen, "Pedagogical Conversions," 142.

some may question not only the educational but also cultural differences between the Philippines and Uganda, for many of these oral champions broad-stroke summations can be made. "Literate approaches rely on lists, outlines, word studies, apologetics and theological jargon. These literate methods are largely ineffective among two-thirds of the world's peoples."[8] Therefore, in the minds of these ION members, the problem is twofold, occurring on a literacy level as well as on a systematic information-processing level. While these proponents do not consider themselves anti-literacy, they are advocating for a change, so that Christian communication, both initial outreach and subsequent instruction, operates on a register that people can receive, understand, and replicate.[9] While one might imagine that the movement's desire to cultivate a communication framework that enables (or encourages) more effective (and reproducible) communication would naturally consider how other social, political, or economic factors may be impinging on local communication patterns and expectations, it appears that such aspects, as of yet, have received minimal attention within the movement's rhetoric. This means that orality, understood here as ION's particularly qualified sense of orality, or what we labeled as **orality$_2$**, often carries a universal tone that can be applied to numerous contexts. Later chapters will suggest that people in different contexts do not necessarily interpret orality in the same monochrome way as those in ION.

Before turning to discuss what kind of changes those within the OM are encouraging, the numerous similarities between the OM and what has been called the Emerging Church movement are worth a brief consideration. This contemporary Christian phenomenon can be understood as a critique arising from within American evangelicalism as participants voice their dissatisfaction with the status quo of conservative Christianity. Emerging responses include a pursuit of authentic Christian life, faith, and community, with emphases on aspects such as simplicity, a renewed interest in pre-Reformation practices, and a high value for contemplation. In his ethnography on this Emerging movement, anthropologist James Bielo identifies the influence of philosophical modernism on conservative Protestantism. Bielo's emergent dialogue partners described with disfavor *"the hermeneutic system of systematic theology"* as the prime example of such philosophical, modern thought with its tendencies towards "rational argument, certainty, proof, and logical apologetics."[10] One is reminded of Steffen's testimony, already

---

8. Lovejoy, *Making Disciples of Oral Learners*, 6.

9. Willis, *Following Jesus*, disc 1, track 3; Steffen, "Clothesline Theology for the World," especially pp. 250–54.

10. Bielo, *Emerging Evangelicals*, 10. Original emphasis.

mentioned, and such parallel concerns suggest a similar distain for propositional apologetics or overtly cognitive rhetoric within both the Emerging Church movement and the OM.

This parallel turn away from what is perceived as cognitive-oriented Christianity has produced within the Emerging Church movement an appreciation for the entire physical sensorium and materiality. Participants have looked for ways to knock down sensory hierarchies and, instead, are exploring ways to design worship encounters intentionally wherein the presence of God is mediated through a wide range of sensory experiences.[11] Naturally, this emphasis has led to a marked engagement with the worshiper's whole body. Alongside this renewed valuing of embodiment, materiality has also received attention with objects such as sponges, lint brushes, or art exhibits being intentionally incorporated into spiritual experiences. Such tendencies within the Emerging movement have all been part of a greater appreciation for practices and liturgies thought to be typical of historic, often Celtic, Christianity, what those within the movement refer to as the *ancient–future* discourse.[12]

Issues of embodiment and materiality were briefly mentioned in the previous chapter and are developed in-depth in chapters 5 and 6 in consideration of the Ugandan Christians' responses to the OM. For now, it is sufficient to recognize that the OM does not have a monopoly on such themes. Movements and institutions borrow themes and practices from each, though it is unclear how far, if at all, the Emerging movement has influenced the members of the OM. Indeed, in interviews with various members of the OM, the Emerging Church did not emerge as a topic of conversation. Likewise, in my analysis of their writings, no evidence appeared suggesting explicit or even implicit connections or influences between the thinking of the Emerging Church movement and the OM. In spite of this apparent lack of cross-pollination, the movements' shared evangelical origins, similar rhetoric, and even some common spiritual practices, such as employing creative arts in worship, suggest that some cross-pollination between movements and their subsequent institutions may have been at work. While not necessarily an antecedent to the OM, the Emerging Church movement is an important parallel phenomenon to keep in mind as this story progresses.

While discourses of cultivating authentic faith are highly valued by members of the Emerging Church, advocates of the OM argue that no such authentic faith is possible if people cannot access God through his word.

---

11. Bielo, *Emerging Evangelicals*, 75–76.

12. See Bielo's chapter 3, "Ancient-Future: Experiencing God," in Bielo, *Emerging Evangelicals*, 70–97.

Therefore, their concern and solution to both the challenge of reading and the issue of differing information processes has been the "recovery" of the power of the spoken word. For those within the OM, this turn back to oral discourse finds its ultimate exemplar in God himself, whom the Bible records as speaking on innumerable occasions. Thus, members of the OM discuss actively seeking to replace print-reliant methodologies that would hinder oral-reliant communicators from accessing or maturing in the Christian message of salvation. Alternatively, they champion *orality*, a broadly defined "complex" that relies, not on the printed word but on the spoken word for communicating information.[13] It is important to recognize that this "complex" understanding of orality only developed later within the history of the movement (as will be described shortly), for what initially excited the pioneers of the movement was oral storytelling. With maturation, leaders within the movement have sought to broaden the concept of orality (into I what I have termed **orality$_2$**), recognizing that it had often been conflated with oral storytelling—an oversimplification that leaders within the movement continue to try to disentangle. Evidence of how hard it has been for them to do so can be witnessed throughout this study, for as discussed in chapter 4, AGC personnel understand orality to be almost exclusively oral storytelling.

Charles Madinger, international director of ION and the founder/CEO of *Institutes for Orality Strategies*, has been a major theorist helping the movement develop what I am labeling as **orality$_2$**, namely ION's ideological understanding of orality as a coherent strategy that is more than just oral storytelling. Currently, Madinger is completing doctoral studies in communications at the University of Kentucky, but he has been involved with helping several organizations implement oral strategies since 2002.[14] In his article "Coming to Terms with Orality—A Holistic Model," Madinger describes orality as "a complex of how oral cultures receive, remember, and replicate (pass on) news, information, and important truths."[15] For Madinger, equating orality and storytelling is "like a coffee lover defining the culinary arts as making a good cup of coffee. The coffee results from successful application of culinary arts but is not exhaustive of those arts."[16] Madinger suggests the need for a more comprehensive understanding, and he proposed seven descriptive disciplines (see Figure 1) with their specific questions, providing

13. Madinger, "Coming to Terms with Orality," 204.

14. Voice for Humanity (http://www.voiceforhumanity.org), Spoken Worldwide (http://spoken.org), Global Impact Missions (http://www.globalimpactmissions.org).

15. Madinger, "Coming to Terms with Orality," 204.

16. Madinger, "Coming to Terms with Orality," 204.

a framework for any communication message intended for oral-reliant communicators. In Madinger's analysis, *culture* influences how a message will be interpreted. *Language* influences whether a message will be received as familiar. *Literacy* relates to whether the audience understands. *Social networks* relate to how the message will spread. *Memory* describes whether the message will be retained. The *arts* are the message's packaging, connecting the message to the deep places of the audience's minds and hearts. Finally, *media* determines how the message will be delivered.[17]

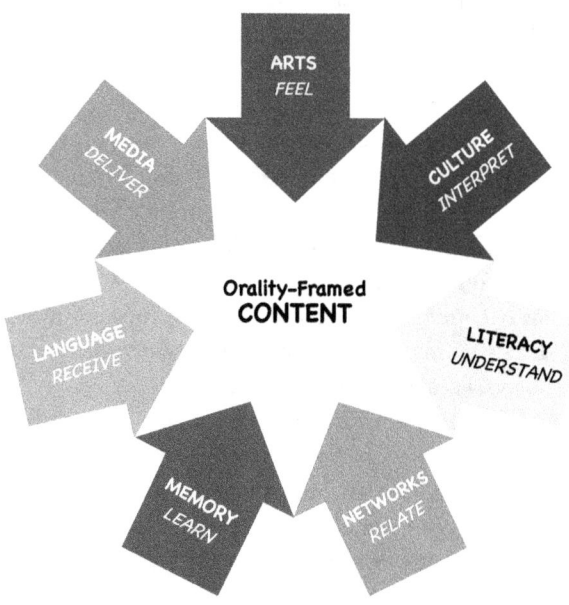

The seven disciplines of orality. Designed by Charles Madinger. Used with permission.[18]

Whereas previously many within the OM had typically only contrasted orality with literacy, Madinger's holistic framework provided a broader conceptualization with issues of literacy being only one element of the larger communication process. Furthermore, the seven descriptive disciplines highlighted the multidisciplinary nature of orality, influencing many within ION to reconceptualize orality as a much larger communication complex.[19] There is a question whether Madinger's seven disciplines

---

17. Madinger, "Coming to Terms with Orality," 204–11; Madinger, "Recap of the Seven Disciplines of Orality."

18. Madinger, "Coming to Terms with Orality," 205.

19. Madinger, "Literate's Guide to the Oral Galaxy."

define orality so broadly that it dissolves any distinction between different modes of communication. Are those seven disciplines inherently related to oral communication, or are they, in fact, related to *any* communication experience or event, whether oral, print, or digitally-based? This question illustrates a theme that runs throughout this work regarding the difficulty of establishing precisely what "orality" means, in this case, to members of the OM, but also elsewhere among those who are supposed to be the recipients of this oral presentation of Scripture.

Naturally, the question emerges of whom ION classifies as an oral-preferenced communicator. As thinking within the movement has matured from drawing a sharp contrast between illiterates and literates, its adherents, influenced in part by Madinger, have adopted a more holistic understanding of orality to include *primary oral* communicators—those who rely on the spoken word—as well as secondary oral communicators. *Secondary orality* includes "people who have become literate because of their job or schooling but prefer to be entertained, learn, and communicate by oral means," relying specifically on "electronic audio and visual communications (multimedia)."[20] Not insignificantly, members of the movement have noted, "In some developing countries people are moving directly from primary orality to secondary orality without passing through an orientation to print."[21] In light of this broader conceptualization of orality, incorporating both those who cannot read but also those who do not or will not, the OM claims that over 80 percent of the world's population prefers oral to literate-based communication.[22] Thus, far from considering themselves as peripheral or confined to working with "traditional" peoples, one leader within the movement states, "There are some who would say that the Orality Movement could *revolutionize the way the Christian world* thinks and acts regarding communicating the Gospel and making disciples."[23] Such claims are quite dramatic, and in even these preliminary observations, definitions, and questions, the reader can sense the fervency with which these oral enthusiasts approach communication. Further exploration requires consideration of the movement's predecessors.

20. Lovejoy, *Making Disciples of Oral Learners*, see section six.
21. Lovejoy, *Making Disciples of Oral Learners*, see section six.
22. Lovejoy, "Extent of Orality," 11–39.
23. Wiles, "Orality Movement," 11. Emphasis added.

ANTECEDENTS

The Literary–Propositional Heritage of American Evangelicalism

While the previous chapter established the prioritized affinity in Protestant history for print in spite of the numerous examples of oral communication, it is now necessary to narrow the concentration in an attempt to explore how that affinity and its philosophical descendants have become, as it were, "the hermeneutical foil" for members of the OM. While already briefly mentioned, its importance necessitates further investigation, specifically considering American evangelicalism and its methods of instruction as the background out of which many of the early OM pioneers emerged. The place to pick up the story is with the emergence of Bible schools in America at the turn of the nineteenth and into the early twentieth century.

The visionaries behind the Bible school movement understood their role as one conservative strategy to counter the growing liberal influence among the mainline denominational institutions.[24] While not necessarily trying to replace existing evangelical seminaries, these Bible schools were designed around the idea of quickly training and sending out men and women to serve and evangelize. Initially, this pragmatic commitment often included lower entrance requirements, intentional opportunities to serve in local ministries and outreaches, and, naturally, a heavy emphasis on studying the Bible. What is of particular relevance for this chapter's interest in the OM is the specific way in which these schools often studied the Bible.

In her seminal study on American Bible schools, Virginia Brereton describes the shift from the nineteenth-century exegetical model of working with a particular passage in the original languages to a new emphasis on understanding the Bible in its entirety and a new appreciation for the validity of studying the English text.[25] Fundamentalist educators, having been influenced, in part, by common-sense philosophy and an empirical approach to theological education as mediated through fundamentalist stalwarts such as Charles Hodge and B. B. Warfield,[26] encouraged students to rely not on commentaries but to think "for themselves" about what the Bible was teaching and how to apply it in daily life.[27] While various methods were employed, Brereton notes that educators began using the term *inductive* to describe this approach of encouraging students to draw their own conclusions after

---

24. Brereton, *Training God's Army*, 33–36.
25. Brereton, *Training God's Army*, 33–36.
26. Noll, "Common Sense Traditions," 216–38.
27. Brereton, *Training God's Army*, 89.

personally engaging with the biblical text. Rather than deductively approaching the text with preconceived notions or ideas, the inductive method was premised on a sincere attempt to let the biblical text, or facts, speak for itself. The Bible student was thus comparable to a scientist, observing the empirical facts, synthesizing them and drawing appropriate interpretations.[28] There are obvious similarities with Hodge's systematic and scientific rhetoric in which the Bible was viewed as a "storehouse of facts."[29]

Brereton acknowledges and agrees with George Marsden's identification of a strong association between the fundamentalist thinking represented in the Bible schools and Baconian science. As "Baconians were taxonomists, categorizers, and classifiers, . . . so also were fundamentalists, and not least of all when they turned to the word of God."[30] Thus, for these Bible educators, inductive Bible study with its appreciation for outlines, defining biblical terms, and explicating general principles of interpretation, became an interpretative system for enabling individual readers of the Bible to observe the spiritual facts, make proper interpretations, and apply such lessons to daily life and circumstances.

This scientific, inductive approach is understood by those within the OM as part of the cause of communication problems in mission contexts. This can be recognized in the experience of the already introduced OM pioneer Tom Steffen. He grew up in the fundamentalist Apostolic Christian Church[31] before attending Dallas Bible College (established 1940, closed in 1985). He later received additional degrees from Biola University,[32] including a Doctorate of Ministry (DMin). Steffen, who remains a professor emeritus with Biola, served for twenty years with New Tribes Mission, fifteen of those in the Philippines.[33] We have already noted his disappointment with systematic communication approaches. The following quotation provides a helpful link between such methodologies and Steffen's Bible school background:

> As my skills in language and culture grew, making public teaching possible, I began to develop a number of lessons following

---

28. Brereton, *Training God's Army*, 87–90; for a more detailed history on the development of inductive Bible study, see Bauer, "Inductive Biblical Study," 6–35.

29. Hodge, *Systematic Theology*, 10–11, 13–15.

30. Brereton, *Training God's Army*, 94; see also Marsden, *Understanding Fundamentalism and Evangelicalism*, 117–19.

31. http://www.apostolicchristian.org.

32. Significantly, Biola was originally established in 1908 as the Bible Institute of Los Angeles. See https://www.biola.edu/about/history.

33. See https://www.biola.edu/directory/people/tom-steffen.

> *the topical outline received in prefield training.* The outline covered the Bible, God, Satan, humanity, sin, judgment and Jesus Christ. . . . I presented the evangelism and discipleship lessons from *a systematic theology* format. I believed these lessons would provide an excellent foundation for the gospel, hence avoiding easy-believism. But as I began to teach publicly, I soon realized that the Ifugao found it difficult to follow my topical presentations, and found them even harder to explain to others. I was astonished and perplexed.[34]

Schooled in a Bible school environment, Steffen was trained in communication methods that relied on outlines, systematic categories, and distilling biblical truth into topical and abstract classifications. When he attempted to reproduce those among an ethnic group that had not undergone similar Bible school-type training, he experienced a communication breakdown. Significantly, although he was communicating orally to his students in the Philippines, the literary and philosophical categories in which he had been trained proved insufficient. Such an example highlights the concern upheld by members of the OM,[35] that "the hermeneutic of systematic theology" as described by Bielo, has indeed permeated evangelical missional communication paradigms but is not necessarily effective for communication in non-western contexts.[36]

Others have noted these systematic or doctrinal emphases within late twentieth-century-American evangelicalism. In his study of the roots of American social reform, Donald Dayton (with Douglas Strong) suggests that two understandings of *evangelical* have emerged, one following that of "the Armenian, pietistic revivalism epitomized in [Charles] Finney" and the other of the "Old School" Presbyterianism as promulgated at Princeton Theological Seminary by Charles Hodge.[37] Dayton suggests that the former represented an eighteenth- and nineteenth-century form of evangelicalism that was "more concerned with the personal appropriation of grace—with conversion and the 'new life' that follows the 'new birth.'"[38] On the contrary, the Princeton school placed a premium on "right doctrine." Dayton argues that Hodge and the Princeton school's doctrinalism have continued

---

34. Steffen, "Narrative Approach," 87. Emphasis added.

35. Other interviewees have been influenced by Bible schools, including Calvin Chong, personal interview, August 5, 2016; Charlie Fletcher, interview via Skype, August 29, 2016; Djibo Isaac Apollos, personal interview, August 10, 2016; Melissa Dueck, personal interview, August 6, 2016.

36. Chiang, August 1, 2016.

37. Dayton and Strong, *Rediscovering an Evangelical Heritage*, 182–83.

38. Dayton and Strong, *Rediscovering an Evangelical Heritage*, 183.

to influence late twentieth-century evangelicalism, resulting in "a growing emphasis on 'right doctrine' (orthodoxy) as the measure of acceptability and a consequent shift away from religious experience (orthopathy) and behavioral norms (orthopraxy)."[39] Strong, in his conclusion to the second edition of Dayton's *Rediscovering a Theological Heritage*, describes how in the 1980s, "'evangelical' became synonymous with a type of Reformed scholasticism and biblical literalism . . . articulated through the lens of modern categories of propositional truth."[40] Strong quotes theologian Roger Olson who describes the proponents of this Neo-Calvinism as tending "to regard right doctrine as the *sine qua non* of evangelical identity; for them . . . . Evangelicalism is primarily a mental category—defined by firm cognitive boundaries."[41] This cognitive-based, propositional articulation of Christianity privileges the mental assent to doctrinal categories that disturbs Steffen and others within the OM. Significantly, Steffen's account illuminates how, for the proponents of the OM, there are two interworking dynamics contributing to contemporary communication failure within evangelical mission endeavors. Part of the problem is the over-reliance on, or expectation of, proficiency with literacy skills. The other central concern is the ubiquitous employment of systematic, often propositional, categories for organizing biblical and theological information.

Nevertheless, the issues are more complex than perhaps Steffen and others have realized. For in spite of Steffen's critiquing the efficacy of systematic hermeneutics within his mission context, inductive Bible study with its supposedly scientific rationale has wielded tremendous influence on the numerous oral Bible study approaches advocated within the OM. Evidence of such influences includes the desire for "oral-preferred" students to "discover" truth for themselves, the interrogative use of questions, albeit orally, and the value placed on working through a particular biblical passage, often a narrative, as opposed to selecting numerous verses from throughout the Bible.[42] When asked about the relationship between inductive Bible study and orality, Lovejoy affirmed the influence of the inductive approach: "When I learned about Bible storying, I realized that the discussion time that followed the telling of the Bible story consisted of the three

---

39. Dayton and Strong, *Rediscovering an Evangelical Heritage*, 179.

40. Dayton and Strong, *Rediscovering an Evangelical Heritage*, 191.

41. Dayton and Strong, *Rediscovering an Evangelical Heritage*, 191. For Strong's quote of Olson, see https://relevancy22.blogspot.com/2013/03/roger-olson-history-of-evangelicalism.html.

42. These elements were evident to me after participating in two *Simply the Story* trainings in February 2016 and June 2017. Specifically, each introductory STS training includes a teaching and drama on the value of self-discovery.

main activities of inductive Bible study: observe, interpret, and apply. I planned Bible storying discussion times with that framework in mind. We often referred to the discussion as the "discovery" period, for that's what we intended and that's what it often was for participants."[43]

Not insignificantly, when encountering resistance to these oral methods, Lovejoy continued, "I sometimes sought to reassure skeptics of *Bible storying* that we were conducting an *oral inductive Bible study* of the biblical story."[44] Such comments reveal an inherent tension experienced by those within the OM regarding their evangelical heritage. Members of the OM are reacting against what could be called a *systematic hermeneutic* and its literary assumptions within evangelicalism, arguing they are advocating something novel. However, testimonies such as Lovejoy's suggest there it is harder for these oral champions to escape a systematic paradigm than they may initially imagine. Such inescapability receives further attention in later text, but attention now turns to the influence of a non-American ecumenist.

Hans-Ruedi Weber

While heavily influenced by the American evangelical movement, one forerunner to the OM who falls outside that category deserves attention, namely the Swiss-born, Hans-Ruedi Weber (1923–). Weber served as a missionary with the Dutch Reformed Church in Indonesia early in his career before becoming an ecumenist with the World Council of Churches. While only in Indonesia for four years, out of his experiences of trying to teach the Bible to "illiterates,"[45] he wrote a short book, which influenced the early practitioners of the OM. *The Communication of the Gospel to Illiterates* describes Weber's journey in seeking to answer a central question that he could find no one else addressing: how do "illiterates" study the Bible?[46] While appreciating the value of promoting theological training, material development, and even the translation of Christian literature, Weber lamented the lack of emphasis, money, or energy put into enabling people to engage the Bible, specifically if they cannot read. He went as far as to chide A. M. Chirgwin and Eugene Nida for declarations such as, "The Bible is for every man," when, in fact, neither author had addressed

---

43. Lovejoy, April 23, 2018.

44. Lovejoy, April 23, 2018. Emphasis added.

45. While recognizing the term *illiterate* often carries pejorative connotations today, I employ it here in adherence to Weber's use.

46. Weber, *Communication of the Gospel to Illiterates*.

the fact that over "half our fellow-men" are "illiterates" and have no access to the printed biblical page.[47]

Thus, in Weber, the OM found the model of someone who valued biblical engagement, questioned a perceived printed bias, and was willing to try new communication methods. As Weber himself said, "The greatest discovery or re-discovery was the Bible itself."[48] Specifically, he discussed how the Bible is God's picture book, revealing pictures of God; it is also about the great drama, "the story of God's mighty deeds"; and, it is the great symbol of God, revealing the deep mysteries not necessarily by words but by signs, such as baptism, the breaking of bread, and the cross.[49] Weber experimented with talk and chalk drawings, participatory group dialogue, community drama, and songs that include bodily rhythm—dance, all of which oriented around engaging the biblical story.[50] Weber reiterated that to change people's thinking, the whole gospel story is necessary, not just the New Testament, if persons are to understand the "redemptive history" of the Bible.[51]

While the echoes of Weber will become self-evident as discussion of the OM unfolds,[52] it is worth highlighting several of his key emphases, namely the concept of "rediscovering the Bible," the significance of story, the role of symbol, the appreciation of participation, and the value of cultural arts. Furthermore, two early pioneers, J. O. Terry and Tom Steffen, have explicitly acknowledged the influence of Weber on their own thinking.[53] Weber noted that India was probably the only country where the problem of "illiteracy" and biblical engagement was being thoroughly addressed as "is shown by Bishop J. Waskom Pickett's book on Christian mass movements in India."[54] Pickett had a remarkable influence on Donald McGavran and the Church Growth Movement.

---

47. Weber, *Communication of the Gospel to Illiterates*, 35–36; Chirgwin, *Bible in World Evangelism*; Nida, *How the Word Is Made Flesh*.

48. Weber, *Communication of the Gospel to Illiterates*, 20–21.

49. Weber, *Communication of the Gospel to Illiterates*, 21.

50. Weber, *Communication of the Gospel to Illiterates*, 15–17, 39–62.

51. Weber, *Communication of the Gospel to Illiterates*, 44–45.

52. Although Weber's book on "Illiterates" was referenced in interviews and publications, surprisingly there seems to be little discussion of his other works. Weber, *Experiments with Bible Study*; Weber, *Walking on the Way*; Weber, *Book That Reads Me*.

53. Steffen and Terry, "Sweeping Story of Scripture," 316.

54. Weber, *Communication of the Gospel to Illiterates*, 34; Pickett, *Christian Mass Movements in India*.

Church Growth Movement

Perhaps the greatest influence on the development of the Orality Movement was the Church Growth Movement (CGM). The CGM developed after the Second World War, but one of its forerunners was the already mentioned—Methodist bishop and church researcher, J. Waskom Pickett. Pickett was committed to challenging mission assumptions for the sake of improving mission results. Under the encouragement of missionary statesman, Dr. John R. Mott (1865–1955), Pickett conducted extensive research on Christian mass movements in India.[55] One young colleague of Pickett's, who wrote a very positive review of Pickett's monograph, was Donald McGavran (1897–1990). McGavran had been born in India to missionary parents, educated at Yale Divinity School, and received his PhD from Columbia University before returning to India as a Disciples of Christ missionary himself. Collaborating with Pickett in subsequent regional church surveys, he became instrumental in investigating people movements of Christian conversion in Madhya Pradesh. This initial analysis by McGavran became the foundations of a life-long commitment to investigate the principles behind how congregations grow.

For McGavran, pragmatism was paramount. He became increasingly convinced that discarding unproductive mission habits would only happen if proper research was conducted to determine what was enabling or hindering church growth. A natural way to assess a church or region was to identify population groups that shared common characteristics, what McGavran called "homogenous units."[56] By clearly demarcating a particular homogenous group, analysis could be more accurately conducted. For McGavran, language was a key way to identify these homogenous groups.[57] Identifying a group's mother tongue, often referred to as the "heart language" because it envisions how one's indigenous, often first, language leads to the heart,[58] was seen as key for analysis and effective gospel communication.

One of the key tenets of the CGM that captures some of the interplay among people groups, language, and conversion is summarized in McGavran's idea: "Men like to become Christians without crossing racial, linguistic, or class barriers."[59] The Christian gospel, according to McGavran,

---

55. Pickett, *Christian Mass Movements in India*.

56. McGavran, *Understanding Church Growth*, 85.

57. McGavran himself spoke Hindi and Chattisgarhee. Tippett, *God, Man and Church Growth*, 21.

58. "Men fight, make love, and mourn in their mother tongue" (McGavran, *Understanding Church Growth*, 193).

59. McGavran, *Understanding Church Growth*, 198.

establishes enough substantial barriers to new believers that any others should be removed if at all possible.[60] Such thinking led to the development of the concept of people groups, which is "an ethno-linguistic group with a common self-identity that is shared by the various members. For strategic purposes it is the largest group within which the Gospel can spread without encountering barriers of understanding or acceptance."[61] Such terms and the emphasis on removing barriers manifests itself clearly in the OM, both in regard to the high value placed by many on translating the Bible into "heart languages" and likewise the foundational conviction that print has remained a "barrier" to Christianity for too long.[62]

Two other aspects of the CGM remain pertinent for discussion, namely the relationship between liturgy and Christian instruction and McGavran's use of Bible stories. In trying to overcome the obstacles of illiteracy, McGavran discussed the need for memorization of Bible passages, creeds, and the use of hymns. Contrary to his own Disciples of Christ denominational tradition, McGavran recommended incorporating these practices into a liturgical style of worship with its emphasis on repetition.[63] Herein, McGavran echoes Weber's experiences with illiterates or oral-preferenced communicators, specifically that liturgy provided a framework of constructing identity, both individually and communally.[64] In chapter 1, we noted the possibility of members of the OM being drawn, perhaps even unconsciously, to Ong's Catholic sacramentality and even to more "Catholic" worship practices that tend to incorporate ritual, liturgy, and embodiment in more explicit ways than many Protestant denominations. While neither McGavran nor Weber had any direct involvement in the OM, their appreciation of liturgy would suggest that such a hypothesis might be moving in the right direction. Nevertheless, AGC leaders seem to have little, if any, patience for anything that resembles Catholic ritual; this is in spite of the denomination's incorporation of orality in recent years.

Returning to the precedent that McGavran established, when evangelizing a new village, he describes how, instead of preaching a sermon with a short text—a method the evangelists found wanting for impacting the people, Bible stories were told. Eight to ten Bible stories were chosen by the evangelistic

---

60. McGavran, *Understanding Church Growth*, 200.

61. http://www.peoplegroups.org.

62. Terry, "Barriers to the Gospel."

63. McGavran, *Satnami Story*, 40–41; this parallels the discussion in chapter 2 on the use of oral repetition in English conventicles. Collinson describes how repetition was essential to the making of "the puritan mind." Collinson, "English Conventicle," 242.

64. Weber, *Communication of the Gospel to Illiterates*, 50–51.

team, usually including the creation narrative, the fall of Adam and Eve, the birth of Jesus, several episodes from Jesus's life, including his crucifixion, resurrection, and present rule throughout the world.[65] This employment of oral methods was not just for evangelization, as McGavran used a similar method oriented around biblical stories, hymns, and memorization for the training of pastors. Thus, the use of oral communication methodologies had been intuitively adapted within the CGM long before the discussion of orality explicitly arrived on the evangelical mission scene.

The other matter that bears relevance for the OM is McGavran's interpretation of Jesus's instructions in Matthew 28:19–20. While the phrase *The Great Commission* was identified with global mission throughout the nineteenth century, it has only been since the early twentieth century that evangelicals have identified it exclusively with Matthew 28.[66] For McGavran, this was a two-part instruction: discipling and perfecting. While acknowledging the importance of perfecting (i.e., of teaching Jesus's commandments and maturing the believer), McGavran believed that for too long mission endeavors had been obsessed with perfecting and had forgotten the discipling. Essentially, the CGM was a pragmatic call for growing the church by "finding" converts, which McGavran interpreted as discipling. While he paid lip service to the importance of medical care, literacy training, and other Christian social welfare activities, the fire in his belly was for growing the church through conversion of all "*ethne*," which he interpreted as discipling all people groups.[67] This is worthy of attention because the language of discipleship appears paramount in later discussion of the OM's central ideologies, although ‚curiously, there seems to be no evidence of members of the OM carrying on McGavran's rather dubious bifurcation between "discipling" and "perfecting."[68]

The influence of CGM on the early pioneers of the OM can be traced through Southwestern Baptist Theological Seminary (SWBTS). The 1960s and 70s were a season of intense, doctrinal dispute as American evangelicals sought to establish (and clarify) their conservative understandings of biblical inspiration.[69] One institution that remained a safe haven for doctrinal conservatism was SWBTS.[70] This institution and particularly

65. McGavran, *Satnami Story*, 54–56.

66. Wright, "Great Commission," 132.

67. McGavran, *Understanding Church Growth*, 31–48, 62; McGavran, *How Churches Grow*, 93.

68. Stanley, "Renewing a Vision for Mission," 194–96.

69. For specific discussion on the doctrinal controversies within the Baptist world, see McBeth, *Baptist Heritage*, 679–82.

70. Baker, *Tell the Generations Following*, 394–96.

its longstanding missions professor, Calvin Guy (1917–2005), has had a significant influence on the OM. Guy, who taught from 1946 to 1982, was committed to promoting the CGM principles in his teaching and travels; he was directly involved in developing church growth strategies in Indonesia and Bangladesh. He was also a personal friend to McGavran, assisting him at one time to obtain a publisher for his *How Churches Grow* manuscript in addition to lecturing at McGavran's School of World Mission.[71] Furthermore, Guy was appointed the founding director of SWBTS's own World Mission/Church Growth Center in 1980, the launch of which included McGavran himself teaching a three-week conference at the seminary.[72] The relevance of SWBTS is that four of the early strategic players in the OM studied at SWBTS, being explicitly influenced by Guy, namely J. O. Terry, Jim Slack, Grant Lovejoy, and Avery Willis.[73]

Two brief observations are necessary. First the CGM, particularly through Guy, strongly influenced the thinking of the early OM practitioners. For example, CGM's deep commitment to pragmatism is evident from the outset of the OM (as discussed shortly). Furthermore, the CGM provided terms and categories such as "people groups," "barrier removal," "heart language," and even the precedent of employing Bible storytelling. In many ways, the OM could be considered an outgrowth or perhaps, more accurately, the fruition of CGM principles put into practice. The second matter is that these early OM pioneers, schooled in such a bastion of conservatism as SWBTS, did not see themselves as radical liberals. They and others following in their stead understood their emerging communication concerns as being methodological, not theological.[74] Thus, while interviews and correspondence bumped into messy doctrinal issues (likewise discussed shortly) and some lateral difference of opinion within the movement was expressed, at no point did I encounter any sentiment that would fall outside of a broad evangelical position. This is an important point to keep in mind in light of ensuing discussions regarding the history of the OM, which is told shortly; however, before turning there, it is important to acknowledge that the cultural turn towards postmodernity has created a philosophical space for the OM to thrive.

---

71. Terry, "Cal Guy and the Church Growth Movement," 67–72.

72. Baker, *Tell the Generations Following*, 465–66.

73. J. O. Terry, email, April 19, 2018; Lovejoy, January 26, 2018; Lovejoy, February 27, 2018; Willis, "Creating the Future," 47–66.

74. Lovejoy, February 27, 2018.

Postmodernity

A full exploration of postmodernity sits beyond the perimeters of this study but several comments are necessary as this phenomenon has been the backcloth for the development of the OM. Postmodernity describes alternative philosophical, cultural, and even theological currents in reaction to post-Enlightenment rationality.[75] Modernity, with its commitments to scientific and verifiable evidences,[76] has been exposed, not as an objective system offering unmediated truth but as a metanarrative in and of itself. Complete with its own assumptions and presuppositions, modernity as a rational-oriented framework has sought to establish its own legitimatization.[77] It is precisely this self-legitimatization that postmodern thought has questioned.

In response to modernity's metanarrative of progress, postmodernity has deemed all metanarratives as obsolete, arguing instead for an infinite number of narratives with infinite meanings. Universals have given way to innumerable particulars, evidenced in the elevation of the consumer's choice. Freedom and truth, severed from any particular tradition, have become understood as pragmatic and purely subjective: "I am free to choose what is true for me."[78]

Ironically, while seeming to dismiss the Christian faith, this challenging of systems that claim their own coherence and legitimacy has leveled the playing field. Now issues of faith and religion have an equal place at the table as they seek dialogue with scientific discourse.[79] Along those same lines, mystery and the unexplained have been invited back into the conversation. Not everything can be or even should be explained in rationalistic terms or by causative relationships. Furthermore, in place of the homogenizing (and hegemonic) tendencies of modernity in "thought, culture, and practice," postmodernity has advocated for discontinuity and plurality.[80] The idea of unmediated reality or objectivity has been shorn of its glory, revealing that all reality assumes interpretation.[81]

This brief sketch of postmodernity is necessary because several of these postmodern shifts in Western (or United States) pop culture have influenced the emergence of the OM as an institutional entity. Immediately, one recognizes the postmodern appreciation of narrative instead of rational syllogism

75. Caputo, "Spectral Hermeneutics," 47–86.
76. Kuhn, *Structure of Scientific Revolutions*.
77. Lyotard, *Postmodern Condition*; Smith, *Who's Afraid of Postmodernism?* 65.
78. Bauckham, "Bible in Mission," 43–55.
79. Guarino, *Vattimo and Theology*, 15.
80. Guarino, *Vattimo and Theology*, 6.
81. Storey, "Postmodernism," 191.

that appears in the OM's own championing of biblical narratives, in its employment of storytelling, and even in its attempts to connect people's stories with the biblical narratives. Doctrinal precepts have been forced to make room for religious experience, as there has been a shift for some from valuing informational content to experiencing relational encounter.[82] The Western missionary or mission agency has been deposed as the assumed authoritative voice as members of the OM movement see in orality an occasion for a plurality of voices to be heard. No longer is the educated missionary or theologically trained pastor the only expert as marginalized voices, empowered through oral methods that do not require facility with literate technology, are being provided with opportunities to contribute to their community's religious and nonreligious discussions.[83] Furthermore, the OM's strong commitment to pragmatism bears postmodern fingerprints, evidenced in the movement's history, to which we now turn attention.

THE HISTORICAL DEVELOPMENT OF THE ORALITY MOVEMENT

Beginnings

With these key antecedents in mind, a brief history of the OM offers a natural way to a more thorough understanding of this mission phenomenon. In the mid-1970s, the American missionary Trevor McIlwain experienced what he considered to be a problem while working among the Palawano ethnic group of the Philippines. McIlwain's mission agency was the New Tribes Mission (NTM), now called *Ethno360*,[84] a United States-based mission agency started by Paul Fleming in 1942. NTM articulated its vision as one of training and sending missionaries to unreached people groups, that is, those communities that had supposedly never heard the Christian message of salvation and had no access to the Bible.

McIlwain expressed a typically evangelical concern related to competing religious ideologies during his encounters with the Palawanos; the converts to Christianity among the Palawanos were mixing their local religious beliefs with their newly adopted Christianity.[85] In his view, the problem originated from the lack of understanding of the Old Testament by the Palawanos.

---

82. Strong's conclusion is particularly illuminating on how this has unfolded upon millennials. See Dayton and Strong, *Rediscovering an Evangelical Heritage*, 187–203.

83. For an account of oral methods being used for non-religious community dialogue, see Min and Wise, "Ten Seed Technique," 49–58.

84. https://ethnos360.org.

85. McIlwain, *Building on Firm Foundations*, 13.

Without a proper foundation to their Christian faith, McIlwain feared the Palawanos were susceptible to constructing what he considered to be a heretical understanding of Christianity. To counter this problem, McIlwain began emphasizing that the Bible was one story, a continuous narrative wherein "the Old Testament is the logical introduction, foundation, and authority for the story of Christ recorded in the New Testament."[86] Such an emphasis led him to develop a sequential or chronological teaching method that began not with Jesus and the New Testament, but with Genesis.

The dual emphasis on the biblical text as one narrative and the need for chronological presentation impacted subsequent practitioners who began to adopt McIlwain's methodology. As is often the case, missionaries and their respective institutions influenced one another. In his work on institutional change in Uganda, Ben Jones refers to this bricolage effect, where no one institution or group can be studied accurately in isolation because institutions develop, change, and remain relevant, in part, by drawing on and reflecting other local institutions.[87] Consequently, in McIlwain and NTM's case, as other missionaries tried out the Chronological Bible Teaching (CBT) method, it became apparent that the material, while narrative-based, retained a heavy emphasis on expository teaching. These early adopters believed more adaptation (or innovation) was needed.

First Followers: International Mission Board of the Southern Baptist Convention[88]

While NTM missionaries pioneered Chronological Bible Teaching and its initial field-testing, it was the International Mission Board of the Southern Baptist Convention (IMB) that became the strategic enthusiasts for this method. Following NTM's emphasis on the chronological order of the Bible and their explorations into biblical narrative, the IMB became the major demonstrator of Bible storytelling, enabling it to become an international phenomenon within the wider evangelical Protestant mission community. Two central figures within IMB who played key roles in further institutionalizing Bible storytelling were Jim Slack and J. O. Terry.

Slack was a former missionary in the Philippines before becoming a church growth consultant for the IMB home office in the early 1980s. Reading Weber's *The Communication of the Gospel to Illiterates* influenced

86. McIlwain, *Building on Firm Foundations*, 63.
87. Jones, *Beyond the State in Rural Uganda*, 27–28.
88. In 1997, the Foreign Mission Board (FMB) of the Southern Baptist Convention was renamed the International Mission Board (IMB). Although anachronistic, IMB is used throughout.

Slack's understanding of oral communication. After he encountered McIlwain's narrative-based CBT, he arranged for McIlwain to conduct two seminars on his CBT method for over 600 IMB missionaries and national leaders in the Philippines in 1983 and 1984.[89] After the seminars in the Philippines, CBT expanded through the extensive IMB international network but not without several adjustments.[90]

Slack, having read and been influenced by Ong's *Orality and Literacy*,[91] recognized that McIlwain's model, while valuable, was too literate reliant. In 1991, Slack invited Terry, the media consultant for the Asia and Pacific regions for the IMB, to develop this storytelling initiative further. Significantly, Terry may have had more influence on the development of Bible storytelling than any other single practitioner.[92] First, he believed in the power of narrative to communicate across literate barriers, wanting not to tell *about* a story but instead simply to tell the story as a story.[93] Second, Terry, who had a background in broadcasting, noted the similarities between audience analysis in broadcasting and what he called, "worldview analysis." According to Terry, not all biblical stories connected with all audiences in the same way. Thus, understanding the cultural and linguistic elements that have shaped an audience's perspectives, what he called "worldview," was a nonnegotiable in selecting which Bible stories to introduce initially.[94] In light of his "worldview analysis," Terry began to drift from a strictly chronological format, emphasizing instead Bible characters and narratives that he believed would most likely engage local audiences. Furthermore, Terry began to experiment with situational storying—telling a particular Bible story for a particular occasion.[95] This put him in a unique position of influence within the fledging storying movement, for he eventually created numerous sets of stories revolving around specific topics that he thought were relevant, including hope, water, food, death, and grief. Thus, CBT had evolved into Chronological Bible Storying (CBS), which eventually morphed into just Bible Storying (BS).[96]

---

89. Steffen, *Worldview-Based Storying*, chapter 2: "Rural Roots."

90. Such adjustments are good examples of what Jones describes regarding the bricolage effect influencing institutional change. See Jones, *Beyond the State in Rural Uganda*, 27–28.

91. Terry, April 19, 2018.

92. Tom Steffen, personal interview, July 27, 2016.

93. J. O. Terry, personal interview, July 25, 2016; Terry, *Basic Bible Storying*, 73–81.

94. Terry, *Basic Bible Storying*, 35–43, 45–49.

95. Terry, *Basic Bible Storying*, 143.

96. Steffen, *Worldview-Based Storying*, chapter 2: "Rural Roots."

Third, Terry appreciated the value of letting the audience discover things in the story for themselves rather than him highlighting certain points. Consequently, this appreciation required a participatory, dialogical process wherein oral learners discovered their own "Aha" moments from discussing Bible stories.[97] Terry expressed appreciation for these moments although one wonders how the people who were actually participating in the discussions were interpreting them. Nonetheless, such an emphasis on self-discovery is reminiscent of the inductive approach already discussed. Fourth, Terry piloted "fast-tracking," a blitz covering the entire biblical narrative in a short, uninterrupted flow. Influenced by anthropologist Jacob Loewen's view of the necessity of a matrix or holistic framework within which to place individual stories,[98] Terry found fast-tracking through the entire biblical narrative provided a panorama effect so that listeners could situate individual stories into the larger biblical drama.[99]

The Development of the International Orality Network

While cross-fertilization between different missionary institutions such as NTM and IMB may have happened more by happenstance in the 1980s, by the 1990s, Terry and Slack were intentionally wielding their knowledge and experience to influence the training institutions that were preparing missionaries. Beginning in 1995, along with Grant Lovejoy—the homiletics professor-turned-IMB orality consultant introduced in chapter 2, they began teaching masters-level modules on cross-cultural communication that was, essentially, a class on CBS. By the late 1990s, other American mission organizations such as Scriptures in Use (SIU) were cultivating their own storytelling adaptions, curricula, and even storytelling networks. Between 1999 and 2001, oral enthusiasts (representing the IMB but also other organizations such as the JESUS Film Project) decided to pull together an informal group of people who were interested in sharing what they were learning about orality. This group met informally for several years and eventually named themselves, the Oral Bible Network (OBN) after the phenomenon already introduced in chapter 2 called the

---

97. Terry, July 25, 2016.

98. Loewen was both an anthropologist and a Mennonite Brethren missionary. The particular book that Terry acknowledged was Loewen, *Culture and Human Values*.

99. Terry, "Fast-Tracking the Bible." In January 1994, Terry began a quarterly publication called the *Chronological Bible Storying Newsletter*. Similarly, in July 2004, he also began producing the *Journal of Bible Storying*. While the newsletter is discontinued, editions of the journal still appear semi-sporadically.

Oral Bible.[100] Lovejoy discussed how the phrase *Oral Bible* had an arresting effect on some conservatives who feared its proponents were devaluing the entirety of the biblical canon.[101] Critique and changing circumstances led to the OBN getting a new name.

In 2000, the Billy Graham Evangelistic Association hosted a conference in Amsterdam for 10,287 Christian evangelists from 209 nations and territories.[102] At this conference, several significant things happened that coincided with and influenced the development of the OM. First, a group of particular senior organizational leaders, who were sitting at or adjacent to "Table 71" in a conference room, decided that they would commit their organizations to engage the remaining people groups without any Christian witness or church initiative. This group included leadership from IMB, Campus Crusade for Christ (now Cru), Youth with a Mission (YWAM), Wycliffe Bible Translators (WBT), and Transworld Radio (TWR). Over the course of the next few years, this "Table 71" collaboration of evangelical organizations would give birth to several significant initiatives, particularly aimed at evangelizing, discipling, and planting Christian churches among the remaining unreached people groups of the world.[103]

Second, at the same conference, Avery Willis, the then vice-president of overseas operations for IMB and responsible for approximately 5,500 IMB missionaries worldwide, was asked, "How do you disciple oral learners?" This was a historic question within the development of the OM. Up until then, oral Bible storytelling had been used primarily for evangelism. As author of *MasterLife*, a discipleship curriculum that has been translated into fifty languages,[104] Willis was well acquainted with literary methods of discipleship and instruction. After that question, Willis realized he did not know how to disciple or educate individuals and groups to learn more in their understanding of Jesus and the Bible without relying on literate methodologies. One recalls Weber's similar inquiry. Thus, a significant, and possibly novel, shift took place within the movement as Willis began to mobilize his influence within IMB to researching, resourcing, and implementing discipleship schemes for oral communicators. To Willis's surprise, he came to believe that the concern for oral discipleship had relevance not

---

100. Steffen, *Worldview-Based Storying*, chapter 2: "Rural Roots"; Steffen, "Tracking the Orality Movement."

101. This was discussed in chapter 2. Lovejoy, August 31, 2016; for critique of the concept of an Oral Bible, see Yoakum, "Spoken Word," 193–228.

102. Olson, "Amsterdam 2000."

103. http://www.table71.org.

104. Willis and Brown, *MasterLife*.

only in non-Western contexts but even in the United States with people who cannot or just do not want to read.[105]

In 2002 the "Table 71" group decided that orality was a relevant category for their communication strategies to unreached people groups, many who still relied heavily on oral communication. Furthermore, similarly to Willis's discovery, there was a growing sense of the relevance of oral communication, not only for "traditional" societies but also for Western ones, as well. For organizations such as Cru who worked primarily on university campuses in what traditionally would be understood as a print-saturated environment, employing methodologies such as oral Bible storytelling was a radical paradigm shift. Yet by 2005, Steve Douglas, the president of Cru, was leading oral Bible studies with American university students.

Out of the ferment of excitement about the possibilities of oral discipleship, Willis and others gathered as a special interest group on making disciples of oral learners at the Lausanne Committee for World Evangelization in Pattaya, Thailand, in 2004. The book *Making Disciples of Oral Learners* was produced, representing a summation of thinking within these evangelical mission circles regarding orality.[106] While elements have since been disputed, it remains the seminal work for introducing central concepts for those interested in the movement.

Consequently, the Lausanne Special Interest Group (#25) and the Oral Bible Network merged, resulting in the formation of the International Orality Network (ION). In early 2005, Willis retired from IMB and took up the mantle of executive director for ION. In the foreword to *Orality Breakouts: Using Heart Language to Transform Hearts*, Willis, after briefly describing the development of ION, summarizes its mission: "To radically influence the way oral preferred communicators are evangelized and discipled in every people group. ION exists to accelerate the process of making the Gospel available to all oral learners in their mother languages and to do it better, faster, cheaper, and more effectively than when literate methods alone are used. The orality movement mobilizes mission organizations and denominations around the world to work together to share oral strategies, to disciple oral preference learners, and to accomplish the vision of reaching all unreached people groups."[107] Such sentiments continued to motivate those within the movement.

---

105. Willis and Snowden, *Truth That Sticks*, 22.

106. Lovejoy, *Making Disciples of Oral Learners*. This has been translated into Chinese, Arabic, Indonesian, French, and Russian.

107. Chiang and Willis, *Orality Breakouts*, viii.

The Maturation of the Orality Movement

In 2010, Samuel E. Chiang, former chief operating officer for TWR, succeeded Willis as ION's executive director. A central concern for Chiang was to address the pervasive misconception that orality equaled storytelling, an association that was thought to limit the full understanding and impact of oral communication. Here is where the shift from orality as understood for evangelistic outreach to orality as legitimized for theological education seems to have been properly established. Willis's passion for discipleship had extended orality beyond mere evangelistic purposes to incorporate spiritual formation or making disciples, but Chiang sought to establish orality as immediately relevant for theological education stakeholders. According to Chiang, the training institutions that produced the pastors, missionaries, and other cross-cultural workers remained almost exclusively attached to print-based communication models.[108] Mission organizations with ties to Chiang and ION began expressing frustration that the traditional Western, and often systematic, literate-based curricula were not preparing students to engage with their oral-preferred audiences. They felt a paradigm shift in theological education was needed.

Leveraging personal relationships, extensive global networking, and what those within the movement interpreted as divine opportunities, Chiang set out to facilitate theological consultations revolving around central concerns related to orality and research, pedagogy, learning styles, and oral assessment. Ironically, those connected to ION realized that if they wanted to cultivate a greater awareness of orality, more writing was going to be necessary to disseminate ideas and provoke academic engagement across a wide spectrum of disciplines. Therefore, by design each of the consultations produced a subsequent collection of essays.[109]

Chiang envisioned another critical component for this reconceptualization, namely the development of another multipurpose platform to stimulate conversation. The *Orality Journal* was launched in 2012, a semi-annual online publication of ION, which "aims to provide a platform for scholarly discourse on the issues of orality, discoveries of innovations in

---

108. Steffen applauds several brave innovators, including Biola University, Fuller Theological Seminary, and Oklahoma Baptist University. For others, see Steffen, "Orality Comes of Age," 139–47.

109. The first consultation was held at Wheaton College (2012), see Chiang and Lovejoy, *Beyond Literate Western Models*; the second was held at Hong Kong Baptist University (2013), see Chiang and Lovejoy, *Beyond Literate Western Practices*; the third was held at Houston Baptist University (2014), see Chiang and Lovejoy, *Beyond Literate Western Contexts*; the most recent was held at Oklahoma Baptist University (2015), see Madinger, *Oralities and Literacies*.

orality, and praxis of effectiveness across multiple domains in society. This online journal is international and interdisciplinary, serving the interests of the orality movement through research articles, documentation, book reviews, and academic news."[110] With the appointment of David Swarr as the new executive director of ION in 2015, the movement yet again reached a hinge point in its development.

Swarr saw his challenge as globalizing the movement. He elaborated that although orality has been pervasively used in mission endeavors around the globe, it has been largely pushed by North American agencies. Herein lies the explanation for part of the title of this book: *Western oralities*. With the Global South assuming the majority status in the world church, Swarr believed representatives from the Global South should lead this global oral initiative.[111] Here was an implicit acknowledgment of the unequal balance of power and authority within the network's history, wherein, those making decisions of influence regarding Christian communication have not been those on the receiving end of this oral phenomenon, but rather those promoting a particular oral agenda. How successful Swarr and his team were in globalizing the OM remains open for discussion. Swarr tried to facilitate this globalizing process by implementing several structural and philosophical changes. A global leadership team was established, and while the North American imprint remains vivid, 50 percent of the team's representatives come from Australia, East Africa, Latin America, and Southeast Asia. Furthermore, the leadership has taken additional, intentional steps, including implementing regional events, developing accessible "gateway" points of entry for people who are interested in orality, seeking strategies that appeal to a younger generation, and exploring ways to leverage the power of technology (e.g., new website design). What none of these steps address is the question raised in chapter 5 regarding the social stigma that is associated with orality in certain contexts such as AGC's. In many ways, the findings of this research may complicate Swarr's articulated desire to pass on the leadership role to a representative from the Majority World, because, at least in certain social contexts, the title of executive director of the International *Orality* Network may not be desirable because of the negative social conceptions of orality.[112]

---

110. This is taken from the title page printed in each journal edition. Archival editions can be accessed at https://orality.net/library/journals/.

111. Swarr, August 18, 2016.

112. Swarr, August 18, 2016.

NOTABLE FEATURES AND IDEOLOGIES

While the foregoing discussion of the history of the OM naturally provides glimpses into the demographic and ideological constitution of this community, a more intentional consideration of the movement's "cultural" beliefs and practices allows for greater understanding.[113]

Notable Features of the Orality Movement

ION's vision is to make disciples of all oral communicators through a wide spectrum of oral and also digital means.[114] While evidence discussed in chapters 5 and 6 problematize this label of "oral communicators," what is important to note at this point is that David Swarr, the then executive director of ION, was seeking to take practical steps to fulfilling the network's vision by encouraging members to pursue three inter-related objectives: to create channels for involvement with oral-preferred people, to champion local Christian initiatives with oral peoples, and to provide information and resources to fuel the movement.[115] The use of the term "movement" is significant because, technically, ION has no official authority within the mission community. Rather than being another Christian mission organization, ION is intentionally structured as a network that seeks to resource a wide spectrum of evangelical mission-interested entities (including individuals, churches, and mission organizations). While there are certain institutional characteristics about ION, it is "institutionally-lite." ION does not have any full-time employees or staff members, nor it does not operate its own office. There is a global leadership team (GLT) who handle immediate decisions regarding the network, and the international council (IC) handles core functions for the network, including communication, prayer, and financial matters. Most of these matters are handled virtually as personnel live in various geographical regions (such as Florida, Virginia, Israel, etc.) These ION team members volunteer their time and energies for the network but all of them have responsibilities in other non-profit organizations and have been granted permission to donate time to ION. A good example of this partnership was Swarr, the then executive director of ION, but who served also as the president and CEO of the 4.2.20 Foundation, a Christian non-profit organization committed to, among other things, helping encourage more translation of the Old Testament into indigenous

---

113. Part of this research is based on my attending ION's North America Regional Conference in Houston, Texas, September 12–14, 2016.

114. Swarr, August 18, 2016.

115. Swarr, "Future of the Orality Movement."

languages. 4.2.20 was Swarr's primary organization but it has freed him to also provide oversight to ION. In like manner, when ION hosts conferences, the responsibility for organizing and funding such events falls on regional and local personnel who invite individuals, churches, and organizations to participate. Thus, ION's existence relies on these partnerships, none more evident than in the area of finances. A partnership has been arranged with the National Christian Foundation (NCF), a Christian charity that provides oversight for monitored giving. Monies given for ION resources or conferences either passes through an account at NCF or volunteers simply utilize their primary organizations' accounting systems. Hence, ION ultimately relies on other institutions for its existence.

Before elaborating on the movement's central ideologies, their key practices deserve brief consideration. While increasingly qualified by other emphases, oral storytelling has been, without question, the premier practice of the movement. The movement values experimentation and adaptability and these characteristics have nowhere been more clearly expressed than in the variety of storytelling approaches that have cropped up. While CBS was the initial storytelling approach cultivated within IMB, different organizations such as God's Story (their method is called Simply the Story), Story Runners, OneStory, and SIU have all developed different storytelling approaches and methods. Each of these approaches reflects aspects of the inductive approach, only on an oral register. The format typically involves the performing of an oral Bible story, followed by a group discussion around particular questions. The primary difference between these various approaches relates to the degree of "exactitude" of fidelity to the written biblical text and the different sets of questions used both before and after the story presentation to stimulate discussion.

While the emphasis on storytelling does not seem to be diminishing, the embracing of other oral genres has become a recent focus of attention within the OM.[116] Specifically, the subject of orality and the arts has been emphasized through a collaborative partnership between ION and the International Council of Ethnodoxologists (ICE).[117] The ICE network "exists to encourage and equip Christ-followers in every culture to express their faith through their own heart music and other arts."[118] Members of ICE have found that the promotion of cultural arts and music often relies

---

116. From my observations and conversations at the ION conference in Houston in 2016, storytelling remains a central cornerstone for ION members. I heard numerous stories shared in the official program including Luke 16:19–31, Acts 10:1–23, and Acts 10: 24–48.

117. https://orality.net/library/journals

118. http://www.worldofworship.org

primarily on oral communication. One unique expression that epitomizes the interrelationship among orality, the arts, and embodiment is the use of henna body painting for the telling of Bible stories.[119] Understanding the mind-set behind the employment of henna for creating occasions for people to access the Christian message necessitates giving attention to ION's core ideologies.

"Washing in the Word"—A Reconceptualization of Biblical Engagement: An Ideological Framework of the Orality Movement

This section presents the conservative evangelical ideological framework that sustains the OM. The central ideology of the movement is a commitment to *biblical engagement*, wherein an individual or a community has the opportunity to encounter God through his word (understood here as the Bible), gain understanding, and respond as the Holy Spirit guides. This commitment to engaging God's word results in three subsequent ideologies, namely, replication of disciples, effective communication, and consideration of other people's communication preference.

CENTRAL IDEOLOGICAL COMMITMENT: A PASSION FOR BIBLICAL ENGAGEMENT

"I call it a washing in the word because we listen to the whole Bible in ninety days."[120] Such was the declaration by a senior ION associate who, as part of her personal, regular, worship routine, audibly listened to instead of read the entire Bible over a period of three months. While participation in such intense oral "washing" may not be a regular occurrence for all members of ION, such an account captures the fervor or spirit of devotion for the Bible amidst this movement.[121] Another such example of this enthusiasm for the Bible occurred when, during one interview, the interviewee (re)told portions of no less than six different Bible stories or teachings, including an impromptu acting out of Exodus 17:1–7. The spontaneous performance was such that it prompted another patron in the coffee shop to stop and express her interest in what was happening.[122] Such examples testify to the

---

119. Rayl, "Sharing Faith through Contextualized Visual Arts"; Ferguson, "Church Planting," 63–66.

120. Bemis, July 26, 2016.

121. For instruction and inspiration regarding a personal ninety-day biblical "listening" experience, see Bemis, *Praying*.

122. Bryan Thompson, personal interview (1st), September 14, 2016.

core conviction that permeates the OM, namely these people have a passion for the Bible and they want to create opportunities for others to encounter it because they believe God speaks through it.[123] The term *passion* is employed intentionally because it captures this unique combination of belief, intense emotion, and enthusiasm that one encounters while engaging these oral champions. Furthermore, in light of this project's emerging interest in embodiment, the passion I encountered in such incidents as in the coffee shop was not one operating on a cognitive or theoretical level but an embodied–imaginative one.

To understand this passion for the Bible, it is helpful to establish that for proponents of the OM, a foundational conviction exists that God is a creative, oral communicator, who speaks to people through multiple ways, including messages from nature and experience.[124] Those within the movement believe that all people are created in the image of a creative, oral communicating God; therefore, they uphold that all people are inherently oral communicators. This ideology (or theology) is captured most succinctly in the *Master Storyteller* project. Swarr and others created the *Master Storyteller* project as a multifaceted platform that includes a website and a digibook, which incorporates literary content, embedded videos, and end-of-the-chapter discussion questions. The project itself witnesses to the attempts within ION to harness digital media in digit-oral ways. Such ways include the printed word but within a much wider mediascape.[125]

In the *Master Storyteller*, Swarr states, "We are all oral learners. We didn't lie in our mother's arms learning our first words from the dictionary."[126] Such an observation has implications: "Since God created us as oral learners he uses oral ways to communicate with us. This may seem like an obvious observation, and yet the way most Christians communicate God's Word relies foremost on a culture of dependence on written text—words on a page. But God's Word is bigger than the constrictions of text. God chose an oral communication master plan through which anyone anywhere could know him [sic]."[127] According to Swarr, Araujo, and Gidoomai, this master plan was modeled in the Garden of Eden in God's original communications with the first man and woman: "The foundational instruction to the parents of

---

123. Bemis, July 26, 2016; Dueck, August 6, 2016; Thompson, September 14, 2016; Apollos, August 10, 2016.

124. Members of the OM uphold an orthodox Christian understanding of the doctrine of the Trinity.

125. Regretfully, due to the digibook format of this book, no page numbers are available. Swarr et al., *Master Storyteller*.

126. Swarr et al., *Master Storyteller*.

127. See "Introduction" in Swarr et al., *Master Storyteller*.

humankind was entirely oral. It was conducted in the context and for the purpose of relationship. Relationships are to be experienced. They are not predominantly a textual exchange. Rather, intimate communication is primarily oral."[128] Thus, a foundational conviction for these proponents is that God seeks interpersonal discourse with all people.

Those within the movement such as the authors of the *Master Storyteller* acknowledge that due to the finitude of humanity, physical texts, whether in manuscript, print, or digital form, are necessary: "When a story is conveyed verbally, where does the authenticating authority lie? Is it with the storyteller? What is to prevent the story from being changed in the telling from one person to another, or from one culture to another? The written Bible is God's solution to this problem."[129] Thus, the physical text became "a means for God to give us an authoritative record, the final authority for life and practice."[130]

Significantly, Swarr maintains that the physical text, though necessary, has created barriers: "Too often we communicate using a medium that does not allow people to learn and relate to the power of God's Word, alive and active in the world, not just stagnant on a page [sic]."[131] Therefore, for these evangelical enthusiasts, what is important to recognize is that "the story doesn't end with the text."[132] While the authors acknowledge the importance and necessity of the written text, they place much of their theological weight on the understanding of the Hebrew word *davar*, an understanding that they argue informed the discussion about the *logos* in John 1:

> *Davar* is Hebrew for "word" and is used to refer both to the Incarnate Word, Jesus, and to the Scriptures. The Davar—The Word—is an extension and manifestation of the person of Jesus. The Word of God is a deposit of the very being of the God of the universe—a repository of his person, bearing his likeness and reflecting his glory. It is alive and active, creative and powerful.
>
> In this way the words "Bible" and "Scripture," which both refer to a written text, are inadequate to represent the Word of God, for they merely indicate its *packaging*. The Word of God was before and will be after script and the printed or digital text, for it is the living essence which is in, and which speaks and

---

128. Swarr et al., *Master Storyteller*.
129. Swarr et al., *Master Storyteller*.
130. Swarr et al., *Master Storyteller*.
131. Swarr et al., *Master Storyteller*.
132. Swarr et al., *Master Storyteller*.

creates through, what we read or hear. God's Word speaks every language, in every time, to all humanity.[133]

Such statements represent leaders within the OM attempting to probe the theological boundaries as their pragmatic-driven practices, initially oriented around more effective communication, are demanding more nuanced articulation regarding the relationship between two central pillars of evangelical faith: what is the relationship between the Bible as the word of God and Jesus Christ as the word of God?

For Swarr, the textuality of the word of God (i.e., the Bible) plays an important role in preserving and authenticating the reproduction of God's word. His argument is that while the textual nature of a printed Bible is important, the word of God does not possess an inherently written textual nature. The movement's *Audio Scripture Engagement Declaration*, a document published to encourage the global church to take oral communicators seriously, states, "The Word of God is unchangeable; the manner or method in which it is communicated does change [sic]."[134] Such theological understanding allows for Swarr and others to suggest that the word of God operates on a kind of universal communication register, accessible and understandable to all humanity (the language is universal: *every* language, in *every* time, to *all* humanity). Such an understanding opens the door for OM proponents to explore nontextual expressions of the word of God, effectively separating the word of God from the written or printed (textual) medium. Consequently, such a conceptual move reduces the printed textuality of the Christian message to the status of "packaging." Such conclusions, while useful for justifying oral explorations in communicating Christianity, raise theological questions. The idea of discarding the printed textual packing of the message, while perhaps motivated by a concern to communicate the gospel more effectively regardless of literacy proficiency, sounds remarkably similar to nineteenth- and twentieth-century liberal scholarship and its attempts to discern the historical kernels amidst the oral traditions within biblical texts. Such a position would fly in the face of the evangelical moorings, which those within ION have continued to affirm.

For the current ION leadership, the solution to the concern that God's word will atrophy without a printed anchor is digital media. As the *Declaration* exhorts, "We call upon the Body of Christ to devote energies, strategies, and resources to provide access for all oral learners to engage the entire Word of God through audio-digital means, so that every tribe, every tongue, and every people group may hear, understand, and have the

---

133. Swarr et al., *Master Storyteller*. Italics added.
134. "Audio Scripture Engagement Declaration."

opportunity to respond [*sic*]!"[135] Thus, in their minds, ION members are not recasting a form of nineteenth-century higher criticism but instead are redefining, or broadening, a strict understanding of orality to include digital media. It should be acknowledged that such a digital perspective represents a progression within the movement's development. For the early pioneers, Bible storytelling was confined to oral performance. With technological advancements, personnel within the movement, such as Swarr who was the executive director of *Davar Partners International*, a Christian technology and media organization, before assuming the helm of ION, have actively incorporated digital media into the movement's discourse. Thus, within ION, digital–oral media is the new print, a supposedly more oral-friendly means of enabling people to interact with the word of God.

Subsequent Ideological Commitment 1: Disciple-Making

The enthusiasm of the members of the OM for biblical engagement results in a corollary commitment to disciple making. Two qualifiers are, however, necessary. First it needs to be reiterated that while a logical flow can be discerned in this framework, in actual practice, these subsequent ideologies happen almost simultaneously and sharp demarcation becomes difficult. Second this discussion is in no way suggesting that the members of ION have a monopoly on these ideas. Discussion of similarities with the Emerging Movement has already touched on this but the OM sits amidst a broad religious landscape wherein traffic in similar ideas and practices is not uncommon. Discipleship, for example, is a standard Christian trope among almost all branches of Christianity; the reason it receives special attention here is because not all Christian groups give it the same emphasis. Among my interviewees, discipleship emerged as a central theme and thus, it deserves attention so as to better understand how members of ION prioritized their evangelical values.

Discipleship, as defined by the senior leader of the OM, refers to the experience and process where a person responds to Jesus Christ with faith and becomes a follower of him.[136] This following requires learning to mirror Jesus's character, a transformation process believed to happen through the power of the Holy Spirit. Growth in understanding is typically associated with the Spirit revealing or speaking to the believer as he or she engages the Scriptures, often within a community of other Christians.[137] One informant

---

135. "Audio Scripture Engagement Declaration."
136. Swarr, August 18, 2016.
137. Bemis, July 26, 2016.

described discipleship as "a relational process, which allowed another person to be close enough to experience and discover scripture together, [involving] walking together, helping to put obedience into practice."[138] For members of the OM, experience rather than informational content was highlighted in this relational process called discipleship, creating an ethos more akin to a journey than a classroom.

The interconnectivity for the OM between discipleship and biblical engagement or adherence to the biblical commands is worth reiterating. Based on passages such as Matthew 28:19–20, and in line with the emphasis of church growth theory, members of the OM have a comprehensive understanding of their mission—to fulfill the biblical command to make disciples of all nations.[139] This is standard Christian rhetoric but for Djibo Isaac Apollos from Niger, oral storytelling is the answer for an "oral community like my country."[140] For Apollos and others within the movement, reproducibility, that is, the ability of disciples to be able to disciple other persons is important, and oral methods were reported as lending themselves to such disciple multiplication.[141] For one pastor, valuing reproducibility meant reshaping his confirmation classes so that rather than just divulging information, he taught the students through Bible storying. He claimed that the students not only grew in their Christian faith but also likewise were equipped with a tool to share their faith and instruct other young people. The pastor recalled one student's testimony after completing the course: "I learned how to be a disciple that makes disciples."[142]

Intentional pressure or coercion, whether physical, verbal, or in any other way, is not considered by the OM to be a legitimate strategy for replicating the discipleship experience in another person.[143] Instead, members seek communication experiences whereby a voluntary decision, a conscious choice to trust in God, can be made after non-discipled persons "encounter Jesus Christ as revealed by the Holy Spirit through the Bible."[144] Therefore, the passion for biblical engagement results in a desire to see the discipling process replicated in another person or group of persons, leading to the second subsequent commitment, namely effective communication.

138. Stan Wafler, personal interview, August 24, 2016.
139. Bemis, July 26, 2016.
140. Apollos, August 10, 2016.
141. Thompson, September 14, 2016.
142. Jason Boetcher, personal interview, September 14, 2016.
143. Stanley, "Conversion to Christianity," 315–31.
144. Handman, *Critical Christianity*, 65.

Subsequent Ideological Commitment 2: Effective Communication

Effective communication, for those within the OM, can be understood simply as the successful interchange of messages so that all persons are able to receive and understand God's word and make a decision, if any so desire, to begin the Christian discipleship process. Three key emergent categories of effective communication received particular accent within the OM, namely pragmatism, narrative, and orality. Narrative and orality have already been briefly introduced, yet, testifying to the continual interaction between the core ideological tenets, they can be most helpfully elaborated within the context of effective communication.

A short account from a Venezuelan interviewee proves illustrative. Pastor Abiel first heard of orality after the Lausanne Movement's Cape Town meeting in 2010. He decided to try an oral discipleship experiment, since many in his community lacked much education and were marginalized by the often exclusively literate church materials. He began by selecting several men to join him for a discipleship group; none had more than a primary education. Each week they developed stronger relational connections as together they discussed their lives before Abiel would tell the group a Bible story. Abiel himself learned the story in language the men would easily recognize, practicing first with his wife and children. He wanted the men to understand the story and to "know God, to meet him" through the story. His initial questions resulted in awkward silences, but over time, he discovered other questions regarding the biblical story and its characters that led to more practical application questions such as, "How is God in this story?" or, "How am I in this story?" As Abiel said, "In the story, I can know Jesus better." This understanding was central for him because he described discipleship as "growing in obedience with Jesus." In time, he started sharing the responsibilities of telling the story and facilitating discussion with the group members so that he could launch a second group.[145]

Pragmatism. One recognizes in Abiel's story the OM's commitments to biblical engagement and disciple making. He wanted that group of men to encounter the word of God and to replicate the process, yet this account also illuminates what effective communication means for the OM, namely a commitment to pragmatism, narrative, and orality. First, Abiel exhibited the OM's trial-and-error pragmatism. Numerous informants described a willingness to experiment with different communication methods when their

---

145. Abiel Herrera, personal interview, August 8, 2016.

previous ones seemed to have failed.[146] Thus, according to Abiel, his first stories were clumsy and his first attempts at follow-up questions failed to generate the discussion he desired. Nevertheless, instead of resorting to previous printed methods, his solution was to try something else. This "hurry up and fail so you can do it better" mentality relates to an open-sourcing mentality in the movement that values adaptability.

A second distinctive of the OM's commitment for effective communication is the tremendous value placed on narrative. Contrary to methods often found in oral catechisms, Abiel was not offering propositions each week for the men's group to memorize or even doctrinal questions for them to answer. Instead, he wanted to tell them a biblical story.[147]

Narrative (and dialogue). As has already been introduced, many in the OM believe the Bible models a method of communication as well as offering a message. They argue that narrative is central to the biblical model. Judgments vary among members regarding how much of the Bible is categorized as narrative, but for some it is as high as 70 percent. For instance, *Simply the Story*, one of the storying training programs within the OM, argues that 70 percent of the Bible is narrative, including the prophets; 15 percent is songs or proverbs, often considered originally oral in nature; and, only 15 percent is expository, primarily the New Testament epistles. They argue that too many evangelical sermons are based on the epistles, which tend to be heavily propositional rather than narrative in content. Not only do such members of the movement believe the Bible is predominantly narrative, but they also uphold Jesus as a communication model. In the view of the movement's adherents, the biblical record of Jesus's employment of narrative, primarily in parables, affirms the necessity of story for effective communication.[148]

Significantly, this understanding of effective communication does not uphold that storytelling alone is sufficient but rather, storytelling combined with dialogue is when transformation is most likely to happen. Repeatedly, informants described how important they viewed the post-story questions for stimulating discussion, oriented around the biblical story that allowed for persons to discover "truth" for themselves.[149] This understanding needs

146. Chiang, August 1, 2016; Ellen Marmon, interview via Skype, August 17, 2016; Dueck, August 6, 2016.

147. I use story and narrative interchangeably.

148. While Pentecostals tend to place a high value on narrative, both within the Bible but also personal testimonies, none of my interviewees discussed the cross-pollination between Pentecostalism and the OM. For an example of orality and storytelling in Pentecostalism, see de Matviuk, "Latin American Pentecostal Growth," 205–22.

149. Andrea Menkin, personal interview, September 13, 2016; Marmon, August 17, 2016; Chong, August 5, 2016; Herrera, August 8, 2016; Thompson, September 14, 2016.

to be qualified because within these members' ideological paradigm, it is the Holy Spirit who illuminates and reveals spiritual truth from within the biblical narrative.[150] Thus, Abiel did not just perform a story but instead facilitated a discussion using questions to probe for spiritual connections between the biblical story and each person's own consciousness.

Members of the OM recounted how narrative, more often than proposition, evokes the intended religious response in their audience. Such comments are reminiscent of the Emerging Church's critique of the "systematic hermeneutic" as discussed earlier. These OM proponents described how story allows for an indwelling or inhabitation of the biblical narrative wherein the hearer sees him- or herself within the stories. For these members, propositions, even biblical propositions, do not lend themselves to emotional engagement in the same way. Thus, for members of the movement, stories create immediacy to characters in the storying event.[151]

This appreciation for narrative involves both a self-visualization and, consequently, a reimagining of one's identity. As one discusses and envisions oneself in the story, a reimagining of one's identity can take place whereby an individual's religious comportment towards his or her self, towards God, and towards his or her community can undergo a transformation.

This dialogical, narrative method exhibits a tension regarding authority. On one hand, for proponents of the OM, the Bible is the final authority, and they maintain a firm belief in the universal relevance of its message. On the other hand, instead of directly telling their audiences what they consider to be true, typically a more propositional approach, these proponents desire for individual persons or communities to experience their own self-visualization and reimagined self-identification by encountering the biblical narrative themselves. Therefore, for adherents of the movement, narrative plus dialogue together create a critical distance wherein audiences are empowered to encounter God on their own.[152]

Orality$_2$. While one might expect orality to be a high value for a movement that bears such a name, it is critical to understand how orality fits into the much broader ideological matrix. It is necessary to emphasize that this is not the generic orality (or **orality$_1$**) that stands in for any communication operating on a verbal register. Rather, this is the OM's particular version of orality, what we have labeled as **orality$_2$**. There are variations in interpretation of orality within the movement, such as the differences discussed earlier

---

150. Bryan Thompson, personal interview (2nd), June 30, 2017; Dueck, August 6, 2016.

151. Bemis, July 26, 2016; Thompson, September 14, 2016; Herrera, August 8, 2016.

152. Handman, *Critical Christianity*, 72.

regarding literal and crafting approaches to storytelling. The movement is not monochrome in its ideological framework. In this sense, orality within the OM might be better defined in plural terms as oralities$_2$. What emerged from the interviews with OM participants was that, while they may have some differences of opinion, there remains a core of mutual commitments.

It is fundamental to recognize that members of the movement are committed to orality (or **orality$_2$**), but not as an end in itself.[153] Instead, they desire to create communication experiences, whereby, according to their theology, persons can be changed by accessing the word of God and having been transformed, to likewise see such a transformation reproduced in another person or community of persons.[154] Thus, within this framework, **orality$_2$** is merely a tool for the purposes of effective communication, affording an even more likely occasion for biblical engagement.

The idea of affordances proves valuable in understanding that members of the OM,[155] before they even knew to call it orality, realized that performed storytelling and subsequently other oral communication applications such as dance, drama, song, and proverbs afforded a multisensory communication event that was not always possible through a print-oriented medium.[156] Thus, they turned with pragmatic vigor to oral communication, which by definition required an embodied communicator.[157] This shift towards oral communication allowed for multiple semiotic systems to be employed at once, namely the linguistic, visual, audio (includes tone and rhythm), gestural, and spatial.[158] Naturally, the use of inter-semiotic systems increased the likelihood of messages being received and understood, enhancing the opportunities for people to encounter God through the biblical story.[159] Not incidentally, it is argued that this use of multiple means for communication reflects God's multimodal communication pattern as described in the Bible, including direct oral address, signs in

153. Menkin, September 13, 2016.

154. Marmon, August 17, 2016; Jay Moon, interview via Skype, July 27, 2016.

155. The theory of affordances developed out of studies in environmental psychology, specifically considering "action possibilities" or affordances by an organism with an object or its environment. See Gibson, "Theory of Affordances," 127–43.

156. The multi-sensory nature of orality was introduced in chapter 2.

157. One recalls the discussion of Whitefield's dramatic embodied preaching in chapter 2. For an excellent discussion on the importance and need for embodied, multisensory preaching, see Mitchell, *Visually Speaking*, especially chapter 8, "The Translated Word," and chapter 9, "The Embodied Word."

158. Anstey and Bull, "Helping Teachers."

159. Kress and van Leeuwen, *Multimodal Discourse*; for specific discussion of multimodality in the Orality Movement, see Calvin Chong, "Encountering Text as a Multimodal Experience."

nature, symbols such as the tabernacle and temple, ceremonial rituals such as the Passover and Eucharist, and even printed texts.[160] Such an admission that God uses the printed text highlights two things, namely, the seeming unaddressed role of texts in the lives of OM members and the reoccurring pragmatic emphasis evident throughout my interviews. Regarding the former, all of the people I interviewed who are actively utilizing **orality$_2$** in their ministry context have, at the minimum, a Bible college education and some, such as Swarr, Lovejoy, Stan Wafler, and Gilles Gravelle have completed PhDs. Thus, while many, if not all, of the interviewees seemed to describe some kind of awakened appreciation for oral communication, it needs to be acknowledged that literary, formal education has directly influenced every one of their experiences. Significantly, I did not hear any one express antagonism towards reading, as if he wished that he was not literacy proficient or hoped to keep others from becoming so. Interviewees did express concern, and this relates to the latter issue of pragmatism, that, in their experience, many people do not understand God's word when it is communicated through literate and systematic reliant strategies. An illustration came during a storying training course that I attended. The trainers raised the question of whether unaware missionary agents have too often assumed their audiences were spiritually "unreceptive" or "hard ground to till," when, in actuality, it was not a spiritual matter but a (mis)communication issue.[161] In the minds of these OM personnel, the pragmatic solution is to try a particular form of oral communication that privileges narrative and utilizes dialogue—what we have defined as **orality$_2$**.

Subsequent Ideological Commitment 3: Communication Preferences

The movement's core ideological passion for biblical engagement fuels a third subsequent commitment, namely to award a high value for other people's communication preferences. In many ways, this third category could easily fall under number two—effective communication; however, it deserves its own attention due to the significance of two prioritized issues: "mother tongue language" and translations.

For members of the OM, communication preference relates to the construction of meaning. One particular interviewee, Gilles Gravelle, a Bible translator who has written on behalf of the OM, provided a glimpse of how at least some within the OM approach the relationship between language and meaning. In Gravelle's understanding, meaning in

---

160. Moon, July 27, 2016.
161. Simply the Story Workshop, June 26–30, 2017, Paisley, Scotland.

a structuralist theory of language is strongly tied to grammatical structures themselves. While such thinking has significantly influenced Bible translators in the past, Gravelle expressed appreciation for recent studies in cognitive science which, he suggested, have helped members of the OM better appreciate how culture, and not only grammatical structures, influence the construction of meaning.[162] Gravelle is suggesting that whereas print is constrained by linguistic signs, oral communication tends to be more holistic, drawing on both linguistic but also nonlinguistic signs such as gesture, movement, and tone. Such nonlinguistic signs are understood to impact the development of meaning.

This issue of meaning has immediate relevance as members of the movement seek to make the Christian message relevant and meaningful for other persons. Thus, the question arises, "How does the other person or community of persons construct meaning within their own context?" According to Gravelle, one has to understand another person's context and the semiotic systems that persons use to construct meaning so that the Bible can be effectively communicated. The irony of such an understanding is that my research suggests that at least some within the OM have not taken Gravelle's recommendation and have failed to fully appreciate how the OM's **orality**$_2$ carries certain negative contextual meanings.

None the less, one of the areas where those within the movement have attempted to understand another person's context and semiotic processes has been in the OM's commitment to translating the Bible into mother tongues or heart languages. A helpful way to understand this concept of heart language is through anthropologist Courtney Handman's study of translation and conflict in Papua New Guinea in the mid-twentieth century. Handman discusses how SIL International (formerly the Summer Institute for Linguistics) missionaries conceptualized "the self" linguistically, rather than culturally, so as to avoid problematic moral issues such as polygamy. This linguistic defining of the self allowed SIL personnel to understand one's native language as the idealized pathway to the heart, defining both oneself and oneself in relationship to the community.[163] From the missionaries' perspective, they wanted to create occasions for people to encounter God. They believed that such encounters, when transacted through one's own heart language, offered "nothing but the Bible in locally appropriate fashion."[164]

---

162. Gravelle, "'What Do You Mean?'" 13–28.

163. Handman, *Critical Christianity*, 74, 81.

164. Significantly, Handman acknowledges McGavran's influence on SIL in this part of her discussion. Handman, *Critical Christianity*, 71.

Such an ideological approach echoes that of many within the OM, but there is a difference. The SIL translators in Papua New Guinea were seeking to create a literate translation of the Bible and, thus by default, were constraining themselves to linguistic signs. Members of the OM want to broaden such an approach. Language remains central, but, they would argue, something is incomplete in defining the self exclusively through linguistic symbols. The OM's adherents exhort that persons are more than their words reduced to writing. Orality, as understood by those within the OM, allows for an understanding of the self that incorporates linguistic but also nonlinguistic semiotic systems. Thus, while still deeply committed to the value of heart language (as reiterated by informants[165]), proponents of the OM, such as Gravelle, are attempting to enlarge the understanding of the self, seeking to unite the linguistic and nonlinguistic (i.e., cultural) elements in an attempt to create a more holistic communication paradigm and, consequently, a more holistic encounter with the word of God. Considering how else the Bible might be encountered without relying on literate and propositional means has led to an exploration of various oral communication genres, namely performance, drama, dance, music, and even visual art. Understanding such communication events as orality is a further illustration of the particular way those within the OM are defining the term (what I have labeled as **orality$_2$**). The exploration and incorporation of such expressions (such as drama, dance, etc.), by those within the OM, are attempts to leverage the advantages of the various semiotic elements inherent in such expressions as means to more effectively translate the printed biblical text into non-print reliant media.

Such explorations are not unproblematic, particularly regarding the issue of spiritual authority. As already introduced in chapter 1, questions have emerged within the movement regarding the evangelical commitment to remain faithful to the biblical text. Does a summarized oral Bible story or a film depicting a Bible story qualify as an authentic biblical translation? While translation is usually construed as being from one text to another, the issues are complicated by the presence of the embodied performer. What degree of literal adherence to a textual translation is necessary for an oral performance to remain biblically authentic and authoritative? Such inquiry may not sit well with certain evangelicals.

Lovejoy noted that in his experience, those from a conservative Reformed background who tend to value the pastor–theologian leader predictably have the hardest time overcoming these and other doctrinal concerns about orality and their expectations for formally (i.e., literary)

---

165. Wafler, August 24, 2016; Chiang, August 1, 2016; Bemis, July 26, 2016.

trained pastors.[166] Such sentiments exemplify what Dayton and Strong describe as "evangelicals" coming from the "Reformed scholasticism and biblical literalism" tradition and relates to the earlier discussion in chapter 3 regarding preaching. With its emphasis on doctrinalism, it is not hard to imagine how sermons from within this particular tradition could easily tend away from dramatic, imaginative preaching to more concise, cerebral argumentation, seeking not so much an embodied change as a convinced mind. Such cognitive, propositionalized preaching, in spite of its oral delivery, is anathema for most members of the OM.

That being said, theological tensions over issues of authority and literal interpretation have emerged within the movement itself, particularly evident through the differing "storying" approaches that have developed. For some, the *crafting* of Bible stories represents a legitimate translation of the Bible. A specific story is scrutinized for the purpose of removing any potential confusing or culturally unfamiliar elements. Often longer narratives will be summarized so as to make them easier to remember and items such as geographic locations or measurements will be left out. When a series of oral stories are put together, an "oral Bible" is formed, and for many within the movement, this oral Bible carries the authority of a printed biblical text.[167]

However, as one informant declared, "It's all God's Word, even the place names and measurements. Who is to say that God might not use some detail that is not important to me in the life of someone else?"[168] Thus, there is a countering group among the OM who advocate a stricter, more *literal* adherence to the printed biblical text. Emphasis is placed on learning the story in its entirety and lengthier passages are either bypassed altogether or divided into more manageable portions for learning. Ironically, the *crafters* argue that the *literalists* are denying whole portions of the biblical narrative to audiences simply because those longer sections become unwieldy for learning by heart or take too much time.[169] The literalists respond that at least they are offering the Bible and not a paraphrase.[170]

In the interviews, several informants offered similar paradigms for navigating this seemingly problematic tension between competing ideologies regarding the perceived authority of the Bible. They suggested turning

---

166. Lovejoy, January 26, 2018.
167. Leatherwood, "Case and Call for Oral Bibles."
168. Thompson, September 14, 2016.
169. Terry, July 25, 2016.
170. Thompson, September 14, 2016; for a sample of internal discussion within the movement regarding literal/crafting approaches, see Miller, *Simply the Story Handbook*, 136–37.

to Christian preaching or proclamation for a mediating paradigm.[171] While the Greek and Hebrew original manuscripts of the Bible are traditionally understood within conservative groups to be the bearers of divine authority, evangelical preachers do not typically read and preach in the original Greek or Hebrew but in the language of the people. This practice suggests that evangelical preaching assumes some form of translation *and* commentary. These informants suggested that both the literal story and the crafted story are, likewise, translations with the literal one including less commentary and the crafted one being more akin to a paraphrase. Both could be understood as the word of God.

While the literalists might not agree that a paraphrase is ever appropriate, this discussion of translation brings together multiple dynamics. Jesus is understood within the movement as the translation par excellence, meditating divine and human communication. Furthermore, translation has played a fundamental role in Christianity as the language and cultural idioms of the Jewish people gave way to the Greek and Roman patterns of the day.[172] The understanding of language shown by members of the OM and their attempt to value communication preferences results in an idealized understanding that requires translation of the biblical message if effective communication is going to transpire, yet, uniquely, their translations are not from the printed word to the printed word but from the printed word to the spoken word. Therefore, this theme emerges once again that the OM's commitment to other people's communication preferences raises questions about the nature of translation and the authority of such translations, highlighting the ideological tension, at times, between commitments to the Bible and a desire to communicate effectively with others.

CONCLUSION: THE **ORALITY** MOVEMENT —ECHO, REVOLUTION, OR RENAISSANCE?

This chapter has introduced the OM as a particular phenomenon in Protestant evangelical history. By discussing the movement's antecedents, history, and ideologies, the ground is prepared to return to the opening inquiry regarding whether this movement is revolutionary: Is it unique in Protestant history or rather only a contemporary echo of oral methodologies that have been historically employed? In reality, such either/or mentalities are not particularly helpful. Rather than being construed as binary opposites between total revolutionary and mere replication of historical precedent, it

---

171. Lovejoy, August 31, 2016; Lovejoy, February 27, 2018; Fletcher, August 29, 2016.

172. Sanneh, *Translating the Message*.

is advantageous to conceptualize the issues more on a continuum with the OM reflecting an in-between renaissance position.

One way to approach this issue is to acknowledge several reasons for justifying the revolutionary rhetoric. First, proponents of the OM use the revolutionary trope within their own discourse. Just as the Gutenberg printing press was a part of a "Scripture literacy revolution," so the OM's *Audio Declaration* proclaims, "We stand today at another *seminal point in history* where digital technology makes it possible for every oral learner to engage with God's Word in audio and audio-visual formats."[173] Jerry Wiles, ION's North America regional director, affirms this revolutionary paradigm: "My vision for the Orality Movement overall is . . . that it would *revolutionize* the way the Christian world thinks about communicating the gospel."[174] Samuel Chiang, when he began to understand the breadth of orality, testified, "I could give my life to this because you could make over industry after industry. We could change the face of missions."[175] Elsewhere, in discussing the history of the movement, he noted, "The ION developments really focused on something totally 'new,' and that has to do with 'orality.'"[176] Such comments indicate an element of revolutionary rhetoric within the OM.

Second, while oral methods of communication have been well established in Protestant persuasion strategies, as detailed in chapter 2, one might label the concerted effort of a wider cohort of organizations, churches, and individuals specifically to promote and champion orality as revolutionary. The OM's particular vision for using oral strategies, incorporating both the method of delivery and the style of the message not only to evangelize but also to instruct and mature Christians, represents an intentionality at a corporate level that one could argue has not always been aggressively promoted historically. Such a statement is in no way making some sort of claim to originality for the movement as literacy barriers have been present from the days of the early church and many Christian leaders have experimented with various oral media. In this way, one could say that Protestants have always been interested in the spoken word (or **orality**$_1$). The difference, one could argue, is that such practices seem to have operated more on an ad hoc or individual basis (one thinks of Weber) and often have been reluctant to deviate far from script/print (as discussed in the previous chapter). In contrast, proponents within the OM question the Protestant print affinity, arguing instead that oral-oriented methods,

173. "Audio Scripture Engagement Declaration." Emphasis added.
174. International Orality Network, "Orality."
175. Chiang, August 1, 2016.
176. Chiang, email (1st), January 26, 2018.

that is, their **orality**$_2$ understanding, have a much wider application than previous Christian generations have perhaps acknowledged. Furthermore, while previous historical attempts have tended to emphasize the oralness of delivery in an effort to overcome literary barriers (e.g., the sermon), these oral enthusiasts would argue their additional attention to the oral style of a message and the way information is processed are unique.

A third way that the movement could be described as revolutionary is their seeking to pry apart an evangelical view of God's word from its traditional association with the printed biblical text. Herein is the challenge to the concept of *Protestant orality* developed in the previous chapter. These OM members are not like the Friday Apostolics in Matthew Engelke's study, who have no place for the Bible in their pursuit of "live and direct" encounters with God.[177] The revolutionary aspect of the OM members' belief and practice is that, as evangelicals, they are committed to the Bible as being God's word yet are willing to conceptualize God's word as being something other than a printed text. Driven by their commitment to facilitate biblical engagement, these oral proponents seek to contextualize the word of God among people for whom print proves a hindrance. Significantly, members of the OM "viewed this as a methodological issue more than a theological one."[178] Therefore, they are not seeking to abolish or recast the canonical biblical deposit but are probing how they as evangelicals can retain their firm commitment to God's word even as they explore oral and digital expressions of this divine revelation that are non-textual reliant.

In reality, such claims and explorations, in spite of appeals to "mere" methodology, are theological. Lovejoy's experience of resistance to orality by those from a strong Reformed background has been countered by a typically warm reception among African-Americans and Pentecostals, for whom, Lovejoy notes, oral tradition does not seem as threatening.[179] Again, such comments highlight how the OM sits within a broader evangelical landscape, but they also emphasize that the differences in reception by such groups hinge precisely on differences in theology. Therefore, one natural area for further study within and regarding the movement is whether the elasticity of evangelical faith can endure the theological probing and its implications as personnel within the movement try to maintain their canonical commitments that uphold their evangelical identity even as those same commitments compel them to fresh contextualized communication considerations.

177. Engelke, *A Problem of Presence*, 3–10; see also 171–99, 200–223.
178. Lovejoy, February 27, 2018.
179. Lovejoy, January 26, 2018.

Such justifications for classifying the OM as *revolutionary* give credence that the OM is not a mere echo of Protestant historical precedent. Nevertheless, *revolution* carries connotations of a severe "break" with the evangelical establishment and historical Protestant tradition, more severe than perhaps those within the movement are necessarily trying to make. Rather than oscillating between revolutionary or echo, Jay Moon, missionary-turned-professor and a thought leader within the OM, uses the word *renaissance* to capture the renewal aspect that he argues undergirds the movement.[180] There are several reasons why this term is more appropriate. First, members of the OM consistently use *rediscovery* or *recovery* rhetoric in appeals to turn back to oral methodologies. In the opening of his book on orality in North America, Avery Willis, Jr. writes, "I invite you to *discover* with me how the fundamentals of *first-century discipleship* affect our efforts to make disciples *as Jesus did—in the twenty-first century*."[181] Not insignificantly, Chiang could affirm the revolutionary nature of the movement in his comments but then he could also reiterate a sense of recovery when he talked about people beginning to "recognize something has been lost in history. They are discovering or finding a renewal of orality."[182] For members of the OM, this "something lost" relates to the prevalence of orality within much of the early church contexts: "The early Church could not have developed as it did if it required literacy of its adherents or made literate forms of training a prerequisite for its leaders. This realization has major implications for how we teach preaching both here and in overseas seminaries surrounded by oral cultures."[183] Such comments suggest that rather than being revolutionary in the sense of launching an entirely new phenomenon, the adherents see themselves amidst a renaissance or renewal of "the old paths"[184] that for too long have been overgrown and unused. Therefore, they appeal both to Jesus and the early church as models for how to engage contemporary audiences.

There is a second reason why the term *revolution* fails to represent accurately the OM and *renaissance* is preferable. In spite of their rhetoric about orality and their desire to overcome literacy requirements and foreign (i.e., Western) information processes, many members of the OM have been indelibly shaped by a Western, print-oriented paradigm. Observation of ION's practices suggests that the adherents are less revolutionary and

---

180. Moon, "Fad or Renaissance?" 6–21.
181. Willis and Snowden, *Truth That Sticks*, 22. Emphasis added.
182. Chiang, August 1, 2016.
183. Lovejoy, "But I Did Such Good Exposition," 7.
184. Jeremiah 6:16.

less oral than they realize. This observation is no more evident than in the failure of the numerous developed oral Bible study methods to disassociate themselves completely from a literary "systematic hermeneutic."[185] While claiming to be oral in nature, the "oral Bible study methods" display literary and Western, systematic fingerprints in relation to the inductive method originating in American Bible schools.

One recalls how the inductive Bible study method was promoted among fundamentalist Bible institutions as a scientific means to ascertain the factual meaning of the text personally. Methods such as biblical exposition relied on dissecting the biblical text into terms, categories, and outlines in attempts to expose the true divine meaning. Such practices assumed both high proficiency in literacy, as well as the mental apparatuses, shaped by particular American social and cultural contexts, necessary to process the biblical information in such a particular way. The relationship between inductive Bible study and the OM is that while advocating for a fresh appreciation to both oral delivery and the oral style of a message, proponents of these new oral Bible study methods have inadvertently appealed to their inductive training. Consequently, the various methods of *oral* Bible study, such as CBS or Simply the Story (STS), all possess a strong inductive, sequential, and, consequently, systematic nature. The generalizing of worldviews into outline summaries, the classifying into sets and selecting of appropriate stories, and the employment of systematic questions to access the true meaning of the narrative suggest not an oral hermeneutic based on indigenous meaning-making or logical processes but a particular Western systematic and propositionalized mind-set being overlaid with an oral rhetoric.[186]

Therefore, such methods, according to an **orality**$_2$ framework, can be understood as oral in their delivery and in the dialogical or participatory nature of the communication event. Nevertheless, practitioners of oral Bible storytelling are actually executing an inductive process, only dialogically. Lovejoy explicitly justified such methods on the grounds that they are really "inductive oral Bible study."[187] The appeal to the inductive method was an attempt to reassure critics that biblical meanings were being accurately interpreted. Rather than letting the story stand on its own, the use of directed questions (different groups use differing questions) is a means to interrogate the text in attempting to discover its spiritual treasures. The unintended

---

185. Curiously, I do not know of any oral Bible study method developed without the influence of western (American) personnel.

186. Steffen does seek to address some of the issues of oral hermeneutics in his recent book, *The Return of Oral Hermeneutics*.

187. Lovejoy, April 23, 2018.

implications of such an approach are that rather than the story being understood as true in its entirety, the narrative can easily become construed as simply the vehicle (packaging?) for transporting the true meaning. Furthermore, the designated questions, while dialogical in nature, are only thinly veiling the inductive exegetical tools deemed essential for personally extracting deep (propositional?) treasures of truth. Once again, it needs to be clear that the issue is not whether the inductive method is or is not an appropriate way to engage Scripture; rather, what is being highlighted is that these champions of orality have struggled to escape the American evangelical, systematic, literary influences they are decrying.

Such observations point to conceptual complexities within the movement. Within the OM, the term *orality* has been loosely defined to incorporate not only an oral delivery method but also the way the content of the message is organized; thus, orality has been enlarged conceptually to incorporate not only a way of communicating via the spoken word but also a way of processing information, specifically a narrative-oriented way of making sense of the world. ION's understanding of orality, while conceptually designed with local communicators in mind, seems to reflect the priorities of an American evangelical context, only now with a universal application. Rather than nuancing understandings of oralities to different contexts, orality within ION (or **orality$_2$**) becomes essentially a one-size-fits-all orality that can be plugged-in and played in almost any context. The field research in chapter 5 reveals that such universal conceptions of orality will not always reflect social expectations and experiences from on-the-ground communicators.

Therefore, while these proponents of orality want to go beyond *Protestant orality* with its textual tether, evidence suggests that these oral champions have struggled to recognize the influence of a particular systematic (or literary) hermeneutical orientation on their own understanding of orality. Furthermore, in their eagerness to critique that very systematic hermeneutic, they tend to conflate ways of communicating with ways of processing information. Such observations expose concerns that reemerge as this discussion continues; for now, it can be acknowledged that while the OM is revolutionary in particular ways, its oral-advocating activities should be interpreted as a twenty-first-century oral renaissance. To understand how that renaissance and its complexities are being played out within a local context, chapter 4 introduces Africa Gospel Church Uganda.

4

Africa Gospel Church

Antecedents, History, and People

INTRODUCTION

THE OVERALL INTEREST OF this project lies in the relationship between cultural expectations of modernity and the communication complexities facing local Christian communities in Majority World contexts. Attention now shifts from the international, global perspective to a localized, denominational context, from ION to AGC. This chapter contributes to this overarching goal by accomplishing two objectives: First, it offers a historical consideration of how print-oriented communication played an essential role in the development, particularly in the early years, of Ugandan Christianity; second, it introduces AGC as a unique and appropriate case study. Understanding the premium placed on literacy in Uganda provides the means to situate AGC into the contemporary communication context. Thus, the first half of this chapter establishes the high value of print-reliant communication within early Protestant Christianity's development among the Baganda before exploring the emerging tensions related to the establishment of formal (i.e., literary) education within colonial and then independent Uganda. The second half of the chapter documents the historical development of AGC and its founding organization, WGM, and considers AGC's holiness theology alongside the historic impact of the holiness tradition in Uganda before exploring AGC's own literate-oriented turned oral-oriented pastoral training program.

A further word on the relationship between these two parts of the chapter is necessary. Appreciation of the tensions that have emerged with the intentional championing of orality by the OM within the contemporary Ugandan Christian context (AGC, specifically) can only be properly understood in light of the long historical associations between Ugandan Christianity and literary communication. While the arrival of Christianity has often been followed with literary communication and education, Uganda provides a fascinating case study of print-preference communication, for early Ugandan Christians were known simply as "readers." This legacy of print-oriented communication has shaped the Protestant (Anglican) Church of Uganda (COU), and while challenged by emerging Pentecostalism, the COU continues to wield tremendous influence within Ugandan Christianity. Therefore, it is necessary to explore this rich, literary-oriented Christianity so as to appreciate the uniqueness of AGC within Uganda's historically shaped contemporary communication landscape. Once the historical backcloth and contemporary picture are clearly in view, the subsequent chapter will delve into the data accumulated from the field work, thus preparing the way for a comparative assessment of the influence of an international communication movement on the communication praxis of a local faith community.

THE DEVELOPMENT OF CHRISTIANITY AND FORMAL EDUCATION IN UGANDA

Christianity's Early Literary Development within the Buganda Kingdom

While the entire story of Christianity's arrival and eventual acceptance in Uganda does not need to be retold,[1] a brief historical recount and discussion of several distinct literary features deserve attention for understanding the communication environment within which AGC operates today and into which the OM has sought to promote oral methodologies. Fascinatingly, the phrase *literate conflict* would not be farfetched in describing the introduction of foreign religions to the Buganda kingdom. Arabs from the coast arrived in the 1840s, trading in ivory and slaves. They also brought with them Islam and introduced Buganda, the largest kingdom in what is now Uganda, to the Qur'an. By the 1860s, the ruler of the Baganda,

---

1. For classic texts on early Christianity in Uganda, see Pirouet, *Black Evangelists*, 1–38; Taylor, *Growth of the Church in Buganda*, 1–105; Tuma and Mutibwa, *Century of Christianity in Uganda*. For a shorter but insightful overview, see also Ward, "History of Christianity in Uganda." While this chapter focuses on Protestant Christianity, for parallel developments among Catholic Christianity in Uganda, see Tourigny, *So Abundant a Harvest*; Waliggo, *Catholic Church in Buddu Province*.

Kabaka Mutesa,[2] employed two Arab scribes and, in time, came to read and speak in Arabic and Kiswahili.[3]

In 1862 European explorers began venturing further down the Nile River, beginning with the Scotsman Samuel Baker who represented the expansionist ambitions of Khedive Ismail of Egypt to the north.[4] In that same year Captain John Speke and Captain Richard Burton were the first Europeans to reach Mutesa's court, searching for the elusive source of the Nile River. While Speke encouraged Christian missionaries to go to Buganda as early as 1864, it was not until after Henry Morton Stanley visited Mutesa in 1874 that a letter to the Queen appeared on November 15, 1875 in the London *Daily Telegraph*, requesting "practical missionaries" to come to Uganda.[5]

Mutesa expressed a great eagerness to learn from Stanley, particularly taking an interest in the Europeans' religion. In time, Stanley offered to have his English Bible translated, first into Kiswahili and then into Arabic script. In Stanley's account, Mutesa's decision of whether to adhere to Mohammed or Jesus was based largely on the comparison of their holy books. Stanley records that Mutesa discussed with his chiefs, saying, "'Stamlee' has come to Uganda with a book older than the Koran of Mohammed, . . . and this boy and Idi have read to me all that Stamlee has read to them from this book, and I find it is a great deal better than the book of Mohammed, besides it is the first and oldest book."[6] While acknowledging this is Stanley's interpretation of what happened, the subsequent growth of the number of Christian followers in Uganda suggests other Baganda came to agree. Thus, from its inception, the bookish or literary nature of Christianity was a powerful agent in establishing its religious authority in Uganda.

While Mutesa's interest in Stanley seems to have included curiosity in European religion as well as the hope of political advantage against threats from Egyptian expansion, he did welcome two Church Missionary Society (CMS) missionaries in 1877 from London and two French Catholic missionaries in 1879.[7] In the early days after the Europeans' arrival, the Catholics, Protestants (CMS), and Muslims vied not only for favor with the Kabaka but often also sought to undermine the reputation and activities of

---

2. For a helpful introduction to Mutesa, see Gray, "Mutesa of Buganda."
3. Manarin, "And the Word Became Kigambo," 22–25.
4. Mutibwa, *History of Uganda*, 3–7.
5. Livingston, "Paradox in Early Mission Education,"162.
6. Idi was one of Mutesa's scribes. Stanley, *Through the Dark Continent*, 323; Manarin, "And the Word Became Kigambo," 32–33.
7. Stock, *History of the Church Missionary Society*, 97–106.

the opposition parties. This animosity would eventually erupt into full-scale war,[8] but many of the early converts to these foreign religions were the young elites, sons of chiefs sent to train in the royal court. Whether initially spiritually interested or just curious of the visitors, the young courtiers began gathering at the missionaries' homes. Over time the missionary compounds became sites of literacy training and religious learning.[9]

Thus, this relationship between Christianity and literacy soon manifested itself in what has been called *kusoma* Christianity.[10] *Kusoma* or reading became associated with those following after Christianity. While the term *reader* was originally dubbed for the early adherents to Islam in the previous generation because of the introduction of literacy due to the association with the Qur'an, the term soon came to include the young Christian pages that learned to read the Bible.[11] Therefore, for the early Ugandan Christians, literacy was a means to shape their Christian identity. This observation should not be missed in light of the forthcoming discussion regarding orality: To be an early Ugandan Christian was to be a reader.

The CMS missionaries expressed their amazement at the eagerness at which the Baganda sought out literacy skills. Particularly, those near the royal court seemed to recognize such abilities could serve not only religious but also political ambitions. Bartolomayo Zimbe Musoke, an early Baganda mission student, declared, "Learning to read became a fashion in Buganda and the subject of conversation where two people met."[12] Louise Pirouet notes, "To be able to read and write quickly became a necessity for anyone aspiring to become other than the most junior of chiefs, and to possess a book and a Christian name was to show oneself a progressive."[13] Such comments reveal something of the role of printed communication in establishing both religious and political identities. Recognizing the early relationship between printed communication and being considered a "progressive" further extends the issue of identity. Thus, reading became a means to distinguish and even reimagine one's identity. While the relationship between politics and texts within East Africa lies beyond the immediate interest of this inquiry,[14]

---

8. Mutibwa, *History of Uganda*, 2.

9. Stock, *History of the Church Missionary Society*, 108–10; Manarin, "And the Word Became Kigambo," 60, 66.

10. See chapter 12, "Kusoma Christianity," in Anderson, *Church of East Africa*, 111–17; See also Pirouet, *Black Evangelists*, 29.

11. Vilhanová-Pawliková, "Biblical Translations of Early Missionaries, 199.

12. Manarin quotes Musoke. See Manarin, "And the Word Became Kigambo," 66.

13. Pirouet, *Black Evangelists*, 29–30.

14. For the influence of Christian texts on political imaginations in East Africa, see Earle, "Political Theologies in Late Colonial Buganda"; Peterson, *Creative Writing*.

it is worth noting how mission activity and the growth of literacy happened simultaneously, enabling local Baganda to craft new identities amidst their unprecedented changing social realities.[15]

While Catholic missions are more often associated with oral catechisms, the White Fathers published the first book in the Luganda language—a catechism—in 1881. In spite of this work, over time, the Bible became more identified with the Protestants.[16] In a bold but perhaps not inaccurate assessment of the necessity of reading for early Ugandan Christians, one scholar says, "Faith alone was not sufficient."[17] As evidence, by 1908 Bishop Tucker could write about the standing rule of the church being that the ability to read the Four Gospels in Luganda was a prerequisite for baptism, a measure of each candidate's sincerity and pure motive.[18] In other words, the early Ugandan Church's understanding of the relationship between salvation and printed communication can be summed as such: "Thus from the very beginning in Buganda, reading was of much more than utilitarian importance. It was the way to salvation."[19]

In 1884, Mwanga became the new Kabaka and while his father Mutesa had managed to navigate and maintain some control over the various religious factions and political dynamics, including the possible threat from Egypt, Mwanga failed.[20] Frightened by the approach of the newly appointed Anglican Bishop James Hannington from the eastern Busoga region, Mwanga ordered him to be executed in 1885. By the end of 1886, over fifty young Christians, many of them pages of the royal court, were, likewise, put to death. Those executed have become known as the Ugandan Martyrs, representing many young readers and leaders within both Catholic and Protestant parties.[21]

In 1888 a coup took place wherein a joint alliance of Muslims, Catholics, and Protestants overthrew Mwanga but this partnership could not last and the Muslims emerged victorious. This rule was short-lived, as by February 1890, the Christians had toppled the Muslims, only then to be hampered by their own internal Catholic–Protestant animosity.[22] In

15. Livingston, "Paradox in Early Mission Education," 163.

16. Openjuru and Lyster, "Christianity and Rural Community Literacy," 100; Manarin, "And the Word Became Kigambo," 45, 48.

17. Livingston, "Paradox in Early Mission Education" 163.

18. Livingston, "Paradox in Early Mission Education," 163.

19. Rowe, "Myth, Memoir and Moral Admonition," 19.

20. Kiwanuka, "Kabaka Mwanga and His Political Parties."

21. Kiwanuka, "Kabaka Mwanga and His Political Parties," 4; Faupel, *African Holocaust*.

22. Tuma and Mutibwa, *Century of Christianity in Uganda*, 9–11.

December 1890, Captain Lugard arrived with the Imperial British East African Company, and with the help of his Protestant sympathies and superior firepower, Protestant Christianity emerged victorious in 1892 from a civil war with the Catholics.[23]

African historian Adrian Hastings, in discussing the significance of the martyrdom and the subsequent wars that took place, first between Christians and Muslims and then later between Catholics and Protestants, made several keen observations. During this time, there was minimal involvement by the European missionaries. The Catholics departed across the lake for a time from 1882 to 1885 and apart from Alexander Mackay who did persevere, the CMS presence was slim. However, Hastings notes that through the wars, Christianity spread from being primarily contained to the elite young people in training at the royal court to the masses. Furthermore, these Christians embraced a deep devotion, not only to the biblical teachings but also to a high moral code. Hastings adds that while this interreligious conflict is usually presented problematically he suggests it represents a robust intellectual achievement whereby Christianity enters into a pre-colonial Buganda society, largely unaided by European missionaries.[24]

What deserves reiteration is that literate (i.e., print-reliant) communication made such an intellectual achievement possible. The missionaries had upheld a fierce "commitment to the medium of literacy for evangelism."[25] Thus, by as early as 1879, reading sheets of the alphabet and short words and even the Apostles' Creed were printed in Luganda. By 1883, Mackay[26] had printed *Bigambo bya mu Kitabu kya Katonda* (*Words from the Book of God*), a Luganda reading primer that began with the Ten Commandments.[27] Such publications were all part of a larger literary communication strategy of the missionaries. As Manarin comments, "With the time and resources the CMS mission invested in producing a vernacular translation of the Christian Scriptures, *the ultimate goal* of missionary instruction lay with enabling the

---

23. Low, *Fabrication of Empire*, 3–4.

24. Hastings, *Church in Africa*, 371–85.

25. Manarin, "And the Word Became Kigambo," 78.

26. It should be noted that Livingston makes a case that Mackay was the epitome of the "practical" missionary that Stanley had requested for Uganda. As the quote indicates, Mackay was committed to literacy but he also sought to promote technological skills and in his workshop, "ironwork, carpentry, and other artisan skills" could be learned. This valuing of practical education as exemplified in Mackay struggled to maintain momentum. Livingston, "Paradox in Early Mission Education," 164–67, 170–71. The Phelps-Stokes Commission lamented that Mackay's "interest shown in technical pursuits" had not been emulated. Jones, "Education in East Africa," 163.

27. Manarin, "And the Word Became Kigambo," 79; Welbourn, "Missionary Methods I," 82.

Baganda to have *the most direct and unencumbered access to the Bible in their own language*. To this end, Mackay wrote that they 'aim steadily at presenting the Word of God both proper, and push forward every means of *enabling them readily to read it for themselves*.'"[28]

While acknowledging the missionaries' ultimate intention and involvement in creating Bible-reading Ugandans, the Ugandans themselves played a significant role in reproducing literate-proficient Ugandan Christians as they adopted Christianity for their own. The mobility of Ganda society in relation to the royal court, whether as a result of persecution for Christian beliefs or merely displeasing the Kabaka, was a key factor that led to the dispersal of literate communication. While the missionaries seemed to have been largely restricted to the capital, mobile Christian readers simply took their newly printed texts with them. This migration resulted in the circulation of differing printed texts. Furthermore, the recurring communication phenomenon was that these Christian readers taught other Ugandans to read, regardless of whether the missionaries were present or not.[29]

Mackay captures this hunger for printed communication when he notes, "Again and again I have seen the various stores and other houses at court, literally converted into reading rooms, . . . lads sitting in groups or sprawled on the hay-covered floor—all reading, some the book of the Commandments and other texts, some the church prayers, and others the Kiswahili N. T. They are besides very eager to learn to write and at all times are scribbling on boards or any scrap of paper they can pick up."[30] Thus, the *Church Missionary Intelligence* for August 1900 printed correspondence with Bishop Tucker recounting that in 1899, the CMS sold 60,338 books in Uganda, including 10,266 New Testaments and 16,005 portions of Old and New Testaments.[31] Book sales were not necessarily the goal, but the literary strategies of evangelism enabled the missionaries to achieve their ultimate goal for the Baganda people: *direct and unencumbered access to the Bible in their own language*. It is important to note that the push forward aimed at enabling young Ugandan Christians to *read* the Bible *for themselves*. Furthermore, the CMS missionaries maintained this biblical encounter needed to happen not in English or even the trade language of the region (Kiswahili) but in the local vernacular of Luganda. Despite challenges, the missionaries remained committed to translating the Bible into Luganda,

28. Manarin, "And the Word Became Kigambo," 77. Emphasis added.

29. Manarin, "And the Word Became Kigambo," 96–101.

30. Manarin quotes Rowe. Manarin, "And the Word Became Kigambo, 97; for the original article and quote, see Rowe, "Mika Sematimba," 185.

31. "The Uganda Mission—The Mission Field"; I am indebted to Peterson for this source. See also Peterson, "Politics of Transcendence in Colonial Uganda," 206.

convinced that encountering the printed biblical text in one's own language was most likely to lead to salvation.

Before turning to the development of education, a comment on literacy and Christian maturity deserve attention. It should be understood that the early literary infatuation was not neatly ordered along clerical or laity lines. Those were only beginning to even develop. The CMS missionaries promoted literacy for anyone, as it was understood to be the key to enabling Christian maturity. This observation parallels and yet contrasts with the OM in the twenty-first century. The OM is likewise seeking to enable *direct and unencumbered access to the Bible in [people's] own language.* They too want to see such encounters happen at both pastoral and laity levels. Furthermore, adherents of the OM would love to see similar local initiatives as those witnessed by early CMS missionaries, whereby communication skills and the Bible are shared and reproduced widely among relational networks. The radical difference is that the OM is promoting oral instead of printed engagement with the biblical texts. Whereas those within the OM would argue that literate skills are not necessary for maturing as a disciple of Christ, the early CMS missionaries believed that, except for the blind or infirm, reading the Bible was essential for establishing young Ugandan Christians in their new faith.[32]

Christianity, Colonialism, and Education in Uganda

In his article on the early mission education among the Baganda, Thomas Livingston discussed how "the missionaries did not see themselves primarily as teachers; though they were constantly engaged in teaching activities, and certain levels of educational development were regarded as manifestations of parallel religious development."[33] This initial parallel development of Christianity and formal print-reliant education necessitates considering Uganda's educational development as a means of better understanding the communication dynamics both at the end of the nineteenth century but also leading up to the establishment of AGC at the end of the twentieth century. Specifically, to understand the communication backcloth for Christianity in Uganda, attention must be given to the high value Ugandan cultures have consistently placed on literary skills since their introduction. Therefore, while an exhaustive treatment of the historical development of Uganda's

---

32. Livingston, "Paradox in Early Mission Education," 163.

33. It is in this context that Livingston highlights the fact that the church established that the ability to read the Four Gospels as necessary before baptism. He specifically notes that this was not ncessarily considered an educational activity but an evangelistic one. Livingston, "Paradox in Early Mission Education," 163.

educational system is not necessary or possible in this setting,[34] components of the story have directly influenced the communication environment within which AGC finds itself today.

Indigenous Education

Before turning to the story of the establishment of mission schools and their influence, the topic of indigenous education deserves attention. In his work on the history and development of Ugandan education, J. C. Ssekamwa opens with a chapter on education before the arrival of formal literary schooling.[35] He notes that education was indeed nonliterate, but, contrary to the early missionaries' understanding of education before they arrived, learning was happening.[36] Due to the similarities in communication praxis with the arrival of the OM over a century later, understanding indigenous education is paramount for understanding early Ugandan Christianity.

The primary teachers in traditional Ganda society were parents, along with other adult community members, and the primary classroom was the fireplace, the center of much of daily life. It was not regimented with daily schooltime hours, but learning happened at any time, on any number of topics. Teaching methods often included explanation followed by immediate practice. Activities such as plays, games, songs, rhymes, and storytelling were introduced early, and then as children matured, idioms, proverbs, and riddles were introduced. Ssekamwa argues that in the interaction between the pupils, adults and other age-mates, a whole spectrum of "philosophy, psychology, sociology, economics, politics, history, and culture" was imparted. Furthermore, this allowed for the children to develop skills in "imagination, thinking, inventiveness, shrewdness, literature, composition, and the art of public speaking."[37] This situation-based (or situation-driven) learning style fulfilled the educational purpose of preparing a pupil so that when he or she came of age, the necessary skills and knowledge to participate and contribute in community life had been attained.[38]

Significantly, not every community's educational experiences were the same. Depending on the environment and other cultural elements,

---

34. For a helpful, albeit dated introduction to Ugandan education, see Hindmarsh, "Uganda," 135–63.

35. Ssekamwa, *History and Development of Education*, 1–24. See also Ssekamwa and Lugumba, *History of Education*; Ssekamwa and Lugumba, *Development and Administration of Education*. Tiberondwa's opening chapter on indigenous education is also helpful. Tiberondwa, *Missionary Teachers as Agents of Colonialism*, 1–14.

36. Ssekamwa, *History and Development of Education*, 21–24.

37. Ssekamwa, *History and Development of Education*, 5.

38. Ssekamwa, *History and Development of Education*, 3–4.

indigenous education systems flexed to provide each community's members with the knowledge and skills that were necessary for handling daily realities and enabling community life to happen. For example, communities that valued cattle keeping crafted educational experiences differently from those living in the forests. Ssekamwa underscores the importance for indigenous education of situating learning within a particular environment so that the needs of that particular community are met.[39]

This issue of environmentally based education deserves keeping in mind, as it became a point of tension with the arrival of foreign educational expectations. How far did European education praxis and theory fit into a Bugandan and later Ugandan learning environment?[40] Furthermore, it holds relevance for the concerns expressed by members of the OM, that the majority of the world's population prefers oral communication. The curious question is whether oral communication methods, such as the ones that Ssekamwa described as already incorporated into indigenous education practices are appropriate for the print-saturated and now digitally fused Ugandan communication environment.

Formal Mission Education

In his thought-provoking book *Missionary Teachers as Agents of Colonialism in Uganda*, Ado K. Tiberondwa describes how education and evangelization were intertwined: "When we talk about the spread of missionary education in colonial Africa we normally mean the spread of Christianity as well, because education was part and parcel of the pastoral work."[41] Therefore, proficiency in literacy was the valued communication skill for early Ugandan Christians. As the number of interested students continued to grow, it became apparent that formal schools were going to be necessary, for, as one CMS missionary writes, "The Bible means readers, and readers mean schools and schools mean teachers."[42] Until the establishment of these formal schools, the literary training was for the purpose of Bible reading and Christian instruction. Attitudes began to change as the missionaries believed there was a need for formal schooling to shape

---

39. Ssekamwa, *History and Development of Education*, 8, 15–17.

40. Ssekamwa, *History and Development of Education*, 17. For a helpful discussion on indigenous curricula, see pp. 8–16.

41. Tiberondwa, *Missionary Teachers as Agents of Colonialism*, 34–35.

42. Ssekamwa quotes J. Steward of CMS at Namirembe. Ssekamwa, *History and Development of Education*, 39.

students' character as well as equip them for "a wider and fast changing world" in which they would live.[43]

Bishop Tucker, arriving in Uganda in 1890 as the third Anglican bishop, played a key role in establishing the mission education system. He appointed C. W. Hattersley to set up a system of primary schools and to begin training teachers.[44] Thus, while some steps were taken beforehand, from around 1898 formal schools were established, and by 1925, eight different types of formal schools could be identified. The *catechist schools* prepared people for baptism. The *village schools* (or *bush schools*) were taught by Ugandans and offered a limited curriculum that mixed practical skills, labor, and literary pursuits. European missionaries with Ugandan assistants managed *vernacular schools*, offering Christian instruction and a more developed literary curriculum. Contrary to the vernacular schools, *central schools* offered English in their literary topics and were seen as helping to build a cadre of students prepared for clerical positions within government posts. *High schools* drew their students from central schools and were originally for society's elite, primarily sons of chiefs or clan heads. *Makerere College* was established in 1922 as the first school opened by the government, and it became the highest academic institution. A few *technical schools* were also set up but in conjunction with missionaries for meeting practical parish needs. Finally, *normal schools* were set up for training teachers.[45] Therefore, within twenty-five years, a multifaceted, albeit not always polished, education system was in place. While presumably the mission expected to draw its leadership from the developing mission schools, what seems to be apparently lacking within this education system was a prioritization of theological education.

In the first decade of the twentieth century, missionaries became convinced that boarding schools were the way forward for the future leaders of the country to appropriate the necessary "Christian and European" values.[46] The establishment of boarding schools ensured, according to the missionaries, that the young pupils remained focused, undistracted by traditional values or their home environment.[47] An argument can be made that the European missionaries essentially disregarded the Ugandan agrarian environment of these young elites, as the new boarding schools were modeled on the image of the British public schools. However, as Gordon P. McGregor

---

43. Ssekamwa and Lugumba, *History of Education*, 40.
44. McGregor, *King's College Budo*, 2.
45. Ssekamwa, *History and Development of Education*, 40–42.
46. Welbourn, "Missionary Methods I," 84.
47. Livingston, "Paradox in Early Mission Education," 175.

points out, in the minds of missionaries such as Tucker, these schools offered Britain's best to the Ugandan young people.[48] Whereas indigenous education sought to foster a synthesis of education and environment, from the start of formal literary education, a tension developed between literary education and the realities of the pupils' environment.

This tension became an ongoing strain in the development of Ugandan education, but even those not interested in Christianity per se were attracted to the schools. Literary education afforded advantages in a developing Ugandan society. Identification as a Christian began to carry not only religious but also material benefits, including at times socioeconomic opportunities on mission stations.[49] Thus, once again, this relationship of identity and print-oriented communication emerges as literary education afforded a means to shape one's material identity. These two emerging issues—environment and materiality—appear very early in the narrative of Ugandan Christianity's understanding of communication and education, becoming core concerns that continue to influence people's attitudes regarding preferences towards religious education and modes of communication. As will become evident, chapters 5 and 6 reveal how questions of materiality and identity are at the heart of AGC's concerned reception of orality in the twenty-first century.

Colonial Education

While Buganda had become a British Protectorate in 1894, the colonial government remained largely uninvolved in education, seemingly grateful to the different mission groups for shouldering both the responsibility and expense of such an endeavor. However, in 1924 the first report of the Phelps-Stokes Commission was released and while overall appreciative of the initial efforts of the missionaries, it called for a much stronger government involvement. The Commission was the result of the work of a philanthropic foundation in the USA with strong concerns for the education of Africans and African–Americans.[50] The report called for the immediate establishment of a department of education within colonial governments to give oversight to the educational developments.[51]

---

48. McGregor, *King's College Budo*, 12.

49. Tiberondwa, *Missionary Teachers as Agents of Colonialism*, 38–39.

50. Jones, "Education in East Africa," xvi–xvii. For a more in-depth discussion on the influence of African Americans, particularly Booker T. Washington and his Tuskegee Institute on African education, see Barnes, *Global Christianity and the Black Atlantic*.

51. Jones, "Education in East Africa," 162–68.

The Commission critiqued the mission schools for the lack of practical education. It is imperative to recognize the early origins of this issue because it has direct bearing on AGC's reception of orality almost ninety years later. The Commission believed the missionaries had been "exclusively literary," neglecting to develop practical skills, lamenting how in spite of Uganda's fertile soil, "they have made practically no provision for agricultural education."[52] The Commission, while trying not to diminish the value of reading, writing, and mathematics, encouraged the immediate development of technical and agricultural education.[53] Since there were limited clerical positions within the government, practical education (or what was called adaptive education) was encouraged based on the assumption that the majority of the students would return to life on the land after school.[54] By 1930, the idea of an increasingly large cadre of well literary-trained young people who did not have designated employment was a matter of colonial concern.

E. C. Morris, the second director of education in Uganda, said, "A policy which had tended to give a purely literary training to the masses in order to serve a small minority, which might benefit by higher education and qualify for semi-professional careers could, if persisted in, only lead to the creation of a discontented community divorced from its own heredity and environment with no outlet for its energies but political intrigue and the flouting of authority."[55] It is worth noting again this theme of the relationship between education and environment: Morris was concerned that purely literary education would divorce pupils from their heredity (traditions) and environment. The solution, according to the Phelps-Stokes Commission and men such as Morris, was more practical education, meaning agricultural or technical training.[56] Attempts were made to encourage

52. Jones, "Education in East Africa," 162.
53. Jones, "Education in East Africa," 7–8, 168.
54. Ssekamwa, *History and Development of Education*, 60; Barnes, *Global Christianity and the Black Atlantic*, xi.
55. Ssekamwa, *History and Development of Education*, 60–61.
56. Ssekamwa, *History and Development of Education*, 61; Barnes's study, while not directly related to Uganda, situates the question of industrial education into a larger framework. Booker T. Washington's teaching at Tuskegee maintained that rather then openly confront white domination, industrial-minded African Americans who succeed economically would have more political capital. While claiming to represent Tuskegee and Washington, Thomas Jones of the Phelps-Stokes Commission subverted Washington's education philosophy dramatically by promoting adaptive education, where Africans needed to "adapt to the niches whites designated for them." Thus, caution needs to be taken regarding terms like "practical," "technical," or "industrial." While the Commission's call for agriculture and technical schools would seem to be promoting Washington's call for industrial Africans, in reality Jones understood this as not about enabling or enhancing African economic well-being but better suiting Africans to fit

practical courses, including the opening of post-primary schools that focused on agricultural and technical skills.[57] Significantly, the simple fact was that neither the students nor their parents who paid their school fees wanted practical (adaptive) training.[58] Manual labor, handicrafts, and farming were associated with the previous way of life—their indigenous environment. The adaptive education philosophy of the colonial government wanted to educate students so they could better adapt in the local agrarian-based environment,[59] but no one understood better than the students that education and environment are related. They intuited that the colonial winds of erosion were drastically changing their environmental landscape. Thus, they were not interested in a practical educational system that did not empower and prepare them for the potential opportunities that now awaited them within a developing colonial environment. They knew well that the gateway into such a new "modern" environment was proficient literary skills.[60] Ssekamwa summarizes this tension well, and due to the relevance of this tension between practical and literary education for subsequent discussions of the OM and AGC, it is worth quoting in full:

> But the cause of the desire for literary education by the people of Uganda is not far to seek. The colonial situation brought in new values and, in order for a person to gain out of that changed situation, he had to avail himself of the literary education that the colonial masters seemed to have gone through. Comfort and the opening up of new horizons meant getting away from the village routine. Therefore no other kind of education but the literary type appealed to the people more because it was the road leading to a new kind of life. Education for adaptation did not excite them, and any one who preached the gospel of education for adaptation was a prophet of doom. By clamoring for literary education, the students were trying to adapt themselves to changed circumstances and to progressive ideas, as they thought.[61]

---

into colonial endeavors. Barnes, *Global Christianity and the Black Atlantic*, 154–55.

57. For a helpful discussion on the paradoxes in early mission-colonial education in Uganda, see Livingston, "Paradox in Early Mission Education."

58. Ssekamwa, *History and Development of Education*, 59–71.

59. Tiberondwa discusses the Phelps-Stokes Commission's recommended "Jeanes schools," which were intended to help "the Africans in the rural areas to love the rural way of life and to strive to improve conditions in the village instead of running away from villages in search of office jobs in towns." See Tiberondwa, *Missionary Teachers as Agents of Colonialism*, 77–80.

60. Tiberondwa, *Missionary Teachers as Agents of Colonialism*, 77–80.

61. Ssekamwa, *History and Development of Education*, 62.

Once again, literary communication was understood as a means to reimagine one's identity and establish one on the road to "progressive ideas." Furthermore, no matter how much the colonial administrators argued for the practical advantages of agricultural or technical education, they and the missionaries with their literary education background were the point of reference for the Ugandan students. While some missionaries dabbled in farming, it was only primarily in the role of supervising Ugandan laborers. Thus, neither farming nor technical know-how had empowered the Europeans but, instead, literary schooling and the Ugandans wanted nothing less.[62]

While the historical details of this recurring theme regarding the preference among Ugandans for literary over practical education throughout the colonial enterprise are not necessary for the purposes of this study, it has remained an ongoing tension in Ugandan education.[63] Recognizing this tension is particularly relevant for understanding subsequent discussions regarding the reactions of AGC church members to oral methodologies. These oral methods were justified as "practical" ways to communicate across barriers, whether educational, economic, or generational. Significantly, the disturbing question emerges of whether twenty-first-century Ugandans have thought, at times, that in oral methodologies they are being offered a form of early twentieth-century "adaptive" education.

Post-Independence Education

In 1963, the independent government under President Milton Obote passed the Education Act, placing all schools receiving government assistance under government control. This mandate included all the religious schools operated by the Church of Uganda, the Roman Catholics, and the Uganda Muslim Education Association.[64] While these and other religious groups have continued to be heavily involved in schools since independence, the government has assumed responsibility for controlling the education system. In reality, the quest for a holistic approach to learning, integrating both practical and academic pursuits, has continued to be a challenge for those involved in Ugandan education.[65] Ssekawma offers an optimistic viewpoint by suggesting that contemporary attitudes towards practical or technological training are more accepting. He notes that Makerere University today offers courses in the Faculty of Technology for "candidates with a bias to practical

---

62. Ssekamwa, *History and Development of Education*, 63–64.

63. For example, see the discussion in the Binns Study Group in the 1950s. Ssekamwa, *History and Development of Education*, 79–83.

64. Hindmarsh, "Uganda," 149.

65. Ssekamwa, *History and Development of Education*, 186.

skills." Nonetheless, even he has to concede that concerns such as the expense of practical education—both tools and materials, the lack of qualified practical teachers, and society's continued prejudice against practical training in favor of literary knowledge are all factors continuing to influence educational attitudes in twenty-first-century Uganda.[66]

Theological Education

Protestant theological education has certainly not escaped some of these emerging issues of identity, environment, and questions of practical versus literary education. With the formalization of education, the attention shifted, inadvertently perhaps, from religious instruction for anyone, clergy or laity alike, to the material and societal advantages of literary education. Thus, the CMS missionaries prioritized their mission schools over training their clergy, which had unintended consequences.

Although Bishop Tucker rather quickly commissioned several Ugandan church leaders and even appointed the first Ugandan priest by 1896, the Anglicans did not prioritize formal theological education. By 1913 the CMS missionaries had begun to establish a theological training school in Mukono to train ordinands and lay readers as well as primary school teachers. Significantly, while enormous energy was devoted to establishing formal mission schools and training the future leaders of the country in Protestant values, little more was done by way of improving clerical education.[67] With time, the CMS missionaries accomplished their goal of establishing a Protestant elite from which the colonial government had ample choices for employment. Shockingly, Hansen notes that at education conferences in 1915 and again in 1921, the missionaries had to acknowledge that no one from their mission schools had joined the ministry of the Anglican Church.[68] This remarkable statistic haunts theological education in Uganda.

Hansen ascribes this growing dichotomy between pastoral (practical) and educational (literary) work within the mission-church-society relationships to two factors still relevant today, the first being the lack of respect afforded to church leaders. Ugandans employed as mission-school teachers or colonial civil servants carried much more social status than the clergy. In his work on Christianity among the Busoga of Uganda, Tom Tuma notes that whereas initially the catechist and schoolteacher were understood as of equal authority, over time a gap grew as the schoolteachers distanced

---

66. Ssekamwa, *History and Development of Education*, 186, 196–97.
67. Slater, "Ownership of Knowledge," 38–39.
68. Hansen, *Mission, Church and State*, 250–54.

themselves from the poorly trained catechists.[69] People trained in formal mission schools had increasingly less respect for church leaders who often possessed inferior education. The second and related factor was economics, an issue that would also reemerge in the twenty-first century. People trained in formal mission schools could make more money in government service than as church leaders. This phenomenon only contributed to the stigma that began to develop in relation to the clergy; not only were they uneducated but they were poor.[70]

Although the missionaries eventually recognized the problem, their commitments to establishing a self-funded indigenous church made them reluctant to consider reorienting the paradigm by improving funding for the clergy or developing more prestigious theological education options.[71] This issue of self-funding reflects the continuing influence on CMS policy of the well-known CMS secretary Henry Venn.[72] Venn believed national churches should be self-governing, self-supporting, and self-propagating. Seen within the broad view of history, the "three-self" paradigm has enabled Ugandan Protestant Christianity to establish its own identity. However, Hansen notes, "Adherence to the principle of self-support made it almost impossible to obtain an educated ministry which could keep up intellectually with the generation being educated by the other sector. This was a hindrance to the Africanization of the church leadership, and thus caused a significant postponement of the realization of the ideal of self-government."[73] Therefore, at times, rigid adherence to the self-reliant model has proved counter-productive.[74]

The Anglican Church's answer to this problem seemed to be to focus on spirituality and hope for the best: "Increased spirituality, and a consequent increase in contributions, were assumed to be the proper way of tackling the problem. This precluded any suggestion of seeking support to break the vicious cycle. The upholding of the principle of self-support limited the Church's range of action considerably."[75] Thus, Bishop Willis declared, "The most essential thing is the revival of spiritual life in the

69. Tuma, *Building a Ugandan Church*, 85.

70. Hansen, *Mission, Church and State*, 252–53, 256.

71. Hansen, *Mission, Church and State*, 254.

72. For detailed consideration of Venn and his influence, see Williams, "'Not Transplanting'"; Williams, *Ideal of the Self-Governing Church*.

73. Hansen, *Mission, Church and State*, 255.

74. Anderson, *Church of East Africa*, 48. To see a brief discussion on Bishop Tucker's disagreement with Venn, regarding whether missionaries should leave (Venn) or remain (Tucker); see pp. 91–92.

75. Hansen, *Mission, Church and State*, 254.

Uganda Church; the giving will follow."[76] Therefore, a paradox had emerged wherein the church wanted to uphold its self-funding commitment but doing so had dramatic implications.

These implications revealed themselves in that those with higher levels of education spurned church positions with their meager salaries; likewise, the up-and-coming educated class distained giving their tithes and offerings to support church leaders whom they regarded as uneducated. While the mission had envisioned drawing leadership from the formally educated class, they found that newly mission trained pupils turned to the colonial government for employment instead. This issue of self-funding and theological education remains a sensitive topic within Protestant evangelical mission endeavors today. Furthermore, the issue of the missionaries emphasizing the spiritual over physical or financial matters reveals a dichotomy in the missionary social imaginary. Such perspectives emerge in chapter 6 as being not just historical phenomena, but ones that prevail today with substantial implications in AGC's relationship with its founding mission, WGM. Such differences in understanding affect communication praxis and reception.

Observations Regarding Christianity, Literacy, and Education in Uganda

Theological education in Uganda will continue to be a subsequent interlocutor, but for now, several observations regarding communication within early Ugandan Christianity deserve highlighting in anticipation of discussion that follows. First, the residual influence of the CMS and both the direct and indirect influence of the Anglican Church permeate Ugandan Christianity today. This is worth developing in order to appreciate the way in which the subject matter of the first half of this chapter has prepared and influenced the context in which AGC emerges.

It is hard to overestimate the influence the Anglican Church (Church of Uganda) has had on Uganda. Paul Gifford observes, "The Anglican and Catholic Churches are an essential part of the social fabric, and have become fixed at a deep level into political, social, and cultural life."[77] While Pentecostalism has exploded on the contemporary Christian stage in Uganda, this phenomenon has been predominantly since President Museveni's coming to power in 1986.[78] Kevin Ward noted the continued Anglican

---

76. Hansen, *Mission, Church and State*, 254.
77. Gifford, *African Christianity*, 61.
78. Ward, "Eating and Sharing," 106.

influence even within the growing Pentecostal upsurge as today's Pentecostals are often still baptized, married, and buried by the Church of Uganda (COU) in spite of worshiping regularly in Pentecostal churches.[79] While the Catholics have outnumbered the Protestants, from their early aligning with the British colonial administrators, the Anglicans have maintained a decisive political advantage. Gifford states bluntly, "The COU has been intimately tied to the state";[80] thus, all of the heads of state except for Amin have come from an Anglican heritage. Summarily, Ward likewise writes, "The Catholic and Anglican Churches remain the most powerful institutions in Ugandan society, deeply embedded in all aspects of Ugandan life." Therefore, while the political and social influence of Pentecostal churches continues to grow, one has to recognize that AGC operates within a political, cultural, and religious environment, which remains visibly marked by direct and indirect Anglican fingerprints.

AGC and COU have several direct connections, which are illustrative of the visible and residual Anglican fingerprints to which both Gifford and Ward allude.[81] For example, part of the initiative to establish WGM Uganda, discussed in more detail on the following page, was in response to several former COU exiles in Kenya requesting WGM Kenya to come and plant an AGC church in Kampala.[82] Furthermore, when WGM and AGC began to explore adopting a program called Community Health Evangelism (CHE),[83] a team from COU came and provided not only the initial training but also the subsequent coaching on facilitating CHE training and outreach. While perhaps not speaking for the entire denomination, one WGM missionary declared during a recent "Farming God's Way" training, "We praise God for Church of Uganda within AGC and we look for ways to partner with them."[84]

There are also residual ways that the Church of Uganda has shaped AGC's thinking. For example, Anglican thinking seems to permeate the

79. Ward provides a very helpful overview of the unique emergence of the Protestant (Anglican) and Catholic duopoly in Uganda. Ward, "Eating and Sharing."

80. Gifford, *African Christianity*, 62, 84.

81. Gifford suggests this issue of identity helps explain why AICs have never taken root, "it was simply too important for one's identity to be either Catholic or Anglican." Gifford, *African Christianity*, 62; for more on AICs in Uganda, see Mwaura, "African Instituted Churches in East Africa," 160–84.

82. Jonathan Mayo, WhatsApp, August 25, 2017.

83. Some organizations call it "Community Health Empowerment."

84. Farming God's Way (FGW) is associated with CHE, only specifically teaching biblical principles for farming. In the last few years, AGC has begun to offer FGW training to pastors and church members within several of the AGC areas. Muehleisen, "Farming God's Way Training."

subconsciousness of Ugandan Christians. When WGM missionaries first started looking for plots of land in Kampala to plant their church, local neighbors inquired which diocese they represented. This association between the COU and the purchasing of land and the constructing of buildings seems to have an indelible impact. In discussing the relationship between COU and AGC, the AGC assistant bishop commented, "The positive influence I see is not on the spiritual aspect, but it's on physical things like they have built many primary and secondary schools in which our children go to acquire education. They have also built hospitals, which has [sic] helped many of us when we are sick. That is why many people see COU as of more help than AGC. They have built universities and guesthouses. This creates job opportunities, which our people run to."[85] Along those same lines, one AGC church leader stated, as a matter of fact, that AGC does not yet provide houses, salaries, or pensions like the COU does.[86] The actual extent to which the COU is able to provide such things today is almost irrelevant. What is relevant is that for these AGC leaders, COU still provides (or projects) a standard benchmark (i.e., the possession of land, salaries, schools, and retirement) of what Ugandan Christianity is supposed to look like in the twenty-first century.

Furthermore, when the time came for submitting the official church constitution, the church leaders decided to adopt an episcopal form of church polity. While this observation is elaborated shortly, it is significant to note that the AGC leaders even overturned the missionaries' preference for the senior church leader being called "general overseer," arguing such a term would not be recognized within Ugandan society. The church leaders explained that the cultural expectation was for the church leader to be a bishop, possessing and wielding religious authority, a precedent long established by both COU and the Roman Catholic Church. Thus, Kefa Masiga was appointed the first AGC bishop in 2011.[87] AGC did not arrive in a political or religious vacuum and, in light of even cursory examples, one can sense how COU has been the predominant Christian influence in shaping the Protestant landscape, whether positively or negatively, directly or even indirectly, within Uganda.[88]

The second observation highlights several of these emerging tensions that have already been identified: education and environment, practical and literary education, and spiritual and material advantage. The first of these

85. Owor, email, August 31, 2017.
86. James Ouma, personal interview (1st), March 31, 2017.
87. Emy, "Constitution of Africa Gospel Church Uganda."
88. Further influences of COU are discussed below.

tensions relates to the interchange between education and the environment of the students. Indigenous education was oriented towards the local environment, situating the learning in practical and immediately contextualized experiences. A cleavage between the learning experience and the local environment began to develop with the organization of formal schooling that then was only exacerbated by the ascendancy of boarding school. As discussed in shortly, promoting the use of oral Bible stories was, in essence, an adaptive communication strategy, introduced as a means to fit into the more rural, often oral-oriented environment within which many of the AGC pastors were operating. While many people found the Bible stories effective, and perhaps it could be acknowledged that the twenty-first-century missionaries were at least trying to be more sensitive to issues related to education and environment, the church's response has not been univocally positive. A deeper understanding of the sources of this resistance requires considering a second tension that has historical roots.

This second tension extends from the developing issue regarding education and environment, namely that of literary versus practical education. While initially, mission education energetically aimed at instruction in literary skills with an eye towards reading the Bible and other religious material for the purpose of developing Christian identity, the Ugandan Christians employed their own "adaptive" interpretation on the purposes of literacy. As the colonial government became more involved, practical instruction, often associated with agrarian labor or traditional crafts, was encouraged. However, to return to Ssekamwa's quotation, "Education for adaptation [practical education] did not excite them [Ugandans], and any one who preached the gospel of education for adaptation was a prophet of doom."[89] The colonial government saw practical education as a natural solution for many students who would return to a traditional and agrarian way of life. In similar ways, the OM's championing of oral communication methodologies has been understood as a natural solution for many of the pastors who communicate predominantly in rural and often more oral-oriented communities. However, there has been surprise among some missionaries that local Christian communities such as AGC have not univocally received these oral methodologies, but at times have interpreted them as "prophecies of doom." As one missionary leader admitted, he had received accusations from some pastors that the missionary did not believe the pastors were capable of more literary-oriented learning or that the missionary was trying to keep the pastors from literate resources.[90] Thus, while oral Bible storytelling seemed a

89. Ssekamwa, *History and Development of Education*, 62.
90. Jonathan Mayo, personal interview (1st), March 23, 2017.

practical tool for the more rural environment and has even been appreciated by church members at some level, resistance has emerged. In some way, the issues sound remarkably similar to what Ssekamwa discussed as happening in the early twentieth century: "By clamoring for literary education, the students were trying to adapt themselves to changed circumstances and to progressive ideas, as they thought."[91] Apparently, communication complexities do not necessarily fade with time.

The third tension that deserves highlighting, that of spirituality and materiality, builds on issues of environment and practical, or traditional, versus literary education. Depending on whose perspective is adopted, either a corruption or an adaption of the initial literary expectations has occurred. While the early missionaries were originally promoting literary skills for the purposes of developing spiritual maturity, such as being able to read the Bible for oneself, Ugandans adapted their own literary purposes, recognizing that literate proficiency afforded more possibilities for economical and material benefits. There is not a one-to-one correlation between literary education and material benefit, nor between practical education and spirituality; however, the categories do parallel and overlap, at times, as Ugandan Christians have seen the economic or material value of literary education. In an inverse manner, AGC pastors have questioned how orality could impact their material identities (as explored in chapter 5).

Issues such as materiality and the continued influence of COU echoed in some form or fashion throughout the field research in Uganda in 2017. These historical issues remain of critical importance for understanding not only communication complexities in the twenty-first century but also how dynamics from the pre-colonial and colonial contexts continue to influence church–mission relationships operating in today's postcolonial context. Before investigating these issues further, a greater understanding of AGC is necessary.

THE DEVELOPMENT OF AFRICA GOSPEL CHURCH UGANDA

Post-Independence Uganda

This section of the chapter explores the historical development of AGC, its holiness theology, and the unique communication case study that its pastoral training program presents. In order to situate WGM and its establishing of AGC in Uganda towards the end of the twentieth century, it is necessary to remark briefly on the nature of the Christianity that had developed

---

91. Ssekamwa, *History and Development of Education*, 62.

within Uganda since the nation's independence in 1962. At the time of independence, a flood of new mission groups and denominations entered the country, although some such as Seventh-Day Adventists and the Salvation Army had arrived much earlier.[92] However, in 1971 Idi Amin assumed power of this nascent African nation. Amin's brutal rule, coupled with his paranoia about any religious threat to his authority, resulted in a persecution of all forms of Christianity and even Islam at times, finding perhaps its most vehement public expression in the murder of Church of Uganda Archbishop Janani Luwum in 1977.[93] American evangelical denominations such as the Southern Baptists and Conservative Baptists, who had arrived since independence, were forced to leave, and Amin eventually banned twenty-seven different religious organizations.[94] Amin was overthrown in 1979 and the country suffered a series of stop–start governments, including the return to power of the first president, Protestant Milton Obote. Finally in 1986, the National Resistance Movement emerged victorious and Yoweri Museveni came to power.[95] Thus, while Uganda had been independent for thirty years, by the time WGM arrived in 1992, the country had experienced only a few years of relative stability.[96]

History of AGC

AGC Uganda grew out of the endeavors of WGM missionaries in Kenya. WGM was founded in Chicago in 1910 under the auspices of the Missionary Board of the National Holiness Association. In 1937, the mission renamed itself the National Holiness Missionary Society and then again in 1954 it became World Gospel Mission.[97] In its infancy, WGM worked in China, beginning with five American missionaries partnering with two Chinese nationals

---

92. Slater, "Ownership of Knowledge," 43.

93. While understood to have been a Muslim, Pirouet points out that Amin's persecution was liberal, whether towards Christians, Asians, or Muslims. Pirouet, "Religion in Uganda under Amin," 13–29.

94. Slater, "Ownership of Knowledge," 43; Ward notes that the only religious groups allowed to remain were the Catholics, Protestants (Anglicans), Orthodox Christians, and Muslims. Ward, "Eating and Sharing," 118; Pirouet, "Religion in Uganda under Amin," 24.

95. Mutibwa, *History of Uganda*, 334–73.

96. Pirouet's article, published in 1980, ends with a somber forecast. "In church life, as in political life, there are hard times ahead for Uganda." Pirouet, "Religion in Uganda under Amin," 26.

97. https://www.wgm.org/history. While used anachronistically at times, from now on, I will use WGM throughout to avoid confusion.

to launch an evangelistic work. China remained WGM's single focus until 1932 when an opportunity in Kenya opened.

A pioneering missionary named William Hotchkiss, who had previously worked with the Africa Inland Mission (AIM) and the Friends Africa Industrial Mission, asked WGM if they would take over Lumbwa Industrial Mission that he had started in Kenya.[98] While initially reluctant due to the mission's concentration on China as well as the apparent lack of funds and interested missionary personnel, the leadership changed its mind when both funds and personnel were surprisingly made available.[99] From the beginning of their work in Kenya, WGM involved itself with evangelism, discipleship, starting churches, and medical outreach. Tenwek Hospital became and continues to be the mission's largest hospital, continuing to expand its healthcare services today.[100]

Thus, Africa Gospel Church (Kenya) began from the evangelistic efforts of WGM's missionaries. On the eve of the nation's independence (1962), AGC Kenya received its own independence from WGM in August 1961. The church, often in conjunction with WGM, has grown to over 1,900 congregations with over 500 secondary and primary schools. In addition to Tenwek Hospital, other ministry and development projects have occurred, including Kenya Highlands Bible College (now Kenya Highlands University), the AGC Baby Centre, and the AGC Kaboson Pastors School.[101]

Beginning in 1990, WGM Kenya leaders Dean Strong and Terry Duncan began to make fact-finding trips over from Kenya to investigate the possibility of opening WGM work in Uganda.[102] This work was done in conjunction with AGC Kenya leadership, and several AGC leaders joined the WGM missionaries on the initial survey trips to Uganda.[103] The interest

---

98. Lang'at, "Holiness Historiography," 181; for more on Hotchkiss's involvement with Africa Inland Mission, see Watson, "Foundational History of the Africa Inland Church," 45–54.

99. After the FGW training, WGM missionary, John Muehleisen discussed at length about the history of WGM Kenya. Muehleisen, "Farming God's Way Training"; see also Cary, *Story of the National Holiness Missionary Society*, 327–42.

100. http://www.tenwekhospital.org. For discussion on the influence of WGM, and specifically Tenwek Hospital, on Kenya's health care system, see Hearn, "Invisible NGO," 32–60.

101. http://www.agckenya.org.

102. Larry McPherson and Joy McPherson, interview via Skype (1st), July 12, 2017; Stanfield and Stanfield, May 9, 2017.

103. In 1998, the second floor of the AGC Kisugu Church was dedicated. In anticipation of the visitors coming for the dedication, Joy McPherson wrote up a short report on the history of WGM and AGC in Uganda. McPherson, "AGC Kisugu Church Second Floor Dedication Service," 1.

Africa Gospel Church 139

in this mission expansion was in part a response to the request of several Ugandan refugees, whose families had been impacted by AGC, particularly those who had joined AGC's Good Shepherd Church in Nairobi. When these families returned to Uganda, they asked the WGM Kenya leadership for a Good Shepherd congregation to be established in Kampala.[104]

The result of these requests and subsequent investigating visits was that in March 1992, WGM received its Ugandan registration. Larry and Joy McPherson, having already demonstrated something of a pioneering spirit by working with AGC Kenya in Eldoret and Kitale, moved to Kampala in August of that year. They immediately set to work by starting a Bible study in their home and, by January 1993, they had rented a semi-constructed house in the Kisugu area of Kampala as the location for their first church plant. Within a few years, several other missionaries joined them, and by 1999, two AGC churches had been planted in Kampala.[105]

Although church planting was a major focus, the Ugandan government refused to register new religious organizations unless they included a social development aspect to their work.[106] With experience in healthcare work in Kenya, the WGM team began a community health outreach program, which was co-led by Joy McPherson and Connie Ojiambo, another former Ugandan exile who had worked as a nurse at Tenwek.[107]

In 1999 Jonathan Mayo, former WGM missionary to Tanzania, replaced Larry McPherson as the country director.[108] In the course of exploring new possibilities, the Mayos (Jonathan and Lisa) and former WGM Tanzania missionaries Philip and Carolyn Knight began "to sense God was leading them to try something new," specifically to establish a new church planting and pastor training model.[109] Jonathan Mayo related how, with limited personnel, he and the Knights decided to develop a more aggressive training model that trained Ugandan church leaders even while they were simultaneously pastoring.[110] The McPhersons had imported a model of church planting wherein

104. The two initiators were Tom Kayongo and Florence Mabonga. Jonathan Mayo, personal interview (2nd), April 4, 2017; McPherson, "Dedication Service," 1.

105. McPherson and McPherson, July 12, 2017; Mayo, April 4, 2017; McPherson, "Dedication Service," 1–3.

106. Gifford discusses this "development" condition for the registration of NGOs. Gifford, *African Christianity*, 99.

107. McPherson and McPherson, July 12, 2017; Mayo, April 4, 2017.

108. It should be noted that this was at McPherson's request. McPherson and McPherson, interview via Skype (2nd), July 13, 2017.

109. Mayo, April 4, 2017.

110. When asked about the shift in strategies, McPhersons expressed their desire for Ugandans to pastor the local churches. Thus, they became heavily involved in the

the missionary established a congregation, pastored for a time while raising up a local leader, before passing on the pastoral responsibilities and moving on to a new location. Mayo believed a dramatic change was needed; thus, beginning in March 2000 with a first class of nine pastors, the AGC Uganda pastoral training program was launched.[111]

Several factors contributed to this adoption of a different church-planting strategy.[112] First, as they investigated ministry opportunities, the WGM Uganda team thought that there was a need for pastoral training. While the COU and Catholic Church had their own theological education schemes, for anyone wanting pastoral training outside of those denominations, the WGM Uganda team believed the options were limited. Both missionaries and several AGC church leaders, while acknowledging there were, and are, born-again believers within the COU, expressed a strong sentiment that many people did not believe COU preached salvation by faith but through works. Thus, even if a pastor could enter the COU training schemes, it would not be desirable. Therefore, the WGM pastoral training was intended to meet a felt need within the Christian community, albeit outside of the dominant denominations.[113]

The second factor relates to institutionalization and the familiar issue of education and environment. Almost all of the WGM Uganda missionaries had worked in other WGM fields, primarily Kenya but also in Tanzania. Beginning work in 1932 among the Kikuyu, WGM Kenya had, along with starting a holiness denomination, begun Tenwek Hospital and established the Kenya Highlands Bible College. These two institutions were the backbone of WGM Kenya's work, requiring continuous human and financial resources. The WGM Uganda missionaries had an aversion to such an institutional model, having witnessed the stress of trying to maintain such work. Furthermore, they had experienced relationships with Kenyan friends wherein a pastor had been sent to Bible school for training away from his or her home environment only to refuse to fulfill the agreement of returning to a village congregation upon graduation. Thus, for the WGM Uganda missionaries, there was an intentional desire to keep the students as close to their home environment as possible so that local churches could benefit from the pastoral training. This intentionality was not only to hedge against what they believed was the tendency of trained pastors not

---

new pastoral training scheme. McPherson and McPherson, July 12, 2017.

111. Mayo, April 4, 2017.

112. Mayo, personal interview (3rd), May 22, 2017.

113. Revs. Owor and Dhikusooka affirmed Mayo and McPhersons's testimonies. Owor, email, August 31, 2017; Dhikusooka, email, September 15, 2017.

to return to their home villages but also because the missionaries hoped that being close to home would foster immediate practical experience for the students in the local community.[114]

Third, the missionaries thought that the rural areas outside of Kampala had been overlooked in the postwar missionary activity. Mayo describes how as more NGOs entered Uganda at the turn of the millennium, the emphasis seemed to be on urban settings, namely Kampala. He and the other WGM missionaries believed a legitimate need existed for a pastoral training program that would reach men and women in these expansive rural areas of Uganda.[115] Therefore, the pastoral training program came about as a desire to provide theological education for those outside of the established denominations that was more rural-oriented and intentionally practical.[116]

The practicalities of the pastoral training will be discussed shortly in more detail, but for now, it will suffice to mention the training's parallel growth with that of AGC and the issue of language within the training. Ironically, in light of their rural focus, the first training was held in Kisugu (an area in Kampala). Nevertheless, by the end of 2000, twenty new churches had been developed and training had spread to additional training sites near the towns of Kayunga and Soroti as well as on Buvuma Island in Lake Victoria.[117] The class sizes were approximately ten to twelve, and the denomination added an approximate twenty churches per year for the next few years. By 2006, there were approximately 120 AGC churches with between 120 to 150 pastors, assistant pastors, and youth pastors who either had been or were in training. Nevertheless, such growth was not sustainable,[118] and the approximate numbers in the spring of 2017 were 154 churches with another thirty to thirty-five preaching points (see Figure 2). Enrollment in the pastoral training hovered around 300 students, having dipped slightly from the 330 students who had participated in 2016. There are currently nine different training centers, but due to costs of transport,

---

114. Beth Muehleisen, personal interview, March 31, 2017; Stanfield and Stanfield, May 9, 2017; Mayo, April 4, 2017.

115. Mayo, April 4, 2017; Stanfield and Stanfield, May 9, 2017.

116. In his correspondence discussing the relationship between AGC and COU, Owor noted AGC's vision to start churches in the villages as contrasted to the COU. Owor, email, August 31, 2017.

117. Due to fluctuating transport and housing costs, training for the pastors on Buvuma Island has alternated between being held on the island and the pastors coming in to Masese (near Jinga) for training.

118. Some of the causes of this plateau effect will be discussed in chapter 6.

subtraining centers have emerged, resulting in training happening in thirty-seven different locations throughout the country.[119]

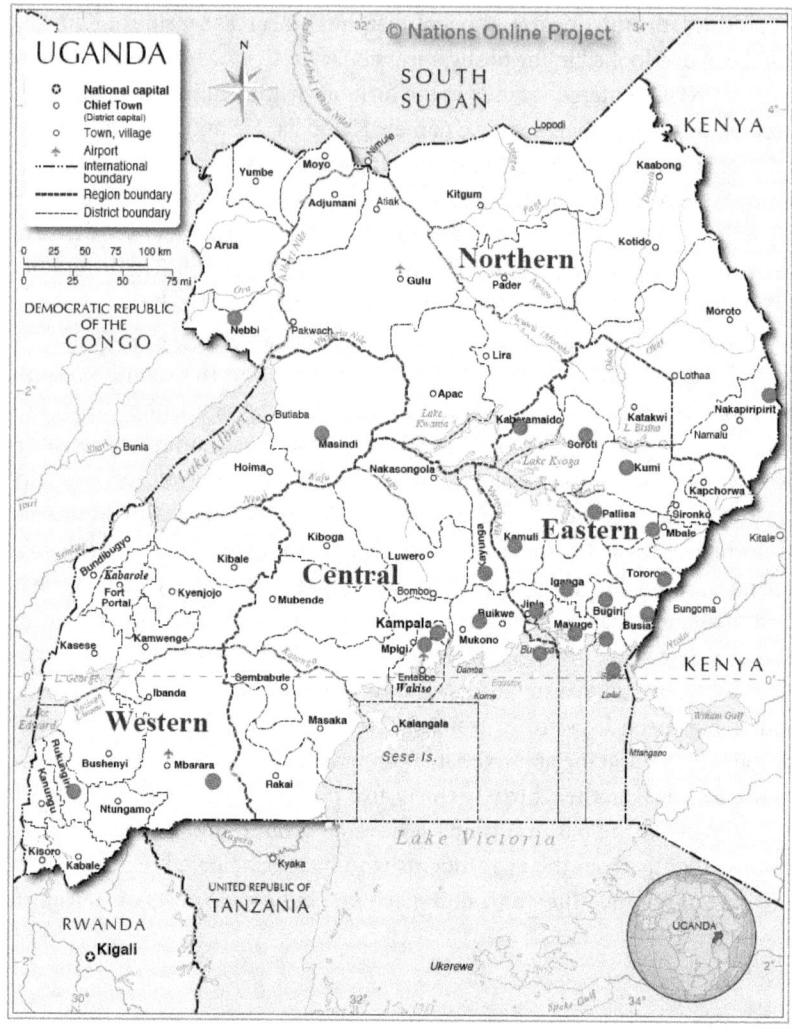

Locations of Africa Gospel Church congregations in Uganda.[120]

119. Regarding transport, with increasing financial constraints, AGC has found it cheaper to transport the trainer to multiple locations, rather than pay for all the students to travel to single site. Ouma, March 31, 2017; Jonathan Mayo, WhatsApp, July 13, 2017.

120. The solid dots indicate the (approximate) areas with AGC representation. Courtesy of Jonathan Mayo. A dot may represent numerous churches within that "area" as the following account about the Masindi area indicates.

The widespread geographic extent of AGC and the multiethnic nature of Uganda result in the pastoral training taking place in a variety of languages, including English, Kiswahili, Luganda, Alur, Runyankole, and Lusoga. While many of the central and eastern ethnic groups within AGC can understand and use the Bantu-related languages, primarily Luganda and Lusoga, the Alur speakers from West Nile and the Ateso speakers from eastern Uganda do not necessarily understand them. Thus, English or Kiswahili is employed although neither is always understood particularly, by those in the more rural settings. This phenomenon presents challenges because, at times, church members in relatively close proximity utilize different languages.

I witnessed this language confusion when I visited the western region of Uganda near the municipality of Masindi with Rev. Miria Mukisa and her husband, Pastor Steward Stephen Mukisa.[121] Rev. Miria is the AGC overseer for "Kampala and beyond," a loosely affiliated area of AGC churches, including those in Masindi, Lugazi (in central Uganda), and Rakai (in south-western Uganda). The church members of Kafu AGC, located fifty kilometers east of Masindi, facilitated the entire service and discussion in Luganda. Those at Bulyango AGC, located twenty-five kilometers west of Masindi, conducted the day's program in Alur, and the two days' activities in Kahara AGC, some seventy kilometers north of Masindi, were spent communicating in Kiswahili. While these churches are all within one hundred kilometers of each other, Rev. Miria discussed not only the transport cost challenges of bringing people together but also the tension of sorting out which language to use during training.

To bring the history of AGC up-to-date, in 2011 AGC received its registration from the Ugandan government as an officially independent entity, separate from WGM. Ward notes that current legislation requires all religious groups to register with the Nongovernmental Organizations Board. Since both the COU and Catholic Church predate that legislation, they jealously guard their non-NGO status.[122] AGC and WGM had been working together for some time to facilitate the denomination's registration. This registration process provided an occasion to clarify the denomination's polity further.

Although there would have been no escaping the precedent of COU's episcopal polity as the standard of Ugandan Protestantism, AGC claims to have looked to their big brother denomination next door, AGC Kenya,

---

121. The issue of language was a reoccuring topic during our travels. Mukisa and Mukisa, April 27, 2017.

122. Ward, "Eating and Sharing," 118.

for inspiration. AGC Kenya had adopted an episcopal form of polity with their registration in 1961 and AGC Uganda decided to follow their example.[123] Such adaptations often have a life of their own as Stanley has highlighted in regards to the adaptation of denominational traditions in mission contexts. He quotes Bishop Bengt Sundler's statement in relation to the Church of South India: "Transplantation means mutation."[124] Stanley makes the case that transcultural experience reshapes Christian tradition, specifically denominational polity, wherein congregational voices have tended to admit the appeal of the episcopal system (e.g., G. Sherwood Eddy), while those from an established and episcopal tradition have tended to express an increasing openness to the involvement of the lay congregation (e.g., Henry Whitehead, Edward Steere).[125]

This tendency towards adaptation can be witnessed in AGC (Uganda) where the modified nature of the church's episcopal polity has more of a pragmatic (almost a Methodist connexional) feel.[126] The head of the denomination is an elected bishop, but there is only one bishop. Instead of dioceses with individual bishops, the denomination has areas (similar to Methodist districts)[127] spread across the country with an area council giving leadership to that region. Practically, much of this area leadership is provided by the area overseer (again, similar to a district superintendent within Methodism), the head of the area council, who provides oversight for the churches and pastors in that particular region, which includes facilitating pastoral training for local pastors, handling conflict, and communicating successes and needs from the area to the General Church Council. The General Church Council includes area overseers, two women representatives, WGM's country director and one other WGM missionary, the department council chair, and the church officers, including the bishop (chairperson), assistant bishop, general secretary, and general treasurer. An Executive Committee ensures the General Church Council fulfills its responsibilities. In addition to the area councils answering to the General Church Council, there is a department council, headed by the General Secretary, which includes various interest groups, such as agriculture and livestock, health and community development, youth, and Christian education. There is also a Trustee Board, which is responsible for all church properties, answering to

---

123. David Dhikusooka, personal communication via Skype, September 15, 2017.
124. Stanley, "Reshaping of Christian Tradition," 408.
125. Stanley, "Reshaping of Christian Tradition," 411.
126. http://www.umc.org/who-we-are/constitutional-structure.
127. http://www.umc.org/who-we-are/organization-church-as-connection.

the General Church Council.[128] Figure 3 provides a flow chart of the AGC's organizational structure.

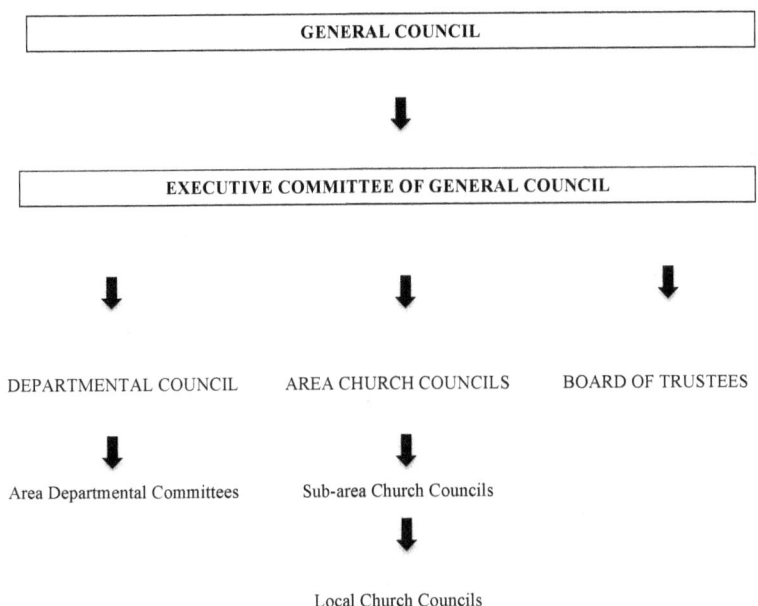

Organizational structure of AGC as depicted
in the AGC constitution, article X.[129]

Thus, AGC's first bishop, Kefa Masiga, was the former area overseer for Busia. Rev. James Ouma, the senior pastor of the original AGC church at Kisugu, became the denomination's first assistant bishop. Not insignificantly in light of the discussion of the historical value placed on education, when the AGC gained its independence from the mission, Ouma, Kennedy Kirui (pastor of United Faith Chapel[130] and the church's General Secretary) and Rev. Emy Mugisha (assistant pastor at AGC Kisugu), were the only three

---

128. Emy, "Constitution of Africa Gospel Church Uganda," 3–4.

129. Emy, "Constitution of Africa Gospel Church Uganda," 6.

130. Kirui pastors the inter-denominational university student church, United Faith Chapel (UFC). While it has maintained an inter-denominational status so as to appeal to all students, WGM missionaries have heavily invested in UFC and AGC considers it part of its "student outreach." Kirui is currently pursuing a PhD from Africa International University (formerly Nairobi Evangelical Graduate School of Theology—NEGST).

pastors to hold bachelor's degrees.[131] While the bishop and at least two other pastors have attained bachelor's degrees since independence and two are currently pursuing bachelor's degrees, post-secondary education remains rare within a denomination with over 150 churches.

Holiness Theology in Uganda and AGC

THE HOLINESS MOVEMENT

The guiding principles of AGC's doctrine grew out of the distinct holiness theology of WGM. An understanding of these holiness theological distinctives necessitates some further historical background. In 1890 William Asbury Dodge and several other men gathered to begin a holiness camp meeting in central Georgia (USA). These men, mostly affiliated with the North and South Georgia Conferences of the Methodist Episcopal Church, had been influenced by John Inskip, the president of what became the National Holiness Association Movement.[132] Inskip and others such as William B. Osborn had established a camp meeting in Vineland, New Jersey, in 1867 and out of that came the "The National Camp Meeting Association for the Promotion of Christian Holiness."[133] These men and women felt a particular conviction to promote the message of holiness of heart and life.[134] They saw themselves following in the theological footsteps of John Wesley, the founder of Methodism in England in the eighteenth century. He believed that a sanctifying work of the Holy Spirit was necessary after one had been born again. This "second work" of grace perfected or purified not just one's sinful actions but could actually purify one's heart so that one's motive and will were holy. As Wesley himself said, "Thus doth Jesus save his people from their sins, not only from outward sins but from the sins of their hearts."[135]

---

131. Shockingly, Mugisha died very suddenly within a year. Thus, not only was AGC deprived of his vision and charisma, but also his academic certification. Mugisha, Winnie, personal interview, May 22, 2017. It should be noted that Ouma has a master's degree from Africa Nazarene University and has completed a DMin degree from the same institution.

132. Synan, *Holiness-Pentecostal Tradition*, 29–30. See also http://indiansprings-campmeeting.org/about-us/history-heritage/.

133. Dieter, *Holiness Revival of the Nineteenth Century*, 86–89.

134. For an interesting consideration of how Dodge's holiness theology of "perfect love" influenced his masculine identity, see Chapell, "Sanctified Manhood," 465–90. See also Dieter's extended discussion of Palmer and her influence. Dieter, *Holiness Revival of the Nineteenth Century*, 22–42, 50–55.

135. Wesley, "Plain Account of Christian Perfection," 366–66.

Dodge's camp meeting, the Indian Springs Holiness Camp Meeting, met in hot central Georgia for the 128th time in July 2018. As in years past, missionaries were an integral part of the ten-day holiness-message program. The missionaries approved to participate throughout the ten days, soliciting prayer and funds for their work, traditionally represent holiness-related mission agencies. The two primary mission groups recognized by the camp's leadership today are One Mission Society and WGM.[136] In many ways, as will be evident, the Indian Springs Camp meeting with its distinct evangelical, Wesleyan-holiness, and missional emphasis captures the spirit behind the theological distinctions of WGM and consequently, AGC Uganda.[137] Before turning attention to the particularities of how WGM's holiness theology has influenced AGC, it would be negligent not to acknowledge the different streams in the holiness tradition and recognize Uganda's strong historical connections with one of those particular branches.

Holiness and the East African Revival

Consideration of the influence of the holiness tradition in Uganda provides a further opportunity to recognize the continuity that flows between the early CMS and later COU endeavors (the first half of this chapter) with the emergence of AGC (the second half of this chapter). With that in mind, in Robert Lang'at's study of the impact of the holiness movement on African Christianity, he distinguishes two subdivisions of Wesley's holiness theology, which emerged in the nineteenth century. Lang'at calls the first Wesleyan holiness, heavily influenced by the American holiness movement, and the second Keswick holiness, also influenced by the holiness movement in America but with different developments. Elaboration on the difference between the two understandings has immediate relevance for recognizing the slightly different holiness traditions as represented by WGM and the East African Revival.

---

136. Traditionally, One Mission Society missionaries are featured on odd years and WGM is featured on even years.

137. The relationship between the holiness movement and missions in Africa is a part of a larger narrative that has interested recent scholarship. Cabrita, *Text and Authority*; Mohr, "Out of Zion," 56–79; for an extended review of Cabrita's work on "Text and Authority," relating it to the East Africa Revival in Uganda, which was heavily influenced by the holiness movement, see Ward, "Review of Joel Cabrita, Text and Authority"; in more directly related fashion, Robert Lang'at, the current bishop of AGC Kenya, argues in his doctoral thesis (Drew University) that the doctrine of holiness provides a theological framework for understanding the emergence of African Christianity. He traces the influences of German pietism and the holiness and revivalist movements on mainline, Pentecostal, and Independent (AIC) denominations. See Lang'at, "Holiness Movement in Africa."

Indian Springs Camp Meeting is a prime example of what Lang'at differentiates as Wesleyan holiness. Regarding the traditional Methodist doctrine of entire sanctification, the camp meeting's website reads, "We believe that entire sanctification is that act of divine grace, by which the heart is cleansed from all rebellion toward God (sin) and filled with the pure love of God. This is a definite cleansing work of grace in the heart of a believer subsequent to conversion, resulting from full consecration and complete surrender and faith in the cleansing merit of the blood of Jesus Christ."[138] It is important to note the language of the cleansing of the heart of sin and the filling of pure love, epitomized in what the confessional statement later calls "holiness of heart and life." Furthermore, this "definite cleansing work of grace" is "subsequent to conversion." As already acknowledged by the close association between WGM and Indian Springs, the mission's theological position lies squarely within this Wesleyan holiness understanding.

Lang'at contrasted this with Keswick holiness, a tradition that emerged with the establishment of the Keswick Convention in the Lake District of England in the 1870s. While also influenced by the American holiness movement, Lang'at suggests that Keswick holiness upheld a gradual sanctification or simply an emphasis on the higher life.[139] Ian Randall, in his study of evangelical experiences, provides even more illumination on the nuances of Keswick thought, noting it was intentionally constructed so as to be "consonant with the Reformed sympathies of much of British evangelicalism."[140] Furthermore, Randall explains, "Keswick denied traditional Wesleyan convictions that Christians could experience entire sanctification, teaching instead that through entry into 'the rest of faith' sin was not eradicated but 'perpetually counteracted.'"[141] Ward elaborates how "the main stream of the Revival rejected decisively any additional experience of 'second blessing' leading to some higher plane of Christian life, beyond the decisive and primary conversion experience of being saved by the blood of the crucified Christ, and in the light of that experience living a life of continual "brokenness" and daily repentance."[142] Furthermore, Randall's work highlights a pneumatological shift that happened, particularly during the interwar period within Keswick, wherein its theology transitioned from the more Wesleyan-holiness emphasis on the Holy Spirit to a more

---

138. http://indianspringscampmeeting-org.secure50.ezhostingserver.com/about-us/statement-of-faith/.

139. See footnote 2. Lang'at, "Holiness Movement in Africa," 2.

140. Randall, *Evangelical Experiences*, 14.

141. Randall, *Evangelical Experiences*, 14.

142. Ward, "'Obedient Rebels,'" 216.

Christological focus, from a filling (or even baptism) of the Holy Spirit to the Lordship of Christ. Thus, Keswick holiness became a moderate holiness, "standard evangelical thinking on consecration, seeing it as commitment to the rule of Christ in everyday life."[143]

While there are incidental examples of the Wesleyan-tradition language being used, it is important to recognize that the Keswick understanding of holiness carried the predominant influence among those involved in the East African Revival.[144] This is nowhere more clearly expressed than in the revival anthem *Tukutendereza, Jesu* (We praise you, Jesus), which was originally called, *Cleansing Blood*, adopted from the Keswick hymnbook. *Tukutendereza* is the hymn mentioned in chapter 2 that exemplifies the intermodal nature that often accommodates hymns. This hymn was published in a (British) Keswick hymnal, but as often happens, the more a hymn is sung, the less the community relies on the printed text. In this way *Tukutendereza* quickly became fixed in the revivalists' oral discourse, and for those touched by the revival message, singing this anthem became a form of identifying with the revival throughout East Africa.[145]

In Uganda, the call for revival began less than two decades after the first CMS missionaries arrived. In the early 1890s, George Baskerville and George Pilkington were consciously aware of the need for a spiritual renewal among both the missionaries and the Ugandan Christians.[146] At the time, Baskerville was reading a book written by a Keswick missioner,[147] but Pilkington, while away on a spiritual retreat, "learned the great secret of the indwelling power of the Holy Spirit, which transformed his whole life."[148] He became convinced that the Holy Spirit was what the church needed first,

---

143. Randall, *Evangelical Experiences*, 30–33.

144. For an example of more "Wesleyan" holiness language, note Pilkington's testimony below, in spite of his Keswick connections. However, his experience was over thirty years prior to what is traditionally called the East African Revival. For the standard treatment of the Revival, see Ward and Wild-Wood, *East African Revival*; for a more detailed consideration of Keswick's influence on the Ruanda Mission missionaries, see Stanley, "East African Revival," 10–11; for more recent scholarship, see Bruner, *Living Salvation in the East African Revival*.

145. Lang'at, "Holiness Movement in Africa," 205–6; Peterson discusses the use of the hymn as a means of identification among the Gikuyu in Kenya. Peterson, *Creative Writing*, 178–79; for his extended treatment on the Revival, see Peterson, *Ethnic Patriotism and the East Africa Revival*.

146. Although Pirouet's understanding of evangelical revival seems rather reductionistic, she does discuss missionaries' dissatisfaction with the spiritual state of affairs in the early 1890s. Pirouet, *Black Evangelists*, 22–26.

147. The book was, "What Hath God Wrought?" by George Grubb. See Lang'at, "Holiness Movement in Africa," 168.

148. Lang'at, "Holiness Movement in Africa," 168.

middle, and last, not just to be with the Ugandan Christians but "to dwell in them."[149] Lang'at notes that Pilkington had direct ties with Keswick, having been influenced by the "Cambridge Seven" in the 1880s, a group that owed much to "Keswick higher life."[150]

Lang'at argues that it was the seeds of Pilkington's revival that eventually sprouted into the East African Revival in the 1930s.[151] Ward observes that while at times in the 1940s, it seemed as if the revivalists, often called the *Balokole* ("Saved Ones" in Luganda), might be thrown out of the COU or leave on their own accord, this schism never happened. He suggests the continued unity of the COU was "partly because of the immense social standing of Anglicanism within Ugandan society."[152] Not insignificantly, by the 1970s, numerous COU bishops as well as many training to be clergy acknowledged having revivalist backgrounds.[153]

Thus, consideration of the holiness movement's influence on Uganda provides a further occasion to understand the influence of the COU on the Christian communication context within which AGC was established and continues to communicate. Having said that, it may come as a surprise that the initial response by several WGM missionaries and AGC members alike, when asked whether they knew much about the revival or had seen much influence from it, was a resounding "no."[154] The former WGM country directors, Jeff and Christine Stanfield (who also have twenty years of mission experience in Kenya) acknowledged that they had heard the *wazee* (elders) in Kenya discuss the revival and heard it alluded to while visiting western Uganda. But with such limited encounters, they could give little testimony of how an understanding of the revival had impacted or was impacting AGC, in particular, or even Uganda Christianity, at large, today.[155]

As it turned out, follow-up conversations to such interactions exposed perhaps more of an understanding than the interviewees may have realized, most clearly seen in the fact that almost every one of those who said the revival had no remaining influence knew and could sing *Tukutendereza*. Furthermore, they recognized it as the revival anthem.[156] The second indication

149. Lang'at, "Holiness Movement in Africa," 169–70.
150. Lang'at, "Holiness Movement in Africa," 169.
151. Lang'at, "Holiness Movement in Africa," 190.
152. Ward, "Obedient Rebels," 113.
153. Ward, "Obedient Rebels," 113.
154. Muehleisen, "Farming God's Way Training"; Caroline Ouma and Lillian Kirui, personal interview, May 17, 2017; Stanfield and Stanfield, May 9, 2017.
155. Stanfield and Stanfield, May 9, 2017.
156. Omri, May 12, 2017; Ouma and Kirui, May 17, 2017; Muehleisen, "Farming God's Way Training."

that the revival has had more influence in shaping AGC than perhaps is realized relates to the Luganda term *Balokole*. The name *Balokole* (the saved ones) emerged during the revival as the defining identity for those involved. It continues to maintain currency in Ugandan Christianity today, although with some adaptation (as will be noted).[157]

Miria and Steward Mukisa informed me that if one is seen carrying a Bible, one is immediately identified as a *Mulokole* (the singular of *Balokole*). They went on to define *Mulokole* as a born-again person, "someone who has surrendered to Christ, given their life to Christ." Steward then quoted Romans 10:9 as the final word: "'If you believe with your heart and confess with your mouth that Jesus is Lord, you will be saved,'—you are a *Mulokole*."[158] While these AGC pastors wanted me to understand that a *Mulokole* is not ashamed to carry and be associated with the Bible (specifically they were talking about the difference between a printed and digitalized Bible), what stood out was that their very language betrayed the residual influence of the Revival. The importance of being identified as a born-again person emerged in correspondence with missionary Jonathan Mayo. He relayed how in the early days of AGC, almost all of the pastors coming and asking to join AGC were from the COU, looking for a born-again church. The reaffirming testimony among them was that they did not believe COU to be a born-again church anymore.[159]

Inquiry into whether COU is considered born-again or not remains beyond the interest of this project. Nevertheless, these vignettes reveal several relevant elements. First, there is a significant holiness tradition that runs through Ugandan Christianity. This tradition seems to be

---

157. In his discussion on Balokole, Ward mentions that while the Revival was influenced by Keswick, it had "a very distinctive African feel about it." His example is that instead of emphasizing Keswick's "second blessing" experience, they focused on a deeper conversion experience. This would seem to contradict Lang'at's (and Randall) differentiation between Keswick-holiness and Wesleyan-holiness. However, Randall's discussion about the "pneumatological shift" of the Keswick understanding makes clear that, while there had been a "second blessing" (more Wesleyan-tradition) understanding, that changed during the inter-war period under the auspices of men like W. Graham Scroggie (1872–1958). The Convention's thinking shifted to more of a "Lordship" and consecration emphasis, which can be seen in much of the Revival language and literature. Thus, Lang'at's distinction between the two holiness strands, aided by Randall's explanation, seems to remain helpful as the Revival emerged in the inter-war period during the late 1920s and 1930s. See Ward and Wild-Wood, *East African Revival*, 1, 5–10. Scroggie is a major voice in Randall's analysis. See Randall, *Evangelical Experiences*, 25–39.

158. Mukisa and Mukisa, April 27, 2017.

159. Mayo, July 13, 2017; Owor and Dhikusooka reaffirmed Mayo's understanding. Owor, email, August 31, 2017; Dhikusooka, email, September 15, 2017.

predominantly influenced by a later Keswick holiness emphasis, stressing not so much a subsequent work to conversion but a rest of faith and walking in the light of daily repentance. In light of the ensuing discussion regarding AGC's concern for holiness theology, this historical Keswick tradition seems to have carried little influence, if any, among the WGM missionaries who established and continued to work alongside AGC. Relevantly, Gifford argues that the revival movement had essentially run out of steam by the mid-1980s.[160] This phenomenon might explain why the McPhersons acknowledged that they had heard about the revival on occasion and even heard the term *Balokole* when they first arrived. Surprisingly, the doctrine associated with the *Balokole* whom they met in the early 1990s smacked more of the prosperity gospel than holiness; thus, they actively sought to distance themselves as an evangelical denomination that believed the Bible and emphasized evangelism. Significantly, the McPhersons acknowledged, "It may have just been the ones [the *Balokole*] that we interacted with."[161] To associate the *Balokole* with prosperity teaching would have been *anathema* for the original revivalists,[162] suggesting that the definition of *Balokole* has perhaps undergone some adaptations with diminished influence of the revival and the influx of other Spirit-oriented (e.g., Pentecostal) teaching. Ultimately, the important point to note is that the original WGM missionaries did not believe the *Balokole* they encountered reflected the holiness ethos that WGM upheld.

Second, in spite of the lack of direct association by WGM with the previous existing holiness tradition, an argument can be made that part of the influence of COU on the communication context in which AGC operates today is because of its *Balokole* holiness tradition. While waning in influence perhaps, there remains residual evidence that the impact of the *Balokole*, most of whom remained within the COU, continues to permeate Uganda Christian discourse. Thus, this reaffirms the reality that the COU (and *Balokole*) have shaped and continue to shape the communication environment within which AGC operates. While having discussed WGM and Uganda's holiness traditions, it is time to address how holiness theology has impacted AGC as a denomination.

Holiness and AGC

Upon arriving in 1992, the WGM missionaries did not think COU, or any other denomination or other local mission organization, adequately

---

160. Gifford, *African Christianity*, 97–98.
161. McPherson and McPherson, July 13, 2017.
162. On this very issue, see Ward and Wild-Wood, *East African Revival*, 7.

reflected WGM's theological emphasis. The McPhersons described how some of the early AGC members believed that there were those within COU who were "not true Christians."[163] When asked about the holiness tradition within the Anglican Church, Mayo replied, "Not only was holiness buried but salvation by faith in Jesus" seemed to have given way to "being Anglican."[164] Furthermore, the McPhersons acknowledged some fear of trying to work with an existing body (e.g., COU) due to negative experiences in Kenya, only for matters to get confusing down the road if a separation became necessary due to theological (or practical) reasons.[165] Therefore, to minimize potential denominational and theological confusion, and perhaps because of the pattern of WGM establishing AGC in Kenya, WGM Uganda started a holiness denomination in 1993.

To everyone's surprise, when the registration finally came back from the government, WGM was classified as a Pentecostal group. Initially, this was disturbing to the early WGM missionaries because of particular associations with Pentecostalism, namely spiritual manifestations, such as speaking in tongues or other teachings, including the Reformed emphasis on "once saved, always saved."[166] Pentecostalism in Uganda is an important interlocutor in Ugandan Christianity; thus, in light of the intention of the early WGM missionaries to distinguish themselves from emerging Ugandan Pentecostalism, several initial comments are in order.

Pentecostal denominations had emerged after independence but then were almost completely suppressed during Amin's regime. Not until 1986 did Pentecostal churches slowly begin and then quite quickly (re)emerge and develop. The McPhersons talked about arriving in 1992 with only a few Pentecostal churches present, yet today, they are on every street corner.[167] Furthermore, far from remaining estranged from worldly affairs in pursuit of holiness or spiritual manifestations, recent research indicates that the Pentecostal churches today wield an increasingly powerful social voice.[168]

---

163. McPherson and McPherson, email, August 22, 2017.

164. Mayo, August 25, 2017.

165. McPherson and McPherson, July 13, 2017.

166. "Once saved, always saved" or what is often called the doctrine of eternal security is not necessarily "Pentecostal." However, in conversation with the McPhersons, it was apparent this issue and that of speaking in tongues were two teachings associated with Pentecostalism from which they were trying to distance themselves and AGC. McPherson and McPherson, July 13, 2017.

167. McPherson and McPherson, July 13, 2017; Gusman, "HIV/AIDS, Pentecostal Churches," 69.

168. Gusman, "HIV/AIDS, Pentecostal Churches"; Bompani and Brown, "A 'Religious Revolution'?" 110–26.

Significantly for this discussion, the relationship between Pentecostalism and speaking in tongues has its roots in the modern American holiness movement.[169] While holiness camp meetings were known to have spiritual manifestations of varying types, only after the Azusa Street Revival started in 1906 under the preaching of William Seymour did speaking in unknown tongues became regarded as doctrinal proof of experiencing the baptism of the Holy Spirit.[170] While charting the divergent and overlapping history of holiness and Pentecostal churches is beyond the scope of this work, what remains important to recognize is that WGM maintained and still maintains a strong doctrinal stance against speaking in tongues as being the necessary evidence of the Spirit-filled life. While they are not necessarily against speaking in unknown languages, they neither seek nor encourage such experiences. Thus, for the early WGM Uganda missionaries, there was a strong reaction to being labeled as Pentecostal although in the end, the registration was not contested with the government.[171] The significance of demarcating differences between Pentecostal and holiness theology became all the more important when the young mission field began to train its own leaders.

In 2000, the mission launched a pastoral training program for empowering new AGC pastors. Although this was an education experience designed to impact the church leaders, aspects of the training have spilled over and provided opportunity for the laity as well.[172] Naturally, the missionaries desired for AGC leaders and members both to experience the sanctified life as well as be able to articulate AGC's holiness distinctives. As developing Pentecostal churches became more prominent, AGC personnel found themselves continually pressured to validate their holiness by speaking in tongues.[173] To help strengthen the church leaders' understanding and

---

169. Lang'at, "Holiness Historiography," 31.

170. See Synan's chapter 5, "The American Jerusalem—Azusa Street." Synan, *Holiness-Pentecostal Tradition*, 84–106.

171. Influenced by Amin, it seems the government ministry at the time classified religious groups as Muslim, Catholic, Anglican, Orthodox, or Pentecostal. Since AGC was clearly not any of the first four, it was "labeled" Pentecostal by default. The mission's legal counsel advised the missionaries to not contest the registration as the lawyers feared it might raise suspicion on part of the government. McPherson and McPherson, July 13, 2017.

172. From visiting and observing leadership in such as AGC Kahara, it would appear the dividing wall between pastors and laity is rather flexible and any lay person who shows initiative can often become involved in the local church's leadership. Site visit, Kahara, April 29, 2017.

173. AGC's distinct theology on tongues came up in conversation as in comparison with local Pentecostal teaching. Ouma and Kirui, May 17, 2017.

resolve in the face of such pressures, Mayo and other WGM missionaries employed several strategies.

First they wrote a discipleship manual in the early 2000s.[174] This handbook of approximately thirty lessons provided the basic theological teaching of AGC with no less than three lessons on holiness, including *Full Surrender*, *Sanctification*, and *Victorious Living*. For example, it states, "We believe the Bible teaches that after we have repented of our sins, received God's forgiveness and are saved, we need to go on to receive a second work of grace in our hearts and lives. The Bible uses several terms to refer to this experience. One term used is sanctification."[175] Likewise, the teaching regarding speaking in tongues comes under the chapter on "Common False Teachings," wherein it reiterates that while they recognize there is "a true gift of tongues," they note Jesus is not recorded as having spoken in tongues.[176] Completing this manual with an AGC pastor or WGM missionary was (and remains) a requirement for church members, thus allowing laity to receive some intentional doctrinal instruction. Likewise, pastors or other leaders have to complete the manual before enrolling in the pastoral training program. This requirement provided the opportunity for students to understand WGM's distinctives as well as opt out of the training if they could not agree to their theology.

The second and third strategies they used to promote WGM and AGC's distinct theology were interrelated—the preaching of holiness and the establishment of holiness camp meetings.[177] The missionaries themselves took opportunities to preach holiness messages when visiting among the budding churches. Furthermore, money was given by WGM to the developing areas for organizing holiness camp meetings. Often the AGC leaders of a particular area would invite the missionaries to come and preach at these camp meetings. Thus, while the camp meeting concept was both new and, at times, not easily adapted into Ugandan communities because feeding and housing people was often a problem, the missionaries were clearly trying to follow in their holiness forefathers' footsteps.[178]

---

174. What is now called the discipleship manual was originally called the membership manual. It has gone through numerous revisions although the core curriculum seems to have remained largely unaltered. Metz, *Church Discipleship Manual*.

175. Metz, *Church Discipleship Manual*, 71.

176. 1 Corinthians 14:27–28; Metz, *Church Discipleship Manual*, 125.

177. Jonathan Mayo, WhatsApp, July 19, 2017.

178. Lang'at discusses the role of holiness camp meetings in Africa, specifically Alexander Reid and the Methodist revivals in Congo as well as the Quessua Camp Meeting in Angola. Lang'at, "Holiness Movement in Africa," 171–74, 213–20, 224–27.

Observations Regarding AGC's History and Theology

Several factors are worth highlighting from both AGC's history and doctrine before considering the content of the AGC pastoral training program in more detail. First AGC Uganda was birthed out of the WGM Kenya missionary impulse and in collaboration with AGC Kenya. As has already been mentioned, the Ugandan missionaries' experiences in Kenya influenced the development of the Ugandan work. AGC Kenya continues to play an almost big brother role for AGC Uganda. Several gestures of goodwill have been extended by AGC Kenya towards AGC Uganda, including the sharing of an older church vehicle and the sponsoring of AGC Uganda's former bishop, Kefa Masiga, to complete a bachelor's degree at Kenya Highlands University. This big brother relationship likewise has resulted in AGC Uganda feeling both inferior in comparison with AGC Kenya's development as well as desirous for such development to happen within Uganda.[179] For example, WGM Uganda missionaries shared about complaints they have had from church members: "Why don't we have a Tenwek hospital or Bible college?"[180] Likewise, one pastor and his wife expressed their wish for AGC Uganda to cultivate projects such as the guesthouses in Kenya that are run by AGC Kenya. It was argued that such development would surely produce both prestige for the church and provide employment for AGC Uganda church members.[181]

The second factor relates to this very issue of institutional development. AGC Uganda was deeply influenced by missionaries who resisted the stereotypical expectations of building institutions such as training schools or hospitals. While WGM has partnered with institutions within Uganda, Heritage International School being the primary example,[182] they have intentionally tried to keep the AGC and its leadership close to the local communities. This design was to facilitate greater grassroots impact wherein pastors could receive training and still participate in family business and cultivation. In other words, although the available missionary personnel for such institutional projects were drastically limited, the decision not to establish institutions was intended to be an act of generosity, wherein church leaders could receive pastoral training while remaining within their local environment with minimal disruption to their family, church, and community relationships and responsibilities. Furthermore, it placed the bulk of the financial burden of travel costs and accommodation on the missionaries

---

179. David Dhikusooka, personal interview (2nd), May 10, 2017; Muehleisen, March 31, 2017.

180. Muehleisen, March 31, 2017.

181. Dhikusooka, personal interview (1st), April 23, 2017.

182. http://www.heritage.co.ug.

instead of the student. At the time, this action was meant as a service for those with restricted (denominational) access to theological education; however, the unintended consequence of a dearth of higher education certification has proved to be a dramatic handicap for the church amidst the cultural communication values of today.

The third factor is that AGC's theological position on matters such as holiness results, at times, in widening an already unhelpful dichotomy. Holiness theology, with its emphasis on the purity of the interior of one's heart, can easily be interpreted as emphasizing a person's spiritual rather than physical concerns. Such (mis)interpretation becomes an explicit issue because the field research revealed that personnel from within the church and mission seemed to place differing emphasis on these two interrelated domains. Ultimately, rather than being peripheral to the discussion, AGC's holiness theology complicates their reception of orality as church personnel find themselves in tension between societal expectations and a theological position that, at times, can be understood to downplay physical or material realities. Such discussion foreshadows the forthcoming analysis in chapter 6.

The Uniqueness of AGC's Pastoral Training

The influence of the OM has been most tangible on the AGC's pastoral training program; thus, elaboration on its development merits attention. It is imperative to recognize the print-reliant nature of the original pastoral training scheme. The initial curriculum for the training program was loosely constructed by the various missionaries assigned to designated training areas. Eventually, uniform lessons were typed up, and by 2002 there was a printed curriculum that included subjects on five key areas: Bible, theology, preaching, evangelism, and practical skills. Bible as a subject surveyed the various genres of the biblical text, while theology articulated a Wesleyan-holiness position. Preaching discussed sermon preparation according to various sermon types, including expository and topical. An adapted form of Evangelism Explosion and the Roman Road were taught in evangelism courses.[183] Finally, practical skills addressed issues such as health, marriage, partnering, baptism, communion, funerals, and church finances.[184] Ideally, each month's training would cover at least one lesson from all five major areas.

---

183. For the historical background of the Evangelism Explosion method developed by Dr. James Kennedy, see http://evangelismexplosion.org/about-us/history/. For a helpful overview of the "Roman Road," see http://www.allaboutgod.com/the-roman-road.htm.

184. Mayo, WhatsApp, July 21, 2017.

Each month the missionaries would drive out to different training locations, such as Masese, Soroti, Bugiri, or Busia, and usually spend the afternoon and then all the next day with the students. Different lessons were taught using a lecture style but with time for interaction and questions. Printed lesson notes were handed out after each session, and even a printed outline cheat sheet was used for evangelism so that students could recall verses and illustrations. Evangelism was an integral piece of the training, particularly in the early years, both instruction on its importance as well as live practice. After teaching, reviewing, and practicing in pairs, the students and the missionaries would go to visit surrounding houses or neighbors within the nearby area to practice sharing their faith. Mayo reiterated how he believes the lack of this teaching on evangelism, monthly review, and live practice (what he called OJT—on-the-job training) within the current training model is why the church has recently experienced minimal numerical growth.[185]

In addition to an active evangelism emphasis, accountability was a key component within the early years of pastoral training. Each student was expected to complete written reports, including documentation of sermons preached, offerings taken up, and, among other things, the number of times a pastor went out for evangelism. Homework was assigned each month and, in time, written exams were proctored. Thus, the training possessed a formalized nature, not in an institutional classroom sense, but the curriculum topics, the reliance on print-oriented lessons, the use of written accountability forms, the expectation of written homework (as in sermon outlines) and, finally, written exams all assumed a formal, literate-skilled learning environment.

In her work, Karin Barber has developed the now familiar concept of "tin-trunk" libraries, hidden stores of printed material that has been kept for a variety of reasons.[186] The print orientation of the AGC pastoral training program allowed for the accumulation of such valued printed artifacts that could be stored and referenced as needed. For at least one AGC family, these printed treasures were not stored in tin trunks but in sugar (i.e., gunny) sacks. On one occasion, I spent a morning with the already introduced pastor–couple, Steward and Miria Mukisa. Discussion turned to the older, more formal, print-oriented pastoral training, and they spoke fondly of the notes that were passed out at the end of each lesson. The formal, printed notes contrasts to the more recent pastoral scheme in which all note-taking is done by hand by the students. This development is partly the result of the

---

185. Mayo, April 4, 2017.
186. Barber, *Anthropology of Texts*; Barber, *African Hidden Histories*.

Africa Gospel Church 159

inclusion of oral Bible storying but also reflects the limited funds available for printing since the church's independence from WGM. When I expressed interest in seeing some of the old notes, Steward and Miria immediately set to work to locate their cache. After some brief discussion, two large sugar sacks were dragged out from the corner of the room. The initial contents were rifled through before several large three-inch binders were victoriously pulled out of one of the sacks and immediately wiped clean of a healthy layer of dust. These were offered to me for perusal with an obvious sense of pride and accomplishment. Page after aging page of formally typed lesson notes were perused, complete with handwritten scrawls adding more personalized reminders. Sermon outlines, accountability forms, and even a few written exams were displayed for my curiosity (see Figures 4 and 5). While both Miria and Steward confirmed that they did, at times, reference those old notes, the layer of dust that had been wiped clean caused some question as to how often that practice happened. Nevertheless, the fact that Miria had her lessons from 2002 when she started the training program, treasured away now for all these years, speaks of the high value that printed materials continue to maintain within AGC.

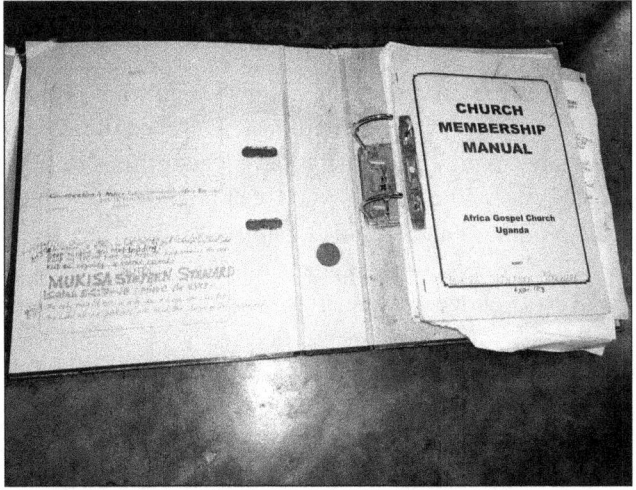

Pastor Stephen Steward Mukisa's pastoral training binder. The AGC Church manual is on top.[187]

---

187. Picture by the author.

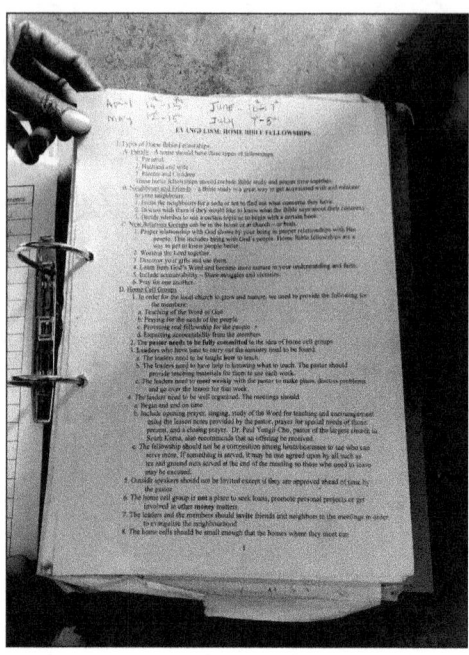

A printed page from Mukisa's former pastoral training lessons.[188]

Over time, the missionaries could not keep up with the demand for this print-reliant pastoral training. Reminiscent of the early CMS missionaries, who began to recruit particularly clever young men due primarily to the lack of other personnel, so the WGM staff began to share the teaching responsibilities with up-and-coming Ugandan leaders. Thus, the missionaries were doing less teaching and more coordinating. Not insignificantly, with the arrival of younger missionaries, fresh from American evangelical seminaries in 2004, the curriculum was deemed not academic enough and was refurbished by the new missionaries. By 2006–2007, complaints were being raised, arguing the teaching had become too academic with almost no room for discussion or questions. Thus, while the training continued to be delivered orally, it tended to be monological with the teacher merely lecturing to the students and the content itself oriented around propositional (i.e., printed) outlines. Therefore, while oral in delivery, the communication and education were not oral in style (as discussed in chapters 1 and 2). It was into such an environment that orality as understood by the OM was introduced.

188. Picture by the author.

In January 2008 a new AGC training center began with a collection of pastors and churches from the Nebbi district area; they had heard about and requested the AGC training.[189] Working with several WGM missionaries based in Arua instead of Kampala, the group of students completed Level 1 of the AGC pastoral training program. However, there were complications. Certain pastors struggled to read the English lessons; consequently, when it came to written exams, those students required a translator/scribe. Furthermore, while the pastors were very eager to learn and expressed appreciation for the teaching, when in-the-field evaluations or church visits were conducted, questions emerged regarding how much of the training was impacting the pastor's attitudes and behavior. Pastors seemed to understand in the formal training session but then were not translating the material into practical engagement with daily relationships and situations.[190] Therefore, it was in the context of this frustration with the topical-oriented, print-based curriculum that a more oral approach began to be explored.[191]

In June 2008, the WGM missionaries were introduced to the OM and the discipline of orality, specifically Bible storytelling. The WGM team was first trained in Simply the Story, an outgrowth of God's Story, an evangelical nonprofit organization out of California that has been a significant player within the OM network. Personnel within *God's Story* had developed an eighty-minute movie, providing an overview of the Bible.[192] As the movie's popularity grew, people began asking *God's Story* for discipleship material. Often the *God's Story* movie was shown prior to the *Jesus Film*, and organizations and churches found that providing the Old Testament background was helpful for many audiences to be able to situate the *Jesus Film* plotline. This pattern led to the development of STS, a five-step oral process designed to enable someone to facilitate an in-depth conversation, whether one-on-one or in a group setting, around a biblical narrative for the purpose of spiritual change, whether first-time conversion or spiritual maturity for those already Christians.[193]

189. This was typically how a new training location started; someone would hear about the training and request WGM to come and establish a new pastoral training program in their location. In this regard, the training followed the requests of Ugandans.

190. Slater deals with the difference between knowledge acquisition and knowledge formulation. The Nebbi pastors privileged knowledge acquisition but then struggled to connect such acquired information with the realities of their communities. See Slater's chapter 2: "Orality and Literacy: Positioning Adult Theological Education for Impact." Slater, "Ownership of Knowledge," 51, 52–100.

191. For an initial discussion on these complications, see Coppedge, "Overcoming Complications to Oral Methodologies."

192. http://www.gods-story.org.

193. http://simplythestory.org/oralbiblestories/.

Due to the ensuing embedded nature of STS in the AGC pastoral training program and its variance with some of the other educational practices and expectations within the Ugandan communication environment, it is worth elaborating on the five-step STS process.[194] *Step one* is the telling of a Bible story, usually limited to ten to twelve verses, which is ideally performed with engaging hand motions and body movement. *Step two* asks for a volunteer to retell as much of the story as can be remembered, thus inviting the audience to begin capturing the story in their own minds and imaginations.[195] In *step three*, the facilitator retells the story a third time, inviting the audience to assist in the retelling by answering simple yes/no or fill-in-the-blank questions. This step allows for the facilitator to correct anything that may have been left out or added by the volunteer in step two. Furthermore, it provides a third retelling of the story so that the audience becomes fairly familiar with the content and feels more comfortable to discuss the story in-depth.

While the story can be told in conversational language, it should not be overlooked that STS stresses accuracy to the details in the biblical text. While other Bible storytelling methods allow for crafting or summarizing a story as described in chapter 3, STS maintains a firm (i.e., literal) view that all of the details of the story are included for a purpose and carry divine authority. To avoid confusion on behalf of the listener, any necessary historical context or possibly unfamiliar terms are explained in a brief introduction before the initial telling of the story. Oftentimes the subsequent discussion will draw on the knowledge or contextual factors of the introduction to enable broader and more in-depth discussion.

Step four shifts into a dialogue facilitated by the storyteller who draws from a variety of questions as she or he asks the audience about various sections of the story. The training stresses moving slowly through each section.[196] Not all of the questions have to be asked for every section of the story, and the storyteller does try to adjust the questions and facilitate the discussion to meet both the time constraints and the interests or

---

194. A STS manual has been produced by God's Story that walks through the five-step process, the rationale behind each step, and offers answers to common questions. Miller, *Simply the Story Handbook*.

195. The facilitator does not usually ask for a volunteer when performing a one-on-one story. Along those same lines, if no one volunteers to retell for a whole group, the facilitator will often invite people to just share with their neighbor what they remember from the story.

196. These questions include: What was said? What was done? What choices were made? What other choices could have been made? What were the results of the choices made? What was the broader impact of those results? Where was or what was God doing in this story?

needs of a particular audience. Nevertheless, it should be reiterated that while the facilitator will have explored and studied the story in-depth in preparation and may be aware of and will try to draw out specific points of interest, the atmosphere, ideally, is more of dialogue and discovery. In a formal STS training, it is stressed that STS storytellers are neither police, scowling around the room to see if anyone got the right answer, nor professors, paternalistically enlightening the ignorant pupils.[197] STS storytellers are encouraged to be fellow mountain-climbers, journeying to discover together what God has for them personally as well as the audience. This participatory, dialogue dynamic, while popular among certain educationists such as the American Jane Vella,[198] is not always perceived in the same warm manner as became apparent from the field research.

Finally, *step five* moves from looking for spiritual observations to asking four specific questions in an attempt to apply in a personal way the lessons that have been discovered from within the discussion of the story.[199] In good evangelical Protestant fashion, the desired STS response is an interiorizing of the biblical truth, wherein some component of the story aligns with circumstances in one's own life and one acknowledges that spiritual change is necessary, resulting in changed thinking, feeling, and behavior. Thus, while acknowledging the source of the stories is the printed Bible, these five STS steps create a communication experience with a portion of the biblical text that does not necessarily require the immediate proximity of a printed Bible. It is precisely this feature—non-print-reliant communication events that engage the Scriptures—that characterizes the OM and became a distinct feature of AGC's pastoral training program. Thus, the STS method, along with its five steps to engage a Bible story orally, was incorporated into the AGC pastoral program.

In 2009 WGM and AGC facilitated an oral Bible storytelling pilot program in Nebbi district. Whereas the first year's training (2008) in Nebbi had included the established AGC pastoral training lesson handouts, written exams, and accountability reports, no printed training materials were handed out in the second year.[200] Instead of monthly training sessions for

---

197. The classic line often quoted although by no means original is, "The professor must die."

198. Vella, *Learning to Listen*.

199. These questions include: Does this (situation, instance, problem, etc.) happen today? What are some examples of this (situation, instance, problem, etc.) today? What about for you—has something like this every happened to you or to someone you know? What can we learn from the story the next time we find ourselves in this (situation, instance, problem, etc.)?

200. A one-page document was handed out on heresies in light of doctrinal

1½ days, training happened every one or two weeks for a morning. Each session included reviewing the last story, learning and practicing a new story, a lengthy discussion regarding key observations in the story, and finally some possibly relevant applications.

Accountability did play a role but in a modified way. Instead of each pastor submitting a written accountability report, a single school exercise book served as the record keeper. Pastors and missionaries had to report to the group how many stories they had told in the previous week(s) and how many they were committing to tell in the upcoming week or weeks. Evaluations were conducted orally, with the pastors being evaluated on their ability to tell stories and facilitate discussion. Furthermore, in an effort to evaluate whether the pastors were reproducing the stories for others to learn, each pastor had to bring one other person on evaluation day whom he or she had been training by using the stories. These disciples were asked to retell various stories and questioned on how well they understood them. Thus, by the end of the year, the pastors had learned twenty different stories from the Gospel of Mark and had opportunities to reproduce their storytelling skills in at least one other person.

The result of this training was mixed. On the one hand, the stories were well received by the pastors and community. The students were eager to learn new stories and appreciated the in-depth discussion regarding treasures within them. They found having a tool to share a portion of biblical text, even without a printed Bible, to be valuable. Bible stories were told in the garden, in the market, at home with the children, and while at work in town. The pastors were delighted to find that people enjoyed the Bible stories. For example, during one training session, Pastor Andrew Piboth recounted visiting a church member in the hospital. He shared a Bible story with the patient, and after discussing briefly, he prayed for the person and prepared to leave. A patient in a nearby bed caught his attention as he was leaving and complained about not being able to hear the story well. So Pastor Andrew repeated the story and, likewise, had a brief discussion and prayer. He tried to leave a second time only to get caught by another patient asking for the story. Thus, when asked to share how many stories he had told at the next training session, he spoke of the patients' interest in the story and concluded by saying, "I lost track of how many times I told the story before I got out of the ward, maybe eight, ten, twelve times."[201]

---

questions that were brought by one particular pastor, who eventually left the training program. Technically, this document was not a planned part of the designed curriculum for the year.

201. I was present when Pastor Andrew Piboth shared that story at a pastoral training session in the spring of 2009.

On the other hand, there were also critiques of the exclusively oral training. Although the pastors found the stories effective for engaging their community members in a conversation about a Bible story, the oral training did not carry respect among the community. Pastors asked for printed artifacts, and it became apparent that the oral training did not carry the same value as that of literary training. Thus an oral–literate tension became apparent. People enjoyed the oral component and found the stories engaging, but they persisted in asking for print-based materials and training because such carried more weight in society.[202]

By 2010, Ugandans were assuming more control of AGC's leadership, including decisions related to the pastoral training curriculum. The AGC pastoral training committee, which included a mix of church leaders and missionaries, decided to pursue expanding the orality training, incorporating it into its other training centers. This decision involved training the Ugandan pastoral trainers in orality and helping to introduce Bible storytelling throughout the denomination. As in Nebbi, enthusiasm for the joy of stories was experienced, but many of the pastors requested continuation of the former topical-oriented, print-based method alongside orality. Therefore, in 2013, the training committee launched a new integrated curriculum. Year/Level one was approximately 80 percent story based but with printed lessons for the facilitators. In addition, some practical lessons were also included that were not story based. Level two sought a mixture, continuing with storying but incorporating more topic-oriented lessons. Level three was almost exclusively print based, as the students have to complete a series of "theological education by extension" booklets, which are written in English.[203] Therefore, one can see from the history of AGC's experience with both print-reliant and oral-reliant curricula, it provides an ideal case study for exploring the nature of communication complexities in Uganda Christianity.

CONCLUSION

This chapter has accomplished two objectives. First, it has highlighted the privileged status that literary (i.e., print-reliant) communication assumed from the earliest days of Christianity in Uganda. Several tensions were identifiable, namely formal education's relationship to the environment, practical versus literary education, and spiritual versus material advantages of education. Furthermore, it has affirmed the influence of the COU (and the *Balokole*) in shaping the communication environment within which AGC

202. Coppedge, "Overcoming Complications to Oral Methodologies."
203. Ouma, March 31, 2017.

operates today. Second, it has introduced AGC with its history, holiness theology, and the uniqueness of its pastoral training scheme. The purpose behind the extended recounting of the historical development of AGC's pastoral training, particularly considering the introduction of oral methodologies, has been to provide the backcloth for a more intentional consideration of what have been the responses and influences of these oral strategies within a Ugandan denomination. AGC's pastoral training scheme has not followed the typical Western, missionary-led, institutionalized process. This phenomenon makes for a unique consideration of how members of AGC are navigating the complexities of communication as they seek to balance the cultural expectations of modernity with supposedly innovative Western ideas of oral education for biblical engagement. While some of those preliminary tensions have already begun to emerge, attention now turns to understanding in more detail and with greater clarity, how local Christians in Uganda are learning, earning, and communicating the gospel message.

5

Communication Complexities in the Africa Gospel Church

INTRODUCTION

THIS CHAPTER TURNS ATTENTION to the research data collected from the fieldwork done in Uganda. The chapter is divided into two sections with the first portion offering some initial observations regarding the varied nature of AGC's valuing and engaging with the Bible. This discussion is important to establish because failure to recognize the value of the Bible may result in underestimating the influence of the medium by which it is engaged. The second portion examines in detail the different modes of AGC's communication, including consideration of oral-reliant, print-reliant, and digital-reliant communication. It also incorporates a category that surprised me. The fieldwork revealed that the church members valued another communication medium, namely material-reliant communication. Thus, discussion includes an exploration of the nonverbal role of materiality within AGC's communication framework and practice. Establishing a comparative assessment of these various communication modes is imperative for the ensuing analysis regarding the claims the OM makes in championing the value, and necessity in some cases, of communication on an oral register. In essence, the central inquiry of the chapter is whether the OM's particular conception of orality (**orality$_2$**) is as prevalent and popular as the OM seems to suppose and what AGC personnel think of these other modes of communication. Therefore, while this chapter provides access to what I learned from the field, or the data itself, the next chapter offers an extended analysis of what this data means.

COMMUNICATION PRAXIS

If the broader investigation of this research revolves around the reception of particular communication practices in light of modernity, considering how AGC members engage the Bible offers a natural point of entry into the discussion. The initial, or primary, sense behind the idea of *biblical engagement* is the act of relating with or to the biblical text, whether reading, hearing, or watching the text being performed live or on a screen. There is also a secondary sense of engagement that incorporates any action that includes a Bible, such as acquiring, possessing, wielding, reverencing, beholding, storing, carrying, or sharing. This double sense of engagement allows for appreciating not only how people relate to the biblical message but also how they relate to the Bible as a material object.[1] Approaching communication complexities through the lens of how local Christians relate with their Bibles is natural for two reasons. First, the OM and AGC share a strong doctrinal stance on the Scriptures as the source of divine authority and norm for Christian understanding and experience. Second, proponents of the OM are encouraging a particular kind of engagement with the Bible. Thus, collecting data of how local Christians and churches engage or interact with the Bible, through differing media and on differing registers, provides a means to gain further understanding into how these Ugandan individuals and communities navigate the construction of their own Christian identities amidst Western stereotypes as well as their own cultural expectations and associations with modernity.

A Variety of Engagers, Places, Times, and Languages

Simply put, members of AGC relate to the Bible in a variety of places, at a variety of times, in a variety of languages. The spectrum of AGC members engaging their Bible was broad: male and female, young and old, educated and uneducated, urban and rural.

---

1. Engelke refers to this as "the dual character of Scripture" as both word and object. See Engelke, *Problem of Presence*, 20–28; for another helpful, recent discussion on the material power of the Bible as an object, see McMahon, "Analysis of the Reception," 195–201.

Communication Complexities in the Africa Gospel Church 169

An older man and woman with their Bibles
during a sermon at Bulyango AGC.[2]

While I was largely limited to witnessing Bibles being read at church, the focus groups and interviews testified to biblical engagement happening at a variety of locations. Church,[3] Bible studies,[4] home fellowships,[5]

---

2. Picture by the author.
3. Focus Group: Kafu, April 27, 2017; Fred Okello, personal interview, March 15, 2017.
4. Mugisha, May 22, 2017; Mukisa and Mukisa, April 22, 2017.
5. Dhikusooka, May 10, 2017; Tonino Pasolini, personal interview, March 16, 2017.

work/school,[6] in the taxi,[7] and at home[8] were all discussed as places where people either read or listened to the Bible. Likewise, interaction with the Bible occurred at any number of times throughout the day, whether before and after work,[9] early in the morning,[10] after lunch,[11] in the evenings,[12] after a conflict,[13] at the office at 9:00 a.m.,[14] before school,[15] or on Sunday afternoons.[16] Naturally, these encounters with the Bible incorporated different engagement practices, whether reading a chapter a day,[17] listening to the radio "to pick some verses,"[18] or participating in the discussion at the church's mid-week Bible study.[19] Furthermore, no dominant genre of the Bible seemed to be preferred above others. People expressed preference(s) for the historical books,[20] stories from the Old Testament,[21] the Psalms,[22] the New Testament in general,[23] the Gospels ("because of the teachings of Jesus"),[24] and the epistles.[25] Finally, engaging the Bible happened in a

---

6. Mukisa and Mukisa, April 22, 2017; Joshua Kinaalwa, personal interview, May 11, 2017.

7. Omri, May 12, 2017; Focus Group: AGC leaders, April 5, 2017; Imam Otafiire, personal interview, April 1, 2017.

8. Focus Group: Masese, April 23, 2017; Martin Owor, personal interview (1st), March 21, 2017; Focus Group: Nebbi, March 19, 2017.

9. Focus Group: Masese, April 23, 2017.

10. Focus Group: Masese, April 23, 2017; Focus Group: Bugiri, May 14, 2017.

11. Focus Group: Bugiri, May 14, 2017.

12. Okello, March 15, 2017; Focus Group: KIU, May 5, 2017; Focus Group: Bugiri, May 14, 2017.

13. Focus Group: Masese, April 23, 2017.

14. Focus Group: KIU, May 5, 2017.

15. Mukisa and Mukisa, April 22, 2017.

16. Owor, March 21, 2017.

17. Owor, March 21, 2017.

18. Kinaalwa, May 11, 2017.

19. Mukisa and Mukisa, April 27, 2017; Focus Group: Masese, April 23, 2017.

20. Kennedy Kirui, personal interview, March 28, 2017.

21. Kisugu AGC Bible Study (3rd), participatory observation, May 11, 2017; Focus Group: Kahara, April 29, 2017.

22. Kirui, March 28, 2017; Focus Group: Bugiri, May 14, 2017; Ouma and Kirui, May 17, 2017.

23. Kisugu Bible study, May 11, 2017; Owor, March 21, 2017.

24. Okello, March 15, 2017.

25. Owor, March 21, 2017; Okello, March 15, 2017.

host of different languages, including Alur,[26] Luganda,[27] Swahili,[28] Ateso,[29] Lusoga,[30] Runyoro,[31] Lugisu,[32] Acholi,[33] Lango,[34] and English.[35]

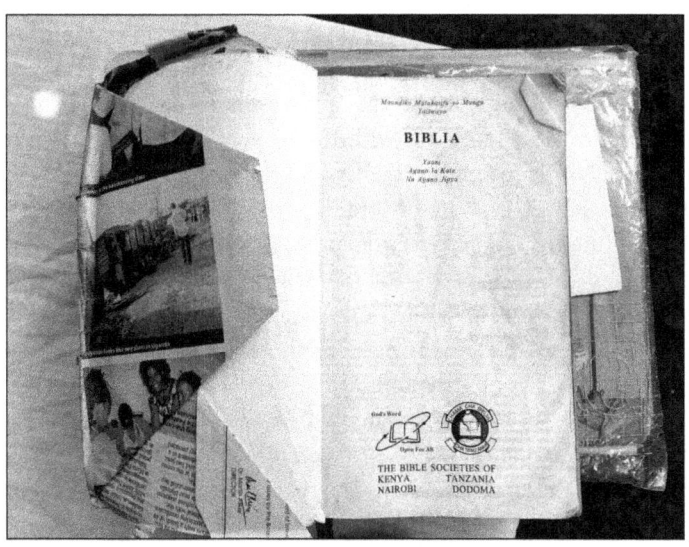

A Swahili Bible wrapped in newsprint. Kahara AGC.[36]

The Value of the Bible

On the one hand, this variety of biblical engagement, this broad spectrum of people, places, times, habits, languages, and even preferred texts, resists any sort of monochromatic classification. On the other hand, when

26. Site visit: Nebbi AGC, participatory observation, March 19, 2017.

27. Site visit: Kisugu AGC, Participatory observation, May 21, 2017; Site visit: Bukasa AGC, participatory observation, April 2, 2017; Site visit: Kafu AGC, participatory observation, April 27, 2017.

28. Focus Group: Kahara, April 29, 2017; Site visit: Kahara AGC, participatory observation, April 30, 2017.

29. Focus Group: Bulyango, April 28, 2017.

30. Focus Group: Kamuli, April 7, 2017; Site visit: Bugiri AGC, participatory observation, May 14, 2017.

31. Focus Group: Bulyango, April 28, 2017.

32. Focus Group: Kahara, April 29, 2017.

33. Focus Group: Bulyango, April 28, 2017.

34. Focus Group: Bulyango, April 28, 2017.

35. Site visit: Kisugu AGC, participatory observation, May 21, 2017; Site visit: United Faith Chapel (UFC), participatory observation, May 7, 2017.

36. Picture by the author.

asked about why the Bible was personally important, a resounding theme emerged. Plainly, the Bible is important because it "does" stuff in people's lives. Such an observation is not necessarily new. Philip Jenkins in his own research on biblical engagement in what he calls the Global South quotes Martin Luther: "The Bible is alive—it has hands and grabs hold of me, it has feet and runs after me."[37] This active, almost aggressive, encounter with the biblical text resonates with the response of AGC church members. Jenkins's work, in essence, seeks to illuminate this "direct relevance of the Bible to the lived realities of contemporary society" within the Global South.[38] He quotes Grant LeMarquand: "African exegesis does not seek to understand the text merely for its own sake or out of an intellectual curiosity. African exegesis is need-driven and faith-oriented." Jenkins reiterates, "Texts are adapted to the needs of the Church's situation."[39] My data aligned with Jenkins's observations.[40]

Admittedly, in a few incidents within the fieldwork, the Bible was described in more intellectual or even cerebral tones, such as, "It is a place for truth,"[41] but these were limited. The typical response affirmed Jenkins's observations, involving action verbs such as, "The Bible directs, teaches, reveals, shows, counsels, guides, convicts, promises, restores, gives, increases, helps, equips." Such descriptions, while perhaps overlapping at times, provide a snapshot of how AGC members perceive the "doing" value of the Bible. Essentially, the Bible's "doing" is intimately related to the mediation of identity. Therefore, a woman in Kafu AGC noted that when she reads John 14 about "the way, the truth and the life," she knows she is one in Christ and there is no condemnation.[42] Likewise, a university student declared that the Bible "helps me know who God is and who I am; if he's father, I am son. It opens my eyes to see who God [is]."[43] For this woman living in rural western Uganda and for this university young man in the urban capital, the Bible was a source of understanding their own identity in relationship to God. They were in different environments and even understood their identities as Christians differently: one under no condemnation

---

37. Jenkins, *New Faces of Christianity*, 18.

38. Jenkins, *New Faces of Christianity*, 18.

39. Jenkins, *New Faces of Christianity*, 35.

40. One of the ways this project enriches Jenkins's otherwise superb research is through its ethnographic perspective. In contrast, Jenkins's seems to draw almost entirely on secondary sources.

41. Not incidentally, this comment came from the university student focus group. Focus Group: KIU, May 5, 2017.

42. Focus Group: Kafu, April 27, 2017.

43. Focus Group: KIU, May 5, 2017.

and the other as a son. However, for both of these AGC Christians, the Bible provided the lens through which they understood their personal identities. The intimate association between the Bible and identity was not just for church members but also church leaders. This observation was brought home to me while attending a Bible study at Kisugu AGC. The evening's study had come to an end and Pastor James Ouma closed an enormous study Bible, set it on the small table in the middle of the circle of seven adults, and while patting the Bible he said, "That is why he created me—to know him."[44] This rather strong proclamation of purpose, a declaration of personhood, by the church's training coordinator no less was quietly declared in direct association with the Bible. Ultimately, the Bible mediates identity for AGC. While perhaps sounding simplistic, if this point is not reiterated, one might overlook the fact that if the Bible is essential for identity construction, then how the Bible is communicated within church praxis is of paramount importance. In essence, consideration of how the Bible is mediated through different communication modes has relevance not only for communication concerns but also implications related to perceptions of personhood within a particular context.

DIFFERING COMMUNICATION MODALITIES

The remaining portion of the chapter explores four different modes of communication that emerged from spending time with AGC. This categorization (oral, print, electronic/digital, and material) is used somewhat heuristically. The goal is not to set up false or arbitrary binaries or flimsy stereotypes but to explore how different modes of practice can or cannot make meaning. In other words, what are the affordances and limitations of differing modes? Understanding the different nuances is necessary if the further analysis is going to interpret how different modes interface with differing cultural expectations. Furthermore, this approach provides an occasion to consider how the differentiation as articulated by the OM regarding the differing modes (oral, print, digital) holds up in the midst of a live contemporary communication context. Since orality is the primary concern for the OM, this overview begins there before moving on to print-reliant, digital-reliant, and, finally, material-reliant modes of communication.

---

44. Kisugu Bible study, May 18, 2017.

Oral-Reliant Communication

ORAL AFFORDANCES

Several of the affordances that emerged from the field research were not necessarily surprises. Oral storytelling lends itself to a certain sense of familiarity with cultural traditions. As one leader said, "People come from a tradition of orality.... It resonates with them as part of their background."[45] Likewise, the spoken word can transcend certain barriers. Since skills such as literacy are not necessary, when dialogue and participation is encouraged, as in discussing a Bible story, many who might otherwise be marginalized can contribute. This capacity was particularly appreciated as beneficial among women; in Uganda, they typically have less literary education. In this way, oral Bible storytelling with its emphasis on discussion was understood as an empowering communication tool.[46]

What the research revealed was that orality's premier affordance is the possibility of affective engagement wherein an audience's emotions, imaginations, and even, at times, bodies are stimulated.[47] This characteristic relates to oral communication's unique relationship with the body. No matter how clear the font on a printed page or the amount of pixels on a digital screen, neither print nor digital media can reproduce a physically embodied communicator. The advantage of the inherent presence of physical bodies within the oral communication event is that it affords the possibility of a multisensory dynamic wherein communication happens on a variety of sensory levels, whether visually, audibly, or spatially, through gestures or even touch. While not all oral communication practices involve all senses, the embodied nature of such practices lend them to incorporating multiple senses.

It is imperative to clarify the limited claim that is being made here regarding oral communication's relationship with embodiment. While literate-reliant and digitally mediated communication can also be embodied, they afford or allow for a disembodiment of at least one party. This is one of their strengths; they transcend space and time. Orality does not possess this luxury. In this way, embodiment is inherent in an oral event for both parties in a way that is not necessarily the case for either a digital or printed experience. There is neither screen, nor microphone, nor page to distract, distance, or serve as proxy for either party. Therefore, in this limited sense, orality brings the body to the fore of the communication experience.

---

45. Kirui, March 28, 2017.

46. Muehleisen, March 31, 2017; Mugisha, May 22, 2017.

47. Focus Group: Kamuli, April 7, 2017; Focus Group: Kahara, April 29, 2017; Omri, May 12, 2017.

Consequently, this tendency of oral communication to be multisensory increases the likelihood of understanding transpiring between parties, tending to foster greater engagement. As Rev. Martin Owor reported, "When they read, they all doze but when I [the pastor] tell a story, they wake up."[48] This multisensory engagement appears throughout a wide variety of oral practices, including storytelling, but also drama,[49] song,[50] dance,[51] and even preaching.[52] While analysis of the genre of sermons can be complicated as discussed in chapter 2, it needs to be reiterated that the best preaching of a traditional, expository kind uses the whole body, such as gesture, movement, drama, and varieties of tone of voice. Consummate preachers in Protestant history such as Whitefield, Spurgeon, and even Graham exemplify this point very well. In this regard, one thing that made such famous preachers effective communicators was not whether they did or did not use manuscripts but how they embodied their oral proclamation so as to have an affective impact on their listeners.

A brief incident from a site visit to Bulyango AGC demonstrates the power of orality's embodied, multisensory affect. On the visit to Masindi with Miria and Steward Mukisa, I had the opportunity to spend a day with Bulyango AGC.[53] The church itself consisted of mud-covered walls and a tin sheet roof situated among several thatched houses. The program for the day's church activities included sermons, worship, prayer, eating together, and an afternoon crusade in the town center.

48. Focus Group: AGC leaders, April 5, 2017.

49. Site visit: UFC, May 7, 2017.

50. Site visit: Kisugu AGC, May 21, 2017; Site visit, Nebbi AGC, March 19, 2017; Site visit: Kahara AGC, April 30, 2017; Site visit: Bugiri AGC, May 14, 2017.

51. Site visit: Kafu AGC, April 27, 2017; Site visit: Bulyango AGC, participatory observation, April 28, 2017.

52. Site visit: Masese AGC, participatory observation, April 23, 2017; Site visit: Bukasa AGC, April 2, 2017.

53. Site visit: Bulyango AGC, April 28, 2017.

176   African Literacies and Western Oralities?

Bulyango AGC. A wooden chair and several branches were used to shade the generator at the corner of the church building from the sun. The generator powered the electric sound system.[54]

During one of the worship sessions, the entire congregation was on their feet, dancing, singing, and clapping as different congregation members took turns pounding a traditional skin-covered drum. Suddenly, to my surprise, the entire company of joy-filled, sweaty bodies picked up the scant possessions near at hand, whether their chairs, benches, or Bibles, and swayed their way out of one of the side entrances of the church building. I was at a loss for what was happening until Steward explained that the song (being sung in Alur) was "a song of Egypt," and the people were fleeing Egypt as they were "marching to the promised land." Although the few Bibles present in the church had been scooped up and carried out, this was not a print-oriented occasion, for up to this point in the service, I had witnessed no reading of the biblical text.[55] It became apparent that the Bibles, chairs, and benches were being reimagined as props in the performance, representing the scant possessions the Israelites had when they escaped from Egypt.

For a short few moments, other visitors and I were left in a practically empty church except for several elderly women. While temporarily

54. Picture by the author.

55. I acknowledge that a text may have been read before my arrival but from my participating observation throughout the morning, there had been no reading prior to this song.

not visible, the ensemble of clapping, stomping, and singing could be heard encircling the church building before the procession reentered the opposing side door of the church and, consequently, the Promised Land. This reentry incited fresh energy from the drum player and the volume of praise, clapping, singing, and stomping reached an even higher intensity. For all practical purposes, Miriam herself could not have celebrated with any more vigor,[56] for it was as if I had passed from a small rural village church and into the Promised Land with the children of God themselves.

According to the OM's understanding of orality (or **orality$_2$**), this was an oral communication event par excellence. Granted, the song found its inspiration from the book of Exodus, which has been transferred down through the generations through the resource of the written and later printed word. In light of this textual residue, the experience could also be conditioned as a "Protestant oral" event, to draw on the earlier taxonomy (illustrating also how at times **orality$_1$** and **orality$_2$** can overlap). Nevertheless, on this particular occasion, there was no reading of the Exodus story; there was no filling in workbook pages on the theology of pilgrimage. Rather, the message was embodied through a *multisensory* and what those within ION would call an *oral* communication event wherein the church community imagined themselves in the biblical narrative. The audience was seeing the pilgrimage take place (visual), hearing the pounding of the drums and raised voices (audible), moving not only through but around the church (spatial), and waving, clapping, and dancing (gestural). Furthermore, the clapping of hands and the holding on to one's chair or the drum stick were tactile experiences, while the mixed aroma of swirling dust and sweaty bodies permeated the olfactory senses. Herein was a robust, full-body and full-sensory engagement communication activity, and while acknowledging textual influence (i.e., the account recorded in the book of Exodus), for those within the OM, such an event epitomizes an embodied oral phenomenon.[57] The point of discussing such an event is not to suggest such embodied worship experiences are exclusive to AGC; on the contrary, they are common in Ugandan worship, particularly among more Pentecostal communities. Rather, the point is to recognize that such events illustrate ION's broad understanding of orality, understood here as **orality$_2$**. While perhaps fused together, such a communication event showcased what members of ION would describe as numerous oral genres,

---

56. Exodus 15:20–21.

57. In a similar worship time, although without the "Egypt song," the physicality of the communication event was underscored when three different drummers were cycled through due to fatigue. Site visit: Kafu AGC, April 27, 2017.

including storytelling, drama, testimony, dance, and singing.[58] Granted, this was an extraordinary communication event, quite a bit more dramatic than some other oral storytelling experiences that I observed. The point is not to argue that AGC alone demonstrates these "oral" features in their worship or that every oral event contains such dramatic multisensory dynamics, but that the embodiment inherent to this particularly defined orality (or **orality**$_2$) encourages greater understanding due to the multisensory channels along which meaning can be conveyed.[59] Consequently, due to its embodied, multisensory nature, oral communication, as understood by the OM, affords a more affective engagement wherein the audience's emotions and imagination are stimulated, often leading to a more effective communication experience, simply by multiplying the number of bodily senses involved in transmitting the message.

There are several important corollaries to this embodied, multisensory tendency of oral communication. The first is that orally communicated messages can be easier to remember.[60] This idea was counter-intuitive for me because I regularly use pen and paper to remember. On the contrary, Rev. Martin Owor talked about the unreliability of paper, which can easily be lost. If one knows the message (or story) by heart, it can be recalled, even if the original paper becomes misplaced.[61] A prime example came when I attended Kahara AGC and was privy to no less than six oral storying performances.[62] Granted, a textual presence was implicitly felt in that all the stories were derived from the Bible, and thus, presumably, the storytellers had read or been read aloud to at some point in the memorization process. Nevertheless, on that Saturday afternoon and Sunday morning, not one of the six storytellers read from a printed Bible or even referred to written notes. Instead, the stories were performed orally, emerging from the tellers' memories. Not incidentally, the memorization process had been mastered by the whole gamut of ages, including a fifteen-year-old young man, two young mothers, a middle-aged male pastor, and two elderly women.

58. Moon, "Fad or Renaissance?" 8–9.

59. Gravelle, "'What Do You Mean?'" 21, 24.

60. Kirui, March 28, 2017; Focus Group: Kahara, April 29, 2017; Focus Group: Kamuli, April 7, 2017; Site visit: Masese, May 16, 2017, Muehleisen, "Farming God's Way Training," participatory observation. After observing a development training, I chatted with on pastor named Silver Wakoko. In discussing storytelling, he mentioned that when the stories are in one's "heart pocket," they can be remembered at any time.

61. The unreliability of oral methods also emerged as will be discussed below. Owor, March 21, 2017.

62. Focus Group: Kahara, April 29, 2017; Site visit: Kahara AGC, April 30, 2017.

A second corollary of orality's tendency for embodied, multisensory engagement is simply that oral communication affords spiritual change. Embodied oral storytelling impacts people's lives.[63] Textual or digital communication can also impact people but the church members articulated an appreciation that the oral Bible storytelling generates spiritual transformation: "People feel excited and feel like learning more when you step through [the story]." This is more than mere entertainment, as they elaborated: "They [the stories] encourage us that if it happened to them [characters within the Bible stories], it can happen to us."[64] This is a significant claim. The biblical text is interpreted to offer hope; thus, telling a story becomes an occasion where people can identify with the characters in the story and envision the possibility of change for themselves and their community.[65]

In some incidents, this is a positive anticipation such as with the Kahara focus group expressing, "It can happen to us." On other occasions, the identification is negative—such as when Owor quoted a portion of the story from Luke 10:38–41 about the sisters Mary and Martha who welcomed Jesus into their home. Owor lamented that with the church and family responsibilities along with his own return back to school, he had been more of a distracted "Martha" than a listening "Mary."[66] Owor used the characters from the story at his own initiative (I did not bring up the story), identifying his negative counterpart in the story even as he likewise acknowledged how he wanted to be more like the character whom Jesus valued. Herein the pastor critiqued his own identity even as he articulated how he wanted to change to be like another character in the story.

Once again, it needs to be reiterated that spiritual change can happen through reading the Exodus account, and certainly one's imagination can be actively employed through reading (or engaging digital media). What remains important to understand is that the church discussed these spiritual changes happening through oral Bible storytelling in a way that they did not recognize as happening as easily or naturally when encountering the story (or scriptural passage) by reading a printed text.

One more interesting affordance that necessitates brief consideration is that orality was perceived by some of the church members as the cheaper mode of communication. On the one hand, this observation counters the

63. Focus Group: Kamuli, April 7, 2017.

64. Focus Group: Kahara, April 29, 2017.

65. Ouma and Kirui, May 17, 2017; although she is considering Pentecostals on the Zambian Copperbelt, Haynes likewise notes the significance of characters in biblical narratives in forming and transforming personal identity. See Haynes, "Theology on the Ground," 272–73.

66. Owor, March 21, 2017.

understanding within much of historical Protestant mission endeavors as printed texts and tracts have typically been understood as much cheaper for propagating the gospel than the cost of establishing and sustaining a missionary presence. One could rather convincingly argue that feeding and housing, much less paying, a trainer or the students themselves would be well beyond the cost of printed notes for a Bible course, but for Rev. James Ouma, the denomination's pastoral training coordinator, the shift from printed curriculum to oral communication has saved the church money. Granted, the trainer receives a printed one-page lesson plan, but its cost is drastically lower than paying for the reams of printed lesson plans, notes, and exams that the church had previously been issuing. Thus, if one sets aside the fact that all communicators, regardless of what means they use, require physical and, consequently, financial upkeep, then, in a conditional sense, orality is cheaper in that there are no additional financial costs necessary for oral communication to transpire, which is not the case with regard to print and digital communication.

This overview of the affordances of orality as perceived by the church has focused on the premier affordance related to orality, namely that its necessary embodiment lends it to multisensory and affective engagement. While not an absolute, this embodiment can aid in memory retention and result in spiritual change. Furthermore, while embodied communicators require certain financial considerations, orality has no additional media expense.

Oral Hindrances

In exploring hindrances to oral communication, aspects internal to the communication event are considered first before attention shifts to external or social dynamics. The prominent internal hindrance that the pastors and other church leaders raised with regard to oral communication was its methodological difficulty.[67] While initially seeming overly simplistic, what I found was a whole complex series of issues involved, not so much in relation to orality in general but rather in regard to oral Bible storytelling in particular. It is important to notice here again, the tendency by the church to conflate "orality" with storytelling. One of the first concerns was the time necessary to prepare an oral Bible story. As one pastor admitted, one cannot just sit down on Saturday night and string some verses together for a sermon. This is an interesting perception, revealing perhaps more about what the pastor believes is a "good sermon." His point seemed to be that if one is going to tell a story, then one has to prepare in advance and know the story

---

67. Owor, March 21, 2017.

well.[68] One might hope (expect) a pastor would do as much to prepare a nonnarrative sermon, but the implication of his words was that storytelling takes more work. Former AGC bishop Kefa Masiga affirmed this impression: "Orality is challenging because you have to memorize something. For some, this is very hard; hard work is needed. . . .This memorizing these words is the hard part of orality that many fear."[69] This expressed concern about orality and the difficulty of remembering would seem to counter the previously mentioned affordance that oral, embodied communication can help memory. Indeed, such a tension suggests that the issues may be more complex, necessitating elaboration.

Learning the biblical material was one of the major purposes behind instituting oral Bible storying, namely, to empower pastors with limited education to have a tool that would enable them to engage the Bible and use it among their communities. Nevertheless, learning the story for those who do not read well has proved to be a challenge. As the administrative secretary paradoxically noted, "It [oral storytelling] favors those who are a bit literate."[70] When pastors cannot read, they lose morale and then are reluctant to come to the pastoral training for fear they will be called upon to retell the story.[71] Thus, ironically, the oral method is having the exactly opposite effect on those with limited education to that which was intended. Furthermore, even if pastors learn the story, telling the story takes some skill, as does facilitating the appropriate discussion questions.[72] Therefore, while oral Bible storytelling was intended to remove print-reliant obstacles for those with limited literacy skills, the process, in its particular format, has introduced its own obstacles, specifically with regard to how people can learn the Bible stories without being able to read themselves.

It is important to make the caveat that this critique seemed related to the STS training method used for learning the stories and, thus, should not necessarily be applied to all OM praxis. That being understood, the STS method and its proponents maintain a high profile within the broader OM landscape; thus, it stands as a legitimate representative of how orality is approached by some within the movement.[73] According to the STS method, learning a story can be done either by reading aloud and then retelling what

68. Dhikusooka, May 10, 2017.
69. Focus Group: AGC leaders, April 5, 2017.
70. Dhikusooka, May 10, 2017.
71. Dhikusooka, May 10, 2017.
72. Focus Group: Kamuli, April 7, 2017.
73. This was reiterated for me while attending the North American regional ION gathering in Orlando, Florida, September 17–19, 2018.

one remembers aloud, a process repeated until the story is learned, or one can listen to another person read aloud and then one retells as best as one remembers, likewise repeated until the story is learned. Both approaches require a printed Bible (or a digital recording), although in theory, the latter is for those who cannot read well.[74] I suspects that part of the pastors' frustration was that there had been a breakdown somewhere in the training chain in teaching how these two methods worked. This frustration may have also been exacerbated by the reiteration throughout the STS methodology that the story has to be learned accurately. Details, while they may be expressed in one's own words, have to be included and summarization is not permitted.[75] Thus, while "oral" in a sense of being spoken, there is a sense in which this valuation of textual accuracy reveals an a priori ideology by those who initially developed the STS method.

The biblical text is understood as God's literal words and thus, all the words of the text are thought to form part of revealed truth. Such a perspective shapes the way one approaches oral storytelling, for the focus of the storytelling event is less on the artistic nature of the oral performance and more on the accuracy of the text. Historically, the pastoral training program has stressed such accuracy, which may have inadvertently created an obstacle for those with limited reading ability. Rather than allowing a certain degree of oral improvisation or poetic license for those who cannot easily verify the biblical details by rereading the page, the STS method and, consequently, the AGC training program have stressed textual accuracy. This *accuracy over accommodation methodology* allows for a literal view of the biblical text, but in light of the voiced concerns, it has apparently discouraged some pastors from engaging the Bible at all.

The difficulty of oral storytelling lies not only in the preparation, the performance, and the facilitation of discussion but also, as the pastors noted, in the lack of an artifact after the communication event, which might be referenced.[76] When people can read a printed text, then they can naturally go back and review anything they may have missed. Without a copy of the printed text, such referencing is not possible. This lack of material artifact was also noted in complaints about the loss of printed notes for each lesson within the pastoral training program. People expressed a desire to have a hard copy.[77]

74. An audio Bible could also be used as Fred Okello affirmed, although I did not find any AGC pastors who were learning via audio Bible. Okello, March 15, 2017.

75. One will recall from the relevant discussion in chapter 3 that unfamiliar terms or necessary historical information is supposed to be supplied in a brief introduction before the story.

76. Omri, March 19, 2017; Kirui, March 28, 2017.

77. Mukisa and Mukisa, April 22, 2017; Focus Group: Kamuli, April 7, 2017.

Furthermore, the pastors have requested books on storytelling—a strong and ironic indicator that while appreciative of aspects of orality, there remains a strong valuation of literary material and learning.[78]

Along those same lines, several within the church and mission discussed the limited knowledge that can be covered orally.[79] While good for activities such as evangelism, oral Bible storytelling tends to remain almost exclusively in one portion of text with only rare references to other passages. This is intentional on the part of the STS method, to try and encourage "deeper" engagement and understanding of a particular narrative instead of merely picking a verse here or a few verses there. Significantly, the cost of such depth is the loss of scriptural breadth (as well as other historical background information).[80] One woman in a silver gomez (i.e., traditional dress) described how she liked looking at a variety of different verses as any one might edify her.[81] The lack of an artifact to reference, cross-check, or provide additional information leads to another reason that orality is considered difficult, namely, maintaining orthodox interpretation.

As already introduced, the tension of maintaining orthodox interpretation while also enabling contextualized application is not new to Christianity. What exacerbates this tension is when the communication event is oral without a printed biblical text. For WGM missionary Nathan Metz, who has been involved with the church, the issue of safeguards within interpretation is precisely his concern with oral biblical engagement. In an impassioned tone of voice, Metz talked about the danger of oral exegesis, the discussing of a passage of Scripture within a small group setting, as giving way to a dangerous subjectivity wherein the Bible means whatever each individual wants it to mean. By way of illustration, Metz made reference to one occasion that he had heard that a group of pastors had made some rather unorthodox applications after discussing the story from Genesis 12 about Abram, Sarai, and Pharaoh. In the story, Abram lies about Sarai being his wife to Pharaoh, only for God to intervene. In the end, Pharaoh releases Sarai, whom he had taken into his harem, and gifts Abram with many livestock. Metz was indignant about the report he had heard wherein the pastors' application had been that God blesses lying.[82]

---

78. Mukisa and Mukisa, April 22, 2017.

79. Owor, March 21, 2017; Focus Group: Kamuli, April 7, 2017; Mukisa and Mukisa, April 22, 2017; Nathan Metz, interview via Skype, April 25, 2017.

80. Mukisa and Mukisa, April 22, 2017.

81. Focus Group: Bugiri, May 14, 2017.

82. This was a self-conscious moment for me, as Metz did not realize that I had been present for that discussion regarding Genesis 12 in 2009. Presumably, another missionary had recounted the episode to Metz although the version that had been passed on to

To prevent such aberrant exegesis, Metz argued that orthodox interpretation requires access to background information on historical and biblical culture. Such information is accessed via print; thus, to promote orality was to deny these pastors the tools they needed for properly interpreting the word of God.[83] Furthermore, when asked about the issue of illiteracy within the denomination, Metz retorted, "Too often we talk about illiteracy, it is, 'Let's find a way around it.' Orality is presented as, 'This helps with illiteracy.' But what else helps—literacy helps!"[84]

Herein was the most articulated and rather scathing critique of orality or, rather more accurately, oral Bible storytelling from a missionary. The primary concern was the misunderstanding and application of the Bible. This problem, yet again, reveals a deep theological and ideological commitment regarding the authority that the Bible holds. For at least some such as Metz, orality not only fails to provide access to the necessary information for proper biblical engagement, but the use of oral methodologies can potentially skew biblical understanding and application within the life of AGC. Not insignificantly, his proposed solution was text-reliant communication methodologies. Before turning to consider the printed mode, several external forces emerged that, likewise, raised rather strong concerns for the promotion of oral methods, such as storytelling, within AGC.

The shift to consideration of external hindrances to orality involves redirecting attention from the immediate oral communication event to the cultural forces shaping the context within which the event itself is happening. Bluntly stated, orality is often perceived as a social stigma. There are several issues involved, but it seems to originate in the historical association between literacy and Christian practice.[85] Such an association is in no way exclusive to Uganda, for in Madagascar, as Jennifer Cole recounts, Catholic and Protestant missionaries were, likewise, first in promoting literary education. One Protestant missionary, discussing the revolutionary aspect of the arrival of formal schools in Madagascar, noted that the possessing of a certificate "confers a certain prestige and opens the door to numerous

---

him seemed slightly embellished. Regardless, I validate Metz's concern, for the group discussion was rather vigorous. It became necessary to break the STS protocol and step out of the immediate story and consider several additional biblical references before finally coming to an accepted but also "orthodox" understanding of the story.

83. By way of comparison with Engelke's study of the "liberal" Friday Apostolics, although they do not believe in a biblical text but rely on the Holy Spirit speaking directly through a prophet, they do not avoid the issue of interpretation. A *mumirir wemweya* or an "interpreter of the spirit" interprets and proclaims to the audience what the Holy Spirit says to the prophet. Engelke, *Problem of Presence*, 171–74, 185–88.

84. Metz, April 25, 2017.

85. See the relevant discussion in part one of chapter 4.

jobs." Therefore, "schooling is synonymous with modernity."[86] The similar sentiments, discussed at length in chapter 4 in the Uganda context, now emerge with intense vengeance in regards to attitudes towards orality. AGC pastor Benson Omri, commenting on early Christianity in Uganda said, "When the gospel was first introduced, what was introduced was reading, not telling."[87] In a similar vein, former bishop Masiga highlighted the value of literary education: "Current education pushes people toward printed material. Orality-oriented person is someone who has not gone to school. . . . A person who has not gone to school has no message, nothing to offer or deliver to us."[88] Such a comment reveals how being oral-reliant, lacking proficiency in literacy skills, equates with, essentially, being a non-person. Literacy proficiency achieved through formal schooling confers personhood, providing credibility within the community, a social capital that orality simply cannot deliver. Omri provided a poignant example from his own life. Now that he has started studying for a degree in theology, when the local pastors' association gathers, he and the other pastors possessing more education are honored by being invited to sit down first. He described this as breaking the local barrier, for when one has more education, he or she can talk about things beyond the local context.[89]

Part of this issue of credibility relates to the traditional nature and associations of oral communication. While several church members nostalgically compared Bible stories to cultural stories, such as those involving the traditional character "Mr. Hare," that same group likewise acknowledged that questions have been raised about the trustworthiness of the Bible stories. If the cultural stories are made up, then does that mean the Bible stories are, likewise, purely imaginative, more fairy tale than history?[90] Similarly, Omri observed that in his context in Nebbi among the Alur people, stories are associated with "making or creating something" that is untrue. Furthermore, they are typically understood as meant for children.[91] This evident association between orality, specifically storytelling, and the traditional forms of communication means that it is considered outdated.[92] Caroline Ouma and Lillian Kirui commented that while storying may be good in the church

86. Cole, *Sex and Salvation*, 30–31.
87. Omri, May 12, 2017.
88. Focus Group: AGC leaders, April 5, 2017.
89. Omri, May 12, 2017; this was affirmed in conversation with Ouma, March 31, 2017.
90. Focus Group: Kahara, April 29, 2017.
91. Omri, May 12, 2017.
92. This was Bishop Masiga's comment. Focus Group: AGC leaders, April 5, 2017.

for ministry, "for building for the future or continuing your education, it is limited."[93] Herein lies the heart of the issue. Orality, specifically oral storytelling, often works as an affective and, thus, effective mode of communication; however, it fails to mediate a particular understanding of one's personhood, namely, the highly valued educated or schooled identity. In this way, orality is understood as unable to build progressive or modern social capacity in the lives of the pastors or the church members in ways that society recognizes. This concern regarding how orality fails to empower a person within one's social network highlights a phenomenon evident in other African contexts, namely, the integrated nature of social networks, identity, and even material goods. This merits elaboration so as to understand how AGC's communication praxis is a part of a wider socioeconomic imaginary.

Jennifer Cole discusses the integrated nature of these factors in relation to their embeddedness in traditional values and practices. She contrasts this with what she calls the process of disembedding. Her concern is where people in Madagascar move from rural environments to more urban ones, and thus, break old traditional attachments in the process of forming new, modern ones.[94] For Cole, the breaking from the traditional and the embracing of the modern involves this process of disembedding. In this sense, AGC has interpreted orality as perpetuating an embeddedness within traditional oral communication frameworks when at least some of the church personnel are looking for ways to disembed themselves as they seek to achieve particular identities within their "modern" context.

This integration of identity and social networks is likewise evident in Naomi Haynes's discussion of how the value of "moving in the Spirit" on the Zambian Copperbelt is realized in one's societal networks through dependence and asymmetric relationships. Her development of the concept of *moving* is not merely forward momentum but "recognizable—usually visible—progress, capable of being 'graded and profiled' and 'recognized in small nuances by others.'"[95] Significantly, Haynes discusses how the value of moving is actualized through a whole series of overlapping metrics such as with the body—gaining weight—in transportation—riding the bus instead of walking or purchasing a car so one does not have to take a taxi any more—or the purchase of some material marker—whether a television or a new set of cooking pots. Attaining such moving milestones or material markers is only possible through one's social networks so people "are

---

93. Ouma and Kirui, May 17, 2017.
94. Cole, *Sex and Salvation*, 46–50.
95. Haynes, *Moving by the Spirit*, 37–40.

always on the lookout for potential patrons or networks through which they might make moving happen."[96]

The importance of material objects in constituting social relations and the defining of one's identity has received emphasis elsewhere in Zambia. Pritchett notes this phenomenon among the Lunda wherein "to be human, the Lunda believe, is to be socially connected," and "to be without social linkages is akin to being lost in the deep forest."[97] Social networks provide meaningful direction for one's life. Once again, as in Haynes's observations, such social embeddedness, to use Cole's phrase, operates on a system of material exchange. As Pritchett notes, "Physical goods must change hands if a relationship is to endure," and "one 'talks' with transactions."[98] Such sentiments are reflected well in Pritchett's discussion of LeVine's observations regarding general traits that can be ascribed to an African personality. While Pritchett questions whether *personality* is the accurate term, he does appreciate LeVine's observation that "material transactions are emphasized in interpersonal relations. That is to say, relationships can frequently be characterized in terms of the type of material exchanges involved: who gives what, to whom, when, and under what conditions."[99]

While acknowledging the differences among peoples in contexts as diverse as Madagascar, Zambia, and Uganda, such examples from Cole, Haynes, and Pritchett highlight the integrated nature of material goods, interpersonal relationships, and social expectations of progress or movement. The implication of such discussion is that any attitude or practice that fails to move one forward (i.e., one remains *stuck*[100] or *constrained*[101]) is to be avoided. It is important to recognize the inherent corollary to this understanding, namely that any action that fails to generate material goods that can be incorporated into one's social network is of little value. Here is the connection with orality and, specifically, storytelling, for, to paraphrase Kirui and Ouma's previous quotation, orality fails *to move* one towards the future. AGC's social context is seeking new, modern attachments that will move an individual forward; in essence, they are looking for material markers that represent a disembedded, reimagined identity. Orality cannot produce such markers and remains embedded in a traditional, outdated,

---

96. Haynes, *Moving by the Spirit*, 37–56, quote on p. 56.
97. Pritchett, *Lunda-Ndembu*, 84–85.
98. Pritchett, *Lunda-Ndembu*, 84, 120.
99. Pritchett, *Lunda-Ndembu*, 11–12; LeVine, "Patterns of Personality in Africa."
100. Haynes, *Moving by the Spirit*, 39.
101. Cole compares "to spread one's wings" or "to move" with the idea of being "constrained" or "crushed." See Cole, *Sex and Salvation*, 66–67.

and limited discourse that no amount of appreciation for its affective engagement possibilities can dissipate.

Orality's inability to achieve these disembedded, modern identities was identified in several ways. On the one hand, the lack of formal, literary learning precludes one from participating in certain civic activities or leadership, such as registration with the government, whether of a local church or the denomination as a whole. In today's context, a village elder is now expected to be able to read and write. Likewise, communities expect their government's local counselor to be able to write a letter on their behalf.[102] The government certifies literary education, and society has come to expect such skills.

On the other hand, and even more practically, the emerging concern focused on whether oral storytelling can build economic capacity. Essentially, people were wondering or perhaps, doubting, "How is orality going to help me?"[103] This issue seemed to be related to the association between formal education and increased financial opportunity. Since the oral storytelling training is not certified other than internally by AGC, it counts for nothing when applying to go on for more formal education.[104] Several times, the comparison was made between training in oral Bible stories and a proper Bible school. Each time, the theme emerged that no matter how well a pastor may know the oral material, without proper formal certification, society will scoff at such a pastor.[105] Ouma recounted, "If I have orality and no formal papers, then the church is not able to support me and so I need to go for further education." Thus, ultimately, having oral skills does not meet the literate-educated-economic expectations within the pastors' context.

Rather tellingly, although church leaders such as former bishop Masiga and Rev. James Ouma have received training in and have even facilitated training in oral Bible storytelling, several missionaries noted that they had never witnessed either leader using the storying approach.[106] In a revealing statement, Jonathan Mayo, who has generally been an enthusiast for orality since 2008, admitted that the church is not asking for orality. He elaborated, saying that for many, orality "does not count as pastoral training because it is not formal education."[107]

---

102. Kirui, March 28, 2017.
103. Ouma, March 31, 2017; Omri, May 12, 2017.
104. Ouma and Kirui, May 17, 2017.
105. Mayo, March 12, 2017; Ouma, March 31, 2017.
106. Stanfield and Stanfield, May 9, 2017.
107. Mayo, March 12, 2017.

Such commentary explodes any naïve understanding that AGC has consistently warmly welcomed **orality**$_2$ as championed by the OM. While there have been numerous aspects to orality, and specifically storytelling, that the church has appreciated, particularly related to its embodied, multisensory affect, negative reactions were expressed in relation to orality as a mode of communication weighted down with strong social stigmas. With associations of being outdated or traditional, orality fails to *move*, not meeting the literary and economic expectations within AGC's social context. Consequently, the church expressed fears that, in spite of being affective (and effective) at times on the ground, the future lay not with oral Bible storytelling but with formal, literary training. While not asking for an elimination of all things oral, they expressed a desire for a greater emphasis on alternative modes of communication that will move and empower them forward educationally, socially, and economically. While it might be tempting for some to quickly suggest such things are "unspiritual" or irrelevant for engaging the Bible and processing the Christian message, the analysis in chapter 6 reveals that for these Ugandan Christians such rigid categories (as spiritual and secular) are unhelpful binaries that do not match their holistic (and embodied) understanding of Christian salvation.

Print-Reliant Communication

Print-reliant communication, as understood by the OM, involves both a reliance on the printed word as well as a particular way of structuring the message's information, typically exemplified in a systematic and/or propositional manner. Already introduced, this conflating of the distinction between the means of communication and the way of organizing information is parallel to the OM's understanding of orality. This tendency is important to keep in mind as the subsequent discussion considers the affordances and hindrances that print-reliant communication, as particularly defined, offers within the AGC community.

PRINT AFFORDANCES

A natural place to begin discussing the advantages of print is WGM's own *The Print Shop*, run by missionary Kenneth Hopson. I was able to spend a morning with Hopson, which included a tour of the small but active shop.[108] Hopson has converted an office and garage into his workspace and has filled the shop with printers, copiers, cutters, staplers, and binders. Leonard, a university student who is also an AGC member, serves as Hopson's right-hand

---

108. Kenneth Hopson, personal interview, March 23, 2017.

man in the shop. Together, they displayed a whole cache of books, pamphlets, and workbooks that were in various stages of completion.

Kenneth Hopson and Leonard in *The Print Shop*.[109]

For Hopson, printing is more than a job; it is interpreted as a vocation. He described how printing was a means for him to contribute to getting Ugandans out of the village and away from a life of "digging." He elaborated, noting that unless people "by some miracle" acquire a little capital or have formal literary training, they will never leave the village. For Hopson, the link between printing, reading, and modernity was immediate and direct; without literate skills, he could see no hope of Ugandans establishing themselves with a proper job, purchasing a plot of land, building a house, or getting married. Thus, according to Hopson, printing was

109. Picture by the author.

directly related to personhood and the construction of one's identity. With emotion in his voice, he described how grateful he was for people who had empowered him, and he expressed his excitement at what he understood to be a chance to empower Ugandans. His immediate example was Leonard, a member of Kisugu AGC. Leonard uses his salary from the shop to help with his university expenses, and he has even been able to purchase a motorbike. For Hopson, Leonard was a perfect example of how further formal, literary education and the *The Print Shop* are empowering AGC to forge new, hope-filled identities. Rather than be forever stuck in the village as a sustenance farmer, the *The Print Shop* has become a site of identity contruction, allowing an AGC member to imagine a life beyond his rural, agrarian upbringing. Hopson noted, "Education for them [Ugandans], which involves literature, that is the way to improve their lives—even more, their way of acquiring, whether bicycle, gadgets, property, home, . . . that is the measure of success. That improves your status, shows others that you are not a poor worthless digger. So literature plays an important role in that approach—to improving their life. People who do not have those things are looked down upon. Money gets you things. How do you get money? Education."[110] The relationship between education, literature, and acquiring is further analyzed in chapter 5 but for now, Hopson's perspective, while enthusiastic, illustrates how printed communication is perceived as carrying social, economical, political, and personal value. In Leonard's case, this printed communication, which includes formal literary education, is interpreted as the opportunity to (re)imagine one's own identity. Therefore, this mini case study provides an ideal backcloth upon which further exploration into the affordances of print communication can take place.

The affordances of print-reliant communication emerged from its artifactual (i.e., material) nature. Strictly speaking, there is one grand affordance, the artifact of a printed text, that then enables a series of consequent sub-affordances. Contrary to a strictly oral communication experience, a written or printed text provides an artifact that both enables learning and supplants the need for memory. This print advantage emerged in relation to notebooks that were carried by certain church personnel, often in tandem with a Bible.[111] Both pastors and members discussed how these notebooks allowed people to remember what they had learned.[112] One honest participant described his appreciation for the notebooks: "We do not pay attention so then we go in our

---

110. Hopson, March 23, 2017.

111. Focus Group: Bugiri, May 14, 2017; Focus Group: Masese, April 23, 2017; Focus Group: Kahara, April 29, 2017; Focus Group: Kafu, April 27, 2017.

112. Focus Group: Kahara, April 29, 2017; Dhikusooka, May 10, 2017.

free time and learn."[113] In such a testimony, it is possible to identify a certain transcendence that printed texts afford beyond the immediacy of the time and place of the communication event, thus enabling communication and learning to occur at one's personal convenience.[114]

The artifact does not just facilitate memory but also ease of learning. Simply put, people described how it is easier to understand the Bible through printed means.[115] Several specific study preferences were mentioned, beginning with something as straightforward as observing a printed Bible is easier to flip back and forth between differing passages.[116] Often printed Bibles also have an index of topics in the back, which likewise makes for easy referencing.[117] Some church personnel expressed appreciation for footnotes and endnotes, while others noted the advantage of being able to highlight or underline special passages.[118] Furthermore, some acknowledged they like having additional printed study resources when they are studying their Bibles. I was surprised when I first attended Kisugu AGC's Thursday evening Bible study and found the primary text was not the Bible but Rick Warren's *The Purpose Driven Life*.[119] Six worn copies, each with a plastic covering in various stages of peeling off, were read and shared by the participants.[120] Similarly, one university student mentioned preferring "one-on-one time with the Bible," with other study books opened for making notes, which could be used afterwards for sharing with other friends.[121] This concern to share with others what one read or learned relates another affordance—the sociality of texts.

---

113. Focus Group: Kahara, April 29, 2017.

114. Kirui, March 28, 2017; Omri, May 12, 2017; During visits to two churches, part of the worship service involved the pastor acknowledging the reception of letters of invitation from other local churches to join in different outreaches or celebrations. This was an interesting example of printed texts enabling communication to transcend geographical and temporal limitations. Site visit: Bukasa AGC, April 2, 2017; Site visit: Kahara AGC, April 30, 2017.

115. Muehleisen, March 31, 2017; Focus Group: Nebbi, March 19, 2017; Focus Group: KIU, May 5, 2017; Focus Group: Kahara, April 29, 2017; Focus Group: Masese, April 23, 2017.

116. Focus Group: KIU, May 5, 2017.

117. Focus Group: KIU, May 5, 2017.

118. Focus Group: AGC leaders, April 5, 2017; Focus Group: KIU, May 5, 2017.

119. Warren, *Purpose Driven Life*; for a flavor of the extent to which Warren's book has had an impact, see Shellnut, "Celebs from Michael Phelps to Kim Kardashian." Shellnut notes that the book has sold over forty million copies.

120. Kisugu AGC Bible Study (1st), participatory observation, April 6, 2017.

121. Focus Group: KIU, May 5, 2017.

While perhaps contrary to certain stereotypes of the lone reader and a printed text, Hopson articulated his surprise when, early in his printing career[122] (he first worked in Tanzania before coming to Uganda), he realized that one printed text is often read by any number of people. His observation was that East Africans love literature; thus, the correlation was not one text, one person but, one text, many people. Far from being classified as a strictly individualized activity, printed communication affords its own communality that perhaps may not be as immediately recognizable as the sociality of an oral conversation. As one elder noted, he goes through his notebook and it helps him teach others.[123] Thus, the printed word or written note influences one's own self-understanding but also influences a corporate religious identity, empowering people to remember and teach or share with others what has been learned.

While related to the preference for a printed text as easier to study, pastors described how the printed text also affords a particular organization of information by "providing a systematic flow."[124] Granted, oral discourse can be systematic and printed texts do not have to display a systematic or propositional structure; for instance, the printed material can be arranged in a narrative. What was being highlighted was a comparison of the oral storytelling lessons and the formerly-used printed lessons. The original curriculum employed printed, topical lessons that utilized an outline format to present a summation of teachings on a particular subject, complete with a list of relevant Scripture passages.[125] The pastors expressed appreciation for this breadth of biblical material, lamenting that such cross-referencing is usually not presented in an oral Bible lesson where the concentration is on one specific passage.[126] The ability to reference was described as enabling a greater understanding of both church doctrine and discipline.[127] While the oral story provides understanding from a specific narrative, it does not afford a wider foundation for understanding a particular topic. Futhermore, a printed Bible allows the student access to all genres of biblical material, whereas the oral storytelling does not do justice to non-story portions of the Bible.[128] This is not to say that oral stories cannot likewise be organized

---

122. Hopson, March 23, 2017.
123. Focus Group: Kahara, April 29, 2017.
124. Focus Group: Kamuli, April 7, 2017.
125. Focus Group: Kamuli, April 7, 2017; Mukisa and Mukisa, April 27, 2017.
126. Notice here, that what was discussed above as a hindrance for orality is described an affordance for textuality.
127. Focus Group: Kamuli, April 7, 2017.
128. Ouma, March 31, 2017.

and told according to particular themes or topics. The pastors seemed to be identifying an appreciation for the way that the printed, topical lessons presented the information in a succinct, even propositional, way, having drawn on a range of biblical references. Biblical teaching could be distilled and then artifacted in a text that is more conducive to covering a particular topic than if one has to keep retelling a cache of stories to recall one's doctrinal positions. Therefore, the artifactuality of printed communication enables both an ease of remembrance as well as a topical approach to the organization of information that those within the church, particularly the church leaders, appreciated.

Directly related to this categorizing of information is the confidence that printed communication affords, confirming what others have thought or how they interpreted things. In the focus group of AGC pastors in Kamuli, one participant noted that with the former printed lessons, interpretation was made easier because it "comes with an agreed principle for understanding something." This "gives you confidence that others believe this way."[129] Thus, the printed notes afforded an immediately accessible "key," as it were, to understand how things have been and should be interpreted. Oral communication does not necessarily afford such clearly articulated principles in quite the same way. For this pastor, there was something in the principle being written down in the notes that offered reassurance of its veracity.

This observation leads to another sub-affordance related to print's artifactuality, namely, printed communication offers reliability. A printed Bible is understood as not only reliable but also as more authoritative than a digital Bible or an oral portion of the Bible. The historical underpinning for this was recognized by some.[130] As Pastor Omri said, "When the gospel was brought, they [the missionaries] were not bringing their own message. To prove that it was not their own message, it had to be read." Thus, reading carried an authority, establishing the message as of divine origin and not just made up by the early missionaries. This should be highlighted: reading mediated a divine message. Omri acknowledged that he prefers printed communication as "he feels more comfortable and more convinced. With the audio [oral], he feels it is harder to convince if it is the word of God. He likes to read it and know and recognize—this is God's word."

Along this same line, there was a sense in which the printed biblical text provided the reference point for other modes. For example, people talked about watching TV, and if they do not understand something, they

---

129. Focus Group: Kamuli, April 7, 2017.
130. This issue was discussed at length in chapter 4.

will go and read the Bible.[131] Likewise, when asked about where the Bible is kept, one Bible study participant answered, "Next to the radio. My Bible is always next to the radio; when some one is preaching or teaching, I can easily check to see if they are speaking the truth."[132] While acknowleding the radio, an electronic form of communication, was a means to engage and learn about the Bible, the printed version validates other versions. Omri concurred that it was similar in his Alur context. Among such people, "It has to be a printed Bible; only in rare cases will they respect a digital Bible. The learned will respect but not the traditional [people]. The traditional will say, 'This is not the Bible. It is not inspired.'"[133] Otafiire Laurent noted that when someone writes, the message is clearly in the writer's handwriting, identifying the author. Thus, the written word becomes an act of mediating personhood. The digital word, on the other hand, can be deleted or someone could "rewrite my words." This, in Laurent's mind, affirmed that "Print is better than digital."[134]

The final sub-affordance that deserves discussion has already been alluded to throughout but can be plainly stated: Printed communication carries social value. This is intimately tied with formal, literary education, as Mayo acknowledged. Ugandans have requested him for printed pastoral training lessons because the printed lesson is considered a higher level of education.[135] Beth Muehheisen agreed, "Paper has value; something on paper has more value than just hearing."[136] Notably, Hopson the printer, admitted, "One does not have to have paper to hear God's word." With that caveat made, he strongly argued that literary education (i.e., print-oriented communication) is essential for Ugandans to reimagine their lives outside of an agrarian-based identity.[137] Thus, Mayo noted that because of this strong association between print and the students' expectations of "something higher," even if he is preaching a story-based sermon at the university church, he carries written notes to the podium.[138] The written (or printed) words carried a social value that affirmed the validity of the pastor's message.

131. This comment was interesting because the participant claimed they would "go and read and ask some one." This would seem to both reiterate the authority of reading but also leave some space for preferring the directive communication as previously discussed above. Focus Group: KIU, May 5, 2017.
132. Kisugu AGC Bible Study (2nd), participatory observation, May 4, 2017.
133. Omri, May 12, 2017.
134. Laurent, April 1, 2017.
135. Mayo, March 12, 2017.
136. Muehleisen, March 31, 2017.
137. Hopson, March 23, 2017.
138. Mayo, March 12, 2017.

This broad overview has established a series of affordances that emerged from the fact that printed communication includes a material artifact—a hardcopy text. This distinct feature of print-reliant communciation affords numerous advantages related to remembrance, organization, transcendence, reliability, and social value. The broader implications are worked out in chapter 6, but one final field anecdote highlights some of these major issues.

While facilitating a focus group discussion with members from Nebbi AGC, I asked the participants how they preferred to engage their Bible, whether by listening, watching, or reading. A sizeable majority indicated that they preferred to read the Bible, but to my surprise, Pastor Willy Manano stood up and addressed me in front of the entire audience, saying, "Even many of the church members cannot read well but they can listen very well."[139] This was a slightly awkward encounter for me as the pastor had seemed to counter the participants' expressed preference. When I asked the pastors (Manano and Omri) about it later over lunch, Manano remarked that he appreciated the bravery of one church member named Kristen who had admitted she prefers to hear the Bible rather than read it. When pressed to explain, both Manano and Omri discussed how members of the group want to be readers even if they cannot; thus, they voted for reading. The pastors continued by saying that to acknowledge that one does not read might make one feel degraded or inferior. Thus, Kristen's confession was an act of courage wherein she admitted her preference for listening, being oral-reliant.[140] Such a story offers a small window into how one woman's communication preference have implications regarding her identity and relationship with her community. Significantly, the pastors were praising her bold self-description in light of the fact that her preferred mode of communication, that of orality, carries negative social connotations. Former bishop Masiga described this desire to be a reader regardless of whether one has literate skills or not as "pride," people wanting "to associate themselves with the elite class."[141] Whether pride or not, the apparent perception among the church is that print communication carries a premier place in society. As Mayo summarized, "Here in this [AGC] community, the clamor is not for more orality, but for more print-based material."[142]

---

139. Focus Group: Nebbi, March 19, 2017.

140. This conversation was initially an interview with Pastor Benson Omri but Pastor Willy Manano joined half way through. Omri, March 19, 2017.

141. Focus Group: AGC leaders, April 5, 2017.

142. Mayo, March 12, 2017.

Print-Reliant Hindrances

Several hindrances to print communication can be easily anticipated. The lack of literacy skills was discussed as an obvious issue and the lack of available tools such as eyeglasses was also a complication. Several other factors emerge that also deserve attention. A primary hindrance to print-reliant communication is the economic factor; it costs money to print and it costs money to buy printed materials.[143] This concern has already been mentioned in relation to the church and the lack of printed pastoral lesson notes, but it has affected the university ministry as well. Mayo described how the leadership team has wanted to use a discipleship curriculum that has been developed in Kenya, but buying the materials has proved to be a tremendous burden on the ministry.[144] This concern, likewise, came up at a *Farming God's Way* training day.[145] This agriculture development program offers training around twelve principles; six are considered spiritual and six are interpreted as practical. According to this model, adhering to all twelve principles provides a biblical approach for growing crops. The problem discussed at the training was the fact that while everyone is given a one-page laminated sheet summarizing the twelve principles, the training manual costs 2,000/= Ugandan shillings. Although this is less than half a US dollar, the cost is prohibitive for some of the trainees. What becomes apparent in these three training examples (i.e., the pastors' lessons, the students' discipleship material, and the farming manual) is that training that relies on printed texts carries an economic burden. The haunting question emerges: Who pays for the training material and, furthermore, how much training material is enough?

A second hindrance to print-reliant communication is its lack of availability. This was most clearly demonstrated by my interaction with Rev. Ouma, who is currently pursuing a Doctor of Ministry degree at Africa Nazarene University. He lamented the challenge of finding access to printed resources for his personal research.[146] While thankful for the Internet, an electronic mode, he has still struggled to find the books and articles necessary for him to complete his thesis. Another way this hindrance was made evident was in the creation of the AGC pastoral library.[147] It has provided some printed resources for pastors to access; however, I was

---

143. Mukisa and Mukisa, April 22, 2017; Dhikusooka, May 10, 2017; Focus Group: Kamuli, April 7, 2017.

144. Mayo, March 12, 2017.

145. Site visit: Farming God's Way, May 16, 2017.

146. James Ouma, personal interview (3rd), May 22, 2017.

147. Site visit: AGC Pastoral Library, participatory observation, April 5, 2017.

surprised to learn that the majority of the books are not for checkout but only for on-site reference. Thus, the pastors have to travel to the church office to access the books in the library.

A third hindrance to print communication is lack of motivation, which has been alluded to before (i.e., the lact of interest), but in light of the discussion on printed communication, a few additional comments are necessary. One pastor recounted how even if people take a printed lesson home, they will return without having finished an assignment.[148] Likewise, reading has the potential to "make people lazy," for "those who read—it eliminates them having to search further for themselves."[149] Furthermore, people tend to have a hard time paying attention: "When you read, they get distracted."[150] Given the option to read or not, at least one church member confessed he would rather play his guitar in the evenings after work.[151] There does not seem to be much of a cultural habit of reading,[152] and if someone does read, for example the newspaper, one pastor argued it will not be the full article as much as it will be the headlines and the pictures.[153] In a similar vein, the general secretary, Rev. Dhikusooka, argued that the former print-oriented, topical lessons tended to minimize student participation in favor of the trainer lecturing through the outlined points. Dhikusooka lamented that the lecture style often resulted in fewer questions being asked to motivate discussion, suggesting that less participation results in less learning. While one may debate how much of a newspaper is actually read or whether participation increases learning, what stands out is that such comments do raise questions about how motivated people are to engage print-reliant communication.[154]

Print-reliant communication, with its distinct physicality, affords numerous advantages not available to an oral communication event. Such a long list of print-reliant affordances, articulated by the church personnel, stymies any blanket categorizations by WGM or the OM that Ugandans, in general, or AGC personnel, in particular, prefer oral instead of print communication. On the contrary, the evidence indicates that the church members have a deep appreciation for printed material. Nevertheless, printed

---

148. Dhikusooka, May 10, 2017.
149. Ouma and Kirui, May 17, 2017.
150. Focus Group: Kamuli, April 7, 2017.
151. Kinaalwa, May 11, 2017.
152. Pasolini, March 16, 2017.
153. Owor, March 21, 2017.
154. Such concern may be related to the tendency of a print-reliant event to be less multisensory than an oral experience, often only engaging the eyes.

communication comes with questions of costs, availability, and motivation, limitations that cannot be easily dismissed.

Digital (Electronic)-Reliant Communication

Digital-reliant communication relies on the immediate presence of an electronic device. Uniquely, spoken words and even printed texts can and often are part of the communication event; however, the communication event itself is tethered to the presence of some form of electronic media.[155] Due to the ever-increasing pervasiveness of digital technology, digital-reliant is used here as a shorthand way of speaking about this broader category of electricity-dependent media. Several general observations are necessary before considering the affordances and hindrances to digital communication within the AGC community.

Upon returning to Uganda in 2017 after having been gone for several years, I was struck by the increased presence of digital technology. This was evident in such processes as my purchasing of a SIM card for my phone or malaria prophylaxis for my children. This influx of digital media was not just in the marketplace, but it became apparent that Christians within the region are using digital media through a variety of ways and on a variety of devices. Rhys Hall, a long-term Episcopal missionary to South Sudan, talked about digital audio players (DAPs), small media devices that could be programed to play audio versions of the Bible. Hall, now located in Arua, Uganda, due to the instability in South Sudan, talked at length about various kinds of teaching they have offered by programing the material onto DAPs, including audio Bibles, but also lessons in peace building, literacy training, and teacher instruction, and they are currently investigating how to implement trauma healing teaching as well.[156] While not specifically a part of WGM or AGC, Hall's testimony and experience provide a glimpse into the possibilities that the versatility of digital media offers for Christians seeking to overcome communication complexities in the region. Furthermore, it parallels similar uses and experiences I observed within AGC.

---

155. Digital-reliant communication is similar to Ong's concept of *secondary orality*. See Ong, *Orality and Literacy*, 11, 133–35.

156. Rhys Hall, personal interview, March 18, 2017.

Four different styles of digital audio players (DAPs).[157]

One such example within an AGC context took place while I attended an AGC *Farming God's Way* training event. WGM missionary John Muehleisen facilitated a conversation on whether the three *Kindle Fires* that he had dispersed among several trainers had been helpful.[158] Discussion ranged from whether the trainers had been able to operate the device and review the training videos, to whether they had found ways to keep the device charged, to a brief demonstration of how to take better pictures of productive gardens with the device's camera. The presence of digital media, or the digital footprint, was further emphasized when Muehleisen pulled out his own computer and speakers and played several particular training videos that he thought might both encourage the trainers as well as remind them of certain aspects of the training. The discussion concluded with Muehleisen reassuring them that he would do his best to try and acquire several more *Fires* for training purposes.

157. Picture by the author.
158. Site visit: Farming God's Way, May 16, 2017.

A digital footprint could be observed in other AGC contexts as well. The presence of radio was a topic of numerous conversations.[159] Likewise, Steward Mukisa shared how he listens to an audio Bible on a DAP while walking to school each morning.[160] The university student focus group talked at length about the use of their smart phones, the various social media platforms they prefer,[161] and whether the cultural differences in American evangelical movies can be overlooked in light of the Christian themes.[162] On numerous occasions, different interviewees or focus groups talked about watching Christian programs or preaching on TV.[163] In two churches, digital projectors beamed messages up on the wall throughout the worship experience,[164] and while attending the Kisugu Bible study, a young man named Michael responded to a particular question the group had discussed by searching on his phone in the midst of the conversation.[165]

Perhaps the most dramatic evidence of electronic media appeared in the sound systems used by the churches in Sunday morning worship. Not every AGC church had an electronic sound system,[166] and the ones that did varied in their sophistication.[167] Not necessarily surprising, the most attention-grabbing experience proved to be the university students' United Faith Chapel (UFC). The service is held in a lecture hall on the fifth floor of a university building. As one walks across the campus towards the building, one is greeted by the sounds of praise and worship band trumpeting into the early Sunday morning air. This worship band included no less than two bass

159. Hall, March 18, 2017; Mugisha, May 22, 2017; Site visit: Kafu AGC, April 27, 2017; Owor, March 21, 2017; Kinaalwa, May 11, 2017; Winifred, personal communication, personal conversation, April 2, 2017.

160. Mukisa and Mukisa, April 27, 2017.

161. While Twitter and Instagram were mentioned, the overwhelming majority use both Facebook and Whatsapp.

162. The students mentioned appreciating various Christian movies, including several by Sherwood Pictures, a company that was established by Sherwood Baptist Church in Albany, Georgia. Focus Group: KIU, May 5, 2017.

163. Focus Group: KIU, May 5, 2017; Focus Group: AGC leaders, April 5, 2017; Beth Muehleisen recounted visiting an overseer's home with two other women leaders and while they waited for the meal, the women turned on the overseer's TV and watched a preaching show. Muehleisen, March 31, 2017.

164. Site visit: Kisugu AGC, May 21, 2017; Site visit: UFC, May 7, 2017.

165. Kisugu Bible study, May 4, 2017.

166. Focus Group: Nebbi, March 19, 2017; Site visit: Kafu AGC, April 27, 2017; Focus Group: Bugiri, May 14, 2017; Kahara was unique in that on Saturday, during the program, a sound system was set up and used. However, during Sunday morning worship, there was no sound system. Site visit: Kahara AGC, April 30, 2017.

167. Site visit: Bukasa AGC, April 2, 2017; Site visit: Bulyango AGC, April 28, 2017; Site visit: Masese AGC, April 23, 2017.

guitars, one acoustic guitar, a set of electric drums, six microphones, one electric keyboard, one soundboard, and a computer hooked up to the projector. Six men and four women made up the worship team; furthermore, a designated cameraman roamed throughout the service with an expensive looking digital camera, snapping pictures of both the praise team and the worshipers. This was a digitally oriented worship experience, complete with digitalized Bibles appearing on both smart phones and tablets.[168] Not insignificantly, it should be noted this was an urban student church environment—a far cry from the rural context of Nebbi AGC or Kafu AGC.

It is this last observation, drawing attention to the difference between rural and urban context, that seems to exposes a discrepancy within the constituency of AGC. While radio was discussed as prevalent throughout AGC,[169] digital media devices such as smartphones, computers, or other media players were not common in rural AGC contexts. From the group discussions and my observations, while highly visible in the urban context, such digital equipment has yet to permeate the rural environments. This was reiterated as not being an exclusively AGC phenomenon in a discussion regarding a new telecommunications company called *Africell*.[170] The company's then current special deal offered free data packages for people in Kampala, while offering free talking time packages to people outside of Kampala in areas such as Bugiri. Rev. Martin Owor explained that the urban people use data now more than talking, while people in the village "do not know the Internet" and "no one is on Facebook."[171] Rev. James Ouma summarized this observation by saying that AGC "is not so technological."[172] I did witness AGC church leaders using smart phones in various rural contexts, but what became apparent was that all of these pastors make regular visits to Kampala, and thus, are in and out of an urban environment. Furthermore, it came to my attention that each AGC overseer was gifted a smartphone by one of the WGM missionaries.[173] It important to keep this urban–rural differentiation in mind, as our attention turns to matters of affordances and hindrances, for the observations made regarding advantages

---

168. Site visit: UFC, May 7, 2017.

169. Kinaalwa, May 11, 2017; Owor, March 21, 2017; Mugisha, May 22, 2017; Focus Group: Kafu, April 27, 2017; Focus Group: Nebbi, March 19, 2017; Focus Group: Masese, April 23, 2017; Hall, March 18, 2017; Pasolini, March 16, 2017.

170. http://africell.ug.

171. Owor, March 21, 2017.

172. Ouma, March 31, 2017; Stanfields made similar comments. Stanfield and Stanfield, May 9, 2017.

173. Dhikusooka, May 10, 2017.

and disadvantages of digital communication seemed to come almost exclusively from church leaders and the university students.

Digital-Reliant Affordances

In a conversation about the appeal of digital phones and TV, the former bishop Masiga dramatically summarized his observations: "So people are running away from print."[174] One reason that people appreciate digital media, such as smartphones, is because they offer a variety of research tools, particularly in relation to the Bible. For example, different Bible versions can be toggled back and forth for comparison, and references can be easily found for those who do not know the Bible well. Words in their original languages can be looked up and the search feature enables immediate cross-referencing. Furthermore, commentary is often available and links to specific topics, such as joy or addiction, can reveal a plethora of biblical references. To enhance the worship experience, Christian music can be downloaded and played even while one studies the Bible.[175]

The most dramatic example of digital media affording biblical learning and study came while I met with the church's top three leaders in the AGC pastors' library. I wanted to spend some time investigating the library, so arriving early, I explored what it had to offer. I was surprised to find that since July 2015, only nineteen resources had been checked out by two missionaries and eight pastors. However, two pastors, both pursuing post-secondary education, accounted for nine of the nineteen books. I supposed this was a critical indictment of print communication, as the average number of books checked out per month was less than one a month. However, this turned out to be a false conclusion.

The bishop, assistant bishop, and general secretary all arrived in due course, and I initiated conversation with them on the usual topics of communication and biblical engagement. All three men graciously participated in the conversation, but, to my surprise, they did it while browsing for books, taking notes from various volumes, and finally snapping pictures of differing pages that held their interest. This was unique in my experience, for while none of the men were rude, they simply took turns answering and when someone else was talking, the other two would be busy reading. When finally asked about the photos, the men told me that the majority of the books cannot be checked out, which explained the limited number of checked out items; thus, the leaders use their phones to snap pictures, the contents of which can be read later at their convenience.

---

174. Focus Group: AGC leaders, April 5, 2017.
175. Focus Group: KIU, May 5, 2017; Kinaalwa, May 11, 2017.

This experience opened my eyes not only to the desire for learning and to the appreciation for printed resources but also to the way that those with access to digital media were leveraging it to take full advantage of limited access to printed resources.[176] While the church leaders have such digital tools, the average AGC pastor does not, nor does he or she receive any assistance with transport costs to visit the church office and library. Thus, the affordance made available to these three leaders through digital media belies the shadow of a hindrance. Nevertheless, the fact remains that digital media affords research possibilities that are not available in the same way through oral or print communication.

A second affordance digital communication provides relates to convenience. People talked about how a phone is easier to carry than a Bible as it can fit more comfortably into a small handbag for a wedding[177] or while traveling.[178] It offers a replay feature that can happen at one's convenience.[179] Furthermore, there are times when a device such as a phone is less threatening, particularly among certain groups such as refugees who adhere to another religion.[180]

Digital communication also enables people to cross boundaries. This third affordance, the transcending of borders, is both similar to and different from that of oral and print communication. It transcends time and space as does a printed text, but it also has the potential to reach a much wider audience. Thus, Father Tonino, responsible for the Catholic radio in Arua, described how before the radio, ecumenical meetings happened on occasion, but the Catholic Church's primary audience was Catholics. With radio broadcasts, all that has changed as their several frequencies have the potential to reach ten million people in the region, many who are not Catholic. While much smaller in scope, AGC also has its own, albeit limited, radio presence in the Nebbi district, as Pastor Benson Omri hosts a radio show every Sunday morning.[181] Thus, there is a transcending of geographical and even ecumenical barriers, and also of physical barriers or handicaps. While

---

176. Focus Group: AGC leaders, April 5, 2017; a similar experience happened when I met Pastor Benson Omri at the library. As with the church leaders, Omri was engaged in discussion, but all the while, he was perusing books. Omri, May 12, 2017.

177. Mukisa and Mukisa, April 22, 2017.

178. Focus Group: KIU, May 5, 2017; Mukisa and Mukisa, April 22, 2017; Laurent, April 1, 2017; Hall, March 18, 2017.

179. Hall, March 18, 2017.

180. Stanfield and Stanfield, May 9, 2017.

181. I was able to visit the radio station. For more information, see https://www.facebook.com/rainbowradio88.2fm/. Site visit: Rainbow Radio, participatory observation, March 19, 2017.

this was already mentioned, in cases such as Fred Okello who is visually impaired, his audio player enables him to engage the Bible in ways not possible through printed communication.[182]

A fourth affordance relates to the desirability and social weight that digital communication carries in the community. Some digital media, such as film, affords multisensory engagement; thus, it becomes not only an audible communication event but also a visual one. After the focus group discussion with the pastors from the Kamuli region, they stayed together to discuss some business matters with Rev. Ouma, the training coordinator. One of the items was a specific request for the *Jesus Film* to show in their area. Likewise, in both Kahara and Bulyango, such films were discussed as having had a powerful influence among the community. Thus, people are asking for such digital media experiences. Ouma likewise said that if given the option between a printed Bible and a phone, everyone would pick the phone. It offers a variety of functions and, more importantly, friends will say, "Wow!" whereas a printed Bible generates no such enthusiasm.

Part of the reason digital communication is so desired is because of the strong association between digital media and modernity. The term *digital* is used as an adjective to mean progressive and modern, while *analog* was defined as backward and negative. When I asked for further clarification on these terms, I was told that digital means "touch-screen," while an analog device is any that has "real push buttons." In a self-conscious moment, the pastor picked up my iPhone and said, "If you have this," holding up the phone, "you are so proud of it. It is powerful." While perhaps not universal,[183] one sensed that digital communication within the church represented an orientation towards what was considered sophistication.

Along these same lines and similar to both oral and print communication, a last affordance offered by digital media relates to identity. Digital media enables the reimagining of one's identity, possibly in explicitly Christian terms. I met two women who testified that they had made evangelical confessions of faith and become born again through radio preaching.[184] For both women, their Christian identity was intricately tied to the transcending power of an electronic device to broadcast spoken words into their lives. These words, this digitalized message, transformed their self-understanding and realigned their identity according to the Christian

182. Okello, March 15, 2017.

183. One university student admitted feeling ashamed at reading the Bible on the phone during church. Focus Group: KIU, May 5, 2017.

184. While radio communication would seem to be "oral," it is classified as "digital-reliant" because it relies on electronic-media. Winifred, personal conversation, April 2, 2017; Mugisha, May 22, 2017.

faith. Significantly, this correspondence between digital media and identity is not always explicitly Christian.

Ouma summarized the relationship between digital media, specifically a smartphone, and one's identity in a rather clarifying way: "A phone is not for accessing information; most often a phone is saying something about an individual. It gives me an identity; it is a fashion. It is not just a phone but it is a reflection on who I am."[185] Such comments echo similar sentiments elsewhere, such as in Mozambique. Anthropologist Julie Archambault noted how recent information and communication technologies have been applauded throughout Africa, often seen in close association with development. In such understanding, "the phone, then, stands as both an index of modernization and driver of socioeconomic development."[186] Although Archambault's own interest is in the local use of mobile phones in Mozambique, she observed that when mobile phones started appearing in Inhambane, "they acted as tangible proof of membership to the civilized world. . . . Phones were seen as the veneer of civilization." Phone ownership embedded one in a wider, modern imaginary—a desirable imaginary so that "young people have harnessed the phone for self-fashioning, as the phone is used to express aspects of one's identity, especially in terms of status."[187]

This seems to be what Ouma is describing when he says, "It is not just a phone but it is a reflection on who I am."[188] Ouma's comments situate issues of communication into a more dynamic complex involving digital communication, social value, and identity. Digital communication, as understood within the context that AGC communicates, is an orientation towards life. It affords opportunities to construct one's identity along a modern, seemingly more sophisticated register. Certainly, more than the spoken word and even more than the revered printed word, the digitalized word seems to offer not only ease of communication and access to information but something more desirable, namely, social capital. Nonetheless, there is a price.

Digital-Reliant Hindrances

If oral communication is the most economically viable (at least, regarding the cost of a communication artifact), digital communication tends to be the most cost prohibitive. Jeff and Christine Stanfield commented that the university students access websites and watch Christian films regularly, but the AGC pastors cannot afford the charges to connect to the Internet.

185. Ouma, March 31, 2017.
186. Archambault, *Mobile Secrets*, 2.
187. Archambault, *Mobile Secrets*, 57–58.
188. Ouma, March 31, 2017.

Rev. Dhikusooka affirmed such sentiments, noting that he had been given a smartphone, but it costs money to buy the "MBs" necessary to download items such as a Bible app.[189] The university students did express appreciation that the Bible apps are often free; however, they also were very conscious of the cost of downloading the app in addition to paying for a phone capable of playing it.[190]

Ironically, one way church members save money is to carry multiple phones, each with its own SIM card. Calling or texting within a network is cheaper; thus, a person can identify by the phone number, which line to use to get the discounted tariff. The catch is that multiple phones means paying for more phone credit.[191] Not only do the phones cost money, but other digital audio devices can be expensive. Rhys Hall provided a detailed breakdown of three different DAP options, their prices ranging from twenty-three to sixty US dollars.[192] When one considers that a printed Bible can be purchased from *The Print Shop* for approximately four US dollars, one recognizes the considerable higher expense of the digital version.

The dynamics of the cost of digital communication relate not only to personal communication but also to the possibilities of the church as a denomination. One of the prayer items from Rev. Martin Owor was establishing a radio program with Rev. David Dhikusooka that would cover the Jinga and Iganga areas but also extend out towards the islands in Lake Victoria. With passion in his voice, Owor lamented how the prosperity preachers have the money to be on the radio but do not have "a message," while in contrast, such an AGC ministry would "help so many people who are deceived because we have a message." Nevertheless, the denomination cannot afford the approximately $220 necessary for a sixty-minute weekly time slot.[193]

One final example of the economic dynamics emerged from conversation with AGC church member Joshua Kinaalwa. He discussed how he had recently undergone an operation, and it had been necessary for him to sell his digital phone to pay his medical expenses. He still listens to the

---

189. "MBs" stands for megabytes. The telecom companies sell data by the "MB," which can be deducted directly from one's phone account. Dhikusooka, May 10, 2017.

190. Several free Bible downloads mentioned by focus group participants were the *Holy Bible App* and *eSword*. *Olive Tree* is another one but one has to pay for the Bible download. Focus Group: KIU, May 5, 2017.

191. Owor, March 21, 2017; Omri, May 12, 2017.

192. The equivilant would be approximately 82,500 to 215,000 Uganda shillings. Hall, March 18, 2017.

193. $220 is approximately 800,000 Ugandan shillings. Owor, March 21, 2017. I understood that Pastor Omri's own radio show in Nebbi is due to his relationship with the radio management and thus, such a phenomenon is not necessarily reproducible for the church elsewhere.

radio at work on a rather worn analog phone, but the digital phone had a Bible app. Now, without the digital phone, he does not have a Bible.[194] Such an account provides an inverse illustration of the economic value ascribed to the digital mode of communication.

In addition to cost, another hindrance to digital communication is technical complications. For example, phones require someone to pay for electricity for the phone's battery and as I myself experienced, a phone battery can often quit at inconvenient times.[195] The constant need to top up one's battery was illustrated on one occasion with the church leadership. Upon arriving at my house, two of the three leaders produced either a phone or a battery pack and requested them to be charged during lunch. Thus, unlike a book that can be opened at any time, no matter how many research apps a device such as a digital phone offers, without a charge, its communication value becomes worthless.

Along these same lines is the issue of technical failure. Okello related how his first audio Bible had broken, and while a missionary replaced the device for him, that friend has now left the country. He expressed fear about what will happen if his current device breaks. Likewise, most of the churches that utilized sound systems ran the electrical system from a generator. These do not always operate as smoothly as planned, and during one service, there were constant interruptions as the technician had to scramble back and forth between the soundboard and the generator outside. Although perhaps not exactly technical failure, another incident illustrated how digital media do have limitations. Otafiire Laurent wanted to download a Bible version in his indigenous language only to find out that his smartphone did not have available memory space. Thus, while often advantageous for transcending such barriers as language, digital media are not always the panacea people anticipate.

Another hindrance digital media struggle to overcome is distraction. Precisely because there are so many features on a device such as a phone, reading one's Bible can easily be interrupted. Numerous testimonies were shared about the challenge of being in church or for private reading only to have a Whatsapp message flit across the screen or, more disruptive, an incoming call.[196] Rev. Kennedy Kirui, the pastor of UFC, discussed having tried to discourage the students from doing Bible study on the phone for precisely this reason; however, he immediately noticed that such an

---

194. Kinaalwa, May 11, 2017.

195. Focus Group: KIU, May 5, 2017.

196. Focus Group: KIU, May 5, 2017; Kinaalwa, May 11, 2017; Kirui, March 28, 2017.

approach meant a bifurcation. The students were then "digital in all but analog in their Bible reading."[197]

Finally, in contrast to the perceived reliability of print communication, for some people, digital media are suspect. This was not the perspective of either Rhys Hall or Father Pasolini, who both were convinced that radio and DAPs carry a certain authoritative weight because people associate them with the West. Pasolini stated, "If something is said on the radio, it is the Bible." Not insignificantly, this was the perspective of two expatriate missionaries.[198] Pastor Benson Omri disagreed, noting that he uses a digital Bible only while traveling and never from the pulpit. "People have the perception that this [holding up a phone] is not the true Bible. This is the true one [holding up a printed Bible]."[199] People are suspicious that different versions have been tampered with so that particular verses have been edited out.[200] One pastor expressed this concern in this way: "People are diluting the Bible to run away from conviction."[201] While there was some indication this could happen with printed Bibles, the concern was typically associated with digitalized Bibles, whether apps on smartphones or other media devices. If icons can be created and edited, who is to say that someone is not creating and editing an altered digitalized Bible version?[202] This reluctance by some to embrace digitalized Bibles fully meant that several times the printed version was referred to as the "original."[203] Furthermore, questions emerged about how well the Bible can be studied on a phone and, ultimately, how digital communication is affecting a person's Christian walk. One missionary even expressed concern over the theological implications of various Facebook posts made by AGC church members.[204] These and other related issues all raise substantial questions for the denomination as it seeks to navigate communication complexities within their context with perhaps the greatest being that not everyone is convinced the digitalized word is

---

197. Kirui, March 28, 2017.

198. Hall, March 18, 2017; Pasolini, March 16, 2017.

199. Omri, May 12, 2017.

200. Mugisha, May 22, 2017. I was reminded of the Reformation era's daunting question of whose (and which) Bible is the "real" Bible.

201. Mukisa and Mukisa, April 22, 2017.

202. Laurent, April 1, 2017; Focus Group: AGC leaders, April 5, 2017.

203. Focus Group: KIU, May 5, 2017; for Pastor Steward, this specifically meant the King James Version (KJV). While I noticed a high regard for the KJV, the denomination does not adhere to a "KJV only" policy. Instead, it seemed that pastors and members used whichever version they could access. Mukisa and Mukisa, April 22, 2017.

204. Muehleisen, March 31, 2017; Stanfield and Stanfield, May 9, 2017.

the divinely inspired word.²⁰⁵ Therefore, in spite of its sophisticated allure, digital communication has its own obstacles.

Material-Reliant Communication

The mode of materiality emerged as a surprise category for me. While questions regarding Christianity's understanding of the relationship between the immaterial and material date back to the early church, recent studies have sought to bring the physicality of religion, specifically the role of material objects and bodily actions, into clearer focus.²⁰⁶ In the introduction to their own work on materiality, Minna Opas and Anna Haapalainen note "the human struggle" with the material because "it is always present, yet often bypassed because of its abundance and ongoing presence."²⁰⁷ In many ways, this was my experience. While the issues that emerged regarding whether a pastor drove a sophisticated vehicle or a congregation had a permanent, finished structure were not new, it was only in conversation regarding how the church communicates its faith that I began to realize such issues were matters related to communication. These were not just "prayer requests" for more physical stuff but for church personnel, these material concerns had direct implications on the denomination's ability to communicate winsomely within their cultural context. Thus, the incorporation of the material mode into interviews and conversations afforded an opportunity to understand yet another level of how the church perceives communication in today's contemporary world.

Before turning to the matter of affordances or hindrances of materiality, it is worth reiterating that all communication bears some relation to the material. The spoken word relies on a human body, the printed word implies a physical text of some material substance, and the digital word necessitates an electronic object. Thus, they all could be classified as oral-material, print-material, digital-material. Indeed this chapter has already begun to explore matters of materiality, whether with regard to the lack of a material artifact that seems to stigmatize orality within the AGC context or the social power communicated through the materiality of a digital phone. Nevertheless, there emerged within AGC another mode of communication

---

205. This was likewise confirmed by the church leaders. Focus Group: AGC leaders, April 5, 2017.

206. For recent two recent examples, see Opas and Haapalainen, *Christianity and the Limits of Materiality*; Plate, *Key Terms in Material Religion*; these two works seem to be extensions of what Morgan calls the "cultural turn" in religion and media studies. See Morgan, *Key Words in Religion*.

207. Opas and Haapalainen, *Christianity and the Limits of Materiality*, 1.

that operated on a nonverbal register, what is being called here *materiality*. Material objects communicate messages and convey meaning not through words, whether spoken, printed, or digitalized, but through the physicality of their material essence. What I came to realize was that these material objects are embedded in a socioeconomic imaginary that confers upon them a particular communication significance that transcends or even at times, eclipse verbal-reliant forms.

Unlike the data related to the previously discussed modes, the data related to materiality presented itself not so much as affordances and hindrances as something oriented around two related correspondences: materiality–spirituality and materiality–sociality. Thus, while advantages and disadvantages emerge, the subsequent discussion follows a slightly different pattern than the previous modes.

One approach to exploring the role of materiality as a mode of communication within AGC is through what I call "theology of the belly."[208] Simply put, belly theology in this book describes the direct correspondence between spirituality and materiality. Haynes notes a similar phenomenon among Copperbelt Pentecostals who value "moving in the Spirit." Weight gain is a prosperity metric indicating that one is "moving."[209] Likewise, Jessica Hardin has explored how fatness is perceived by evangelical Christians in Samoa. Although Hardin's discussion is pushing against simple fat-positive/fat-stigma dichotomies, arguing that often ambiguities exist in how fatness is interpreted due to social, economic, and embodied cues, her article highlights how body size possesses communicative properties.[210] Significant to this project, such communication happens on a nonverbal register; it is the physical presence (or absence) of a large stomach that conveys spiritual meaning within the community.[211]

---

208. This is slightly different than Jean-François Bayart's extended political understanding. In his seminal work, Bayart uses the phrase "politics of the belly" to depict the relationship between African leaders and the state. "'The goat eats where it is tethered' and . . . . those in power intend to 'eat.'" The use of the phrase "theology of the belly" in relation to orality and materiality is not intended to echo all of Bayart's observations although there is some natural overlap in his discussion on the relationship between accumulation, social mobility, and materiality. Bayart, *State in Africa*, lxxxv.

209. Haynes, *Moving by the Spirit*, 39, 72.

210. Hardin, "Christianity, Fat Talk, and Samoan Pastors"; for her discussion on learning to read and interpret fat, see pp. 187–88.

211. Site visit: Farming God's Way, May 16, 2017. Here is where the difference between my conception of belly theology differs from Bayart's belly politics. Although belly politics does operate at times within the church domain, I am interested in how the belly communicates on a non-verbal, material register.

An explicit example of how bellies communicate came up in conversation while I was traveling with several missionaries and AGC leaders. In a vulnerable moment of self-disclosure, one of the missionaries acknowledged that he has had to decline preaching invitations from close friends due to the fact that the community will not believe the pastor if the pastor tells them that the missionary did not leave millions of shillings behind for the pastor. This is because of the missionary's large physical stature; people assume he is a very wealthy individual and assume that if he visits the pastor, he (the missionary) will "bless" the pastor with a large financial gift. The missionary acknowledged that he does not have such large financial resources to give out at so many different churches; thus, he has had to say no to invitations that he would otherwise have enjoyed.[212]

On another occasion, belly theology manifested itself through the contents of a sermon. Rev. Miria Mukisa was preaching at Kahara AGC and she exhorted the congregation to give generously so that that the church's storehouse might be filled to help meet physical needs in the community. She continued, urging the people that she wanted to see their pastor grow a big belly by the time of her next visit for that would tell her that the people were giving. Herein the material was related to meeting physical needs, but the measurement of a generous spirit was the size of the pastor's stomach.[213] The belly itself becomes a physical metric, communicating the wealth and generosity of a congregation.[214]

Belly theology does not always necessitate a stomach but is shorthand for describing the relationship between materiality and spirituality. At one of the Kisugu Bible studies, the pastor asked the group what people look for in their coming to church. While the group did discuss reasons, such as "looking for truth" or "because its one's father's religion," they agreed that the majority of people go to church for some material component, whether physical healing, miracles, financial help, job opportunities, and even marriage partners.[215] While I initially interpreted this as church members saying that they valued physical or material realities at least as much as the spiritual, if not more so, further reflection suggested things were more complicated. Rather than being construed as a binary between the privileging of the spiritual or the physical, what the church personnel seemed to be articulating, both explicitly and implicitly, was an integration of values. The

---

212. Anonymous, May 16, 2017.

213. Hardin acknowledges the association between fatness and generosity. See Hardin, "Christianity, Fat Talk, and Samoan Pastors," 180.

214. Site visit: Kahara AGC, April 30, 2017.

215. Kisugu Bible study, May 4, 2017.

whole point of the interchange during the Bible study discussion was that people with physical or material concerns were choosing to come to the church, an overtly spiritual space. The implication of the discussion was not so much materialistic motives rather than spiritual ones as much as it was a window into an imaginary wherein people are not differentiating between a spiritual domain in their lives and a physical one.

Such understanding caused me to reconsider the persuasive powers of materiality, particularly in relation to the other modes of communication. When asked about the relationship between oral, print, and digital modes to materiality, Ouma immediately said, "All of these relate to that one [material]."[216] He illustrated by taking an example from church the previous Sunday morning. A woman named Irene had praised God during the oral testimony portion of the service, all the while holding a brightly colored handbag. Ouma noted that the handbag was the material evidence that God had blessed her: "If you say that God has blessed me, people will say, 'With what?' They will want to see." Thus, two observations can be made. First, from a communication perspective, the *material* handbag substantiated the *oral* testimony, even though it operated on a nonverbal level. The brightly colored handbag communicated something that the oral word did not. In fact, more than merely illustrative, the material object of her handbag communicated something the spoken word *could* not communicate. This leads to a second, closely related, point that I was discovering. For the woman, there was no compartmentalizing her spiritual blessing from the physical object; the spiritual blessing was realized through materiality.

The natural conclusion to belly theology is that the material evidences divine favor. As Ouma said, "A big car means a big God." Such thinking tends to be associated with what has been termed the health and wealth gospel or prosperity gospel. The natural corollary is that no belly means no God. Missionaries recounted stories of people leaving AGC, saying, "How can we follow you [the AGC pastor] if you do not have a car? You are blocking the blessings from flowing from heaven."[217] Likewise, AGC pastors recounted the challenges as people wonder how a poor pastor can bless anyone. The expectation is, "If you are a good preacher and God blesses you, then you have to look like it. And people will listen to you."[218] Such an attitude echoes sentiments expressed through Haynes's experience wherein her host purchased and displayed new cooking pots as material evidence of God's provision and prosperity. Shiny, new cooking pots communicated

---

216. Ouma, May 22, 2017.
217. Stanfield and Stanfield, May 9, 2017.
218. Ouma, May 22, 2017; Mukisa and Mukisa, April 22, 2017.

to all who walked through the kitchen that divine provision was enabling the pastor's family to "live well."[219] In such contexts, whether among Copperbelt Pentecostals or AGC members, material prosperity was not just for materiality's sake, but physical things such as new pots or a vehicle attract attention, becoming a platform for people to listen and witness God's provision. Such understanding has tremendous implications for the way the denomination communicates and is perceived within the local community, particularly in light of the fact that not a single AGC congregation is able to support a full-time pastor financially.

The recognition that material objects and spiritual blessing are always contextualized provides a natural segue, for not only is there a direct correspondence between materiality and spirituality, there is also correspondence between materiality and sociality. Whatever the relationship is between the material and the immaterial in Christianity, it is worked out in the context of a particular community. In AGC's context, materiality not only validates personal spirituality, such as Irene with her handbag, but a denomination's favor with God is demonstrated to society by their physical assets. An illustration came in relation to the physical presence, or lack thereof, of the denomination's bishop.

Dhikusooka recounted to me how a local religious group, what he called a cult, had recently built a new building for the neighboring police force. With frustration in his voice, Dhikusooka described how the country's president had praised the cult because of the physical contribution they had made. "No one touches them," commented Dhikusooka. The materiality of the cult's contribution established the group's identity and ensured that the community would not disturb their religious activities. In contrast, AGC has been disturbed. Dhikusooka had recently found himself in the regional police office due to some legal wrangles between certain local community members and several AGC churches on Buvuma Island in Lake Victoria. To Dhikusooka's frustration, the police commander did not know AGC at all. Instead, the commander demanded, "Who is your bishop? Where is your headquarters?" In this context, the physical presence of the bishop communicates something to the community. It is not on a verbal register, but one of material possession. Dhikusooka explained, "When you look at the bishop, people look at what he has; they look at his car, his education." Dhikusooka recounted how on a visit to Kenya, he witnessed the material presence of AGC Kenya and found himself respecting and admiring their bishop because of his vehicle and education (a PhD awarded from Drew University, USA). In comparison, he described how "he felt small," and confessed he wished AGC

---

219. Haynes, "Pentecostalism and the Morality of Money," 20–22.

Uganda's bishop also had such material assets.[220] For Dhikusooka, the lack of material presence in the community has left AGC vulnerable because people neither know nor respect the denomination. As Dhikusooka said, "Now here we are—who are we?" Such comments raise substantial questions, for the failure to communicate on a material register has, for at least one leader, now placed the identity of AGC in jeopardy.[221]

The relationship between materiality and the denomination's identity expressed itself most vividly and most broadly in relation to physical church buildings. A little background information is necessary to set the stage for understanding the church personnel's perspective on church structures. In the early days of the pastoral training program, the mission had established a roofing assistance scheme. If the local community provided the supplies and labor for the church walls, the mission would help cover the cost of putting on a church roof. This was seen as a cost-sharing venture, dependent upon the initiation of the local congregation but matched by the financial resources of the mission. Inevitably, the mission could not maintain its financial commitments and the scheme essentially collapsed.[222] However, the ghost of such material assistance has been far from exorcised, and several church members discussed how the abolition of the scheme has resulted in churches struggling to afford permanent buildings in their communities.[223]

The lack of financial means and, consequently, lack of material development has had immediate implications for the growth of the church. Maria Mukisa described how the AGC church in Masindi had been offered a plot of ground within the town for development by the municipality for six million Ugandan shillings. Neither the local church nor the denomination could afford the price. In time, the pastor left and the congregation collapsed. Likewise, the Mukisas shared how they have struggled to purchase land for their own church, Bukasa AGC. They currently meet in a former chicken-breeding barn but cannot develop the property until they have purchased it. Lamentably, they have watched as the price has increased from eight to ten to twelve million shillings as real estate values increase. In rather stark terms, they described how without land, there was no future for

220. Dhikusooka, April 23, 2017.

221. Dhikusooka, May 10, 2017.

222. On occasion, special gifts are given to the mission, usually from visitors, to help with a specific local church. These funds are forwarded to the denomination, which distributes them to the local church council.

223. Permanent would be defined as having plastered brick walls and a tin sheet roof. In contrast, a temporary structure uses mud, sticks, or boards for the walls and may include a thatched roof. Focus Group: Kamuli, April 7, 2017; Focus Group: Kahara, April 29, 2017; Mukisa and Mukisa, April 22, 2017; Dhikusooka, May 10, 2017.

Bukasa AGC. The reason is the lack of a material building. It was reported that people get saved and want to come to church only to be discouraged by the temporary nature of the church building. They leave and go find another church.[224] Omri concurred, describing how a government official, such as a resident district commissioner, will not feel comfortable praying under a tree, assuming that people will despise him or her, saying, "My God is not a big God."[225] Dhikusooka agreed, noting that a temporary structure can be easily "swept away by the town council."[226]

Therefore, the lack of proper physical building communicates not only a theological message but it also says something about the direction and movement of the church. As the pastor of Kahara AGC said, "The physical development shows the community we are going forward." This language echoes similar sentiments to the "moving" rhetoric Haynes discovered among Copperbelt Pentecostals. This is a significant element to understanding materiality, for physical development not only communicates theologically but it communicates modernization.[227] A physical building conveys a message to the community that the denomination is embracing modernity. Therefore, Omri acknowledged, "Without a building, people see that there is no vision or future for that church or ministry." Sitting in Kahara AGC's unroofed structure with mud thick underfoot from recent rain, Pastor Samuel linked the lack of materiality directly to the lack of church planting, saying, with frustration in his voice, "How can we open other churches when the mother church is like this?"

Such indicting comments reveal how matters of communication, materiality, sociality, and spirituality are intricately related. While material things communicate on a nonverbal register, those things carry particular associations with modernity and identity. Furthermore, within AGC' social context, these material things reveal something about the nature of God. AGC's lack of material things, such as permanent church buildings, has led to AGC being perceived as not modern. Consequently, such a perception has limited the denomination's opportunities to generate greater spiritual impact among certain communities.

---

224. Mukisa and Mukisa, April 22, 2017.

225. Omri, May 12, 2017.

226. Dhikusooka, May 10, 2017; Haynes, likewise, discusses the desire of congregations to register with the city council so as to secure a plot of land for a building. "This is the great dream of all Pentecostal churches, though few are able to make it a reality" (Haynes, *Moving by the Spirit*, 31).

227. Site visit: Kahara AGC, April 30, 2017.

CONCLUSION

This chapter began with an overview of AGC's appreciation for the Bible. Since the Bible is understood as intricately related to personal identity among AGC members, how it is mediated carries significance for understanding communication dynamics but also for understanding personhood as well. This observation raised the stakes for the second portion of the chapter, which provided a detailed overview of four different modes of church communication. What emerged was that while church personnel appreciated how oral communication necessitates the body (or embodiment) in a unique way, often lending itself to multisensory and affective engagement, the OM's understanding of orality (or what has been labeled as **orality$_2$**) has not been as quite a perfect fit for the AGC context as supposed. Church personnel expressed concerns, both internally—regarding the storytelling methodology, but also externally—related to the church personnel's social contexts. Regarding the former, some of the supposedly oral methods were not as user-friendly as expected and regarding the latter, orality, which lacks any material artifact, failed to achieve or assist in constructing the modern and sophisticated sensibilities, which are valued by the church members' communities. Rather, orality was interpreted as perpetuating a traditional embeddedness with little hope of forward (or modern) momentum.

Although in varying ways and degrees, both printed communication and digital communication were understood as more helpful in achieving this desired disembedding. The material artifactuality of both print and digital communication means that, while both were interpreted as more costly (particularly digital media), their artifactual quality makes them popular for, among other things, Bible learning, referencing, interpreting and remembering. Furthermore, their artifactual nature carried social value for constructing modern identities. Finally, materiality itself was discussed as the non-verbal category, yet a mode that boldly communicated the measure of one's spirituality and social standing. Rather than being interpreted as peripheral, material things were discussed as integral for conveying certain modern sensibilities; consequently, the lack of such material objects was interpreted as hindering not only the church's social standing but also the denomination's spiritual influence.

Along the way, numerous issues have emerged in this chapter as worthy of further analysis in light of this project's overall goal of understanding the reception of the OM by AGC. These issues have included questions about embodiment, identity, affectivity, economics, material objects, and social expectations. It is time to turn attention to further analysis of the interconnectivity of these key themes.

6

Analysis

*Materiality Complexities in
AGC's Reception of Orality*

INTRODUCTION

IN THIS CHAPTER, THE overarching question regarding the reception of the Orality Movement by Africa Gospel Church finally receives a direct answer. Speaking in broad terms, AGC appreciates the embodied and affective nature of oral communication, particularly exemplified in storytelling, for both evangelism and discipleship. Thus, as a ministry tool, oral methodologies were deemed effective. Nevertheless, the OM's understanding of orality (or **orality$_2$**) has, at times, failed to recognize how influential the external social forces are on the church within the context in which they are trying to communicate their Christian faith. Specifically, oral storytelling as introduced by members of the OM has not been able to, or at least has yet to, meet the educational, economic, or social expectations of AGC members. Such unmet expectations have limited the church's spiritual impact. This mixed reception of orality relates to multiple kinds of materiality. Orality affords a *materiality of embodiment* but nevertheless fails to produce another kind of materiality, namely, a *materiality of artifact*. In summary, it is orality's lack of this second kind of materiality, material artifactuality, that carries such concerns within AGC's social imaginary.

This chapter is divided into three sections. The first delves into recent scholarship on the materiality of religion. Scholars from a spectrum of disciplines, including religious studies, anthropology, philosophy, cultural studies, communication, and media studies, have begun advocating for an appreciation and consideration of the essential role that material things play in mediating religious experience. This interest has required fresh inquiry into, among other things, the role of the body and the entire sensorium within religious practice. While one may intuit the connection between materiality, embodiment, and communication, it is worth elaborating why religious materiality proves helpful for analyzing research data on communication.

This book's overarching concern relates to how different modes of communication convey modern, religious identities. In chapter 5, I mentioned that as I conducted interviews and focus group discussions in the field that were oriented towards matters of communication, I was surprised that the conversation kept returning to material issues. Why were material concerns being raised in the context of communication? Were these research conversations becoming merely occasions for church members to share with the outsider different individual or corporate church needs in hopes of some material, or specifically, financial, assistance? Granted, there may have been some of those dynamics at work at times; however, I became convinced that one of the primary results of my research was that matters of communication for the church members often meant an association with material objects. While familiar with requests for material assistance from living in Uganda, I had never considered such material requests in the context of communication. On one level, the request for school fees, assistance with the church building, or even food for hungry stomachs carried an obvious communication message of need for education, shelter, and nourishment. However, on another level, the absence of such material things was communicating something else, something with typically negative connotations about an individual person's identity or even the denomination's own self-understanding. In light of this surprising, for me, link between communication and materiality, this chapter's first section probes into the nature of this religious materiality. Birgit Meyer and James K. A. Smith, along with others, introduce several useful concepts for deepening an understanding of these material dynamics within the religious communication of AGC's context. With a theoretical framework in place, the second portion of the chapter explicitly addresses how the church has appreciated and appropriated orality. The third section examines how particular social forces seem to have been underestimated by those promoting oral communication.

A THEORETICAL FRAMEWORK FOR ANALYSIS

The Materiality of Religion

In the introduction to a volume on religion, media, and culture, David Morgan credits James Carey as effecting a "cultural turn" in religion and communication studies.[1] Carey, in his influential article "A Cultural Approach to Communication," contrasts what he calls the *transmission* view of communication, understood by terms such as "imparting," "sending," or "giving information to others," with a *ritual* view of communication demonstrated in words such as "sharing," "participation," and "association." In spite of being less common today, Carey argues that the ritual view is much older than the transmission understanding.[2] The transmission view arose with the age of exploration and discovery wherein communication and transportation were simultaneously understood. This came to have moral implications so that technology was interpreted as enabling Christians to transmit and spread abroad the knowledge of the kingdom of God.

In contrast, Carey describes the ritual view of communication as "directed not toward the extension of messages in space but toward the maintenance of society in time; not the act of imparting information but the representation of shared beliefs."[3] The accent shifts from the "transmission of intelligent information" through "the sermon, instruction, and admonition," to "the prayer, the chant, and the ceremony," in an attempt to understand "the construction and maintenance of an ordered, meaningful cultural world that can serve as a control and container for human action."[4] This shift in accent, as encouraged by Carey, has informed Morgan and others in exploring religious materiality.

Central to this shift is the development of the concept of mediation within the studies of both culture and religion. Angela Zito argues, "A good deal of human life is about making the invisible visible, that is, *mediating it*." What she and others are trying to emphasize is that there is no unmediated access to reality; all of reality is, in some sense, a process of mediation. Thus, for her, "mediation is the construction of social reality where people are constantly engaged in producing the material world around them, even as they are, in turn, produced by it. Every social practice moves through and is carried upon a material framework or vehicle."[5]

1. Morgan, "Introduction," 2–10.
2. Carey, "Cultural Approach to Communication," 13–19.
3. Carey, "Cultural Approach to Communication," 16.
4. Carey, "Cultural Approach to Communication," 16. Emphasis added.
5. Zito, "Culture," 77; Zito refers to her own definition elsewhere. See Zito, "Can Television Mediate," 724–38.

Far from being dismissed or regulated to second-class, materiality plays an essential role in the process of mediation. Philosopher Charles Taylor talks about how "ideas always come in history wrapped up in certain practices, even if these are only discursive practices."[6] Thus, in much the same way, he is describing how central practice or material form relates to conceptions of the invisible, or in this case, something as seemingly immaterial as a raw idea. Both Taylor and Zito are calling attention to the fact that mediation and the material are necessary to the process of making real, or revealing, the presence of the invisible.

Such an understanding of mediation, when applied to religion, immediately finds a generic definition, such as "a set of beliefs," as not only remarkably inadequate but also tinged with Protestant interiorization overtones.[7] Instead, there has been a reconceptualizing of religion that argues that such ideas are always situated in material forms. Morgan summarizes this renewed interest in the ritual view of religious communication, insinuating that among some scholars, the transmission of belief approach has now become what he calls the "older framework": "Religion has come to be widely understood as embodied practices that cultivate relations among people, places, and non-human forces—nature, spirits, ancestors, saints, gods—resulting in communities and sensibilities that shape those who participate. This departs from an older framework in which religions were defined as systems of ideas to which believers assented."[8] Anthropologist Birgit Meyer would agree with such sentiments.

Meyer notes that media are essential to these embodied practices, including modern (i.e., new) media such as film, television, or computers, but they also include material objects, such as icons, sacred texts, and even the human body.[9] Media are not just carriers of messages or meaning, which is Carey's transmission view, but they themselves shape the participant's religious experience. Therefore, while careful to avoid any technological determinism, such scholars of materiality are trying to expand the aperture of understanding to emphasize how essential material

---

6. Taylor, *Modern Social Imaginaries*, 33.

7. For Asad's classic critique of Clifford Geertz on religion as a system of beliefs, see Asad, *Genealogies of Religion*, 27–54; see also Vries, "Introduction," 1–98.

8. In light of the previous discussion on early Protestantism (see chapter 2), it is significant to highlight that what Morgan describes as the older framework of religion is the new one brought by Protestantism, challenging the older medieval understanding of religion as communal practice embodied in ritual. Morgan, "Religion and Media," 347.

9. Meyer, "Introduction," 11.

objects, discourses, and bodies are to invoking and mediating some sense (or experience) of the divine.[10]

Before continuing, it is necessary to clarify briefly that this renewed interest in material things should not be misunderstood as a philosophical materialism. These scholars are not arguing for a philosophy that upholds only matter nor an understanding that material things are of more value than immaterial or spiritual concerns. On the contrary, this turn towards the material is rather an expression of a curiosity in how materiality, that is the gritty stuff of daily life, plays an inherent role in mediating religious experiences with the seemingly immaterial.

With that clarification in mind, attention returns to Meyer's development of media as embodied practices. This is part of her more ambitious project to refurbish the notion of aesthetics by drawing from Maurice Merleau-Ponty's phenomenology of perception.[11] Merleau-Ponty (1908–61) provided acknowledgement of and argued for the importance of sensory knowledge. Meyer's development of aesthetics is primarily an attempt to counter what she calls an interpretative study of religion. Such a view, also understood as the representational approach, tends to focus its analysis or interpretation upon understanding how religious symbols represent or carry particular meanings.[12] Such an approach tends to dismiss the role of the body in religious experience and, consequently, the affective role that certain objects, images, and other material forms play in religious encounters. Thus, she appeals for an approach to religion that incorporates "the material, bodily, sensational and sensory dimension."[13] She calls this a *religious aesthetic*, "an embodied and embedded praxis through which subjects relate to other subjects and objects and which is grounded in and offers the ground for religious experience."[14] Essential to her definition is an understanding of *formation*, a term she uses rather than community to capture both the social nature of these religious groups but also to give attention to the processes, often performative in nature, that shape (i.e., form) the religious subjects within such groups. Thus, she argues for what she calls

---

10. This not only applies to one's relationship with the divine but also one's relationship with one's self. Miller argues that clothing, rather than being merely superficial, "plays a considerable and active part in constituting the particular experience of the self, in determining what the self is" (Miller, *Stuff*, 40; see also 12–41).

11. Merleau-Ponty, *Phenomenology of Perception*; Merleau-Ponty, *Primacy of Perception*.

12. Notice the similarity to Carey's language mentioned above.

13. Meyer understands sensation to relate to feelings and sensory to relate to the senses. See footnote 27 in Meyer, "Religious Sensations," 19.

14. Meyer, "Aesthetics," 27.

aesthetic formations, a theoretical framework that captures "the formative impact of a shared aesthetic through which subjects are shaped by tuning their senses, inducing experiences, molding their bodies, and making sense, and which materializes in things."[15]

This concept of formations holds promise for forthcoming analysis as AGC's pastoral training could easily be identified as the formational training wherein pastors learn the church's embedded and embodied aesthetic practices. Meyer calls such practices *sensational forms*, "relatively fixed, authorized modes of invoking and organizing access to the transcendental, thereby creating and sustaining links between believers in the context of particular religious regimes."[16] In essence, they are the acceptable religious habits that "bind and bond" those of a particular religious comportment to each other and to God.[17]

Meyer's approach has sought to investigate how various old and new media have influenced different religious groups' sensational forms. She helpfully reiterates that new media never come as "purely instrumental" but always within complicated negotiation processes wherein questions of authorization are in tension.[18] It is these complicated negotiation processes that this current project investigates. While no one in AGC or WGM has used terminology such as sensational forms or religious aesthetics, Meyer's understanding of these ideas provides categories to begin to recognize the material role of the body in religious communication as well as the related but distinct role of material objects in AGC's aesthetic formation. Consequently, the subsequent analysis could be described, at some level, as an attempt to understand how differing sensational forms or religious practices within different modes of communication enable or fail to invoke an encounter with God.

Cultural Liturgies Project (Christian Culture Theory)

While Birgit Meyer is writing as a social scientist within a broad religious framework, James K. A. Smith[19] writes as a Canadian Reformed philosopher with Radical Orthodox sympathies.[20] Smith offers a more concentrated

15. Meyer, "From Imagined Communities," 7.
16. Meyer, "Aesthetics," 27.
17. Meyer, "From Imagined Communities," 13.
18. Meyer, "From Imagined Communities," 14.
19. Smith (PhD, Villanova) teaches at Calvin College.
20. Radical Orthodoxy (RO) emerged in the 1990s as a sharp critique of "the secular" and theology's increasing reliance on and accommodation for modernity's supposedly "neutral" commitments, namely its privileging of the "rational" and "scientific." The

articulation of how one particular religion, namely Christianity, engages with and, at times, counters culture. Smith's "Cultural Liturgies" started out as an apologia for Christian education and, even more specifically, for a Christian university education. However, what unfolds in his ambitious three-volume trilogy[21] is a theology[22] of culture.[23] His concern is to develop a Christian cultural theory that shifts the emphasis off Cartesian understanding of human persons as primarily "thinking beings" or even "believing beings" and instead recognizes persons as "beings of desire" or what he simply calls "lovers."[24] Such a philosophical anthropological reorientation reframes the role of Christian education from merely transmitting information, even what might be called "Christian information or ideas,[25] to the formation of desires, a reemphasis not on the head but on the heart or what he calls the *cardia*, the "gut."[26] Central to this is a shift from an emphasis on worldview, a popular evangelical concept that tends to traffic primarily in concepts and ideas, to Charles Taylor's category of imaginary, that which

---

chief adherents, John Milbank, Catherine Pickstock, and Graham Ward, have sought, on the one hand, to reestablish a theological framework that draws on the church's tradition, particularly Augustine and Aquinas, while on the other hand, addressing realities in today's postmodern context. For key texts, see Milbank, *Theology and Social Theory*; Milbank et al., *Radical Orthodoxy*; Pickstock, *After Writing*; Ward, *Cities of God*. Smith has been strongly influenced by RO as is evident in his own contributions to RO and in his subsequent thinking. Smith, *Introducing Radical Orthodoxy*; Smith and Olthuis, *Radical Orthodoxy and the Reformed Tradition*.

21. Smith, *Desiring the Kingdom*; Smith, *Imagining the Kingdom*; Smith, *Awaiting the King*.

22. It is appropriate to note that, while employed for heuristic purposes in this chapter, Smith's labeling his project as a "theology of culture," may be a slight misnomer. One cannot help but notice his preference for philosophical dialogue partners. While theology is not absent, note his use of Augustine, his use of the biblical text itself is pauce. At least one reviewer noted this may cause consternation among Smith's more conservative Reformed audience. Pitts, "Book Review: Forming Christian Lovers."

23. Anthropologists may quibble with Smith's use of the word "culture" or the phrase, "philosophical anthropology." Perhaps that is fair as he is a philosopher, not a trained anthropologist. Angela Zito's short discussion on culture as meaning, as practice, and finally as mediation may be helpful to locate where to situate Smith's thought. He seems to land somewhere between culture as practice and mediation. One imagines he would be sympathetic to the religion-as-materiality scholars' understanding of culture as mediation. However in personal correspondence, Smith indicated that he only knew of Meyer tangentially. Zito, "Culture"; James K. A. Smith, personal communication, email, November 22, 2017.

24. Smith, *Desiring the Kingdom*, 35.

25. While Smith does not discuss Carey, one senses Smith is reacting to what Carey labeled as the transmission view of communication. See discussion above.

26. Smith, *Desiring the Kingdom*, 35, 37–73.

includes ideas but operates more on the radar of intuition and imagination.[27] Smith, also drawing on the work of Merleau-Ponty,[28] argues that this shift is possible if proper attention is given to the embodied nature of human persons. Meaning happens, at least initially, through the bodily senses, a point, he argues, that the concept of worldview seems often to ignore entirely.[29] Thus, while not anti-rational, Smith, similarly to Meyer, calls for re-appreciation of the role of the body[30] and its ability to perceive meaning, which leads him to argue that the habits (*habitus*) of the body, drawing on the work of Pierre Bourdieu (1930–2002), have tremendous capacity for shaping one's desires or loves.[31] There are regular (thin) practices that everyone has, but there are also identity-shaping (thick) practices, which he calls rituals. These rituals, the ones that give ultimate meaning, are actually, *religious liturgies*.[32] Thus, cultural, secular institutions such as the mall, the stadium, and the university are not just neutral sites of consumerism, entertainment, or information but instead are religious, liturgical sites that shape one's bodily practices and, thus, one's love (or worship) away from God. Smith's proposed solution to this problem is not necessarily an anti-cultural stance but one that is aware and, at times, antithetical, wherein counter-liturgies must be cultivated. Only through such counter-formations, primarily found within the ecclesial context of worship in which he includes both the church and the university, can Christians both form and re-form their own desires rightly towards God.[33]

Smith elaborates this framework, what he also calls a "liturgical anthropology," by suggesting that imagination is the nexus of meaning and, specifically, narrative is the language of the heart: "As we saw with

27. For Smith's specific critique of worldview and his articulation for using imaginary, see *Desiring the Kingdom*, 63–71; for Taylor's own development of imaginary, see Taylor, *Modern Social Imaginaries*.

28. Smith, *Imagining the Kingdom*, 31–73.

29. One is reminded of Meyer's reaction to the "interpretative" or "representation" approach to religion. See above.

30. Smith's attention to embodiment reflects a similar concern in RO thought. For examples, see chapters 7 and 8: "Erotics: God's Sex" by Gerard Loughlin and "Bodies: The Displaced Body of Jesus Christ" by Graham Ward, in Milbank et al., *Radical Orthodoxy: A New Theology*, 143–62, 163–81; "Displaced Bodies" also appears as part of Ward's larger argument in *Cities of God*. The preceding chapter 3, entitled "Transcorporeality: The Ontological Scandal," is also relevant (Ward, *Cities of God*, 81–96).

31. Smith, *Imagining the Kingdom*, 75–100.

32. Here again, one senses Smith's indebtedness to RO as its adherents bestow liturgy a central place in their theological project. See especially Pickstock, *After Writing*.

33. See chapter 5, "Practicing for the Kingdom," and chapter 6, "A Christian University is for Lovers," Smith, *Desiring the Kingdom*, 155–214, 215–30.

both Merleau-Ponty and Bourdieu,[34] stories 'mean' on a register that is visceral and bodily, more aesthetic than analytic, 'made sense of' more by the imagination than the intellect. Stories are something we learn 'by heart' in the sense that they *mean* on a register that eludes articulation and analysis. . . . This philosophical anthropology, which sees the (affective, preconscious) imagination as the center of gravity of human action, thus accords a central role to *story* or narrative."[35] Thus, the imagination allows one to envision the *telos*, the good life toward which one's heart worships (longs or desires).[36] The liturgies of significance (or *habitus* of weighted meaning) are actually compressed narratives, performative actions that invite either an individual or a group to reenact, re-narrate the larger story within which a person or community operates. Therefore, describing what he calls a "general poetics," Smith is trying to establish an "aesthetic understanding," note the similarity to Meyer's own language, of human persons that, giving central place to imagination, is "both poetic and narrative. And this aesthetics is rooted in an embodied comportment to the world, at the nexus of body and story."[37] This is summarily put, "I cannot answer the question, what do I love? Without (at least implicitly) answering the question, what story do I believe? [sic]"[38] Therefore, both the church and the university are sites of formation, where embodied perceptions are sanctified through story and the re-storying of the imagination so that Christians can participate in the kingdom and mission of God.[39]

---

34. While Smith does not dialogue with Meyer or Morgan, it is significant to note that Merleau-Ponty and Bourdieu are his two key dialogue partners in volume 2, both of whom have influenced scholars in areas of religion, media studies, and anthropology. See Morgan, "Introduction"; in her seminal (and already referenced) inaugural lecture, Meyer, likewise, refers to Merleau-Ponty directly, but also includes Roodenburg's article on Bourdieu in her endnotes. Meyer, "Religious Sensations"; Roodenburg, "Pierre Bourdieu," 215–26. Thus, while Smith begins with a philosophical rather than anthropological starting point, it is significant that he and those investigating religious materiality are drawing on the same sources.

35. Smith, *Imagining the Kingdom*, 109. Emphasis original.

36. See Taylor's discussion on what he calls "fullness" and "human flourishing." Taylor, *Secular Age*, 5–20.

37. For Smith's earlier discussion on aisthesis and aesthetics, an account quite similar to Meyer's own analysis, albeit Smith's is in direct dialogue with Augustine, see Smith, "Staging the Incarnation," 123–39.

38. Smith, *Imagining the Kingdom*, 129–30. To avoid confusion that he is inadvertently returning to a more "rational" adherence of belief, in a footnote, Smith clarifies that this understanding of belief is in line with Bourdieu's sense of "practical belief," that is "a state of the body."

39. Smith, *Imagining the Kingdom*, 157. For his rather heavy emphasis on the role of story in sanctifying the imagination, see pp. 160–64.

Smith's cultural theory fills in and enlarges what Meyer has begun to develop in several ways. First his scholarship reaffirms Meyer's emphasis on the significance of aesthetics for understanding culture, in general, and religion, in particular. Neither Meyer nor Smith is interested in nonrational theory; however, they are seeking to address the tendency to conceptualize human beings as primarily rational animals that make meaning within the human mind. Thus, Smith's interest in the role of the human body parallels Meyer's own work, refuting an understanding of religion and, particularly, Christianity that explicitly or even implicitly affirms a mind/body dualism. Both Smith and Meyer reiterate the need to validate the role of the body's sensorium not as an end in itself but in an attempt to develop a more multifaceted, holistic understanding that includes both the cognitive and affective faculties of individual persons and their shared communities.

Second, Smith provides several additional conceptual tools to add to the analytical tool belt. Smith refers to *religious liturgies*—these thick, identity-forming practices or sensational forms that are aimed towards differing visions of human flourishing or what Smith calls *telos*. As discussed shortly, *telos* becomes an analytical means to inquire how orality affords or hinders the process of moving towards the Africa Gospel Church's intended goal(s).

This theoretical section has introduced the developing area of religious materiality, dialoguing primarily with Meyer and Smith. Significantly, these two different strands of scholarship are drawing from similar sources and are seeking to reconceptualize approaches to human persons and religious practice. Furthermore, they help illuminate how two different kinds of materiality, that of material objects and that of the human body enabling religious experience. It is time to see how these ideas play out in the material communication practices of AGC.

AFRICA GOSPEL CHURCH'S RECEPTION OF THE ORALITY MOVEMENT

Esther Atyanga's Story

This section of the book is the culmination of the previous chapters, bringing together the data from the last chapter with the theoretical tools offered by Meyer and Smith in an analysis of AGC's reception of the OM. One particular incident from the field captures the essence behind the church's appreciation of oral storytelling.[40]

40. It is necessary to reiterate that while the OM has conceptualized orality in broader terms, AGC has tended to interpret orality in almost exclusively "storytelling" terms. I acknowledge that the ensuing analysis of oral storytelling as "orality" may not necessarily apply to all other genres of oral communication. Nonetheless, since AGC

While attending the WGM/AGC twenty-fifth anniversary festivities (December 7–9, 2017) in Kampala, I was in mid-conversation with the newly reelected Assistant Bishop Martin Owor when we were interrupted. A girl in a pale green dress came up and she asked if she could tell us a story. We both turned and gave her our full attention, and she proceeded to narrate in English the less familiar biblical story of the prophet Elisha being mocked by a rowdy group of youths (2 Kings 2:23–25). Her performance took less than sixty seconds and, for all practical purposes, was almost 100 percent accurate.[41] Both Owor and I appreciated her storytelling and courage to share and then resumed our conversation.[42] Significantly, such an incident is more than just an endearing research episode; it provides a possible window through which glimpses can be seen of how the church has appreciated and incorporated orality into its aesthetic formation.

From the focus group discussions, personal interviews, site visits, two interrelated positive things became apparent about AGC's reception of orality. First, AGC affirmed that orality, understood most often by the church as oral Bible storytelling, affords affective biblical engagement and even, at times, spiritual transformation.[43] Second, there was evidence that orality as understood by the OM has become authorized as a legitimate sensational form for mediating God's presence within AGC. Both of these deserve elaboration.

AGC's Appreciation of Orality

"When they read, they all doze but when I [the pastor] tell a story, they wake up."[44] This was the observation of Rev. Martin Owor regarding the use of orality in his congregation. If church personnel such as Owor were able to articulate the affective power of oral storytelling to awaken his congregants, then the question emerges: What is it about orality, and storytelling in particular, that causes it to engage audiences affectively? This project suggests that at least part of the answer is the unique, embodied nature of oral communication. At some level, this is true of any generic oral communication (**orality$_1$**), but it is

---

is the object of my analysis, the following discussion uses orality and oral storytelling interchangeably.

41. The only detail I noticed to be missing from her retelling was the mentioning of Elisha visiting Mount Carmel before proceeding to Samaria.

42. After completing the story, I did ask the girl her name, Esther Atyanga. Africa Gospel Church/World Gospel Mission Uganda 25th Year Anniversary Celebration, Participatory observation, December 8, 2017.

43. This was discussed at length in chapter 5's section on affordances of orality.

44. Focus Group: AGC leaders, April 5, 2017.

even more relevant when considering orality within the OM's **orality$_2$** paradigm because their broad conception of orality includes numerous artistic genres, including dance, song, storytelling, and drama.

Qualification of this connection between embodiment and orality (here, I am again focusing primarily on **orality$_2$**) is important, and while this was discussed in the previous chapter, it deserves reiteration. While print or digital modes of communication can and do incorporate the body, orality affords the possibility of a multisensory communication event that is inherent in a way not necessarily found in the other modes. Print and even electronic modes can and often do incorporate the bodies of the communicators; however, the printed artifact or digital screen also allows for a proximity or a distance within the communication event. One can read a letter from a friend and while such an activity would qualify as a communication event, the friend's physical body is not immediately necessary. The physical letter serves as a proxy, enabling a distance between bodies so that at least one party's physical body does not have to be present. Likewise, one can listen to a radio or a podcast, which would be classified as an embodied experience, and yet, at least one of the parties is absent, mediated into the communication event through electronic (i.e., disembodied) means. This is not always the case; often, print or digital media are used to enhance a communication event wherein all the communicators are present. However, while the use of both digital- and print-reliant media can include embodiment, they can also afford a disembodiment for at least one of the parties. This is their strength as they allow a transcendence of both time and space.

Oral communication is different; embodiment is intrinsic to orality for both parties in a way it is not necessarily so in either the digital or printed mode. Communication does not happen if both parties' physical bodies are not present. This is in no way trying to over-romanticize orality. The inability of oral communication to transcend beyond the time and place of both interlocutors is one of its liabilities. That being said, this argument is simply acknowledging that while the body can and does play a role in print and digital media, there are communication events wherein the printed page, the electronic sound wave, or the digital screen allows for an eclipsing of the other interlocutor's physical body. In contrast, oral communication is distinct, guaranteeing personal, embodied, although not necessarily effective, communication.

It is worth a side note here to acknowledge again the complicated nature of a sermon. While one might argue that preaching from a manuscript is technically a print-reliant event, this discussion is not arguing that the body of the preacher does not play a significant role in conveying meaning. Such an example illustrates how an *embodied* print-reliant event can likewise draw on the advantages that the body brings to the communication experience, advantages enumerated below. Where print and digital media incorporate the body, they, likewise, leverage such advantages as oral communication. However, not all print- or digital-reliant events include the body (or bodies) in the same way as oral communication, which always includes bodies. Thus, it is only in this limited sense that this project is highlighting how oral communication uniquely affords the possibilities of capitalizing on the significant role of the body in conveying and constructing meaning in every oral experience.

Having established orality's inherent embodiment, it is helpful to revisit Smith's understanding of the relationship between the body and meaning-making. According to Smith's argument, perception happens initially on a sensory level, in a precognitive way, an intuited sort of "being-in-the-world."[45] Smith comes at this in a lengthy development of Bourdieu's understanding of *habitus*, a disposition in the world that is neither instinctive nor necessarily deliberate.[46] Instead, this *habitus* operates from an in-between place, and, as Smith summarizes, is "the habitual way we construct our world."[47] One's *habitus* cannot be formed without one's social community, for in the social interaction one imbibes the practices that make one "native," a local who knows what to expect in a particular set of circumstances. For Bourdieu and Smith, one has to recognize that this local understanding happens on a *"practical sense"* level, that "know-how that resides in the body, that unique sort of understanding of the world that is identified with a *habitus*." This practical sense is a way of "'making sense of' the world'" but operates more on the level of what Smith calls "the feel of the game" than on a conscious, deliberate register.[48]

What needs to be highlighted for our immediate purposes is that this habitual way of being in the world, of perceiving without even realizing, happens through the body. Furthermore, it is shaped or formed in the body through practice. Thus, no one is born a native, but such a practical-sense orientation is cultivated as one is habituated into the embodied practices of a community.[49] Thus, Smith and Bourdieu are giving the body an intricate role, center-stage in fact, for constructing meaning in the world.

By considering orality's inherent embodiment and by exploring Smith's argument that the body is integral for constructing meaning in the

45. This is a common phrase used by Smith.
46. See chapter 3, "The Social Body," Smith, *Imagining the Kingdom*, 75–100.
47. Smith, *Imagining the Kingdom*, 81–83.
48. Smith, *Imagining the Kingdom*, 85–87.
49. Smith, *Imagining the Kingdom*, 93.

world, we are more equipped to realize why AGC's appreciates orality, specifically storytelling and even how, at times, it elicits spiritual transformation. Smith and Bourdieu argue that meaningful perception happens in the body and orality foregrounds the body in the communication event. This was dramatically demonstrated in the Exodus song witnessed at Bulyango AGC, which incorporated an assemblage of oral song, dance, and drama. But it also appeared in the oral Bible storytelling performances. Whether it was Esther's slip of a young girl physique or Joseph's developing manhood stature,[50] or Mama Annette's weary and worn elderly body,[51] for each of these oral communication events, the storyteller's physical body played a role in how meaning was conveyed. Smith would argue, the body played a role in conveying meaning even if neither the performer nor the audience cognitively realizes it.[52] Granted, I, as a trainer-turned-researcher, would perhaps have encouraged some of the storytellers to utilize more dramatic motions or capitalize on the communication space more intentionally so as to elicit an even greater "affective" impact on the audience but even so, the actual, physical body of each of the storytellers afforded the possibility of engagement with multiple physical senses. Furthermore, this embodied engagement with multiple senses encourages memory, which aligns with the data from chapter 5 where church personnel expressed appreciation for how storytelling makes it easier to remember the Bible stories in one's heart pocket. Thus, maximizing the number of senses creates more possibilities for affective engagement and remembrance and, consequently, more possibilities through which mediation and even transformation between the human worshiper and God can transpire. Do they occur every time? Not necessarily, but Smith would argue transformation may be happening through bodily actions even if one does not realize it.

To understand the connection between oral embodiment, affective engagement, and spiritual change better, it is helpful to reiterate that this kind of transformation happens not necessarily in a *logical logic*, that of the "rational, deliberative, deductive logic of thinking," but in line with Bourdieu's *practical logic*,[53] similar to what Meyer calls *common sense*.[54] Smith

---

50. Site visit: Kahara AGC, April 30, 2017.

51. Focus Group: Kahara, April 29, 2017.

52. Once again, it should be realized that this argument is not suggesting the body does not convey meaning in print, digital or other complicated communication events such as the sermon. As those events include embodiment, they, likewise, leverage the advantages that Smith has been describing regarding the body's intrinsic role in making meaning. Oral communication just does this inherently.

53. Smith, *Imagining the Kingdom*, 90–91.

54. Meyer, "Religious Sensations," 20.

refers to Bourdieu's discussion of the "religion of the knights," which was less about the commitment of a warrior's soul and more about his bodily posture. "When [a knight] stepped forward to become the liege man of a lord, it was again an *attitude, a position of the hands*, a ritual sequence of words which only had to be uttered in order to bind the contract."[55] Such an understanding seems counterintuitive to the typical Protestant emphasis on one's interior belief or motive. Smith anticipates this concern by quickly inserts a retort for those who would question the knight's sincerity, as if it were only his hands and his words, but not necessarily his true heart or conviction. "Such concerns about sincerity are still operating with a dualism that assumes we 'go through' rituals because 'inside' we first *believe* something—that rituals externally 'express' some prior, mental interiority."[56] However, Smith argues this does not honor Bourdieu's *logic of practice* or what Smith describes as "the irreducibility of enacted [or embodied] belief." Summarily, Smith writes, "ritual is the way we (learn to) believe with our bodies."[57]

It is important to note that Smith's use of the concept of belief is qualified—embodied or enacted belief. Instead of reducing Christianity to "a set of propositions to which worshipers give assent," Smith would agree with anthropologist Talal Asad that something more integral is at stake.[58] Far from being merely an interior phenomenon occurring in the disembodied mind, Christianity is, according to Asad, a constituting activity wherein religious knowledge and belief, understood as embodied in practice and discourse, are enacted within particular historical contexts.[59] Smith's overall argument complements Asad, so one suspects Smith is pushing (gently) back on his evangelical audience' for whom belief may typically be interpreted as operating primarily on a "mental, interiority" register. In actuality, Smith is seeking a more holistic understanding, wherein identity is formed and worship realized not through cognitive belief but through a process akin to Asad's embodied, constituting activities of practice and discourse.

Therefore, in light of Smith's argument, one is prepared to recognize how embodied belief and oral storytelling can, at times, produce spiritual transformation. The embodied action (or ritual) taking place through an oral Bible story performance is not merely an expression of AGC's prior mental affirmation or belief in God. Instead, it is, in actuality, habituating or forming a particular desire in the storyteller and possibly in the audience,

---

55. Smith, *Imagining the Kingdom*, 92. Original emphasis.
56. Smith, *Imagining the Kingdom*, 91–92. Original emphasis.
57. Smith, *Imagining the Kingdom*, 91–92.
58. Asad, *Genealogies of Religion*, 41.
59. Asad, *Genealogies of Religion*, 44–47.

as well. Such desires are part of a grander liturgical narrative with a particularly orienting *telos* and, consequently, identity. This helps explain why some church personnel described their excitement regarding storying and how identifying with characters in the stories not only enabled them, and others, "to experience salvation" but also "to get God's power."[60]

The reader may recall several other quotations from chapter 5. "People feel excited and feel like learning more when you step through [the story]" and "They [the stories] encourage us that if it happened to them [characters within the Bible stories], it can happen to us."[61] The tone and wording of the language are significant: people *feel* excited and *encouraged* as they see connections between Bible characters and circumstances in their own lives. Granted, one cannot measure the level of spiritual transformation and I lament not obtaining more testimonies regarding the nature or process of that excitement or encouragement elicited through the biblical stories. Nonetheless, Smith's argument helps illuminate how the body is doing more than that for which it has been given credit in making sense of and constructing meaning in the world. Coupled with the observation that oral storytelling carries an inherent embodiment, one can began to understand why the church recognized oral storytelling's affective engagement and remembrance propensities as well as how, at times, it even elicited spiritual change.

Before continuing, clarification is again appropriate. Other modes of communication have and do produce engagement and even spiritual experiences. This book's argument does not want to diminish such characteristics. The difference relates to orality's dependence on the bodies of the communicating parties, a factor that can be present, as acknowledged, in print and digital events and yet, at times, can be limited or absent all together. I am suggesting that when the body is eclipsed through print or digital media, and only in this limited sense, then a significant means for meaning to be constructed and even belief to be enacted is, likewise, eclipsed. Granted, print and digital media can construct meaning in other ways, and they do afford other positive characteristics as discussed in chapter 5. Nonetheless, when the body is absent, or at least one party's body, such events cannot draw on its unique capacity for making meaning as described by Smith. Oral communication necessitates the bodies of both parties, so only in this limited sense am I arguing that oral communication lends itself to affective engagement and even, at times, spiritual change. My overall argument suggests that these unique meaning-making capacities of the body, which were perhaps not even always recognized by the church, are part of why the

---

60. Focus Group: Kahara, April 29, 2017.
61. Focus Group: Kahara, April 29, 2017.

church personnel described appreciating oral Bible storytelling. This oral method lent itself to a refreshing affective engagement, which was not necessarily experienced in the same way through the printed text.[62]

This extended discussion has explored how AGC appreciated orality, but the subsequent question is how far orality, particularly storytelling, has been actually appropriated into the church's aesthetics or their authorized religious practice. That would be the true measure of how far they have actually sanctioned orality, as understood by the OM, as a legitimate means for mediating God's word and, consequently, God's presence.

AGC's Appropriation of Orality

Indeed, while I cannot speak for the entire denomination, in the churches where I visited or held focus group discussions, oral storytelling was deemed an authorized and relatively fixed mode for mediating an encounter between the AGC Christians and God. It is worth reiterating that storytelling was not absent before the WGM introduced the STS oral storytelling method into AGC's training program. The difference is that rather than being merely illustrative or secondary to print-reliant methods, oral storytelling as a formal communication method has become an acceptable church practice. This does not mean that everyone uses storytelling all the time. On the contrary, most of the pastors still seem to prefer to keep their printed Bibles close at hand, but it was generally recognized that the immediate proximity of printed biblical text is not necessarily required for pastors or church members to encounter God through the Scriptures.

Here is where Esther's performance is once again helpful, for while it is only one episode, it provides a glimpse of one of the ways in which orality, as understood as by those within ION, has infiltrated AGC's aesthetic formation. Esther's story was not a scheduled narration organized by either a pastor or me, but something that spontaneously emerged from the heart of a young person who was eager to demonstrate her own capacity to perform a religious ritual. No doubt there were a variety of motivations (possibly including social, economic, or even political dynamics) behind selecting me to be the one to hear the story. Time could be spent wondering if she had planned ahead or been practicing and memorizing with her friends or family by the chance she would have the opportunity to impress me. Granted, that may have happened; furthermore, one needs to acknowledge that the story itself originated in the biblical text, presumably introduced to Esther by her pastor as discussed shortly. Nevertheless, what stands out is that she

---

62. Once again, see chapter 5's discussion on the possibility of spiritual change and reimagining one's self in the story.

did not read the story of Elisha and the youth to me. No printed Bible was involved in her interaction with me; that particular communication event was exclusively oral. She was able to enact an oral religious practice wherein the word of God was performed accurately. This phenomenon in and of itself bears testimony to how oral storytelling has become part and parcel of at least some of the aesthetic framework of AGC.

Not insignificantly, I had heard that exact story in April 2017 while visiting this young lady's church (AGC Kahara) when her pastor had performed it.[63] Only, eight months later, it was not the church leader but a child of that congregation who recited the biblical drama. This is where both Smith's and Meyer's understandings of formation become helpful. For during the in-between months, some process of formation took place within that church community whereby a junior member not just learned a Bible story but was formed into being an active participant and even performer of the liturgical ritual that she had witnessed embodied and embedded in her pastor and church community. Here is a prime example of how the church's *habitus* or aesthetic disposition, is being formed or reproduced in the life of the next generation of "native" AGC Christians.[64]

For precise research purposes, one wishes for more information on how that formation process happened. Esther could have mastered the story by sitting down to read it nightly or write it out regularly throughout the eight months. More likely, such a *habitus* was formed in the Thursday afternoon Bible storying class held at Kahara AGC, wherein each week the pastor taught stories, that this liturgical practice was honed in this younger church member. Furthermore, I suggests that this girl saw the Elisha story and other stories performed by her church leaders and began to intuit not only the importance of biblical narratives but also that oral storytelling is a valid sensational form for mediating encounters with God through his word.

I heard many people appreciate orality and, as has been described in the previous chapter, AGC members were able to articulate numerous affordances that orality, specifically oral Bible storytelling, offered within the life of the church. Perhaps the clearest picture of such an appreciation and, even more significantly, appropriation of such oral methods, was my experience of Esther's story performance. It should not be missed that this encounter did not take place in the church building or during a regular worship time. Instead, it was a spontaneous oral expression of a sensational habit that had been formed within a church member who has

63. Focus Group: Kahara, April 29, 2017.

64. Native (or nativity) is used here with the shorthand sense of Bourdieu and Smith—a local who can intuit local knowledge. A native "just knows" what should happen next in a particular context. Smith, *Imagining the Kingdom*, 93.

imbibed from AGC's aesthetics that oral Bible storytelling affords mediation between God and church members.

Such explorations into the question of why AGC appreciated orality offers members of the OM some fresh conceptual tools to articulate what so many of them have already intuited. Rather than merely relying on anecdotal stories of appreciation and even spiritual change, I am suggesting that Meyer and Smith provide a theoretical framework wherein we can better understand embodied materiality and its significance in oral communication for the construction of meaning and spiritual identity. In spite of such appreciation and appropriation of oral storytelling, it has to be realized that several significant concerns emerged as well from within the church.

AGC's Critique of Orality

While AGC has adapted orality, specifically oral storytelling, into its aesthetic formation, it has not been the panacea that perhaps some were hoping would overcome all the church's communication challenges. On the one hand, it affords affective engagement as previously described; however, orality carries a liability that does not seem to have yet been fully appreciated by the WGM missionaries. Herein is where confusion regarding materiality becomes explicit. As discussed, members of the OM in general and the WGM missionaries in particular seemed to have intuited the material embodiment of orality—the material (or physical) body affords affective engagement in substantial ways, but they failed to understand the valued role that materialities, specifically material objects or artifacts, play in communication and how communication as a phenomenon is embedded in a wider religious-socioeconomic imaginary. What follows is a brief discussion about the differences between mission and church social imaginaries as well as further consideration of *telos* in an AGC context. With those points of reference in place, consideration turns to three specific ways that orality failed to meet the societal expectations, particularly in regards to theological education.

Social Imaginaries

One way to approach this critique is from the observation that within the differing social imaginaries of the church and mission, physical and spiritual matters seems to receive slightly differing accents. Such a seemingly simple observation places the discussion at the center of Meyer's and Smith's concern for the material or physical reality of the otherwise seemingly immaterial or spiritual nature of religion. Neither Meyer nor Smith is arguing for an inverse privileging of the material over the immaterial. They both are merely calling attention to the material so as to create some theoretical space to give materiality proper attention in light of the relatively recent, and characteristically Protestant, historical tendency to associate religion with the immaterial, exemplified in mere assent to doctrine or belief.[65]

Within the missionaries' social imaginary, one of the primary communication problems within AGC was limited literary expertise. This was hindering spiritual maturity. The missionaries were looking for a communication method that would enable and mediate spiritual maturity but that did not rely on literacy. Orality promised to be the answer. As has been discussed, it afforded affective engagement with the Bible and even elicited spiritual change at times. Nonetheless, in their enthusiasm for spiritual realities, the missionaries neglected to give balanced attention to the physical realities or social dynamics within which the church members were operating. They failed to recognize the influence of materiality in shaping particular associations regarding religious communication, in general, and pastoral training, in particular, within the wider social context. Granted, the WGM missionaries' involvement and championing of the physical-oriented trainings and outreaches, such as *Community Health Empowerment* and *Farming God's Way*, prevent any sort of blanket or over-generalized accusation that the mission does not care for the physical realities. Nonetheless, there seems to remain an implicit dualism within the missionaries' social imaginary between the physical and the spiritual. This deserves further probing because it parallels Meyer's and Smith's discussions regarding the Western tendency to privilege the mind over the body.

One way to approach this issue is to notice that, while perhaps inadvertent, the so-called *transformational ministries* and their subsequent training courses, personnel, and curriculum are clearly distinct from the pastoral training within the church. Transformational ministries is the term used to describe WGM and AGC's collaborative efforts in activities that give specific attention to physical needs, including, *Community Health Empowerment*, *Farming God's Way*, *Women's Cycle of Life*, and *Children's Community Health Empowerment*. Interestingly, many of the pastoral trainers have been or currently are involved in the transformational training

---

65. Here again, it is helpful to recall the brief discussion introduced earlier in the chapter regarding Talal Asad's argument that defining religion in terms of cognitive assent to a set of propositions, transpiring primarily in the disembodied mind, has a "modern, privatized Christian" genealogy. For Asad, religion is a constituting activity in a particular, historical, social context, wherein embodied practices and discourses shape and form the self. Asad, *Genealogies of Religion*, 27–54; for extended treatment on his understanding of the relationship between the body and ritual, see pp. 55–79.

programs; however, the two ministries or programs are distinct, parallel activities within the denomination, and individual pastors and churches and their members are left to identify and sort out any ways the two teachings reinforce and strengthen or contradict each other. Thus, while not necessarily intended, a dualism seems to operate as if the pastoral training conveys knowledge about spiritual matters while transformational ministries convey knowledge regarding physical affairs. This is directly antithetical to the jargon used by John and Beth Muehleisen and others involved with transformational ministries who would argue the whole point of transformational ministries is to be holistic, addressing issues regarding the mind, the body, and the soul within specific communities.[66] I am merely noting that, in actuality, there seems to be a divide between the holistic activities and the pastoral training. Perhaps this separation is merely related to logistics, but a case can be made that it has inadvertently resulted in a bifurcation between physical and spiritual matters.

This is important in light of both Meyer's and Smith's emphasis on formation within their understanding of aesthetics. One can easily imagine how such an apparent dualism, even if inadvertent, acts as a filter, or perhaps more appropriately, a constraint in forming (or even misshaping?) the church's aesthetic practice and understanding. Rather than being a unified aesthetic formation wherein different types of needs are addressed simultaneously or at least in the context of each other, a dualistic framework has developed.

The immediate significance is that in their enthusiasm that orality may meet spiritual goals, the missionaries do not seem to have recognized the depth of the social and physical realities within which the church has operated. Such oversight has meant that the missionaries have not appreciated fully the physical and communal concerns regarding orality within the church. While I did not sense that the church personnel were primarily concerned with physical matters, the limited awareness or perhaps misunderstanding of the actual physical realities on the part of the missionaries seems to have left the church leaders with little choice but to draw attention to the physical or material concerns just out of necessity to keep the denomination operating as a social entity.

This extensive development of an apparent dualism within the church and mission relationship is imperative for setting the stage to understand the subsequent discussion. Two examples will help illustrate such physical accent within the church and the missionaries' limited understanding of the

---

66. Muehleisen, March 31, 2017; John Muehleisen, personal interview, May 18, 2017; Site visit: Farming God's Way, May 16, 2017.

church members' realities. The first came from discussing AGC's problem on Buvuma Island with the local authorities. (This issue was briefly discussed in chapter 5.) Rev. Dhikusooka, the former area overseer for that area and the administrative secretary of the denomination, acknowledged that he does not call his bishop to handle such problems because the bishop has no money to help. Instead, he calls the WGM country director, Jeff Stanfield.[67] In such a situation, the concern was literally for physical, financial help. Stanfield shared in conversation with me that he has sensed he had gathered a reputation in the denomination for being a "no man" to all the church's physical requests. Not insignificantly, Dhikusooka implied as much in conversation.[68] What remains important to recognize is that with limited funds, the church has found that in difficult circumstances where they lack material or financial resources they have to appeal to WGM. For example, the situation on the island required legal advice and, thus, paying legal fees; consequently, Dhikusooka did not know where else to turn but to Stanfield. Such requests reinforce the stereotype that the church is primarily concerned with physical or financial matters.

A second example that addresses how the missionaries seem to have a limited appreciation for the physical realities of the church members came in conversation with Rev. James Ouma. He alluded to a new WGM missionary who had recently begun offering some personal financial training for church members. Ouma expressed his frustration, not necessarily with the new missionary personally, but at the mission in general because the new financial training stressed things such as budgeting and planning. Ouma, in an exasperated tone, noted that the missionaries do not realize the truly impoverished state of the pastors, many of whom have no consistent form of income, a variable assumed in Western models of budget planning. He summarized, "Africans do not have accounts; they live on a daily basis."[69] While Ouma may have generalized for emphasis, his concern illustrates how the church has felt misunderstood by the missionaries, specifically regarding the Ugandans' actual degree of physical need.

This misunderstanding came home to me in a new way while discussing finances with Ouma.[70] The WGM missionaries raise funds while in the United States for anticipated living and ministry expenses and are only then sent to Uganda once the necessary funds have been raised. Thus, the missionaries arrive in Uganda fully funded and do not have to find secular

67. Stanfield stepped down as country director in 2019.
68. Dhikusooka, May 10, 2017; Stanfield and Stanfield, May 9, 2017.
69. James Ouma, personal interview (2nd), April 7, 2017.
70. Ouma, April 7, 2017.

employment to feed their families, pay their children's school fees, or pay monthly rent and vehicle or other transportation costs. All of those things that might be generally classified as secular or physical affairs have been budgeted into the amount raised before arriving. The result is that when the missionaries arrive, they are free to pursue activities that may tend to be classified as more spiritual, such as evangelism, discipleship, or even pastoral training. The mission does not pay any of its pastors, only its missionaries; thus, there are two different financial models in place. The consequence is that the pastors and church leaders have to conduct the supposed spiritual, immaterial church activities amidst the physical, material pressures of feeding families and paying children's school fees, not to mention healthcare costs or caring for aging parents. It is no wonder that under such a bifurcated system the missionaries tend towards a privileging of the supposed spiritual matters while the church leaders are constantly battling to meet physical needs. While such discussion may feel slightly tangential to a discussion of the church's reception of orality, these are the issues shaping the church's religious and social aesthetic within which such reception takes place. Furthermore, one can recognize Smith's and Meyer's concerns that the propagating of such a dualistic paradigm, whether intentionally or not, tends towards a neglect of the physical or material realities.

It needs to be reiterated that I heard discussion of both physical and spiritual concerns from church and mission personnel alike; the difference seemed to be that the missionaries tended to accent the spiritual concerns. This was no more explicitly stated than when one missionary asked me in a rhetorical voice, "Are we physically or spiritually building the church?"[71] The tone in the missionary's voice made it indelibly clear that he was primarily concerned with the latter. Such an emphasis naturally leads to particular interpretations of communication phenomena, interpretations with implications that neither WGM nor members of the OM seemed to have fully realized. It is imperative to recognize this dualistic imbalance if one is to understand the ensuing concerns raised by the church regarding orality properly.

Telos

Before turning to consider the particular critiques that emerged, it is worth returning to Smith's concept of *telos* one more time and asking, what is the end goal or desire that motivates, whether directly or indirectly, Ugandans in general and AGC members in particular. In his discussion of *telos*, Smith is trying to get at the issue of what people desire or love or, ultimately, worship. While granted such inquiry carries Christian overtones, that is not totally

---

71. Anyomous, May 9, 2017.

misplaced, as the central party to this research investigation is a Christian denomination. While a full treatment of such a broad-sweeping categorization of people as Ugandans lies beyond the confines of this project, the initial probing I conducted provides at least a small glimpse into how those within AGC would classify Ugandans' loves.[72]

Although limited in number, I was able to hear a mixture of voices discuss *telos*. In an interview, Ouma talked about something similar to *telos*, what he called the "achieved" life, akin to the idea of human flourishing, as being a life wherein a person was married with children, possessing a job, a house, and a vehicle.[73] Likewise, Rev. Martin Owor replied that Ugandans love land, houses, and vehicles. When nudged to say more on the subject, Owor noted that all such things are owned by money, so he articulated, money is actually the number one love.[74] This sentiment was echoed when I asked two AGC members and they both answered money. The first woman said, "Life will go but if one has money," and she trailed off as if it should be obvious that money makes life worthwhile. The second woman said, "With money, you can get the good life: land, a vehicle."[75] One pastor asked his family on my behalf and they agreed that some mature Christians love "to please God." However, within that same family, they suggested that Ugandans love "true friendship," "money," and "their own lives." Furthermore, the pastor reported that he thought Ugandans love music and entertainment. He argued that on all holidays and weekends, people congregate where there is music; not insignificantly, he added that even pastors must have "good music *equipment* in order to attract people."[76]

While the questions were asked more generally, as in what do Ugandans love most, one cannot help but suspect such answers were a mixture of describing *others* as well as offering some autobiographical reflection on church members. Regrettably, gathering more explicit data on this subject was not possible and this would be a natural opportunity for further investigation in the future. The reason such a limited discussion is worth consideration is that it provides at least a glimpse into the teleological underpinnings

---

72. Due to the multi-ethnic make-up in AGC and my desire to get a sense of the broader social imaginary, I asked about Ugandans in general. Granted, this has limitations and a natural place for further inquiry would be how differing ethnic groups within Uganda in general or AGC in particular might answer such a *telos* question differently.

73. Ouma, March 31, 2017.

74. Martin Owor, personal interview (2nd), December 8, 2017.

75. Janet Nalongo and Joyce Kagoya, personal conversation, December 8, 2017.

76. David Dhikusooka, personal communication, January 1, 2018. Emphasis added to reinforce the materiality of his answer.

that make up the contextual dynamics within which AGC operates. What stands out is that the described *telos* was holistic, incorporating spiritual aspects but also social–relational ones as well. Furthermore, the descriptions were of a very material or physical character. Whether a spouse, a vehicle, a plot of land or even one's own life or body, the measure of a full life, to use Charles Taylor's term included some *material* object. While an extended discussion about Christianity's teaching on the restoration of the physical body and creation are well beyond the scope of this project, it is worth realizing that *telos*, as discussed in an AGC context, connotes an integration of spiritual, social, and material components.[77] While one wishes more could be explicitly affirmed, even this brief discussion provides a glimpse into how material things are part and parcel of the larger teleological imaginary within which AGC operates. Significantly, such an integrated understanding of *telos* is not unique to AGC.

Anthropologist Julie Archambault discusses this issue in Mozambique where her youthful interlocutors talked about *curtir a vida*, enjoying the good life through activities such as enjoying good food, wearing nice clothes, or getting to travel. However, the Mozambican youth continued, describing how "a successful life also meant having something to show for, and ultimately, being considered a person by others as well as by the state. Specifically, this generally entailed building a house, getting married, having children, and maintaining harmonious relations with neighbors and relatives."[78] We should notice the similarities between her descriptions of the successful life and Ouma's definition already mentioned of what counts as an achieved life. The point is that the *telos* or full life described in these accounts carries more than spiritual overtones or, in contrast, merely economic ones; rather, they represent a spectrum of material desires that are realized and manifested in one's relationship with God, family, neighbors, and the state. Ultimately, *telos* in such contexts carries an integrated understanding, incorporating spiritual, physical, social, and political domains. This makes sense when one realizes that within AGC's social imaginary, the integrated *telos* reflects an integrated understanding of personhood.

Such observations regarding the integrated understanding of *telos* align well with the earlier discussion regarding differences between the social imaginaries of the church and mission personnel. The stage is now set to turn

77. One recalls this theme was already introduced in the previous chapter's discussion regarding research done by Cole, Haynes, and Pritchett.

78. Archambault, *Mobile Secrets*, 16–17; Likewise, Cole's research specifically focuses on how women in Madagascar are seeking to achieve their desired telos through either entering the sexual economy or immersing themselves within Pentecostalism. See Cole, *Sex and Salvation*.

attention to AGC's critique of orality. It needs to be understood that while nuancing these various structures or elements assumes a certain degree of academic parsing, for the church members, the elements were often mixed up in the flow of conversation. Consequently, it should be clearly acknowledged that no one provided a tidy three-point critique of orality. Nevertheless, as I listened to the responses of AGC to orality, several concerns emerged that have already been introduced but deserve further investigation, namely regarding education, economics, and social status.

Material Critique #1: The Lack of Educational Value.

In the previous chapter, it was acknowledged that **orality**$_2$ fails to produce formal educational value. One may recall that the WGM missionary and printer, Kenneth Hopson, talked with passion about how he believes formal literary education is crucial for (re)imagining one's identity. His statement is worth repeating and analyzing so as to reaffirm the importance of literary education within the broader Ugandan social imaginary: "Education for them [Ugandans], which involves literature, that is the way to improve their lives—even more, their way of acquiring, whether a bicycle, gadgets, property, a home—that is the measure of success. That improves your status, shows others that you are not a poor worthless digger. So literature plays an important role in that approach—to improving their life. People who do not have those things are looked down up on. Money gets you things. How do you get money? Education."[79] The advantage of Hopson's statement is that he articulates so clearly how education, economics (e.g., money, acquiring), and status or an improved life are interconnected. For immediate purposes, literary education is understood as an essential means to reconstruct an identity, not as a "poor, worthless digger," but as one who does not have to be looked down upon. What is paramount is that literary education assumes a materiality not found in orality. It is not necessarily *the materiality of an embodied communicator*—what we have talked about as possible in a print or digital event but which is intrinsic to oral communication. Rather, the materiality that seems to have been overlooked by those promoting oral storytelling is *a materiality of artifact*. One has only to think of the folders filled with lessons and notes that Miria and Steward Mukisa uncovered from the sugar sacks.[80] These were brown, worn, fading pages; nonetheless, they were actual physical, musty objects that I could touch and turn. No matter how many stories

79. Hopson, March 23, 2017.
80. Mukisa and Mukisa, April 22, 2017.

one has memorized in one's "heart pocket" or how well one can facilitate a post-performance discussion about a story, at the end of the day, orality, as understood so often by AGC as oral Bible storytelling, offers nothing tangible over which to run one's fingers. As Hopson said, education in a Ugandan context involves literature, which by definition includes the physical presence of paper and texts. Therefore, oral communication, without this material artifact, fails to produce or maintain educational value.

A good example can be recalled from chapter 5 regarding the former practice of passing out printed copies of the pastoral training notes. In the focus group discussion with the Kamuli area pastors, a pastor named Monday commented that he liked it best when printed notes were given out. Without the printed lessons, some pastors missed some of the information because they are not able to write notes fast enough on their own. Furthermore, the group noted that with a printed lesson, one can always "pull a file." One thinks again of the Mukisas' sugar sack filing system. Regretfully, with an oral story, there is no physical file to pull. This absence of material artifact was being lamented within the pastoral education program.[81] Rev. David Dhikusooka concurred, noting that when he, as a trainer went to a pastoral training event, the pastors always wanted to return "with some thing."[82] As he said, commenting on the former days with printed lessons, "Then we had files; we got files, and each time you come, you put in their papers; then they return and feel comfortable [at this point, Dhikusooka swung his arms in an exaggerated manner, smiling broadly] and can revise from home. Humans are not computers; you can't store everything. You can go back always and refer, revise, remember."[83] While the role of a material artifact in memory was discussed in the previous chapter, what is worth reiterating here is that orality's absent material presence does not satisfy the church's literary education expectations or desires, particularly in relation to pastoral training. The feeling of being educationally "comfortable" or content came through possession of a material thing.

Another way this manifested itself was in relation to the value that is placed on certification. Orality does not produce or enable one to procure any recognized educational certification. Pastor Benson Omri, who is also a primary school teacher, commented that because of the structure of the educational system in Uganda, orality was not taken as important or as an effective component of education. His reason was that orality lacks

---

81. Focus Group: Kamuli, April 7, 2017.
82. Dhikusooka, May 10, 2017.
83. Dhikusooka, May 10, 2017.

documentation.[84] Once again, no matter the number of stories or songs or even dramas that one can perform, there is no magical number that enables one to obtain a certificate or diploma, much less a degree, in orality or oral storytelling. As Jonathan Mayo commented, even if a pastor had the equivalent of a diploma in biblical orality, people would ask, "Show us the material." He continued, noting that even if the pastor was an expert in biblical orality and knew the information better than a three-year Bible college student, at the end of the day, what would matter was who had material evidence of the education.[85]

Two remaining examples, one positive and one negative, illustrate the power of certification or material credentials and reinforce the assumed interconnectivity between what is considered proper education and materiality. On one occasion, I visited the Mukisas' home and noted that Miria's "AGC Pastoral Training Level One Completion Certificate" hung in a frame on the wall in their sitting room.[86] There displayed for all to see was a printed artifact, a material reminder of her educational accomplishment. Inversely, the apparent lack of certification or creditization within AGC was also testified. The Kamuli area overseer, Ibrahaim Lisok, noted that he would not run for bishop in the December 2017 church elections because he only possessed a diploma. Amidst the discussion, it was stated, "The church needs credentials." Lisok considered himself disqualified from church leadership because of the lack of more recognized education accomplishments and their consequent documentation.

It is worth underscoring that document certification is a high value that has worked its way into the social imaginary of the church. While more exhaustive research could be conducted on where and how this valuing of printed material and accreditation came about, in light of the interrelated historical development of Christianity and literary education in Uganda as discussed in chapter 4, a fair hypothesis suggests that AGC members have seen such text preference modeled in the Church of Uganda. If that is the case, then literary texts themselves were originally alien to the differing ethnic groups in what is now Uganda. Nonetheless, what the OM seems to have failed to realize is that while originally foreign to the different ethnic groups' social imaginaries, over time, what was alien has now become indigenous. While attempting to appeal to what was presumed to be part of the traditional oral social imaginary, the OM, specifically WGM, did not account for the ways that printed materials

---

84. Omri, May 12, 2017.

85. Mayo, March 12, 2017.

86. Miria finished Level 1 in 2003 before orality was introduced to the AGC training scheme. Mukisa and Mukisa, April 22, 2017.

and literary education have become part of the broader, indigenous social imaginary within which AGC functions.

The inability of orality, and particularly the OM, to deliver in this area was raised with some insight by Kennedy Kirui, the only pastor associated with AGC who is pursuing a PhD. He specifically suggested that the OM needed to think about how to provide opportunities to study orality and progress from one level of study to another in officially recognized ways, presumably externally to AGC or the OM itself. He acknowledged the tension of making orality textual, but he argued that unless the OM addresses the lack of accreditation, those in the academy will receive orality with suspicion.[87] Kirui has identified a significant tension for the OM and one that deserves future inquiry: How will the OM maintain its commitment to orality in contexts that value literary accreditation?

For now, it is worth summarizing that for many within AGC's context, education is assumed to be literary; consequently, people value a materiality of artifact, a materiality that neither orality, in general, nor oral storytelling, in particular, can deliver. Significantly, a primary reason for valuing literary education with its physical texts and printed certificates is that, as Hopson noted, it is the means for acquiring wealth.

Material Critique #2: The Lack of Economic Value

As in formal education, there is a materiality to economics that orality fails to deliver. Once again, it is important to highlight a difference in materiality; this is not the materiality of embodiment but *one* of artifact. Numerous AGC members expressed a dissatisfaction with their apparent experience that orality, understood as storytelling, was not building economic value in their lives or families in the ways they believe print-reliant communication does, specifically literary formal education. While this was introduced in the previous chapter, the cultural dynamics are worth exploring so as to understand how church members interpret orality's failure in this regard.

One of the clearest articulations of this issue came while sitting in the home of the Dhikusooka family. Rev. David Dhikusooka pastors the Masese AGC church, which benefited from the mission's early church-building initiative; thus, the congregation has both a well-designed permanent structure as well as a permanent house for the pastor. In the course of the conversation, Dhikusooka talked about the issue of financial need, saying, "With storying, people are equipped for evangelism and can go anywhere; but no one is planting churches because there are no benches or church buildings." He

---

87. Kirui, March 28, 2017.

continued, "Story does not contribute material betterment. You can't sit on a story, nor does it keep off the rain." This was perhaps the clearest indictment of oral storytelling's inability to produce economic benefit. Significantly, Dhikusooka was able to identify the relationship between oral storytelling and the lack of economics as expressed in the absence of material things. For this pastor, storying was able to do what would be considered spiritual work—evangelism; however, it failed to provide the funding for the material objects necessary to mediate that spiritual work among the community, namely, a building or even benches. One may immediately question how other modes such as printed communication or digital communication can "keep the rain off." Such an inquiry requires returning again to the contextual association between literary education and economic empowerment.

Simply put, the more formal literary education one possesses, the more money one can make.[88] This observation was confirmed among the missionaries[89] as a contemporary phenomenon but also has historical precedent as introduced in chapter 4. It needs to be highlighted that what was prevalent was the presumed correlation between formal education and more money, although in actuality, I encountered several individuals who had various post-secondary qualifications but for whom employment had proved elusive. Nonetheless, there is some justifiable rationale behind the rather prevalent association between literary education and money. Omri talked about how when he completes his current studies for a bachelor's degree, he will be eligible for a different class of employment and, consequently, a higher salary.[90] Ouma, commenting on Omri's future prospects, likewise noted that Omri will be qualified for a salary increase whereas there is no such financial incentive with oral storytelling, even if one were to be involved with it for ten years.[91]

While the association between education and economics is by no means particular to Uganda or AGC,[92] the reason it bears highlighting is because for some of the church members, oral communication does not deliver on the literary education; consequently, it cannot deliver with regard to increased employability. While denominational financial struggles are a common church issue throughout the world, what is important to recognize is that numerous AGC church members associated at least some

88. Ouma, March 31, 2017; Kirui, March 28, 2017; Omri, May 12, 2017.
89. Metz, April 25, 2017; Muehleisen, March 31, 2017; Hopson, March 23, 2017.
90. Omri, May 12, 2017.
91. Ouma, March 31, 2017.
92. Cole likewise discusses how the ideology developed with the introduction of formal schooling, wherein it became the pathway to a better job, social prestige, and all things "modern" (Cole, *Sex and Salvation*, 30–33).

of their financial hardships with orality. Not incidentally, at least one missionary shared how she had been asked why WGM Uganda did not open a proper (i.e., literary-oriented) Bible college.[93] One can easily imagine that in the mind of the inquiring AGC member, a Bible college seems like a natural solution. While a literary degree from such an institution cannot, in and of itself, keep off the rain, it might lead to employment, which implies a salary, which could pay for proper housing. While some in Western contexts may wonder how a theology degree might improve employment prospects, Omri discussed how with a bachelor degree's he could leave primary school teaching and apply for higher paying jobs such as a project manager with an NGO or administrator at an orphanage.[94] Thus, while Dhikusooka's earlier comments regarding pastoral housing may seem like a long way from matters of communication, for those within the church, there was an intimate connection.

Part of the explanation for this connection lies in the association within the broader AGC context among economics, materiality, and spirituality. "Belly theology" was introduced in the previous chapter as shorthand for describing how spiritual maturity was often measured by material possession. Herein, AGC leaders and members are struggling to address their own physical needs as well as articulate a response to the pressure of the so-called prosperity gospel. Ouma described how "Africans understand the Bible to say that love and prosperity go together." He noted that they identify well with characters from the Old Testament who had humble beginnings but became "great people." Abraham and David are understood as biblical examples of those who left all to follow God and found that God provided abundantly for them. Ouma articulated this line of thought, that a powerful God should have no trouble providing for someone: "If he [God] loves me, he will provide for me." While God's provision is standard fare within Christian discourse, Ouma elaborated his understanding of how prosperity has escalated the material rhetoric. Thus, this is the context behind his previously referenced comment that a pastor who drives "a big car" or has a big belly reflects "a big God."[95] Elsewhere, in discussion on prosperity, Ouma summarized this understanding of the proportional relationship between spirituality and material prosperity: "The heart of God means material prosperity."[96]

93. Muehleisen, March 31, 2017.
94. Omri, May 12, 2017.
95. Ouma, March 31, 2017.
96. Kisugu Bible study, May 18, 2017.

While a full exploration of prosperity teaching in Uganda lies beyond the confines of this project, several points are worth underscoring. First, whatever one believes or denies about prosperity teaching, it has inextricably linked spirituality with materiality. While AGC would consider itself an evangelical denomination with the stereotypical emphasis on interior transformation, there was a general consensus among the pastors interviewed that they were struggling to articulate for their congregations an appropriate response to prosperity's alluring material promise.[97] The rationale behind this complaint was rather straightforward as the pastors were all bi-vocational; not one is fully supported by his or her church. Therefore, routine matters of physical or material need were raised and discussed with me. AGC finds itself trying to inhabit an in-between or paradoxical space, offering critique of the prosperity teaching on the one hand as being selfish and unbiblical. Jesus himself is never described as having "a big car" or a house to call his own. As one pastor said, "He had to borrow a donkey!"[98] Nonetheless, both pastors and church members alike are daily facing physical needs that demand attention, specifically financial attention. The material lack within AGC has been interpreted within the wider social imaginary as being indicative that AGC has a small God. As Caroline Ouma and Lillian Kirui said, "In Africa, pastors pray blessings and if you do not have the blessings, you cannot pray those over me." In other words, if someone does not have the material evidence, the physical objects (or the belly) that certify his or her God as capable of providing material benefit, then the pastor and his or her God are inferior.

While some of these concepts were introduced in the previous chapter, they are worth developing here because things get more complex before they get simpler. One of the allures of prosperity teaching is that one can achieve a material *telos*; uniquely, it provides an alternative route to such material goals without necessarily achieving the normally assumed educational qualifications. Prosperity teaching offers an avenue to attain the "good life," what was described in terms of a spouse, a house, some land, and vehicles, not through formal literary education with its assumed print reliance but through religious practice or a prosperity aesthetic formation. This is not to argue that prosperity groups do not utilize print or digital modes; a quick glance at websites for any number of such groups dismisses such a thought. What Ouma wanted me to understand is that traditionally, pastors have been perceived as poor. He shared about how

---

97. Mukisa and Mukisa, April 22, 2017; Omri, May 12, 2017; Dhikusooka, May 10, 2017; Ouma, March 31, 2017; Owor, March 21, 2017.

98. Mukisa and Mukisa, April 22, 2017.

when he told his father that God had called him to preach, his father expelled him out of the house for three days. It was only after the community elders sat with Ouma's father and discussed the matter with him that Ouma was welcomed back into the family. While often respected in spiritual and even community matters, one stereotype is that pastors lack material possessions. It was important to Ouma that I understand that preachers of prosperity were seeking to "tell the world that to be a pastor is a good thing; you can prosper."[99] Such a testimony provides a glimpse into the economic imaginary in which AGC operates.

In light of these contextual realities, what makes AGC's response to this prosperity teaching relevant for the present discussion is that, once again, orality is understood as failing to enable people to achieve the desired *telos* that is upheld within the broader social imaginary in which the denomination operates. People are seeking material well-being, whether through literary education with the hopes of employment or through adhering to a prosperity aesthetic. On the one hand, AGC's evangelical doctrinal stance does not allow them to embrace officially what several of the leaders described as misinterpretations of God's promises.[100] On the other, the church's employment of orality, instead of the more formal, literary education model, has not produced any recognized material advantage to the church or its members. Thus, two of the strategic means or channels for achieving the desired integrated *telos* as understood within the wider social imaginary appear inaccessible to AGC.

In light of this, I sensed a general discouragement among both leaders and members. Denominational leaders talked about trying to sensitize church members to the dangers of prosperity teaching.[101] They have tried to maintain the denomination's doctrinal positions on holiness and righteousness, but they admitted that people are much more interested in learning about material prosperity.[102] Not surprisingly, while the pastors discussed warning others of the dangers of prosperity teaching, they also admitted their own material needs and eager availability to receiving any material blessing that God wanted to provide.[103]

Here is where the earlier discussion of holiness theology in chapter 4 finds relevance. Holiness theology tends to be interpreted as emphasizing one's spiritual interior, remaining pure in heart and life amidst the dangers of the world's material temptations. Whether one agrees with the finer

---

99. Ouma, March 31, 2017.

100. Ouma, March 31, 2017; Steward Stephen Mukisa, personal interview (2nd), December 8, 2017.

101. Owor, March 21, 2017.

102. Focus Group: AGC leaders, April 5, 2017.

103. Steward Stephen Mukisa, personal interview (1st), April 29, 2017.

points of holiness discourse is almost beside the point; what matters is that the denomination's understanding (and experience?) of holiness theology has complicated their responses to social expectations for material blessing. It is helpful to reiterate that no one was arguing that the church's use of oral storytelling had made the church materially poor. Rather, what needs to be understood is that for some within a denomination struggling with rampant basic physical needs, oral storytelling was perceived as offering little by way of hope for addressing what were so often such pressing material concerns. Consequently, it was unable to propel one towards a spiritual-socio-materialistic *telos*.

Material Critique #3: The Lack of Social Value

The third critique can already be intuited in light of the first two—orality's lack of artifactual materiality carries negative social connotations. Ouma stated, "Society has expectations that AGC is not fulfilling."[104] It was all too clear that those expectations were material in nature, yet no evidence was produced to show how oral storytelling was rectifying those unfulfilled social expectations.

One specific area where the church seemed to be unable to meet society's material expectations as highlighted in the field data reported in chapter 5 was regarding the communicative power of material buildings. As discussed in chapter 5, the materiality of a church building communicates within the Ugandan Christian discourse; it mediates a space wherein worshipers can encounter God through words and practices but it also mediates a message to the surrounding community not only about God but about the worshipers who belong to that church. The lack of modern physical church buildings has resulted in AGC failing to mediate those opportunities, instead suffering disrespect and discouragement. This appears not just to be a matter of denominational pride. In discussing these matters, Omri talked about the significance of being able to say, "Our church is there." Although the comment was made in relation to the physicality of a church building within the local municipality of the Nebbi community, such a statement carries tremendous weight in regards to identity. A congregation is more than a physical building, but without the physicality of a material structure, it was evident that neither the community nor even the congregation itself has a clear sense of AGC's identity. Thus, the lack of materiality has resulted in limited community respect, which has resulted in limited and, at times, failed spiritual communication. The denomination has missed out on opportunities to mediate between God and their communities because they

104. Ouma, March 31, 2017.

have failed to obtain the material assets that society values. Ultimately, orality has failed to help church personnel achieve the material things that society values. Consequently, this lack of materiality has cast a deep shadow over the denomination, essentially discrediting their social position and calling into question the denomination's own self-understanding.

Regretfully, there seems to be a discernible pattern. In the same way that WGM and the OM seem to have failed to recognize how literary texts and education have become indigenous within the broader social imaginary within which AGC functions, so they also seem to have failed to appreciate how physical structures have become indigenously valued. Religious sites may not have always been associated with permanent structures, but over time and under the influences of both the Roman Catholic Church and the Church of Uganda, religious sites in general, and Christian ones in particular, have come to be understood as necessitating a proper physical building.[105] In light of Meyer and Smith and from what numerous church personnel shared, it seems that the material building itself has become part of broader religious aesthetic, a sensational space wherein other religious practices can mediate encounters with God. This understanding seems to have been misinterpreted by the WGM missionaries who, at least at times, have understood buildings to carry mere physical and, consequently, unspiritual associations. Thus, the (inadvertent?) dualism within the mission, discussed previously, continues to misconstrue communication between the church and mission, regrettably, with seemingly significant ramifications.

CONCLUSION

It is worth re-emphasizing the intertwined nature of these issues: communication, spirituality, education, economics, and social status. What emerged from the research data was a sense of frustration with the lack of pieces of paper (e.g., educational certification) that can function in the wider market place for employment. In its advocating oral storytelling, the mission has been promoting a system of Christian learning or discipleship that traffics not in educational certification but in oral intangibles, affective stories memorized in a heart pocket, but that are not necessarily marketable. In this pattern, WGM seems to reflect the ethos of the OM, searching for effective ways to enable people to engage biblical narrative and their

---

105. There seemed to be a general understanding that the appreciation for physical church buildings finds its roots in the Anglican and Roman Catholic traditions. While living and working in Uganda, it was common to see both Church of Uganda and Roman Catholic church buildings in various communities. Jonathan Mayo, personal communication, January 12, 2018; John Muehleisen, personal communication, January 12, 2018.

truths. Thus, while oral storytelling is a communication strategy, essentially, it is also an educational strategy.

As has become evident, it is an imperfect educational strategy. While AGC has acknowledged the strengths of orality in some ways, the church members and leaders' survival requires a particular, literary educational currency in their contextual marketplace. In other words, within the secular aesthetic formation (i.e., the broader social imaginary) in which AGC operates,[106] certain material objects and practices are authorized to mediate or produce certain teleological goods. Literary educational currency mediates, at least, in theory, economic benefit, which enables material gain and, consequently, social status, all of which contribute to substantiating one's spiritual authority. Here is where orality stumbles. Oral storytelling fails to provide the culturally expected and even, demanded, literary educational currency. This inability was associated with a lack of economic betterment and employment for pastors, resulting in the failure of the denomination to obtain material assets, namely, church land ownership and permanent church buildings. This perception has resulted in some of the church personnel expressing strong negative sentiments towards orality and its seeming inability to enable or empower the church towards an integrated, understood to include materialistic, future. While some within the mission might interpret such a materialist future as unspiritual or unholy, the church seems to be arguing that at some deeper level, such material evidences can, although not necessarily always, mediate truth. Therefore, such concerns are about communication, the underlying theme of this project. Even more, they relate to Christian education and how particular instructional practices fail to achieve the necessary materiality of the economic and social *telos* ascribed to by a wider, secular aesthetic formation.

This conclusion ripples through the entire discussion regarding AGC's reception of the OM. Ultimately, it is not a matter of whether the church prefers orality to print or whether orality is or is not effective for religious communication. What emerges out of the data regarding the denomination's understanding of materiality is that material objects provide fixed reference points for mediating identity and religious encounter within their particular social imaginary. While orality affords an embodied materiality, it fails to offer a material artifact for either the communicants or their immediate community, and this inability seems to have wider implications than the OM has previously recognized.

---

106. Here I am drawing on Meyer's aesthetic formations but in synthesis with Smith's discussion of "secular liturgies." For more on this, see Smith's chapter 3, "Lovers in a Dangerous Time: Cultural Exegesis of 'Secular' Liturgies," in Smith, *Desiring the Kingdom*, 89–129.

7

Conclusion

The Material Implications of Orality

INTRODUCTION

THE INTRODUCTION OF THIS book opened with a quotation from Mitchell and Marriage that deserves reiterating: "Conversation lies at the heart of our human existence, at the heart of our cultural understanding and at the heart of our religious experience."[1] This project has sought to facilitate a conversation between Africa Gospel Church and the Orality Movement as represented by World Gospel Mission. Mitchell and Marriage noted their own interest in conversations happening on the boundaries, those in-between spaces of self-disclosure and discovery of another. Exploring such border crossings has indeed been at the center of this research endeavor as consideration has included parties from the Western context as well as the Majority World, each operating from within their own broader social imaginary. The discoveries have been mixed, as church personnel articulated an appreciation as well as critique of the efforts by WGM to promote particular oral communication strategies within the denomination.

As attention shifts to the broader implications of this project, one way to bring together the various themes that have developed is to return to the two kinds of materiality that have been explored, namely that of embodiment and that of artifacts. Both kinds of materiality have intimate associations with identity; thus, the implications from the analysis of this research are summarized around three broad categories: material embodiment, material things, and material personhood. This conclusion examines how each

---

1. Mitchell and Marriage, *Mediating Religion*, 1–2.

of these interrelated categories carries implications for the OM and AGC but also for Majority World Christians operating in similar contexts.

MATERIAL EMBODIMENT

In exploring the positive responses by the church members to oral communication, the analysis in the last chapter included lengthy discussion on the role of the body. Orality affords a particular kind of materiality, an embodied materiality that is unique among other communication modes in its inherent ability to draw on the multisensory possibilities for affective engagement. The WGM missionaries and others among the OM seemed to have intuited this embodied, affective potential and combined it with the imaginative potential of narrative, resulting in heavy emphasis on one particular genre of oral communication, namely oral storytelling.

At this point, before continuing to proceed with discussion on the implications of the body, it is necessary to address one of the concerns that has emerged from this study. The research revealed that church members as well as many within the OM tend to associate orality with both oral communication and narrative. Such an understanding conflates a mode of communication with a way of organizing information, resulting in a definition of orality (as **orality$_2$**) that blurs two distinct, albeit at times interrelated, processes. Information delivered orally can be organized in narrative, but it can also be formatted in other ways such as in propositions. Although some within the wider OM have sought to conceptualize orality as something other than strictly oral storytelling, what AGC as a denomination imbibed was an almost exclusive understanding of orality as oral Bible storytelling. The problem with conceiving of orality to include both the oral communication mode and the narrative format for organizing information is, at times, communications on the ground apparently are more complex. For although WGM understood AGC church members to be "oral-preferred" communicators according to the OM's particularly definition of orality, these oral-preferred church personnel were requesting literate tools, such as books on storytelling and printed notes,[2] and were complaining about the difficulty of memorizing Bible stories.[3] Rev. Martin Owor was a prime example of a supposed oral person not matching up with the OM's particular interpretation of orality; Owor classified himself as an oral learner, but promptly stated his favorite parts of Scripture were not the narrative

---

2. Mukisa and Mukisa, April 22, 2017. This was discussed in chapter 4 under the section on hindrances to orality.

3. This was likewise discussed under oral hindrances in chapter 4. Focus Group: AGC leaders, April 5, 2017; Dhikusooka, May 10, 2017.

portions but the epistles.[4] Such an incident from the field suggests that these supposed oral communicators are not necessarily fitting into WGM personnel's or OM members' **orality**$_2$ categories.

Consequently, I offer a self-reflexive caution to those involved with the OM that static definitions or generic categorizations of how people communicate need to be reconsidered. It can be acknowledged that mission organizations such as WGM are operating within a particular ideology, one with global implications, and so, its adherents are, at times, looking for some general communication categories to discuss and strategize for their own ends. Nonetheless, this research has revealed that, at least in AGC's context, a universal conception of orality and oral communicators does not always do justice to the communication realities as expressed by those on the ground. Reconsideration of such terms and continued sensitive to local communication frameworks requires thorough research—a luxury that some evangelicals feel conflicts with other theological commitments regarding the impulse to reach as many people as possible before the second coming of Christ. While acknowledging the tension between theological commitments and practical communication realities, this project highlights the irony that miscommunication seems to be happening, at least in this particular Ugandan context, between some of the proponents of these oral communication strategies and the very people that those strategies were designed to reach.

That critique standing, it is worth returning to the significance of the body within Christian communication. I suggest that the proponents of the OM are to be commended for championing oral communication as a legitimate means for engaging with the Bible and seeking to foster religious experience, particularly, as a counter to overly cerebral, propositionally-oriented expressions of the Christian faith. While perhaps without even always realizing it, these oral enthusiasts have intuited something about orality and its affective potential for engaging people in appealing ways that do not rely on cognitive argument. Drawing on the scholarship of those such as Smith and Meyer, I argue that it is orality's unique relationship with materiality, particularly that of the body, that makes the difference. The body makes meaning in ways that doctrinally minded and bound evangelicals have not always acknowledged. Thus, even if the OM's conceptual discourse needs continued refining, especially with regard to defining orality itself, it should be acknowledged that the movement's proponents have actively sought to create new space for alternative ways of engaging with Scripture and encountering God. This has included a heightened sensitivity

4. Owor, March 21, 2017.

to the body as not just illustrative but as central for communicating their gospel message. One has only to recall the emphasis on the body in both editions of the *Orality Journal* in 2016 where various embodied expressions were discussed, including dance, body painting, smelling, and singing.[5] Likewise, within AGC, where orality was understood almost synonymously with oral storytelling, one remembers young Esther's story of Elisha the prophet and the provoking youth calling him "Baldhead." While Esther's performance in and of itself was not particularly dramatic, the fact that she embodied her message afforded a greater possibility for affective engagement, particularly since she herself was a youth and her own head was bald as is typical for many young Ugandan school girls.

Thus, the OM's exploration, incorporation, and even attempts at the authorization of the oral mode of communication have opened up new or, at least, rediscovered avenues for conceptualizing and implementing fresh, embodied, Christian communication discursive practices. This is significant, particularly in light of current scholarship's tendency to conceptualize new media as related to electronic or digital communication while print is old media.[6] Oral communication is indeed older than either of these, but the OM's refocusing attention on orality means that future research cannot simply let oral communication fall by the wayside. This could be important in light of the fervor regarding the possibilities and limitations of the increasingly ubiquitous, disembodied, digital screen.

MATERIAL THINGS

Materialized Orality

One of the major themes that this book has uncovered has been the mismatched understanding between church and mission personnel regarding the ascribed communication value given to material things. While those within the WGM and OM missionary community seemed to have intuited and appreciated the material role of the body in making meaning, there has been a lack of recognition regarding how material and physical objects convey meaning within AGC's wider social context. As discussed in the previous chapter, this difference in value ascribed to material things relates to differences in the socioeconomic imaginaries of the church and mission personnel.

---

5. Chiang and Coppedge, "Arts & Orality Part 1"; Chiang and Coppedge, "Arts & Orality Part 2."

6. For examples, see Meyer, "From Imagined Communities," 12; Mitchell and Kidwell, "Changing Uses of Old and New Media," 419–431.

The mission's tendency towards a dualistic paradigm results in a compartmentalized mentality where the mission leader can ask, "Are we growing the physical or the spiritual church?" implying that these are two distinct entities. In such a framework, it is easy to understand how material objects are deemed less valuable. This is further exacerbated in a theological environment where commitments to personal holiness often stress the need to renounce all earthly (read: material) claims on a worshiper's life. In such a dualistic paradigm, an artifact such as a church building[7] seems to suffer from what Daniel Miller calls the "humility of things."[8] Rather than recognizing how the church building acts as a communication medium in and of itself, shaping and forming what transpires in and around it, the building tends instead to be overlooked, important only as the container where the truly spiritual means are conducted, namely, worship and preaching. One can immediately recognize that the missionaries are not actually without material expressions of their faith; rather, to be more accurate, their sociotheological imaginary prioritizes verbal discursive materialities that are interpreted as optimal for facilitating spiritual experiences. This study is not suggesting that such verbal discourses do not facilitate spiritual encounters; rather, it only seeks to highlight the material nature of even these supposed spiritual or intangible practices.

The AGC personnel seemed to operate with a slightly different approach. They, likewise, incorporate verbal discourse, but the concept of belly theology was employed as shorthand to tease out how physical, material things, communicated spiritual realities. Whether a large belly, an iPad,[9] or a permanent church structure, these tangible, physical objects carried substantial communicative weight in and of themselves among the communities wherein AGC is seeking to serve. Consequently, contrary to being conceptualized as distinct, they were described as interrelated; the material object substantiated a spiritual claim. One recalls Rev. James Ouma's illustration that a bright colored handbag was material proof, validating a woman's oral testimony in church about God's blessings. Thus, the church members described a more holistic or integrated frame, whereby communication matters were embedded in a spiritual-socioeconomic imaginary. In such contexts, material things communicated spiritual, societal, and economic realities.

7. McDannell divides material culture into artifacts, landscapes, architecture, and art. Curiously, according to her taxonomy, a church building could be any number of these. I use "artifact" here as a broad descriptor. McDannell, *Material Christianity*, 2–4.

8. Miller, *Stuff*, 50–54.

9. Steward discussed how iPads have become, for some pastors, markers of God's blessing. Mukisa and Mukisa, April 22, 2017.

This mismatched understanding of how nonverbal materialities matter within a particular socioeconomic context has implications for those within the OM. Simply put, members within the OM are going to have to explore ways to materialize orality in order to address concerns being voiced by those within the AGC context. Strictly speaking, oral communication offers a verbal, material discourse, but in actuality, it affords no physical, material artifact. In contexts, such as Uganda, where at least among the AGC members' communities physical, material things convey spiritual and social realities, orality's lack of a material artifact has to be acknowledged and addressed. The need to materialize orality was the issue that Kennedy Kirui seemed to be raising in his recommendation that the OM needs to find ways to credential orality so as to meet community expectations.[10] Granted, as discussed in chapter 3, some American evangelical institutions are trying to offer various certifications and degrees in orality and other groups within the movement do stress "things" such as storytelling pictures or even a story picture cloth.[11] Such attempts are a step in the right direction to intentionally incorporate material things but they fail to address the larger conceptual understanding of how physical, material things communicate in ways that verbal discourse does not. What is needed is not just material helps to assist the pastor or other church leader in remembering the oral text, whether narrative or otherwise. Rather, consideration needs to incorporate the bringing together of the two kinds of materiality that this project has addressed, linking *embodied* oral communication with material *things* so that a communication event transpires on an affective register as well as in a materially valued or respected way among a particular community.

Significantly, the reality that printed *materials* remain highly valued in many communities, such as in AGC's Uganda, means that, ultimately, members of the OM may have to reconsider incorporating printed materials into their oral strategies. This admission does not necessarily mean an abdication of orality or oral strategies, but this research does suggest that in contexts where material objects communicate loudly on an integrated spiritual-socioeconomic plane, to dismiss the material value of a printed text or even a media device is going to result in ongoing miscommunication.

Materialized Authority

This materiality of things and their perceived social value has implications in regards to a second theme evident in this investigation, namely, authority.

10. Kirui, March 28, 2017.

11. The IMB sells Bible storying scarves depicting scenes of biblical narratives. See https://store.imb.org/bible-storying-cloth-scarf/.

Throughout this project, the issue of authority has emerged at various points, particularly regarding how differing modes of communication convey or fail to convey spiritual authority. In many ways, this issue of authority relates to a theology of translation, only in this case it is not necessarily from one language to another but from one medium to another. For those who believe the Bible is God's word, as members of both the OM and AGC do, one of the theological questions emerging from this research is whether the Bible can be translated into and communicated through alternative media other than print and still be the authoritative word of God.

On the one hand, the previous chapter explored how oral storytelling has indeed become an authorized practice within AGC's aesthetic formation. On the other hand, however, there does seem to be a conscious desire by church personnel to keep the printed text close at hand. I recall two sermons where the biblical story was performed orally—but only after the narrative had first been read.[12] Such examples do not negate the evidence and claims made in the preceding chapter regarding oral storytelling as being an approved way to engage the Bible within AGC. Nevertheless, overall, the printed version remains the authoritative medium.

As discussed in the comparison of differing communication modes in chapter 5, AGC personnel questioned, at times, the ability of oral communication and digital media to convey the authoritative word of God. The church members discussed keeping the Bible close to their radio so they could easily verify if someone speaking was preaching the truth. Likewise, concern was voiced that a digital version could be easily manipulated, thus, corrupting the biblical text. Such manipulation of the biblical text was explained as "People are diluting the Bible to run away from conviction."[13] Regardless of whether that is actually happening or not, the point worth reiterating was: "People have the perception that this [holding up a phone] is not the true Bible. This is the true one [holding up a printed Bible]."[14] Therefore, contrary to David Swarr's and others' sentiments discussed in chapter 3 that it is conceptually possible to prise apart the word of God and the printed medium, for AGC personnel, the printed Bible is the standard medium for mediating the authorized Scriptures.

Such observations suggest that, despite AGC's appreciation and appropriation of oral methodologies as a legitimate means to engage and communicate the Bible, the printed medium still carries a theological authority that neither the oral mode nor digital media can match. Birgit Meyer talks about

---

12. Site visit: Bukasa AGC, April 2, 2017; Site visit: Masese AGC, April 23, 2017.
13. Mukisa and Mukisa, April 22, 2017.
14. Omri, May 12, 2017.

how new media, by which she means electronic media, always require negotiating and navigating issues of authorization.[15] While acknowledging again that orality is the oldest medium, Meyer's comment has relevance for any medium being introduced as new into an established communication context. In that case, orality is *new* in the sense of being introduced in a particular way through WGM and the OM; nevertheless, this research suggests that neither oral nor digital versions of the Bible have yet to successfully negotiate and navigate themselves into the authoritative position within the church's sociotheological imaginary. The printed version of the Bible remains, for most in AGC, the truly authoritative word of God.

As proponents of the OM continue to foster biblical engagement in various communities around the globe, such sociotheological considerations need to be kept in mind. Even if some people and their communities do prefer oral or digital versions of the Bible, whether in portions or its entirety, the movement is going to have to continue to explore ways to help such nonprint versions navigate the authorization process within those broader sociotheological imaginaries.

Materialized Interpretation

A sub-theme related to communication, material artifact, and authority runs throughout this project and consequently, deserves addressing. Historically, the Bible came as a printed text to Uganda, and its artifactuality affords referencing and review. Furthermore, the printed word provided a means to ensure and transfer authorized biblical interpretation. **Orality**$_2$ cannot offer that in the same way. In chapter 4, WGM missionary Nathan Metz forcibly made this observation, noting that without some material means to keep interpretation in check, dangerous exegesis could and already has, according to Metz, infiltrated AGC. Metz's solution to orality's inability to offer an interpretative safeguard was the printed medium.

For members of the OM, this critique cuts deep into their commitment to honor God's word. As discussed in chapter 3, these members are passionate about creating opportunities for people to encounter God through the biblical message and, as discussed in chapter 4, oral Bible storytelling has mediated encounters between AGC personnel and God. Nonetheless, while enabling participants to engage the biblical text for themselves and discover Christian truths, the oral method fails to provide much, if any, access to how the historic church has interpreted that same biblical passage. Furthermore, in spite of the STS's method of including necessary historical or background details in the introduction of a story that may be relevant for the ensuing

---

15. Meyer, "From Imagined Communities," 14.

discussion, one cannot help but recognize such information is dependent on some previous storyteller or trainer being able to access such details through the materiality of print. Without literacy skills, one is dependent on the limited information contained in the storyteller's introduction with little to no recourse for attaining more historically relevant background or linguistic information. The idea that an authorized biblical interpretation requires as much reveals its own ideology; however, even if one grants a generous latitude in defining an authorized interpretation, it still remains the case that without printed material and the necessary literacy skills, one has practically no means to access how previous generations of Christians have interpreted the biblical text.

Members of the OM have indeed embraced digital media as an available resource for capturing and transmitting the biblical text. The next step would be for them to utilize digital media as a means to make historical interpretations of the biblical text by those within the church accessible to their audiences. In reality, one cannot help but anticipate the challenges of creating oral-digital communication platforms whereby additional historical background and linguistic information would be orally accessible. The impracticalities of such platforms, at least, at this point in technology's development, platforms that offer historical insight, yet are not reliant on literacy proficiency, suggest, ultimately, a rather stark conclusion for those within the OM: while oral methods can and do afford engagement with the biblical text, access to additional interpretative tools, historical understandings, and extra-biblical background knowledge requires material artifacts, whether via print or digital media. Consequently, such an admission implies that, in all practicality, accessing such knowledge necessitates literacy proficiency. While one can argue that such extra-biblical information is not necessary for evangelism and even initial discipleship, a strong argument can be made it is necessary, at some level, for developing Christian leaders who can interface between their contemporary, cultural context and the historical, biblical environment. Materiality matters and, for those within the OM, further appreciation and consideration of how things communicate within a broader socio-historic-spiritual-materialistic imaginary will be important.

MATERIAL PERSONHOOD

As has become evident through the course of this discussion, issues of orality are indeed communication concerns, but communication never stands as an isolated phenomenon; rather, it is embedded within a larger social and material imaginary that shapes and forms personal identity. Thus, to talk about orality is to raise questions about how people understand themselves—in short, what it means to be a person.

This has implications because for those within the OM to classify someone as oral-preferred, is to make a statement, not just about an individual's communication style but about his or her identity. While this conclusion has already cautioned against static classifications used by various members within the OM, it is worth revisiting this concern in light of the much larger issue of personhood. On the ION website, the hub of the OM, the question "Who is ION?" is answered with the following statement: "The International Orality Network is an affiliation of agencies and organizations working together with the common goal of making God's Word available to *oral communicators* in culturally appropriate ways that enable church planting movements everywhere."[16] On that same page, one reads: "ION seeks to radically influence the way *oral communicators* are encouraged to follow Jesus."[17] The statement is intended to particularize the network's target audience—communicators who prefer oral rather than literate methodologies. The research in Uganda has illustrated that things are more complicated. These alleged oral communicators are *persons* situated in particular social contexts and in, at least, some of the supposed oral environments such as AGC's, these persons do not want to be identified as oral-preferred. This was most clearly evidenced in the account recalled in chapter 5 from my experience at the Nebbi AGC church.

I asked the Nebbi focus group how they preferred to engage the Bible. The vast majority raised their hands, indicating they preferred to engage the Bible through reading—only to have their pastor stand up and, in front of everyone, address me by contradicting the church members. He declared that most of them could not read well but rather were very good at listening. This contradicting cultural scenario revealed something(s) related to tensions regarding conceptions of personhood as understood by local church members. It is possible that the pastor's classification was false and, in fact, most of the church could read well. Much more likely, it is possible that his statement was accurate, that the Nebbi AGC church community as a whole did not have strong literacy proficiency. If so, then in a technical sense, the church members could be classified as oral-reliant communicators. Nevertheless, regardless of the community's literacy proficiency, or lack thereof, and, regardless even if their pastor thought they were oral-reliant, what mattered was the church members did not want to identified themselves as *oral*

---

16. https://orality.net/about/. Emphasis added. This is the updated version of Willis's original mission statement for ION as presented in chapter 2.

17. https://orality.net/about/. Emphasis added.

communicators; they wanted to be identified as literate communicators, able to read the Bible. Thus, even if the group was technically oral-reliant, they self-identified as literate-preferred communicators.

Such an incident reveals how aspects of personhood can be interpreted differently, sometimes even quite dramatically, by those on the ground. The mission and others within the OM are trying to identify both those who do not possess literacy skills or, if they do, still prefer to communicate on a primarily oral register. In actuality, labeling a person as an oral communicator has broader connotations that may not have been completely thought through. It would seem this is another area where those within the OM have the opportunity to enlarge their understanding of how communication is embedded in and influenced by a broader social, materialistic imaginary. As discussed in chapter 5, I had the opportunity to debrief the Nebbi focus group with the church pastors, Benson Omri and Willy Manano. They discussed the stigma of being identified as unable to read. Regardless of whether individual members could read or not, the majority of the focus group identified themselves as preferring to read their Bible. According to Omri and Manano, this was not merely a matter of whether one had literacy skills, or not, but rather how one's identity was perceived by the community. Raising one's hand to say one preferred to read the Bible was a way to associate one's personhood with a particular socially acceptable, even privileged, identity. Granted, the woman named Kristen did identify herself as preferring oral communication, but the pastors were explicitly noting her courage at making such a public and possibly shameful identification. Therefore, what stands out is that the majority of these alleged oral communicators did not want to be identified as oral-preferred persons.

This identity complication, where local communicators are not actually fitting into the OM's communication classifications, necessitates further research. While perhaps present in interpersonal experiences or discussions, I am unaware of any official discourse within the movement regarding this paradoxical personhood phenomenon and how to address it. Similar to the issues of embodiment and the need to materialize orality, this personhood tension flows out of the interrelated nature of communication within a particular social environment. Future communication approaches within the church and mission are going to require creative discussions that are attentive not only to personal communication abilities and preferences, but also to how such communication abilities and preferences are shaped and formed by the surrounding social imaginary.

In highlighting the way modes of communication are situated within a broader social imaginary, this research has drawn attention to how communication is always related to identity. In many ways, this is very theological, as the WGM missionaries and others involved in the OM desire the transformation of personal identity through encountering Jesus Christ in the Bible. Such issues of identity are not, however, only theological, as this book has explored. Each mode of communication connotes certain sensibilities, particularly in relation to modernity, matters of identity that are situated within a broader socioeconomic and materialistic framework. Thus, in exploring communication complexities, this project has engaged a larger or, perhaps more accurately, a more holistic discourse regarding personhood. Personnel within the mission and the church inhabit different social imaginaries, which, consequently, include differences of understanding regarding the nature of what it means to be a person, particularly a *modern* person inhabiting a particular Ugandan context.

This has larger implications beyond reaching individual persons with the gospel message, for as mentioned in the preceding quotation from the ION webpage, ION members are "working together with the common goal of making God's Word available to oral communicators in culturally appropriate ways that enable church planting movements everywhere." Ultimately, the OM's desire is to see oral communicators following Jesus in reproducing church communities; for that goal to be fulfilled, they are going to have to continue to attune their ears to how personhood is constructed and perceived by both local Christian communicators and their communities. This is not to say that society alone defines the person within the church fellowship, but, as has been explored, failure to recognize how aspects of personhood such as communication are influenced by social realities will stymie efforts aimed at achieving effective communication and flourishing churches.

Appendix A

Oral Sources

INTERVIEWS

Interviews Regarding the Orality Movement

Apollos, Djibo Isaac. Personal interview in Jakarta, Indonesia. August 10, 2016.
Bemis, Linda. Skype interview. July 26, 2016.
Boetcher, Jason. Personal interview in Houston, Texas. September 14, 2016.
Chiang, Samuel E. Personal interview in Jakarta, Indonesia. August 1, 2016.
Chong, Calvin. Personal interview in Jakarta, Indonesia. August 5, 2016.
Dueck, Melissa. Personal interview in Jakarta, Indonesia. August 6, 2016.
Fletcher, Charlie. Skype interview. August 29, 2016.
Herrera, Abiel. Personal interview in Jakarta, Indonesia. August 8, 2016.
Lovejoy, Grant. Skype interview. August 31, 2016.
Marmon, Ellen. Skype interview. August 17, 2016.
McMahon, Wilson. Skype interview. August 29, 2016.
Menkin, Andrea. Personal interview in Houston, Texas. September 13, 2016.
Moon, Jay W. Skype interview. July 27, 2016.
Steffen, Tom. Skype interview. July 27, 2016.
Swarr, David. Skype interview. August 18, 2016.
Terry, J. O. Skype interview. July 25, 2016.
Thompson, Bryan. Personal interview (1st) in Houston, Texas. September 14, 2016.
———. Personal interview (2nd) in Paisley, Scotland. June 30, 2017.
Wafler, Stan. Skype interview. August 24, 2016.
Wiles, Jerry. Skype interview. January 29, 2018.

Appendix A: Oral Sources

Interviews Regarding Africa Gospel Church

AGC Church Members

Dhikusooka, David. Personal interview (1st). April 23, 2017.
———. Personal interview (2nd). May 10, 2017.
Kinaalwa, Joshua. Personal interview in Muyenga (Kampala). May 11, 2017.
Kirui, Kennedy. Personal interview in Muyenga (Kampala). March 28, 2017.
Mukisa, Miria, and Steward Stephen Mukisa. Personal interview in Bukasa (Kampala). April 22, 2017.
Mukisa, Steward Stephen. Personal interview (1st) in Kiryandongo. April 29, 2017.
———. Personal interview (2nd) in Kisugu (Kampala). December 8, 2017.
Omri, Benson. Personal interview (1st) in Nebbi. March 19, 2017.
———. Personal interview (2nd) in Kiwafu (Kampala). May 12, 2017.
Ouma, Caroline, and Lillian Kirui. Personal interview in Kiwafu (Kampala), May 17, 2017.
Ouma, James. Personal interview (1st) in Kiwafu (Kampala). March 31, 2017.
———. Personal interview (2nd) in Buwagi. April 7, 2017.
———. Personal interview (3rd) in Kisugu (Kampala). May 22, 2017.
Owor, Martin. Personal interview (1st) in Muyenga (Kampala), March 21, 2017.
———. Personal interview (2nd) in Kisugu (Kampala). December 8, 2017.

World Gospel Mission Missionaries

Hopson, Kenneth. Personal interview in Kiwafu (Kampala). March 23, 2017.
Mayo, Jonathan. Personal interview (1st) in Muyenga (Kampala). March 23, 2017.
———. Personal interview (2nd) in Muyenga (Kampala). April 4, 2017.
———. Personal interview (3rd) in Muyenga (Kampala). May 22, 2017.
McPherson, Larry, and Joy McPherson. Skype interview (1st). July 12, 2017.
———. Skype interview (2nd). July 13, 2017.
Metz, Nathan. Skype interview. April 25, 2017.
Muehleisen, Beth. Personal interview in Muyenga (Kampala). March 31, 2017.
Muehleisen, John. Personal interview in Muyenga (Kampala). May 18, 2017.
Stanfield, Jeff, and Christine Stanfield. Personal interview in Kabalagala (Kampala). May 9, 2017.

ADDITIONAL INTERVIEWEES

Hall, Rhys. Personal interview in Arua. March 18, 2017.
Laurent, Imam Otafiire. Personal interview in Muyenga (Kampala). April 1, 2017.
Okello, Fred. Personal interview in Arua. March 15, 2017.
Pasolini, Tonino. Personal interview in Arua. March 16, 2017.

FOCUS GROUP DISCUSSIONS

Focus Group: AGC Church Leaders. Personal meeting in Muyenga (Kampala). April 5, 2017.
Focus Group: Bugiri AGC. Personal meeting in Bugiri. May 14, 2017.
Focus Group: Bulyango AGC. Personal meeting in Bulyango. April 28, 2017.
Focus Group: Kafu AGC. Personal meeting in Kafu. April 27, 2017.
Focus Group: Kahara AGC. Personal meeting in Kahara. April 29, 2017.
Focus Group: Kamuli Area Pastors. Personal meeting in Buwagi. April 7, 2017.
Focus Group: KIU Students. Personal meeting in Kansanga (Kampala). May 5, 2017.
Focus Group: Masese AGC. Personal meeting in Masese. April 23, 2017.
Focus Group: Nebbi AGC. Personal meeting in Nebbi. March 19, 2017.

Bibliography

Anderson, W. B. *The Church of East Africa: 1840–1974*. Reprint, Dodoma: Central Tanganyika, 1981.
Anonymous. "A Participatory Approach to Song-Crafting." *Orality Journal* 4.2 (2015) 43–48.
Anstey, Michèle, and Geoff Bull. "Helping Teachers to Explore Multimodal Texts." *Curriculum and Leadership Journal* 8.16 (2010). http://www.curriculum.edu.au/leader/helping_teachers_to_explore_multimodal_texts,31522.html?issueID=12141.
Archambault, Julie Soleil. *Mobile Secrets: Youth, Intimacy, and the Politics of Pretense in Mozambique*. Chicago: University of Chicago Press, 2017.
Arrington, Aminta. "Hymns of the Everlasting Hills: The Written Word in an Oral Culture in Southwest China." PhD diss., Biola University, 2014.
Asad, Talal. *Genealogies of Religion: Discipline and Reasons of Power in Christianity and Islam*. Baltimore: Johns Hopkins University Press, 2009.
"Audio Scripture Engagement Declaration." International Orality Network, 2010. https://orality.net/declaration/.
Austin, Alvyn. *China's Millions*. Grand Rapids: Eerdmans, 2007.
Baker, Robert A. *Tell the Generations Following: A History of Southwestern Baptist Theological Seminary 1908–1983*. Nashville: Broadman, 1983.
Barber, Karin, ed. *African Hidden Histories: Everyday Literacy and the Making of the Self*. Bloomington: Indiana University Press, 2006.
———. *The Anthropology of Texts, Persons and Publics*. Cambridge: Cambridge University Press, 2007.
Barbour, Rosaline. *Introducing Qualitative Research: A Student Guide to the Craft of Doing Qualitative Research*. London: Sage, 2008.
Barnes, Andrew E. *Global Christianity and the Black Atlantic: Tuskegee, Colonialism, and the Shaping of African Industrial Education*. Waco: Baylor University Press, 2017.
Bauckham, Richard. "Bible in Mission: The Modern/Postmodern Western Context." In *Bible in Mission*, edited by Pauline Hoggarth et al., 43–55. Regnum Edinburgh Centenary Series 18. Oxford: Regnum, 2013.

Bauer, David R. "Inductive Biblical Study: History, Character, and Prospects in a Global Environment." *The Asbury Journal* 68.1 (2013) 6–35.
Bayart, Jean-François. *The State in Africa: The Politics of the Belly*. 2nd ed. Cambridge: Polity, 2009.
Bemis, Linda. *Praying for Oral and Oral Bibleless People Groups*. Hong Kong: International Orality Network, 2018.
Bernard, H. Russell. *Research Methods in Anthropology: Qualitative and Quantitative Approaches*. Lanham: AltaMira, 2011.
Bialecki, Jon, Naomi Haynes, and Joel Robbins. "The Anthropology of Christianity." *Religion Compass* 2.6 (2008) 1139–58. https://dx.doi.org/10.1111/j.1749-8171.2008.00116.x.
Bielo, James S. *Emerging Evangelicals: Faith, Modernity, and the Desire for Authenticity*. New York: New York University Press, 2011.
———. *Words upon the Word: An Ethnography of Evangelical Group Bible Study*. Qualitative Studies in Religion. New York: New York University Press, 2009.
Bompani, Barbara, and S. Terreni Brown. "A 'Religious Revolution'? Print Media, Sexuality, and Religious Discourse in Uganda." *Journal of Eastern African Studies* 9.1 (2015) 110–26. https://dx.doi.org/10.1080/17531055.2014.987507.
Botha, P. J. J. *Orality and Literacy in Early Christianity*. Biblical Performance Criticism. Eugene: Cascade, 2012.
Bowman, Carla. *Building Bridges to Oral Cultures*. Pasadena: William Carey Library, 2017.
Box, Harry. *Don't Throw the Book at Them: Communicating the Christian Message to People Who Don't Read*. Pasadena: William Carey, 2014.
Brereton, Virginia Lieson. *Training God's Army: The American Bible School, 1880–1940*. Bloomington: Indiana University Press, 1990.
Brown, Candy Gunther. *The Word in the World: Evangelical Writing, Publishing, and Reading in America, 1789–1880*. Chapel Hill: University of North Carolina Press, 2004.
Bruner, Jason. *Living Salvation in the East African Revival in Uganda*. Rochester: University of Rochester Press, 2017.
Burghardt, Walter J. "The Catholic Concept of Tradition in the Light of Modern Theological Thought." *Proceedings of the Catholic Theological Society of America* 6 (2012) 42–77.
Cabrita, Joel. *Text and Authority in the South African Nazaretha Church*. Cambridge: Cambridge University Press, 2014.
Cannell, Fenella. "Introduction: The Anthropology of Christianity." In *The Anthropology of Christianity*, edited by Fenella Cannell, 2–50. Durham: Duke University Press, 2006.
Caputo, John D. "Spectral Hermeneutics: On the Weakness of God and the Theology of the Event." In *After the Death of God*, edited by Jeffrey W. Robbins, 47–86. New York: Columbia University Press, 2007.
Carey, James W. "The Cultural Approach to Communication." In *Communication as Culture: Essays on Media and Society*, revised, 11–28. New York: Routledge, 2009.
Cary, W. W. *The Story of the National Holiness Missionary Society*. Chicago: National Holiness Missionary Society, 1940.

Chapell, Colin B. "Sanctified Manhood: Theology and Identity in the Southern Holiness Movement." *Journal of The Historical Society* 13.4 (2013) 465–90. https://dx.doi.org/10.1111/jhis.12029.

Chiang, Samuel E., and Avery T. Willis, Jr., eds. *Orality Breakouts: Using Heart Language to Transform Hearts*. Hong Kong: ION/LCWE, 2010.

Chiang, Samuel E., and Grant Lovejoy. *Beyond Literate Western Contexts: Honor and Shame and Assessment of Orality Preference*. Hong Kong: International Orality Network, 2014.

———. *Beyond Literate Western Models: Contextualizing Theological Education in Oral Contexts*. Hong Kong: International Orality Network, 2014.

———. *Beyond Literate Western Practices: Continuing Conversations in Orality and Theological Education*. Hong Kong: International Orality Network, 2014.

Chiang, Samuel E., and William A. Coppedge, eds. "Arts & Orality Part 1: Foundations and Applications." *Orality Journal: The Word Became Fresh* 5.1 (2016). https://orality.net/library/journals/volume-5-number-1/.

———, eds. "Arts & Orality Part 2: Equipping for Ministry." *Orality Journal: The Word Became Fresh* 5.2 (2016). https://orality.net/library/journals/volume-5-number-2/.

Chirgwin, A. M. *The Bible in World Evangelism*. London: SCM, 1954.

Chong, Calvin. "Encountering Text as a Multimodal Experience: Implications for the Educational Ministries of the Church." Paper presented at ION North America Regional Conference, Oklahoma City, 2015.

Cole, Jennifer. *Sex and Salvation: Imagining the Future in Madagascar*. Chicago: University of Chicago Press, 2010.

Collinson, Patrick. "The English Conventicle." In *Voluntary Religion*, edited by W. J. Sheils and Diana Wood, 223–59. Studies in Church History 23. Oxford: Basil Blackwell, 1986.

Coppedge, William. "Overcoming Complications to Oral Methodologies among the Alur People of Uganda." Presented at University of Glasgow, 2010.

Cox, Jillian E. "Martin Luther on the Living Word: Rethinking the Principle of Sola Scriptura." *Pacifica* 29.1 (2016) 3–21. https://dx.doi.org/10.1177/1030570X17690011.

Dawson, Jane E. A. *Scotland Re-formed 1488–1587*. Edinburgh: Edinburgh University Press, 2007.

Dayton, Donald W., and Douglas M. Strong. *Rediscovering an Evangelical Heritage: A Tradition and Trajectory of Integrating Piety and Justice*. 2nd ed. Grand Rapids: Baker Academic, 2014.

Dewey, Joanna. "The Gospel of Mark as an Oral-Aural Event: Implications for Interpretation." In *The New Literacy Criticism and the New Testament*, edited by E. S. Malbon and E. V. McKnight, 145–63. Sheffield: Sheffield Academic, 1994.

———. "Oral Methods of Structuring Narrative in Mark." *Interpretation* 43.1 (1989) 32–44.

Dieter, Melvin Easterday. *The Holiness Revival of the Nineteenth Century*. 2nd ed. Studies in Evangelicalism 1. Lanham: Scarecrow, 1996.

Duffy, Eamon. *The Stripping of the Altars: Traditional Religion in England, c.1400–c.1580*. New Haven: Yale University Press, 2005.

Dunn, James D. G. *Jesus Remembered: Christianity in the Making*. Grand Rapids: Eerdmans, 2003.

Earle, Jonathan L. "Political Theologies in Late Colonial Buganda." PhD diss., University of Cambridge, 2012.

Edwards, Mark U., Jr. *Printing, Propaganda, and Martin Luther*. Berkeley: University of California Press, 1994.

Ellison, Robert H. *The Victorian Pulpit: Spoken and Written Sermons in Nineteenth-Century Britain*. Selinsgrove: Susquehanna University Press, 1998.

Emy, Mugisha. "The Constitution of Africa Gospel Church Uganda." Kampala: Print Shop, 2012.

Engelke, Matthew. *A Problem of Presence: Beyond Scripture in an African Church*. Berkeley: University of California Press, 2007.

Evans, G. R. "Authority." In *The New Cambridge History of the Bible: From 1450–1750*, edited by Euan Cameron, 3:387–417. Cambridge: Cambridge University Press, 2016.

Farrell, Thomas J. "Early Christian Creeds and Controversies in the Light of the Orality-Literacy Hypothesis." *Oral Tradition: Festschrift for Walter J. Ong* 2.1 (1987) 132–49.

Faupel, J. F. *African Holocaust: The Story of the Uganda Martyrs*. Revised. Nairobi: Paulines, 2007.

Ferguson, Tom. "Church Planting with Bible Storying and the Creative Arts." *Orality Journal: The Word Became Fresh* 5.1 (2016) 63–66.

Finnegan, Ruth. "Communication and Technology." *Language and Communication* 9.2–3 (1989) 107–27. https://dx.doi.org/10.1016/0271-5309(89)90013-X.

Furet, François, and Jacques Ozouf. *Reading and Writing: Literacy in France from Calvin to Jules Ferry*. Cambridge: Cambridge University Press, 1982.

Gibson, J. J. "The Theory of Affordances." In *Perceiving, Acting, and Knowing: Toward an Ecological Psychology*, edited by R. Shaw and J. Bransford, 127–43. Hoboken: John Wiley & Sons, 1977.

Gifford, Paul. *African Christianity: Its Public Role in Uganda and Other African Countries*. Kampala: Fountain, 1999.

Glaser, B. G. *Doing Grounded Theory: Issues and Discussions*. Mill Valley: Sociology, 1998.

Glaser, B. G., and A. L. Strauss. *The Discovery of Grounded Theory: Strategies for Qualitative Research*. Chicago: Aldine, 1967.

Goody, Jack. *The Domestication of the Savage Mind*. Themes in the Social Sciences. Cambridge: Cambridge University Press, 1977.

Goody, Jack, and Ian Watt. "The Consequences of Literacy." In *Literacy in Traditional Societies*, edited by Jack Goody, 27–68. Cambridge University Press, 1968.

Gordon, Bruce. "The Bible in Reformed Thought, 1520–1750." In *The New Cambridge History of the Bible: From 1450–1750*, edited by Euan Cameron, 3:462–88. Cambridge: Cambridge University Press, 2016.

Gravelle, Gilles. "'What Do You Mean?' Why Communication Breakdowns Happen." *Orality Journal: The Word Became Fresh* 6.1 (2017) 13–28.

Gray, J. M. "Mutesa of Buganda." *Uganda Journal* 1. 1 (1934) 22–50.

Greeley, Andrew. *The Catholic Imagination*. Berkeley: University of California Press, 2000.

Guarino, Thomas G. *Vattimo and Theology*. Philosophy and Theology. London: T. & T. Clark, 2009.

Gusman, Alessandro. "HIV/AIDS, Pentecostal Churches, and the 'Joseph Generation' in Uganda." *Africa Today* 56.1 (2009) 66–86. https://dx.doi.org/10.2979/aft.2009.56.1.66.
Handman, Courtney. *Critical Christianity: Translation and Denominational Conflict in Papua New Guinea*. Anthropology of Christianity. Berkeley: University of California Press, 2014.
Hansen, Holger Bernt. *Mission, Church and State in a Colonial Setting, Uganda 1890–1925*. London: Heinemann, 1984.
Hardin, Jessica. "Christianity, Fat Talk, and Samoan Pastors: Rethinking the Fat-Positive-Fat-Stigma Framework." *Fat Studies* 4.2 (2015) 178–96. https://dx.doi.org/10.1080/21604851.2015.1015924.
Harrison, Carol. *The Art of Listening in the Early Church*. Oxford: Oxford University Press, 2013.
Hartnell, Malcolm Richard. "Oral Contextualization: Communicating Biblical Truth to the Digo in Kenya 2009." PhD diss., Fuller Theological Seminary, 2009.
Hastings, Adrian. *The Church in Africa, 1450–1950*. Oxford: Oxford University Press, 1996.
Havelock, Eric. *The Muse Learns to Write: Reflections on Orality and Literacy from Antiquity to the Present*. New Haven: Yale University Press, 1986.
———. *Preface to Plato*. Cambridge: Harvard University Press, 1963.
Hawkins, Sean. *Writing and Colonialism in Northern Ghana: The Encounter between the LoDagaa and 'the World on Paper.'* Toronto: University of Toronto Press, 2015.
Haynes, Naomi. *Moving by the Spirit: Pentecostal Social Life on the Zambian Copperbelt*. Oakland: University of California Press, 2017.
———. "Pentecostalism and the Morality of Money: Prosperity, Inequality, and Religious Sociality on the Zambian Copperbelt." *Journal of the Royal Anthropological Institute* 18.1 (2012) 123–39.
———. "Theology on the Ground." In *Theologically Engaged Anthropology: Social Anthropology and Theology in Conversation*, 266–79. Oxford: Oxford University Press, 2018.
Heal, Bridget. "The Catholic Eye and the Protestant Ear: The Reformation as a Non-Visual Event?" In *The Myth of the Reformation*, edited by Peter Opitz, 321–55. Refo500 Academic Studies. Göttingen: Vandonhoeck & Ruprecht, 2013.
———. *A Magnificent Faith: Art and Identity in Lutheran Germany*. Oxford: Oxford University Press, 2017.
Hearn, Julie. "The Invisible NGO: US Evangelical Missions in Kenya." *Journal of Religion in Africa* 32.1 (2002) 32–60.
Hennink, Monique M. *Understanding Focus Group Discussions*. New York: Oxford University Press, 2014.
Hennink, Monique M., et al. *Qualitative Research Methods*. London: Sage, 2011.
Hindmarsh, Roland. "Uganda." In *Church, State, and Education in Africa*, edited by David G. Scanlon, 135–63. New York: Teachers College, 1966.
Hodge, Charles. *Systematic Theology*. Vol. 1. Grand Rapids: Eerdmans, 1940.
Horsfield, Peter. *From Jesus to the Internet: A History of Christianity and Media*. Chichester: John Wiley & Sons, 2015.
Houtman, Dick, and Birgit Meyer, eds. *Things: Religion and the Question of Materiality*. New York: Fordham University Press, 2012.

Howell, Brian M. "The Repugnant Cultural Other Speaks Back." *Anthropological Theory* 7.4 (2007) 371–91. https://dx.doi.org/10.1177/1463499607083426.
Hunt, Arnold. *The Art of Hearing: English Preachers and Their Audiences, 1590–1640*. Cambridge Studies in Early Modern British History. Cambridge: Cambridge University Press, 2010.
Hurtado, Larry W. *Destroyer of the Gods: Early Christian Distinctiveness in the Roman World*. Waco: Baylor University Press, 2016.
———. "Oral Fixation and New Testament Studies? 'Orality,' 'Performance' and Reading Texts in Early Christianity." *New Testament Studies* 60.3 (2014) 321–40. https://dx.doi.org/10.1017/S0028688514000058.
International Orality Network. "Orality: Changing the Paradigm." *YouTube*, November 25, 2015. https://www.youtube.com/watch?v=z6uslWUdHwY.
Iverson, Kelly R. "Oral Fixation or Oral Corrective? A Response to Larry Hurtado." *New Testament Studies* 62.2 (2016) 183–200. https://dx.doi.org/10.1017/S0028688515000430.
———. "Orality and the Gospels: A Survey of Recent Research." *Currents in Biblical Research* 8.1 (2009) 71–106. https://dx.doi.org/10.1177/1476993X09341489.
Jagerson, Jennifer. "Transformation through Narrative: Exploring the Power of Sacred Stories among Oral Learners in Ethiopia." PhD diss., Biola University, 2016.
Janes, Dominic. "The Wordless Book: The Visual and Material Culture of Evangelism in Victorian Britain." *Material Religion* 12.1 (2016) 26–49. https://dx.doi.org/10.1080/17432200.2015.1120085.
Jenkins, Philip. *The New Faces of Christianity: Believing the Bible in the Global South*. New York: Oxford University Press, USA, 2006.
———. *The Next Christendom: The Coming of Global Christianity*. 3rd ed. Oxford: Oxford University Press, 2011.
Jones, Ben. *Beyond the State in Rural Uganda*. International African Library. Edinburgh: Edinburgh University Press, 2009.
Jones, Thomas Jesse. "Education in East Africa." Phelps-Stokes Commission. New York: Phelps-Stokes Fund, 1924.
Keane, Webb. "Materialism, Missionaries, and Modern Subjects in Colonial Indonesia." In *Conversion to Modernities: The Globalization of Christianity*, edited by Peter van der Veer, 137–70. New York: Routledge, 1996.
———. "On the Materiality of Religion." *Material Religion* 4.2 (2015) 230–31. https://dx.doi.org/10.2752/175183408X328343.
Kelber, Werner H. *The Oral and the Written Gospel: The Hermeneutics of Speaking and Writing in the Synoptic Tradition, Mark, Paul, and Q*. African Systems of Thought Series. Bloomington: Indiana University Press, 1997.
Kent, Eliza F. "Books and Bodices: Material Culture and Protestant Missions in Colonial South India." In *Mixed Messages: Materiality, Textuality, Missions*. New York: Palgrave Macmillan, 2005.
Kirsch, Thomas G. *Spirits and Letters: Reading, Writing and Charisma in African Christianity*. New York: Berghahn, 2008.
Kiwanuka, M. S. M. "Kabaka Mwanga and His Political Parties." *Uganda Journal* 33.1 (1969) 1–16.
Koehler, Paul F. *Telling God's Stories with Power: Biblical Storytelling in Oral Cultures*. Trotwood: United Theological Seminary, 2007.

Kreitzer, Beth. "The Lutheran Sermon." In *Preachers and People in the Reformations and Early Modern Period*, 35–64. Leiden: Brill, 2001.
Kress, G. R., and T. Van Leeuwen. *Multimodal Discourse: The Modes and Media of Contemporary Communication*. London: Arnold, 2001.
Kuhn, Thomas S. *The Structure of Scientific Revolutions: 50th Anniversary Edition*. 4th ed. Chicago: University of Chicago Press, 2012.
Lang'at, Robert K. "Holiness Historiography: As a Theological Framework for Understanding the Emergence of Christianity in Africa." *African Journal of Evangelical Theology* 29.1 (2010) 29–52.
———. "The Holiness Movement in Africa: A Historiographical Study of the Quest for Sanctification as a Theological Framework for Understanding the Emergence of Christianity in Africa." PhD diss., Drew University, 2003. https://search-proquest-com.ezproxy.is.ed.ac.uk/docview/305338464?accountid=10673.
Leatherwood, Rick. "The Case and Call for Oral Bibles: A Key Component in Completing the Great Commission." *William Carey International Development Journal* 2.2 (2013) 37–39.
Lee, Kuem Ju. "Bible Storytelling: A Recommended Strategy for Training Church Leaders in Oral Societies." PhD diss., Southern Baptist Theological Seminary, 2005.
Lesage, Julia. "Christian Media." In *Media, Culture, and the Religious Right*, edited by Linda Kintz and Julia Lesage, 21–49. Minneapolis: University of Minnesota Press, 1998.
LeVine, R. A. "Patterns of Personality in Africa." In *Responses to Change: Society, Culture, and Personality*, edited by G. A. DeVos. New York: Van Nostrand Reinhold, 1976.
Livingston, T. W. "Paradox in Early Mission Education in Buganda." *Journal of African Studies* 2.2 (1975) 161–76.
Loewen, J. A. *Culture and Human Values: Christian Intervention in Anthropological Perspective: Selections from the Writings of Jacob A. Loewen*. Applied Cultural Anthropology Series. Pasadena: William Carey, 1961.
Lord, Albert B. *The Singer of Tales*. Edited by S. Mitchell and G. Nagy. 2nd ed. Cambridge: Harvard University Press, 2000.
Lotz, David W. "Sola Scriptura: Luther on Biblical Authority." *Union Seminary Review* 35.3 (1981) 258–73.
Lovejoy, Grant. "'But I Did Such Good Exposition': Literate Preachers Confront Orality." Paper presented at the Evangelical Homiletics Society, 2001.
———. "The Extent of Orality: 2012 Update." *Orality Journal* 1.1 (2012) 11–39.
———, ed. *Making Disciples of Oral Learners*. Pasadena: William Carey, 2005.
Lovett, Ian. "Will There Ever Be Another?" *Wall Street Journal*, February 24, 2018, Section: Review.
Low, D. *Fabrication of Empire: The British and the Uganda Kingdoms, 1890–1902*. Cambridge: Cambridge University Press, 2009.
Lyotard, Jean-François. *The Postmodern Condition: A Report on Knowledge*. Minneapolis: University of Minnesota Press, 1984.
Madinger, Charles. "Coming to Terms with Orality: A Holistic Model." *Missiology: An International Review* 38.2 (2010) 201–13. https://dx.doi.org/10.1177/009182961003800211.
———. "A Literate's Guide to the Oral Galaxy." *Orality Journal* 2.2 (2013) 13–40.

———. *Oralities and Literacies: Implications for Communication and Education*. International Orality Network, 2017. E-book. https://orality.net/library/other/orality-literacies/.

———. "Recap of the Seven Disciplines of Orality." Podcast. International Orality Network. https://orality.net/content/recap-the-seven-disciplines-of-orality/.

Makosky Daley, et al. "Using Focus Groups in Community-Based Participatory Research: Challenges and Resolutions." *Qualitative Health Research* 20.5 (2010) 697–706. https://dx.doi.org/10.1177/1049732310361468.

Manarin, Louis Timothy. "And the Word Became Kigambo: Language, Literacy, and Bible Translation in Buganda 1875–1931." PhD diss., Indiana University, 2008.

Marini, Stephen. "Hymnody and History: Early American Evangelical Hymns as Sacred Music." In *Music in American Religious Experience*, edited Philip Vilas Bohlman et al., 123–54. Oxford: Oxford University Press, 2006.

Marsden, George M. *Understanding Fundamentalism and Evangelicalism*. Grand Rapids: Eerdmans, 1991.

Matviuk, Marcela A Chaván de. "Latin American Pentecostal Growth: Culture, Orality and the Power of Testimonies." *Asian Journal of Pentecostal Studies* 5.2 (2002) 205–22.

McBeth, H. Leon. *The Baptist Heritage: Four Centuries of Baptist Witness*. Nashville: Broadman, 1987.

McDannell, Colleen. *Material Christianity: Religion and Popular Culture in America*. New Haven: Yale University Press, 1995.

McGavran, Donald A. *How Churches Grow: The New Frontier of Mission*. London: World Dominion, 1959.

———. *The Satnami Story: A Thrilling Drama of Religious Change*. Pasadena: William Carey, 1990.

———. *Understanding Church Growth*. Grand Rapids: Eerdmans, 1970.

McGrath, Alister E. *Christianity's Dangerous Idea: The Protestant Revolution—A History from the Sixteenth Century to the Twenty-First*. New York: Harper Collins, 2007.

McGregor, Gordon P. *King's College Budo: A Centenary History 1906–2006*. Kampala: Fountain, 2006.

McIlwain, Trevor. *Building on Firm Foundations: Guidelines for Evangelism and Teaching Believers*. Sanford: New Tribes Mission, 1987.

McIntyre, Roy C. "Using Ceremonies to Disciple Oral Learners among the Tribal People in Bangladesh." PhD diss., Asbury Theological Seminary, 2005.

McLuhan, Marshall. *The Gutenberg Galaxy: The Making of Typographic Man*. Toronto: University of Toronto Press, 1962.

McMahon, Wilson. "Analysis of the Reception and Appropriation of the Bible by Manobo Christians in Central Mindanao, Philippines." PhD diss., University of Edinburgh, 2017.

McPherson, Joy. "AGC Kisugu Church Second Floor Dedication Service." Kampala: World Gospel Mission, March 8, 1998.

Merleau-Ponty, Maurice. *Phenomenology of Perception*. Abingdon: Taylor & Francis, 1945.

———. *The Primacy of Perception: And Other Essays on Phenomenological Psychology, the Philosophy of Art, History, and Politics*. Evanston: Northwestern University Press, 1964.

Metz, Nathan, ed. *Church Discipleship Manual*. Revised. Kampala: Print Shop, 2016.

Meyer, Birgit. "Aesthetics." In *Key Words in Religion, Media, and Culture*, edited by David Morgan, 20–30. New York: Routledge, 2008.
———. "Introduction: From Imagined Communities to Aesthetic Formations—Religious Mediations, Sensational Forms, and Styles of Binding." In *Aesthetic Formations: Media, Religion, and the Senses*, 1–30. New York: Palgrave Macmillan, 2009.
———. "Religious Sensations: Why Media, Aesthetics and Power Matter in the Study of Contemporary Religion." Inaugural Lecture at Vrije Universiteit, Amsterdam, October 6, 2006. http://dare.ubvu.vu.nl/bitstream/handle/1871/10311/oratie%20B%20Meijer%206%20okt%2006.pdf?sequence=1&isAllowed=y.
Milbank, John. *Theology and Social Theory*. 2nd ed. Malden: Blackwell, 2006.
Milbank, John, et al., eds. *Radical Orthodoxy: A New Theology*. London: Routledge, 1999.
Miller, Daniel. *Stuff*. Cambridge: Polity, 2010.
Miller, Dorothy. *Simply the Story Handbook*. 6th ed. Hemet: God's Story Project, 2014.
Min, Lim Su, and Pam Wise. "The Ten Seed Technique with Village Leaders in Southeast Asia." *Orality Journal: The Word Became Fresh* 4.2 (2015) 49–58.
Mitchell, Jolyon P. *Visually Speaking: Radio and the Renaissance of Preaching*. Edinburgh: T. & T. Clark, 1999.
Mitchell, Jolyon P., and Jeremy Kidwell. "Changing Uses of Old and New Media in World Christianity." In *The Wiley Blackwell Companion to World Christianity*, 419–431. Chichester: John Wiley & Sons, 2016. http://dx.doi.org/10.1002/9781118556115.ch31.
Mitchell, Jolyon P., and Sophia Marriage, eds. *Mediating Religion: Conversations in Media, Religion and Culture*. London: T. & T. Clark, 2003.
Mohr, Adam. "Out of Zion into Philadelphia and West Africa: Faith Tabernacle Congregation, 1897–1925." *Pneuma* 32.1 (2010) 56–79.
Moon, W. Jay. "Fad or Renaissance? Misconceptions of the Orality Movement." *International Bulletin of Mission Research* 40.1 (2016) 6–21. https://dx.doi.org/10.1177/2396939315625979.
Morgan, David. "Introduction." In *Key Words in Religion, Media, and Culture*, 1–19. New York: Routledge, 2008.
———, ed. *Key Words in Religion, Media and Culture*. New York: Routledge, 2008.
———. "Religion and Media: A Critical Review of Recent Developments." *Critical Research On Religion* 1.3 (2013) 347–56. https://dx.doi.org/10.1177/2050303213506476.
Muehleisen, John. "Farming God's Way Training." Training seminar attended in Masese, May 16, 2017.
Mutibwa, Phares Mukasa. *A History of Uganda: The First 100 Years 1894–1995*. Kampala: Fountain, 2016.
Mwaura, Philomena Njeri. "African Instituted Churches in East Africa." *Studies in World Christianity* 10.2 (2004) 160–84. https://dx.doi.org/10.3366/swc.2004.10.2.160.
Nida, Eugene A. *How the Word Is Made Flesh: Communicating the Gospel to Aboriginal People*. Princeton: Princeton Theological Seminary, 1952.
Noll, Mark A. "Common Sense Traditions and American Evangelical Thought." *American Quarterly* 37.2 (1985) 216–38. https://dx.doi.org/10.2307/2712899.

———. "The Defining Role of Hymns in Early Evangelicalism." In *Wonderful Words of Life: Hymns in American Protestant History and Theology*, edited by Richard J. Mouw and Mark A. Noll, 3–16. Grand Rapids: Eerdmans, 2004.

———. *The Rise of Evangelicalism: The Age of Edwards, Whitefield, and the Wesleys*. A History of Evangelicalism. Leicester: Apollos, 2004.

Olson, Ted. "Amsterdam 2000 Called the Most Multinational Event Ever." *Christianity Today*, August 2, 2000. http://www.christianitytoday.com/ct/2000/julyweb-only/32.0d.html.

Ong, Walter J. *Orality and Literacy: Technologizing of the Word*. New York: Routledge, 1982.

———. *The Presence of the Word: Some Prolegomena for Cultural and Religious History*. New Haven: Yale University Press, 1967.

———. *Ramus, Method, and the Decay of Dialogue: From the Art of Discourse to the Art of Reason*. Cambridge: Harvard University Press, 1958.

Opas, Minna, and Anna Haapalainen, eds. *Christianity and the Limits of Materiality*. London: Bloomsbury Academic, 2017.

Openjuru, George L., and Elda Lyster. "Christianity and Rural Community Literacy Practices in Uganda." *Journal of Research in Reading* 30.1 (2007) 97–112. https://dx.doi.org/10.1111/j.1467-9817.2006.00325.x.

Ostling, Richard N. "Evangelical Publishing and Broadcasting." In *Evangelicalism and Modern America*, edited by George Marsden, 46–55. Grand Rapids: Eerdmans, 1984.

Parry, Milman, et al. *Serbo-Croatian Heroic Songs: Bihacka Krajina: Epics from Bihac, Cazin, and Kulen Vakuf*. Cambridge: Harvard University Press, 1980.

Peel, J. D. Y. *Religious Encounter and the Making of the Yoruba*. Bloomington: Indiana University Press, 2003.

Peterson, Derek R. *Creative Writing: Translation, Bookkeeping, and the Work of Imagination in Colonial Kenya*. Social History of Africa. London: Heinemann, 2004.

———. *Ethnic Patriotism and the East Africa Revival: A History of Dissent, c. 1935–1972*. Cambridge: Cambridge University Press, 2012.

———. "The Politics of Transcendence in Colonial Uganda." *Past & Present* 230.1 (2016) 197–225. https://dx.doi.org/10.1093/pastj/gtv059.

Pettegree, Andrew. *Brand Luther: 1517, Printing, and the Making of the Reformation*. New York: Penguin, 2015.

———. *Reformation and the Culture of Persuasion*. Cambridge: Cambridge University Press, 2005.

Pickett, J. Waskom. *Christian Mass Movements in India*. Lucknow, India: Lucknow, 1933.

———. *Christian Mass Movements in India: A Study with Recommendations*. Nashville: Abingdon, 1933.

Pickstock, Catherine. *After Writing: On the Liturgical Consummation of Philosophy*. Challenges in Contemporary Theology. Oxford: Blackwell, 1998.

Pirouet, M. Louise. *Black Evangelists: The Spread of Christianity in Uganda 1891–1914*. London: Rex Collings, 1978.

———. "Religion in Uganda under Amin." *Journal of Religion in Africa* 11.1 (1980) 13–29. https://dx.doi.org/10.2307/1580791.

Pitts, Jamie. "Book Review: Forming Christian Lovers: James K. A. Smith, *Desiring the Kingdom: Worship, Worldview, and Cultural Formation*." *The Expository Times* 122.10 (2011) 514–15. https://dx.doi.org/10.1177/00145246111220100713.
Plate, S. Brent, ed. *Key Terms in Material Religion*. London: Bloomsbury Academic, 2015.
Prior, Randall. "Orality: The Not-So-Silent Issue in Mission Theology." *International Bulletin of Mission Research* 35.3 (2011) 143–47.
Pritchett, James A. *The Lunda-Ndembu: Style, Change, and Social Transformation in South Central Africa*. Madison: University of Wisconsin Press, 2001.
Puff, Helmut. "The Word." In *The Oxford Handbook of the Protestant Reformations*, edited by Ulinka Rublack, 390–405. Oxford: Oxford University Press, 2016. http://www.oxfordhandbooks.com/view/10.1093/oxfordhb/9780199646920.001.0001/oxfordhb-9780199646920-e-15.
Randall, Ian M. *Evangelical Experiences: A Study of the Spirituality of English Evangelicalism 1918–1939*. Carlisle: Paternoster, 1999.
Rattenbury, J. Ernest. *The Evangelical Doctrines of Charles Wesley's Hymns*. 3rd ed. London: Epworth, 1954.
Rayl, Scott. "Sharing Faith through Contextualized Visual Arts." *Orality Journal: The Word Became Fresh* 5.1 (2016) 59–62.
Rhoads, David. "Biblical Performative Criticism: Performance as Research." *Oral Tradition* 25.1 (2010) 157–98.
Robbins, Joel. "Continuity Thinking and the Problem of Christian Culture." *Current Anthropology* 48.1 (2007) 5–38.
Robson, Colin. *Real World Research: A Resource for Users of Social Research Methods in Applied Settings*. 3rd ed. Chichester: John Wiley & Sons, 2011.
Roodenburg, Herman. "Pierre Bourdieu: Issues of Embodiment and Authenticity." *Etnofoor* 17.1/2 (2004) 215–26.
Rowe, John A. "Mika Sematimba." *Uganda Journal* 28.2 (1964) 179–200.
———. "Myth, Memoir and Moral Admonition: Luganda Historical Writing 1893–1969." *Uganda Journal* 33.1 (1969) 17–40.
Rubin, Herbert J., and Jane S. Rubin. *Qualitative Interviewing: The Art of Hearing Data*. Second. Thousand Oaks: Sage, 1995.
Rublack, Ulinka. *Reformation Europe*. 2nd ed. New Approaches to European History. Cambridge: Cambridge University Press, 2017.
Sanneh, Lamin. *Translating the Message: The Missionary Impact on Culture*. 2nd ed. Maryknoll: Orbis, 1989.
Schultze, Quentin J., and Robert H. Woods, Jr., eds. *Understanding Evangelical Media: The Changing Face of Christian Communication*. Downers Grove: IVP Academic, 2008.
Seng, Wes. "Symposium: Has the Use of Orality Been Taken Too Far?" *Evangelical Mission Quarterly*, April 2016. https://www.emqonline.com/article/emq_archive/201604.
Shakespeare, Steven. *Radical Orthodoxy: A Critical Introduction*. London: SPCK, 2007.
Shellnut, Kate. "Celebs from Michael Phelps to Kim Kardashian Want a Purpose-Driven Life." *Christianity Today*, August 12, 2016. http://www.christianitytoday.com/news/2016/august/celebs-from-michael-phelps-to-kim-kardashian-want-purpose-d.html.

Slack, James Byron, Sr. "The Development of a Chronological Bible Storytelling Module for Use in Training Literates to Communicate the Gospel among Oral Communicators." DMin diss., Southwestern Baptist Theological Seminary, 1995.

Slater, Brent D. "The Ownership of Knowledge: Literacy and Orality in Theological Education in Uganda." PhD diss., University of Edinburgh, 2002.

Smith, James K. A. *After Modernity? Secularity, Globalization, and the Re-enchantment of the World.* Waco: Baylor University Press, 2008.

———. *Awaiting the King: Reforming Public Theology.* Cultural Liturgies. Grand Rapids: Baker, 2017.

———. *Desiring the Kingdom: Worship, Worldview, and Cultural Formation.* Cultural Liturgies. Grand Rapids: Baker, 2009.

———. *How (Not) to Be Secular: Reading with Charles Taylor.* Grand Rapids: Eerdmans, 2014.

———. *Imagining the Kingdom: How Worship Works.* Cultural Liturgies. Grand Rapids: Baker Academic, 2013.

———. *Introducing Radical Orthodoxy: Mapping a Post-Secular Theology.* Grand Rapids/Milton Keyes: Baker Academic/Paternoster, 2004.

———. "Staging the Incarnation: Revisioning Augustine's Critique of Theater." *Literature and Theology* 15 (2001) 123–39.

———. *Who's Afraid of Postmodernism? Taking Derrida, Lyotard, and Foucault to Church.* Grand Rapids: Baker Academic, 2006.

Smith, James K. A., and James H. Olthuis, eds. *Radical Orthodoxy and the Reformed Tradition: Creation, Covenant, and Participation.* Grand Rapids: Baker Academic, 2005.

Soukup, Paul A. "Contexts of Faith: The Religious Foundation of Walter Ong's Literacy and Orality." *Journal of Media and Religion* 5.3 (2006) 175–88.

———. "In Commemoration: Walter Ong and the State of Theology." *Theological Studies* 73.4 (2012) 824–40. https://dx.doi.org/10.1177/004056391207300404.

———. "Orality and Literacy: 25 Years Later." *Communication Research Trends* 26.4 (2007) 3–33.

Spurgeon, Charles H. "The Wordless Book." In *Metropolitan Tabernacle Pulpit*, 57 (1911). http://www.spurgeongems.org/chsbm57.pdf.

Ssekamwa, J. C. *History and Development of Education in Uganda.* 2nd ed. Kampala: Fountain, 2000.

Ssekamwa, J. C., and S. M. E. Lugumba. *Development and Administration of Education in Uganda.* 2nd ed. Kampala: Fountain, 2000.

———. *A History of Education in East Africa.* 2nd ed. Kampala: Fountain, 2001.

Stanley, Brian. "Conversion to Christianity: The Colonization of the Mind?" *International Review of Mission* 92.366 (2003) 315–31. https://dx.doi.org/10.1111/j.1758-6631.2003.tb00407.x.

———. "The East African Revival: African Initiative within a European Tradition." *Churchman* 92.1 (1978) 6–22.

———. *The Global Diffusion of Evangelicalism: The Age of Billy Graham and John Stott.* A History of Evangelicalism. Downers Grove: IVP Academic, 2013.

———. "Renewing a Vision for Mission among British Baptists: Historical Perspectives and Theological Reflections." In *Truth That Never Dies: The Dr. G. R. Beasley-Murray Memorial Lectures 2002–2012*, edited by Nigel G. Wright, 185–202. Eugene, OR: Wipf and Stock, 2014.

———. "The Reshaping of Christian Tradition: Western Denominational Identity in a Non-Western Context." In *Unity and Diversity in the Church*, 32:399–426. Studies in Church History. Oxford: Ecclesiastical History Society/Blackwell, 1996.
Stanley, Henry Morton. *Through the Dark Continent*. Vol. 1. New York: Harper and Brothers, 1878.
Steffen, Tom. "A Clothesline Theology for the World: How a Value-Driven Grand Narrative of Scripture Can Frame the Gospel." *Great Commission Research Journal* 9.2 (2018) 235–72.
———. "A Narrative Approach to Communicating the Bible (Part 1)." *Christian Education Journal* 14 (1994) 86–97.
———. "Orality Comes of Age: The Maturation of a Movement." *International Journal of Frontier Missions* 31.3 (2014) 139–47.
———. "Pedagogical Conversions: From Propositions to Story and Symbol." *Missiology* 38.2 (2010) 141–59. https://dx.doi.org/10.1177/009182961003800205.
———. "Tracking the Orality Movement: Some Implications for 21st Century Missions." *Lausanne Global Analysis* 3.2 (2014) 21–24.
———. *Worldview-Based Storying: The Role of Symbol, Story, and Ritual in the Orality Movement*. Hong Kong: International Orality Network, 2017.
Steffen, Tom, and James O. Terry Jr. "The Sweeping Story of Scripture Taught through Time." *Missiology* 35.3 (2007) 315–35.
Steffen, Tom, and William Bjoraker. *The Return of Oral Hermeneutics: As Good Today as It Was for the Hebrew Bible and First-Century Christianity*. Eugene, OR: Wipf and Stock, 2020.
Stock, Eugene. *The History of the Church Missionary Society: Its Environment, Its Men and Its Work*. Vol. 3. London: Church Missionary Society, 1899.
Storey, John. "Postmodernism." In *Cultural Theory and Popular Culture: A Reader*, 6th ed. Harlow: Pearson Education, 2012.
Stout, Harry S. *The Divine Dramatist: George Whitefield and the Rise of Modern Evangelicalism*. Grand Rapids: Eerdmans, 1991.
Street, Brian V. *Literacy in Theory and Practice*. Cambridge Studies in Oral and Literate Culture. Cambridge: Cambridge University Press, 1984.
Swarr, David. "The Future of the Orality Movement." Opening Session presentation at the ION North America Regional Conference, Houston, 2016.
Swarr, David, et al. *Master Storyteller*. Richmond: International Orality Network, 2017. http://orality resources.com/read-master-storyteller/.
Synan, Vinson. *The Holiness-Pentecostal Tradition: Charismatic Movements in the Twentieth Century*. 2nd ed. Grand Rapids: Eerdmans, 1997.
Taylor, Charles. *Modern Social Imaginaries*. Durham: Duke University Press, 2004.
———. *A Secular Age*. Cambridge: Belknap Press of Harvard University Press, 2007.
Taylor, John V. *The Growth of the Church in Buganda: An Attempt at Understanding*. London: SCM, 1958.
Terry, J. O. "Barriers to the Gospel." *Bible Storying: Chronological Bible Storying Newsletter* 2.4 (1995). Newsletter personally distributed via email.
———. *Basic Bible Storying: Preparing and Presenting Bible Stories for Evangelism, Discipleship, Training, and Ministry*. Revised. Fort Worth: Church Starting Network, 2008.
———. *Chronological Bible Story Newsletter*. (Alternative titles: *Bible Storying: Chronological Bible Storying Newsletter* and *Bible Storying: Storying the Bible for Today's World*.) 1.1–4.4, 1994–97. Newsletter personally distributed via email.

———. "Fast-Tracking the Bible." *Bible Storying: Storying the Bible for Today's World* 3.4 (1996). Newsletter personally distributed via email.
Terry, John Mark. "Cal Guy and the Church Growth Movement." *Faith and Mission* 15.1 (1997) 67–72.
Thigpen, L. Lynn. "Connected Learning: A Grounded Theory Study of How Cambodian Adults with Limited Formal Education Learn." PhD diss., Biola Universtiy, 2016.
Tiberondwa, Ado K. *Missionary Teachers as Agents of Colonialism in Uganda: A Study of Their Activities 1877-1925*. 2nd ed. Kampala: Fountain, 1998.
Tippett, Alan Richard, ed. *God, Man and Church Growth: A Festschrift in Honor of Donald Anderson McGavran*. Grand Rapids: Eerdmans, 1973.
Tourigny, Yves. *So Abundant a Harvest: The Catholic Church in Uganda, 1879-1979*. London: Darton, Longman and Todd, 1979.
Tuma, A. D. Tom. *Building a Ugandan Church: African Participation in Church Growth and Expansion in Busoga: 1891-1940*. Nairobi: Kenya Literature Bureau, 1980.
Tuma, A. D. Tom, and Phares Mukasa Mutibwa, eds. *A Century of Christianity in Uganda: 1877-1977*. Nairobi: Uzima, 1978.
"The Uganda Mission—The Mission Field." *Church Missionary Intelligencer*, August 1900.
Vella, Jane. *Learning to Listen, Learning to Teach: The Power of Dialogue in Educating Adults*. Revised. San Francisco: Jossey-Bass, 2008.
Vilhanová-Pawliková, Viera. "Biblical Translations of Early Missionaries in East and Central Africa: Translations into Luganda." *Asian and African Studies* 15.2 (2006) 198–210.
Voskuil, Dennis N. "The Power of the Air: Evangelicals and the Rise of Religious Broadcasting." In *American Evangelicals and the Mass Media*, 69–95. Grand Rapids: Zondervan, 1990.
Vries, Hent de. "Introduction." In *Religion: Beyond a Concept*, 1–98. New York: Fordham University Press, 2008.
Vries, Laurens de. "Views of Orality and the Translation of the Bible." *Translation Studies* 8.4 (2015) 141–55. https://dx.doi.org/10.1080/14781700.2014.992463.
Waliggo, John Mary. *The Catholic Church in the Buddu Province of Buganda, 1879-1925*. Kampala: Angel Agencies, 2010.
Walsham, Alexandra. "Holy Families: The Spiritualization of the Early Modern Household Revisited (Presidential Address)." In *Religion and the Household*, Studies in Church History, 122–60. Ecclesiastical History Society 50. Woodbridge: Boydell, 2014.
Ward, Graham. *Cities of God*. London: Routledge, 2000.
Ward, Kevin. "Eating and Sharing: Church and State in Uganda." *Journal of Anglican Studies* 3.1 (2005) 99–119.
———. "A History of Christianity in Uganda." In *From Mission to Church: A Handbook of Christianity in East Africa*, edited by Zablon Nthamburi. Nairobi: Uzima, 1991. http://www.dacb.org/stories/uganda/histories/a%20history%20of%20christianity%20in%20uganda.html.
———. "'Obedient Rebels': The Relationship between the Early 'Balokole' and the Church of Uganda: The Mukono Crisis of 1941." *Journal of Religion in Africa* 19.3 (1989) 194–227. https://dx.doi.org/10.2307/1581347.
———. "Review of Joel Cabrita, Text and Authority in the South African Nazaretha Church." In *Marginalia: A Los Angeles Review of Books*, September 24, 2016. http://marginalia.lareviewofbooks.org/spirit-literacy-prophecy-modernity-south-african-church-kevin-ward/.

Ward, Kevin, and Emma Wild-Wood, eds. *The East African Revival: History and Legacies*. Kampala: Fountain, 2010.

Warren, Rick. *The Purpose Driven Life: What on Earth Am I Here For?* Grand Rapids: Zondervan, 2012.

Watson, A. O. Omulokoli. "Foundational History of the Africa Inland Church, 1895–1903." *Africa Journal of Evangelical Theology* 14.2 (1995) 45–54.

Watson, J. R. *The English Hymn: A Critical and Historical Study*. Oxford: Oxford University Press, 1999.

Weber, Hans-Ruedi. *The Book That Reads Me*. Geneva: World Council of Churches, 1995.

———. *The Communication of the Gospel to Illiterates: Based on a Missionary Experience in Indonesia*. Edinburgh: Edinburgh House, 1957.

———. *Experiments with Bible Study*. Geneva: World Council of Churches, 1981.

———. *Walking on the Way: Biblical Signposts*. Geneva: World Council of Churches, 2002.

Welbourn, F. B. "Missionary Methods I." In *East African Christian*, 79–91. London: Oxford University Press, 1965.

Wesley, John. "A Plain Account of Christian Perfection." In *The Works of John Wesley*, edited by Thomas Jackson, 11:366–466. Grand Rapids: Zondervan, 1872. https://www.ccel.org/ccel/wesley/perfection/files/perfection.html.

Wiles, Jerry. "The Orality Movement." In *Orality in America*, edited by Mark Snowden, 7–13. Mission America Coalition, 2016. https://www.cmalliance.org/ministries/download/OralityinAmerica.pdf.

Williams, C. Peter. *The Ideal of the Self-Governing Church: A Study in Victorian Missionary Strategy*. Studies in Christian Mission. Leiden: Brill, 1990.

———. "'Not Transplanting': Henry Venn's Strategic Vision." In *The Church Mission Society and World Christianity 1799–1999*, edited by Kevin Ward and Brian Stanley, 147–72. Studies in the History of Christian Missions. Grand Rapids/Richmond: Eerdmans /Curzon, 2000.

Willis, Avery T., Jr. "Creating the Future: A Tribute to R. Cal Guy." *Faith and Mission* 15.1 (1997) 47–66.

———. *Following Jesus: Making Disciples of Primary Oral Learners*. Audio CD, 7 modules. Progressive Vision, 2002.

Willis, Avery T., Jr., and Mark Snowden. *Truth That Sticks: How to Communicate Velcro Truth in a Teflon World*. Colorado Springs: NavPress, 2010.

Willis, Avery T., Jr., and Sherrie Willis Brown. *MasterLife: Developing a Rich Personal Relationship with the Master*. Nashville: B. & H., 1998.

Witvliet, John D. "The Spirituality of the Psalter: Metrical Psalms in Liturgy and Life in Calvin's Geneva." *Calvin Theological Journal* 32.2 (1997) 273–97.

Wright, David F. "The Great Commission and the Ministry of the Word: Reflections Historical and Contemporary on Relations and Priorities." *Scottish Bulletin of Evangelical Theology* 25.2 (2007) 132.

Yoakum, Stuart Trevor. "The Spoken Word: God, Scripture and Orality in Missions." PhD diss., Southern Baptist Theological Seminary, 2014. http://search.proquest.com/docview/1541534690?accountid=10673.

Zito, Angela. "Can Television Mediate Religious Experience: The Theology of Joan of Arcadia." In *Religion: Beyond A Concept*, edited by Hent de Vries, 724–38. New York: Fordham University Press, 2008.

———. "Culture." In *Key Words in Religion, Media, and Culture*, edited by David Morgan, 69–82. New York: Routledge, 2008.

Index

accountability, 158–59, 163–64
accuracy, textural, 162, 182
the achieved life, 3, 241–42
aesthetics, 222–23, 226–28, 234–36, 238, 249, 253, 260. *See also* embodiment
affectivity, 64–65
Africa
    anthropological studies in, 16
    communications technologies, 206
    East African Revival, 147, 149–50
    importance of material objects in, 186–87
    oral praxis in, 11–12, 11n26, 12n25
Africa Gospel Church Kenya (AGC Kenya)
    dominance of Kipsigis people in, 32
    independence from the WGM, 138
    influence on AFG Uganda, 156
    Lang'at's views on holiness, 147n137
    materiality and authority, 214–15
    missionary efforts, 32n108, 156
    work with AGC Uganda, 139, 143–44, 156
Africa Gospel Church Uganda (AGC). *See also* pastoral training *and specific forms of communication*
    and the "achieved life," "good life," 241
    adaptations by, 144
    and the AGC Kenya, 156
    Atyanga's identification with, 235
    and biblical authority/standards, 168
    and biblical engagement, 168–70
    certification issues, 188
    and church buildings, 251–52
    church government and organization, 134, 144–45, 157
    communication modes, overview, 173
    Community Health Empowerment program, 8
    compiling history of, 25
    congregations, 142f
    and the COU model, 150, 152–53
    digital communications, 202, 209
    financial limitations, 134
    history, 5–7, 137, 141
    and holiness theology, 152, 155
    impact on Pentecostals, 132–33
    and indigenous education, 128–29
    local focus, 134–35, 156
    local Ugandan leadership, 165
    and materiality, 8, 171–72, 214, 219, 239
    multi-ethnic nature, 32, 32n109
    and the OM, 4, 14–15, 25, 243–45
    and orality, 71, 135, 157, 165, 186, 228–34
    partnership with the WGM, 7–8

288 Index

Africa Gospel Church Uganda (AGC) (*continued*)
   population served by, demographics, 7
   pragmatism, handicaps associated with, 157
   program growth and limitations, 142n119
   recognition by the Ugandan government, 143
   relationship with COU, 133–34
   "reverend" and "pastor" titles, 27n96
   and speaking in tongues, 15
   and spirituality vs. materiality, 136, 211, 238–39, 241–43
   spiritual transformation from storytelling, 231
   and tensions between literacy and practical education, 135
   transportation costs, 143
   use of radios, 201
American Bible schools, 74–75
Amin, Idi, 137, 137n94, 153
Anglican Church. *See* Church of Uganda (COU, Anglican)
anthropology of Christianity, 16, 29, 224, 226n34
the Apocrypha, 45, 65
Apollos, Djibo Isaac, 100
apostolic teachings, 13, 41, 111
Archambault, Julie, 206, 242
art, visual, 24, 39, 70, 72, 107
Asad, Talal, 232, 237n65
Atyanga, Esther, 228, 231, 234–35, 257
Audio Declaration (OM), 110
audio-digital communication. *See* digital-reliant communications
Audio Scripture Engagement Declaration, 98
Azusa Street Revival, 154

Babington, Gervase, 60
Baconian science, 75
Barber, Karin, 158
Baskerville, George, 149
Bayart, Jean-François, 211n208

belly theology (prosperity gospel), 5, 136–37, 211–14, 211n208, 211n211, 247–52
Bemis, Linda, 10–11
Bernard, H. Russell, 31
Bible. *See also* Old Testament
   and the Apocrypha, 45
   canon/authority of, communicating orally, 8–9, 39–40, 65, 106
   carrying, and *Mulokole*, 151
   contextualizing, 45–46
   crafted vs. literalist approaches, 108–9
   and C. Wesley's hymnody, 56
   digital approaches, 199, 203, 209
   engaging with, 74–75
   and evangelical missional communication, 98
   exegetical tools, 46–47
   as "God's picture book," 79
   Kiswahili New Testament, 117, 121
   languages used to describe, 172
   McIlwain's chronological approach to teaching, 86
   Old and New Testaments as continuous, 86
   orthodox interpretations, 183, 194
   personal interpretations, 42–43, 45–46, 171–72
   printed text, as divine authority, 39–43, 97, 194–95
   right understanding of, 44
   Swahili Bible, 171
   value of print-related communications about, 193–94
   vernacular translations, 43, 105–6, 121–22
   versions, choosing one to follow, 45
Bible college, 6, 105, 156, 248
Bible Storying (BS), 87
Bible storytelling
   and accuracy, 182
   approaches to, 77–78, 94–95, 108–9
   arts collaborations, 94
   on college campuses, 90
   as core practice of ION, 94
   and cross-cultural communication, 88

Index   289

emphasis on in the AGC, 228, 234
fast-tracking, 88
and focus on characters, 87
imagination at center of, 226
IMB's demonstrations of, 86–88
limits of as educational currency, 253
and low-literacy, 181–82
Master Storyteller project, 96
participatory discovery, 88
preparation time needed for, 180–81
situational storytelling, 87
spiritual transformation, 231–32
and the STS process, 161–63
value of repetition, 81n63
Bible study. *See also* Bible storytelling
chronological approach, 86
English language, 74
inductive approach, 113
literalism/textualism, 77, 108
orality approach, 113
and printed texts, 11
biblical engagement
Abiel's story, 101–2
approaches to, 168–71
defined, 168
embodied-imaginative, 96
and encountering God, 95, 105–6, 234
in India, 79–80
links with embodiment and spiritual change, 231–32
as need- and faith-driven in Africa, 172
as personal/individual, 168–72
through orality, 48, 95, 168–69, 174, 178, 183–84
and value of multisensory communication, 178
Bielo, James, 29, 69, 76
Bigambo bya mu Kitabu kya Katonda (*Words from the Book of God*; Mackay), 120
Billy Graham Evangelistic Association, 89
Bourdieu, Pierre
on habits that give life meaning, 225–26

habitus concept, 230
influence on Smith, 226n34, 226n38
logic of practice, 231–32
Bowman, Carla and Jim, 11
Brereton, Virginia, 74–75
Brown, Candy Gunther, 57, 63
Buganda kingdom
as British Protectorate, 126
introduction of Islam, 116–17
and *kusoma* Christianity, 118
Luganda translations of sacred texts, 119–22
missionary education in, 122–23
spread of Christianity in, 119–20
system-based education, 124
Building Bridges to Oral Cultures (C. Bowman), 11
Bulyango AGC
approaches to biblical engagement, 168–70
Exodus song, 175–78, 231
languages used in, 143, 170–71
Burton, Richard, 117
Buvuma Island AGC, 7–8, 141, 214, 239

Calvin, John, 43, 47, 54
Campus Crusade for Christ (Cru), 89
Carey, James, 220–21, 224n25
catechist schools (Uganda), 125
Catholic Church
appeal to OM members, 81
authority of oral traditions, 13
and embodied religious experience, 23–24
missionaries in Buganda, 119–21
Celtic Christianity, 70
certification, educational, importance, 146n131, 157, 188, 243–45, 252
CGM. *See* Church Growth Movement (CGM)
Chiang, Samuel E., 91–92
China, WGM's early focus on, 137–38
Christian culture theory, 223–25, 224n232
Chronological Bible Storying (CBS), 87–88, 94, 113
Chronological Bible Teaching (CBT), 86–87

church buildings, as indicators of
    success, 251–52, 252n105, 258
Church Growth Movement (CGM)
    history and influence, 79–83
    pragmatic missionary approach, 100
Church Missionary Society (CMS)
    comparison with OM, 122
    early work in Uganda, 117–18
    emphasis on literacy, 14
    mission schools, 130
    sale of books, 121
    self-supporting missions, 131
Church of Uganda (COU, Anglican)
    as a born-again church, 151
    and certification, 245
    and church buildings, 252, 252n105
    and the East African Revival, 150
    holiness tradition, 152
    impact and influence in Uganda,
        116, 130–33
    links to ruling elites, 133
    principle of self-support, 131
    public views of, 134
    relationship with the AGC, 133–34
    relationship with Pentecostals, 133
    relationship with the WGM, 134
    salvation through works, 140
church planting, 68, 139, 144, 216, 263,
    265
CMS. *See* Church Missionary Society
    (CMS)
Cole, Jennifer, 184–87
colonialism, impacts on education,
    122–28, 127n56, 135–36
"Coming to Terms with Orality—A
    Holistic Model" (Madinger),
    71–72
communication, religious. *See also*
    digital-reliant communications;
    embodiment; material-reliant
    communication; oral-reliant
    communication; print-reliant
    communications
    and biblical engagement, 168–71
    breadth of, 5, 37
    confusing information processing
        with, 113–15
    effective, working to discover, 101–5
    and embodiment, 218–19, 223
    factors that limit, 3
    heart language/mother tongue, 80,
        83, 90, 106–7
    influence of the COU, 150
    and language diversity, 105–6, 143,
        158
    and literacy, 135–36, 121
    and meaning in language, 106
    miscommunication, 3
    and modernity, 168, 190–91, 205–6,
        210
    multisensory, 104–5, 104n155
    as persuasion, 48–49
    and preaching, 49–53
    rediscovery, recovery rhetoric, 112
    and spiritual transformation, 229–
        30, 233–34
    systemic/doctrinal, 76
    through song, 53–58
    transmission vs. ritual view of, 220
    using ordinary spoken language,
        52–53
    Whitefield's skills at, 50
*The Communication of the Gospel to
    Illiterates* (Weber), 78–79, 86–87
community. *See also* Africa Gospel
    Church Uganda (AGC)
    and identity, 222, 230
    and shared faith, 158
    and social networks, 186
Community Health Empowerment
    program (CHE), 8, 133, 237–38
consent forms, 24n87, 28
COU. *See* Church of Uganda (COU,
    Anglican)
Council of Trent, 13, 45
"A Cultural Approach to
    Communication" (Carey), 220
"Cultural Liturgies" (Smith), 224
culture
    incorporating with storytelling
        methods, 94–95
    and oral-reliant communications, 72
    theology of Christian culture, 224

davar (word), Hebrew meanings, 97–98
Dawson, Jane, 8, 54–55
Dayton, Donald, 76–77
Dhikusooka, David

and the Buvuma Island problem, 239
on costs of digital communication, 207
on denominational authority, 214–15, 215n226, 246–47
radio program, 207, 207n193
dialogue. combining with storytelling, 102–3
digital-reliant communications
accessing print media using, 203–4
audio-digital communication, 98–99
for Bible studies, 203
convenience, 204
costs, 206–7, 207n189
and crossing boundaries, 204
digital audio players (DAPs), 199–200
and distraction, 208–9
doctrinal validity of, 209–10
prevalence, 199
and social status, identity, 205–6
and technological failures, 208
tools for, 199–201
urban-rural differences, 202–3
for the visually impaired, 205
Disciples of Christ, 80–81
discipling, discipleship
Abiel's story, 101–2
and the AGC Uganda discipleship manual, 155, 155n174
commitment of the OM to, 99–100, 112
as goal of ION institutions, 10, 68
local focus, 156–57
McGavran's approach, 82
for oral learners, 89–91
doctrine of eternal security, 153n166
Dodge, William Asbury, 146–47
Douglas, Steve, 90
Duncan, Terry, 138

East African Revival, 147, 149–50
education. *See* literacy, literary education; pastoral training
Ellison, Robert, 52–53
embeddedness vs. disembedding, 186–97

embodiment. *See also* communication, religious; faith
and belly theology, 211–14, 211n208, 211n211
and the Emerging Church movement, 70
experiential communication, 50
and material expressions of faith, 258
and multisensory communication, 16, 104–5, 104n155, 175–78
and orality2, 229–31
and religious practice, 218–19, 221–23
as source of meaning, 51, 225, 230–31
and spiritual transformation, 96, 179–80, 231–32
Emerging Church movement, 69–71, 103
engagement, affective. *See* biblical engagement
Engelke, Matthew, 16, 111, 168n1, 184n83
evangelicalism, evangelicals. *See also* Africa Gospel Church Uganda (AGC); missionaries; pastoral training
belly theology, 211–14, 211n208, 211n211
and bridging boundaries, 3
British, and Keswick holiness, 148
dichotomous view of spirituality and materiality, 238–39
doctrinal concerns, 107–8
and education, 77, 124–32
Finney's vs. Hodge's approaches, 76
importance of hymns to, 56–57
and material costs, funding, 131–32, 179–80
neo-Calvinism, 77
revivalist school, 76
and systematic/doctrinal communication efforts, 76
systematic/doctrinal theology communications, 76
Exodus 17:1–7, acting out of, 95

faith. *See also* the Bible
    authentic, 70–71
    communicating, 37, 39
    equating the Bible with, 68, 98–100, 111
    and hearing the word of God, 51
    proclaiming orally, 51, 55, 58, 94, 205–6, 210, 218
    and salvation, 42, 140, 153
Farming God's Way (FGW) program (AGM), 8, 133, 133n84, 197, 200
"fast-tracking," 88
Finnegan, Ruth, 21–22
Finney, Charles, 76
Fleming, Paul, 85
flourishing, human, 3, 227, 241
focus groups, 31–33
formation. *See also* discipling, discipleship
    aesthetic, 222–23, 228, 234–36, 238, 249, 253, 260
    and religious community, 222–23, 235
    spiritual, 91, 224–26
4.2.20 Foundation, 93–94
Friday Apostolics, 111, 184n83
fundamentalism, 74–75

Gadamer, Hans-Georg, 2
Garden of Eden, 96–97
Genesis 12, 183, 183–84n82
Geneva Reformed worship, 54–55
German Bible (Luther), 46–47
Gifford, Paul, 132–33, 152
global leadership team (GLT), International Orality Movement, 92–93
God, encountering. *See also* embodiment; faith; mediation
    creating opportunities for, 95, 103–6, 261
    and engaging with Scripture, 223, 234, 256–57
    oral communications and, 234
God's Story, 11, 94, 161
God's word
    the Bible as, 182
    crafted vs. literalist approaches to the Bible, 108–9
    and print as reliable communicator of, 194–95
    as unchangeable, 98
    as written, spoken and personal, 19–20, 41, 70–71, 96–97
Goody, Jack, 21
Graham, Billy, 50–51
Gravelle, Giles, 105–7
The Great Commission phrase, 82
Guy, Calvin, 83

Haapalainen, Anna, 210
habitus concept (Bourdieu), 230, 235
Hall, Rhys, 35, 199, 207, 209
Handman, Courtney, 106
Hannington, James, 119–20
Hansen, Holger Bernt, 130–32
Hardin, Jessica, 211, 212n213
Hastings, Adrian, 120
Hattersley, C. W., 125
Haynes, Naomi, 179n65, 186–87, 211, 216, 216n226
Heal, Bridget, 59–60
heart language, 80, 83, 90, 106–7
Hennink, Monique, 26n91, 31
Herrera, Abiel, 101
Hodge, Charles, 74–77
holiness movement/theology
    and the AGC Uganda discipleship manual, 155
    doctrine of eternal security, 153n166
    influence in Uganda, 149–52
    Keswick holiness, 147–48
    and material blessings, 250–51
    and orality, 57
    origins and early history, 146, 155
    and Pentecostalism, 154
    underlying belief, 146
    Wesleyan holiness, 147–48
Hopson, Kenneth, 189–93, 195, 243. *See also The Print Shop*
Horsfield, Peter, 42–43, 46–47
Hotchkiss, William, 138
How Churches Grow (McGavran), 83
Hunt, Arnold, 51, 52n41
Hurtado, Larry, 15–16, 59

hymns, hymnals, 55–58

identity. *See also* community
　the Bible as source for understanding, 172–73
　and communication preferences, 196, 219
　and concepts of self, 106–7
　and digital media, 205–6
　and print-reliant communications, 193
　and *The Print Shop*, 191
　role of materiality, 186–87, 215–16
　and sense of belonging, 186, 230
ideological orality, 3–4
Ifugao people (Philippines), theological approaches, 68
illiteracy, 4, 42, 79, 81, 184
imagination. *See also* embodiment
　Catholic, 22–23
　at center of human action, 225–26, 226n39
　in children, developing, 123
　and multisensory communication, 178–79
IMB. *See* International Mission Board (IMB), Southern Baptist Convention
Imperial British East African Company, 120
India, fostering biblical engagement in, 79–80
Indian Springs Holiness Camp Meeting, Georgia (USA), 147–48
indigenous peoples, identifying, 80
inductive approach to Bible study, 74–75, 77–78, 94, 113–14
indulgences, 44
industrial education, colonial, 127–28, 127n56
information processing, 113–15
Inskip, John, 146
Institutes for Orality Strategies, 71
Institutes of Christian Religion (Calvin), 43, 47
International Council of Ethnodoxologists (ICE), 94

International Mission Board (IMB), Southern Baptist Convention, 9n15, 52, 86–90
International Orality Network (ION). *See also* Orality Movement (OM); orality2
　affiliates, 9n16
　Chiang's leadership, 91–92
　discipleship and, 68
　expanded orality concept, 69, 91, 114
　female leaders, 10–11
　financial partnerships, 94
　formation of, demographics, 9–11, 90
　global leadership team (GLT), 93
　mission, 9–10, 90, 93
　multisensory communication, 177–78
　oral-preferenced communicators, 73, 94
　print communications, 17
　relationship with the Bible, 68, 95, 98
　structure, 93–94
　Swarr's leadership, 92
　target audiences, 10
international council (IC), International Orality Network, 93
interview methodology, 24–25
ION. *See* International Orality Network (ION)
Islam, introduction in Uganda, 116–17

"Jeanes schools" (Uganda), 128n59
Jenkins, Philip, 172, 172n49
Jesus Christ, as the personal word of God, 19–20, 41, 97–98, 109
Jesus Film, 161, 205
Jones, Ben, 86, 87n90
Jones, Thomas, 127n56

Kahara AGC
　Bible storying class at, 235
　communications with other churches, 192n114
　desire for digital media, 205
　desire for material development, 216

Kahara AGC (*continued*)
    and the link between pastors and
        laity, 154, 154n172
    location, 143
    manifestations of belly theology, 212
    optimism, 179
    and remembering stories, 178n60
    sound systems, 201n166
    and speaking in tongues, 153n66
    storytelling performances at, 178–79
    Swahili Bible, 171
Kenya. *See* African Gospel Church
    Kenya (UGC Kenya)
Keswick Convention, Keswick holiness,
    147–50, 152
Kinaalwa, Joshua, 207–8
Kirui, Kennedy, 145–46, 145n130,
    208–9, 246
Kirui, Lillian, 185–86, 249
Kisugu AGC, 173, 191–92
Kiswahili New Testament, 117, 121
Knight, Philip and Carolyn, 139–40
kusoma (reading), 118

Lang'at, Robert, 147–50, 147n137,
    151n157, 155n178
Laurent, Otafiire, 35, 195
Lausanne Special Interest Group (#25),
    90
least-reached people, 10
LeMarquand, Grant, 172
Leonard (*The Print Shop* assistant),
    189–91
literacy, literary education
    call for change in approach, 91
    and certification, 146n131, 157, 188,
        243–45, 252
    colonial the mission/industrial
        system, 122–28, 135–36
    confluence with oral modes of
        communication, 16
    cross-cultural limitations, 69
    importance in Uganda, 118, 122,
        128–30, 135–36, 196
    and income opportunities, 247
    and learning Bible stories, 181–82
    and the limits of Bible storytelling,
        253

    vs. orality2, 247–48
    and oral-reliant communications,
        12–13, 72
    overcoming barriers to, 48
    situation-based learning, 124
    and social context, 21, 21n71
    and social status, 184–85
Literacy in Theory and Practice (Street),
    21
liturgical anthropology (Smith), 225–26
Livingston, T. W., 120n26
Loewen, Jacob, 88, 88n98
logos (word), broad meanings, 97–98
Lotz, David, 41n3, 44
Lovejoy, Grant
    classes in cross-cultural
        communication, 88
    on doctrinal concerns, 107–8
    on inductive Bible study, 77–78
    on the language of sermons, 52
    on resistance to orality, 111
Luganda (language), translations of texts
    into, 119–22
Lunda people, Zambia, 187
Luther, Martin
    criticisms of indulgences, 44
    emphasis on written Scripture,
        13–14, 38–39, 41
    exegetical tools, 46–47
    German translation of the New
        Testament, 43
    on the power of music, 53–54
    and the priesthood of all believers,
        41–42
    and right understanding of
        Scripture, 44
    use of vernacular, 42–43
Lutheranism, 59–60
Luwurn, Janani, 137

Mackay, Alexander, 120–21, 120n26
Madhya Pradesh, India, 80
Madinger, Charles, 71–72, 73
Makerere College/University, 125,
    129–30
Making Disciples of Oral Learners
    (ION), 9, 18, 90
Manano, Willy, 196, 264

Marini, Stephen, 57
Marriage, Sophia, 2–3, 254
Marsden, George, 75
Masese AGC, 158, 246
Masiga, Kefa
  as first AGC bishop, 35n116, 134
  on oral-reliant communication, 196
  role in AGC Uganda, 145
  views on storytelling by, 181, 188
Master Storyteller project, 96
materiality, material culture. *See also* modernity; print-reliant communications
  and denominational authority, 214–15, 215n226, 246–47
  and embodied religious experience, 16, 218–19, 222–23
  and the Emerging Church movement, 70
  importance among Ugandan Christians, 2, 5, 16, 126, 186–87, 237, 241–42
  and the limitations of orality, 182–83, 186–88, 250–51, 253
  link with literacy/literary education, 136, 191, 243–44
  material-reliant communication, 210–13, 219, 221
  and printed materials, 243–44
  and social networks, identity, 186–87
  sand spiritual blessings (prosperity gospel), 5, 136–37, 211–14, 211n208, 211n211, 247–52
Matthew 2:19–20, 82
Matthew 28:19–20, 100
Mayo, Jonathan, 139–40, 195, 245
McGavran, Donald, 79–82
McGrath, Alister, 43–46
McGregor, Gordon P., 125–26
McIlwain, Trevor, 85–87
McLuhan, Marshall, 15n15
McPherson, Larry and Joy, 139, 153
media, as embodied practice, 72, 221–22. *See also* digital-reliant communications; print-reliant communications

Mediating Religion (Mitchell and Marriage), 2–3
mediation (making the invisible visible), 136–37, 220–21, 224n23, 231–33, 236. *See also* embodiment; spiritual transformation
memory, orality and, 72, 178
Menkins, Andrea, 11
Merleau-Ponty, Maurice, 222, 225–26, 225n34
Methodism, 56, 144, 146
Metz, Nathan, 183–84
Meyer, Birgit, 219, 221–22, 226–27, 231
Miller, Dorothy, 11
missionaries. *See also* World Gospel Mission (WGM)
  chronological approach to teaching the Bible, 86
  conflicts with pastors, 135
  educational requirements, 6
  emphasis on dispersed literacy, 121
  financing of, 6, 240
  issues of orthodoxy vs. personal interpretation, 46
  mission schools, 122–28, 127n56, 135–36
  sharing of approaches among, 86
  and "The Wordless Book," 60–61
Missionary Teachers as Agents of Colonialism in Uganda (Tiberonda), 124
Mitchell, Jolyon, 2–3, 254
modernity. *See also* materiality
  characteristics and expectations, 83–84, 115, 166, 185–87, 223n20
  and church buildings, 251–52
  and communications, 168, 190–91, 205, 216, 265
Moody, Dwight L., 60
Moon, Jay, 112
Morgan, David, 220–21
Morris, E. C., 127–28
mother tongue communications, 105–6
Muehheisen, Beth and John, 195, 238
Mugisha, Emy, 145–46, 146n131
Mukisa, Miria and Steward
  on carrying a Bible, 151
  display of training certificate, 245

Mukisa, Miria and Steward (*continued*)
    inclusion in study, 26–27, 27n96
    manifestation of belly theology, 212
    on print-oriented pastoral training, 158–59
    work with AGC Uganda, 143
Mulokole/Balokole ("Saved One/s"), 151–52
multisensory communication, 104–5, 104n155. *See also* embodiment
Museveni, Yoweri, 132–33, 137
Musoke, Bartolomayo Zimbe, 118
Mutesa (Kabaka), 117–18
Mwanga (Kabaka), 119–20

narrative communication, dialogue, 101–3
"The National Camp Meeting Association for the Promotion of Christian Holiness," 1, 146
National Christian Foundation (NCF), 94
National Holiness Association Movement, 146–47
National Holiness Missionary Society, 137
Nebbi district, Uganda
    AGC radio presence, 204
    church buildings, 251
    introduction of orality in, 161–65
    and view of stories as fictional/untrue, 185
New Tribes Mission (NTM), 85
Niebuhr, H. Richard, 22–23
Noll, Mark, 50, 56–57, 64
normal schools (Uganda), 125

Obote, Milton, 129, 137
Ojiambo, Connie, 139
Okello, Fred, 34, 182n74, 205, 208
Old Testament. *See also* the Bible
    Apocrypha, 45
    appeal of characters and stories, 170, 248
    importance of understanding, 85–86, 161
    translation into indigenous languages, 93–94

Olson, Roger, 77
Omri, Benson
    on the importance of literacy, 196, 244–45
    on the introduction of Christianity to Uganda, 185
    on printed texts as reliable, 194
    questions asked, 29–30
    radio show, 204
One Mission Society, 147
Ong, Walter
    aural vs. written communication of God's word, 19–20
    and Catholic sacramentality, 81
    on communication and cognition, 18–19
    influence of Niebuhr on, 22–23
    influence on OM, 15
    influence on Slack, 87
    on the psychodynamics of orality, 18–19
    on sacramental thinking, 22–23
Opas, Minna, 210
Oral Bible, 45, 89
Oral Bible Network (OBN), 88–90
orality. *See also* orality2; Protestant orality (orality1)
    as an "adaptive" methodology, 129
    affective impact vs. social benefits, 185–86, 237, 251–52
    ancient, studies of, 15–16
    and breadth of non-verbal communication, 107
    and emotional connection, 174
    and holiness theology, 157
    ideological orality, 3–4
    vs. literacy, as binary stereotype, 12–13
    and material markers, 5, 186–88
    meaning of, 3–4, 52
    and narrative communication, 91, 101
    as "old fashioned," 37
    oral delivery and style, 53
    and oral learning from birth, 96
    vs. orality2, 40
    pastoral education and discipleship, 17–18, 40, 90, 161–64

Index   297

and the power of God's spoken
    word, 71, 112, 228
relationship between spoken and
    written texts, 16
secondary, and digitized/electronic
    media, 18
as social stigma, 184–85
and spiritual authority, 107
traditional, characteristics, 3, 12n25,
    15, 19
value of repetition, 81n63
and the variety of oral practices, 175
orality2. *See also* oral-reliant
    communication; Protestant
    orality
and affective engagement and
    spiritual change, 230–32
challenges of defining, 71–73
and depth of understanding, 178
disciplines associated with, 71–72,
    111
and embodiment, 218, 229–31
emphasis on preaching, 13
example of, 175–78
and expanded concepts of "self," 107
and inductive Bible study, 113–14
within ION, 114
limits, 243–48, 250, 253
and materiality, 246–51
and memorization, 178
moving beyond storytelling, 71
overlaps with orality1, 177
primary and secondary oral
    communicators, 73
strengths and weaknesses, 252–53
and theological education, 40
as tool, not end in itself, 104–5
universality, multi-context
    applicability, 69
*Orality and Literacy: The Technologizing
    of the Word* (Ong), 18–19, 87
*Orality Breakouts: Using Heart Language
    to Transform Hearts* (Willis), 90
Orality Journal (ION), 17, 23–24, 91–92
Orality Movement (OM). *See also*
    orality; orality2; oral-reliant
    communication; Protestant
    orality

American influences, 74–78
and the appeal of oral-based
    communication, 73
Audio Declaration, 110
Bible study, inductive approaches,
    77–78, 113
and biblical engagement, 95, 168
and Catholic worship practices, 81
commitment to Scriptural accuracy,
    45, 111, 113
and communicating the meaning of
    Scripture, 106
and conflating communication and
    information processing, 113–15
and contextual concerns, 45–46, 65
and the continued demand for
    print-based materials, 16–17,
    165
and countering overly print-reliant
    mission endeavors, 40
crafted vs. literalist approaches to
    the Bible, 108–9
criticisms of Ong within, 22
and developing effective
    communication, 101–5
emphasis on discipleship, 10, 82,
    99–100
influence on AGC missions, 14–15,
    25, 227–28
influence of the CGM, 80–83, 122
influence of Hans-Ruedi Weber,
    78–79
influence of Ong, 15, 18, 22–23
integrated preaching with orally
    constructed narratives, 13
lack of materiality, implications, 2
and the literary sermon vs. ordinary
    spoken language, 52
methodological vs. theological
    focus, 83, 111
mother tongue communications,
    105–6, 122
origins and development, 8–9, 71
pastoral training approach, 1–2
placement within the Protestant
    tradition, 68–69
postmodernity and, 37, 84–85
pragmatism of, 101–2

Orality Movement (OM) (*continued*)
  print-reliant communications, 189
  and questions of spiritual authority, 107
  as renaissance, not revolution, 110–12
  similarities with the Emerging Church movement, 69–70
  Swarr's globalizing efforts, 92
  target audiences, 10
  theological conservatism, 83, 97–98, 168
  and the understanding of language, 109
  as unique, examining, 66
  use of narrative and dialogue, 102–3
  value for evangelization and discipling, 67
  and Western-educated missionaries, 112–13
Orality Movement (OM) study, design for, 24–36
oral-reliant communication
  benefits, 174–80
  limitations, 180–89
  and oral preferences, 10, 43–44, 73, 78–79, 81
  and the power of God's spoken word, 69–71
  and the preached word, 39
Osborn, William B., 146
Ouma, Caroline, 249
Ouma, Carolyn, 185–86
Ouma, James
  on the "achieved life" and materiality, 213, 241–42, 248–49
  avoidance of storytelling by, 188
  Bible study, 173
  on finding reading materials, 197–98
  on the physical realities of AGC pastors, 239
  role in AGC Uganda, 145–46
Owor, Martin
  appreciation of orality, 228
  communication of negative attributes, 179
  on orality and memory, 178

  oral-reliant communications, 175
  radio program, 207, 207n193
  on Ugandan value systems, 241
  on use of digital media, 202

Palawano people, 85–86
participant observation, opportunities and limitations, 26–31
participatory discovery, 88
Pasolini, Tonino, 34–35, 209
pastoral training
  as an AGC mission, 139–41
  costs of training material, 197
  and cross-cultural communication, 88–89
  desire for printed materials, 158–60, 193
  discipleship manual, 155, 155n174
  embedded and embodied practices, 223
  integrated oral-literate curriculum, 165
  lectures, 160
  McGavran's approach, 82
  multi-lingual nature, 143
  in the Nebbi region, 161–64
  and negative views of orality, 188–89
  oral communication methodologies, 1–2
  partnership with the WGM, 8
  pastoral leadership/authority, 107–8, 154
  and the poverty of pastors, 247–50
  pragmatic approaches, 135–36, 140–41
  program growth and limitations, 141–42, 141n117
  refurbishment by new missionaries, 160
  and stress on accuracy, 182
  the STS process, 161–64
  vs. transformational ministries, 237–38
  unique elements, 157–58
  use of DAPs, 200
  visual tools, 161
Pentecostalism
  appreciation for orality, 111

equating weight-gain with spiritual
     growth, 211
similarities with the OM, 102n148
and speaking in tongues, 153n66,
     154
in Uganda, 132, 153
people groups
   adoption of term by OM
        practitioners, 83
   Bible-less, as target audience, 10
   commitment to reaching, 89
   defined, 81
personal interviews, approaches and
     analysis, 31, 33–36
Pettegree, Andrew, 48–49, 58–59
Phelps-Stokes Commission reports, 126,
     127–29
Piboth, Andrew, 164
Pickett, J. Waskom, 79–80
Pilkington, George, 149–50
Pirouet, Louise, 118
politics of the belly. *See* belly theology
postmodernity, 84–85
pragmatism
   and effective communication,
        100–102
   handicaps of, in Uganda, 157
   McGavran's emphasis on, 80
   in pastoral training, 135–36, 140–41
preaching
   embodied, multisensory, 50–51, 64,
        104, 104n157
   literary vs. oral, 52, 64
   and oral-reliant communications,
        175
   and orality2, 13
   Protestant emphasis on the sermon,
        39, 49
   status of clergy in Uganda, 131
Princeton school of evangelicalism, 76
the printing press, 42–43
print-reliant communications
   availability issues, 197
   characteristics, 189
   choosing, 243–44
   and conceptual organization,
        193–94
   costs, 197

digital access to, 203–4
economic value, 246
engagement issues, 198
and illiteracy, 42–43, 197
and interpretative texts, 43, 194
and modernity, social value, 190–91,
     195
networking using, 193
pamphlet format, 43
The Print Shop, 189–90
reliance on, 13–14
reliability, 194
and remembrance, 194
written notes/supporting material,
     178, 180–82, 192, 192n114,
     194–95, 197, 244, 255
Pritchett, James, 187
prosperity gospel theology, 5, 213–14,
     249–50
Protestant orality (orality1)
   and affective experience, 64
   approaches to evangelism, 68
   biblical engagement, 48
   and communicating through song,
        53–58
   communication complexities, 39
   dependence on textual modalities,
        63–64
   and electronic mass media, 62–63
   emphasis on the spoken word,
        110–11
   and hymns and hymnals, 55–58
   instructional texts, 47
   and oral persuasion, 40, 48–49
   overlap with orality2, 177
   and qualified orality1, 48
   sermons and preaching, 39, 49–53
   and textuality, 59
   and "The Wordless Book," 60–62
Protestant Reformation, Protestantism
   and canonical authority, 43, 45–46
   and congregational singing, 53–54
   and the elevation of written
        authority, 13–14
   emphasis on literate discourse,
        58–59
   emphasis on written Scripture,
        38–39

300 Index

Protestant Reformation, Protestantism (*continued*)
  inherent textuality, 48
  and personal interpretation of Scripture, 46
  persuasion strategies, 40, 48–49, 56–57, 62
  and the priesthood of all believers, 41–42
  relationship with printing, 4, 42, 45–47
  use of metrical psalms, 54–55
  and visual imagery, 59
  and the word of God in scripture, 41
psalms, metrical, 54–57
The Purpose Driven Life (Warren), 192
purposive recruitment, 25–26, 26n91

Radical Orthodoxy (RO), 223–24n20
radio communications, 205, 205n184
Radio Pacis, 35
Randall, Ian, 148–49
Rattenbury, J. Ernest, 56
Rediscovering a Theological Heritage (Dayton), 77
The Reformation and the Culture of Persuasion (Pettegree), 48–49
religious practice. *See also* Protestant Reformation, Protestantism
  communicating the complexity of faith, 37
  liturgies as compressed narratives, 226–27
  material, bodily, sensational and sensory dimensions, 221–23, 221n8
  and mediation, 220
  Smith's concept, 227
  transmission vs. ritual view of, 220
research methodology, 24–25
Roman 10:14–17, 51
Roman Catholic Church
  and church buildings, 252, 252n105
  communications in Latin, 42
  multisensory communication, 38
  unwritten traditions, 41
Rublack, Ulinka, 41–42, 53, 58

sampling approach, 25–27
Scriptures in Use organization, 11
secondary oral communicators, 73
self-support principle, 131–32
sermons, 39, 49–53, 229–30
Seymour, William, 154
SIL International, 106–7
Simply the Story method, 161
situational storytelling, 87
Slack, Jim, 18, 18n51, 86–87
Slater, Brent, 17–18, 161n190
Smith, James K. A.
  dialogue with Merleau-Ponty and Bourdieur, 226n34
  and enacted belief, 232
  integration of body and meaning, 225, 227, 230–31
  liturgical anthropology, 225–26
  on the materiality of religion, 219
  Radical Orthodox perspective, 223–24, 224nn22–23
  telos concept, 240–41
  theology of Christian culture, 224–25
sola Scriptura, 41
song, music, communicating through, 53–58
Soukup, Paul, 22–23
sound systems, 201–2
Southwestern Baptist Theological Seminary (SWBTS), 82–83
speaking in tongues, 153n66, 154–55
Speke, John, 117
spiritual transformation. *See* mediation (making the invisible visible)
Spurgeon, Charles Haddon, 53, 60
Ssekamwa, J. C., 123–24, 128, 136
Stanfield, Jeff and Christine, 206–7, 239
Stanley, Henry Morton, 117, 144
Steffen, Tom, 68, 70, 75–77, 79
storytelling. *See* Bible storytelling
Stout, Harry, 49–50
Street, Brian V., 21, 21n71
Stringer, Tricia, 11
Strong, Douglas, 76–77, 138
STS (5-step oral pastoral training)
  in the AGC training program, 234
  and encouraging engagement, 183

the five steps, 162–63, 163n199
introduction and development, 161–62
and low-literacy, 181–82
reactions to, 164–65
Sundler, Bengt, 144
Swahili Bible, 171
Swarr, David
  on the barriers of physical texts, 96–98
  on challenges of incorporating women into leadership, 10
  and the 4.2.20 Foundation, 92–94
SWBTS. *See* Southwestern Baptist Theological Seminary (SWBTS)
systematic/doctrinal theology communications, 75–78

"Table 71" collaboration, 89–90
Tanzania, WGM work in, 140
Taylor, Charles, 221, 224–25, 242
technical schools (Uganda), 125
technological determinism, 21–22
telos and human flourishing, 227, 233, 240–42
Terry, J. O., 79, 87–88, 89n99
text-reliant communication. *See* print-reliant communications
Tiberondwa, Ado K., 124
Tonino, Father, 204
transformational ministries vs. pastoral training, 237–38
translation, issues related to, 105–9
Tucker, Alfred (Bishop), 119, 121, 125–26, 130
Tukutendereza, Jesu (We praise you, Jesus; hymn), 150
Tuma, Tom, 130–31
Tyndale, William, 46

Uganda
  colonial opposition to purely literary training, 127–28
  failure to take oral education seriously, 244–45
  government control of education, 129
  Idi Amin, 137
  importance of literacy in, 118, 122, 128–30, 135–36, 196
  language diversity, 143
  materiality, 126, 214–15
  post-independence education, 129
  system-based education, 124
  types of schools, 125
  urban-rural divide, 202
  vernacular and village schools, 125
Ugandan Christianity. *See also* Africa Gospel Church Uganda (AGC); Church of Uganda (COU, Anglican); World Gospel Mission (WGM)
  call for revival in, 150
  and church buildings, 252
  dependence on textual modalities, 67
  and digital audio players (DAPs), 199–200
  early history, 116–17
  impact of the Anglican Church, 124–33, 143
  and the importance of education, 122–23
  and literacy-based communication, 4, 14, 115–16, 118, 121, 135–36, 185
  material culture, 2, 5, 16, 126, 186–87, 237, 241–42
  mission schools, 125–27
  moving beyond faith, 119
  and the *Mulokole/Balokole* holiness tradition, 141–52
  and Pentecostalism, 153
  post-independence mission groups, 136–37
  "readers," 116
  and social status, 126
  suppression of, 119
  teachers vs. clergy, status, 130–31
  and the Ugandan educational system, 123
United Faith Chapel (UFC), 26, 26–27n94, 201–2

Venn, Henry, 131
Vries, Lourens de, 22, 22n74

Index

Wakoko, Silver, 178n200
Ward, Kevin, 133, 151n157
Warfield, B. B., 74–75
Warren, Rick (*The Purpose Driven Life*), 192
Washington, Booker T., 127n56
Watson, J. R., 55
Watts, Isaac, 56
Weber, Hans-Ruedi, 78–79, 86
weight-gain and spiritual growth, 211
Wesley, John, 56–57, 146
Wesleyan holiness, 6, 147–49
"Western oralities," 92
WGM. *See* World Gospel Mission (WGM)
WGM Uganda. *See* World Gospel Mission Uganda (WGM Uganda)
Wheeler, John Butcher, 61
"When Survey" (Watts), 56
White Fathers, 119
Whitefield, George, 50–51, 64, 104n157
Wiles, Jerry, 110
Willis, Avery Jr., 89, 90, 112
Willis, John, 131–32
Wither, George, 55–56
Witvliet, John, 54
"The Wordless Book," 60–62
World Gospel Mission (WGM)
   about, 5–6
   dualism between the physical and the spiritual, 237
   early work in China, 137–38
   emphasis on personal holiness, 6
   financing of missionaries, 6
   founding, 137
   holiness theology, 146–48, 152
   introduction to orality, 161
   and materiality, 237, 239–40, 252
   missionary workforce, 6
   partnership with the AGM, 7–8
   socioeconomic constraints, 8
   transformational ministries vs. pastoral training, 237–38
World Gospel Mission Kenya, institutional model, 140
World Gospel Mission Uganda
World Gospel Mission Uganda (WGM Uganda). *See also* pastoral training, WGM Uganda
   and the church in Kampala, 134
   classification as Pentecostal, 153, 153n166, 154n171
   community health outreach, 139
   early history, 138–39, 139n104
   faith-based missionaries, 6, 8
   and focus on pastoral training, 139–40
   founding, 138–39
   holiness theology, 153
   The Print Shop, 189–90
   and salvation through faith, 140
   and speaking in tongues, 154
   work done by, 6–7, 6–7n6
worldview analysis (Terry), 87
Wycliffe Bible Translators (WBT), 89

Youth with a Mission (YWAM), 89

Zambia, materiality in, 186–87
Zito, Angela, 220–21, 224n32

www.ingramcontent.com/pod-product-compliance
Lightning Source LLC
Chambersburg PA
CBHW050623300426
44112CB00012B/1627